SHEPPARD'S DEALERS
IN COLLECTABLES

Companion Volumes

SHEPPARD'S DIRECTORIES

Directories of Antiquarian & Secondhand Book Dealers

SHEPPARD'S BOOK DEALERS
IN THE BRITISH ISLES

SHEPPARD'S BOOK DEALERS
IN EUROPE

SHEPPARD'S BOOK DEALERS
IN JAPAN

SHEPPARD'S BOOK DEALERS
IN AUSTRALIA & NEW ZEALAND

SHEPPARD'S BOOK DEALERS
IN NORTH AMERICA

SHEPPARD'S BOOK DEALERS
IN INDIA AND THE ORIENT

International Directories

SHEPPARD'S INTERNATIONAL
DIRECTORY OF PRINT AND
MAP SELLERS
A DIRECTORY OF BUSINESSES IN THIRTY-EIGHT COUNTRIES

SHEPPARD'S INTERNATIONAL
DIRECTORY OF EPHEMERA DEALERS
A DIRECTORY OF BUSINESSES IN TWENTY-ONE COUNTRIES

SHEPPARD'S

DEALERS IN COLLECTABLES

A DIRECTORY OF DEALERS IN NEW & REPRODUCTION AND OLD & ANTIQUE COLLECTABLES

FIRST EDITION

RICHARD JOSEPH PUBLISHERS

First Edition published 1996

RICHARD JOSEPH PUBLISHERS LIMITED
UNIT 2, MONKS WALK
FARNHAM, SURREY GU9 8HT
ENGLAND
TEL: (01252) 734347   FAX: (01252) 734307

I.S.B.N. 1 872699 32 4

Database advisor - John Withers
Printed and bound by
Professional Book Supplies Ltd., Abingdon, Oxford, UK.

Compiler's Note. Whilst every care is taken to ensure
that the information given in this Directory is as
accurate and complete as possible, the Publishers
cannot accept any responsibility for any inaccuracies
that occur or for any relevant information that was not
available to the Publishers or its professional advisers
at the time of going to press.

CONTENTS

ALPHABETICAL INDEXES

SPECIALITY INDEX
to the Geographical Directory of Dealers

This index lists dealers under specific subject headings. The following list has been created from the subjects provided by dealers' entry forms.

SPECIALITY INDEX – NEW & REPRODUCTION

SPECIALITY INDEX – OLD & ANTIQUE

COLLECTORS' ASSOCIATIONS

ADVERTISING MUG COLLECTORS' ASSOCIATION, 'Whitecroft', Chandler Road, Stoke Holy Cross, Norwich NR14 8RG. Enquiries to: Peter R. King. Informal group of collectors of advertising mugs & promotional ceramics. (Send S.A.E.)

ANTIQUE COLLECTORS' CLUB, 5 Church Street, Woodbridge, Suffolk IP12 ID5. Tel: (01394) 385501. Fax: 384434. Enquiries to: Sales Department. Publishers of definitive reference books on antiques and collecting, and *Antique Collecting* in which private individual subscribers may advertise collectables free of charge.

THE ARMS AND ARMOUR SOCIETY, Field House, Upper Dicker, Hailsham, East Sussex BN27 3PY. Tel: & Fax: (01323) 844278. Enquiries to: The Hon. Secretary. To encourage the study, collection and conservation of arms and armour. Monthly meetings, journal twice yearly, newsletter quarterly.

BADGE COLLECTORS CIRCLE, 3 Ellis Close, Quorn, Loughborough, Leicestershire LE12 8SH. Tel: (01509) 412094. The Hon. Secretary: M. Setchfield. For collectors of non-military badges (i.e. enamel or button badges).

THE BRITISH ANTIQUE DEALERS' ASSOCIATION, 20 Rutland Gate, London SW7 1BD. Tel: (0171) 589-4128. Fax: 581-9083. Est: 1918. Secretary General: Mrs Elaine Dean. Assistant Secretary: Mr Mark Dodgson.

BRITISH BUTTON SOCIETY, The Old Dairy, Newton, Kettering NN14 1BW. Tel: (01536) 746027. Hon. Secretary: Mr K. Riddle. Membership Secretary: Mrs J. Baron. Tel: (0117) 966-8815. Society for collectors of old and interesting buttons.

BRITISH MATCHBOX LABEL & BOOKLET SOCIETY, 122 High Street, Melbourn, Cambridgeshire SG8 6AL. Tel: (01763) 260399. Secretary: Arthur Alderton.

BRITISH MODEL SOLDIER SOCIETY, 22 Lynwood Road, Ealing, London W5 1JJ. Tel: (0181) 998-5230. Secretary: Mr David Pearce. Est. 1935.

BRITISH NUMISMATIC TRADE ASSOCIATION, P.O. Box 474A, Thames Ditton, Surrey KT7 0WJ. Tel: (0181) 398-4290. Fax: 398-4291. Est: 1973. General Secretary: Mrs Carol Carter.

BRITISH TEDDY BEAR ASSOCIATION, P.O. Box 290, Brighton, East Sussex BN2 1DR. Tel: (01273) 697974. Fax: 626255. An association for collectors of teddy bears.

THE BUTTONHOOK SOCIETY, 2 Romney Place, Maidstone, Kent ME15 6LE. Tel: (01622) 752949. Fax: (01634) 831945. Enquiries to: Paul Moorhead. A society for buttonhook collectors dedicated to research as to their history and origins.

CLARICE CLIFF COLLECTOR'S CLUB, Fantasque House, Tennis Drive, The Park, Nottingham NG7 1AE. Est: 1982. Chairman: Leonard Griffin.

THE COMMEMORATIVE COLLECTORS SOCIETY, "The Gardens", Gainsborough Road, Winthorpe, Near Newark, Nottinghamshire NG24 2NR. Tel: (01636) 704179/71377. Secretary: S.N. Jackson. International Society of private collectors of commemorabilia of all kinds, in ceramic, glass, printed ephemera, enamels, woven and printed textiles etc.

CORGI COLLECTORS CLUB, P.O. Box 323, Swansea SA1 1BJ. Tel: & Fax: (01792) 476902. Enquiries to: The Secretary. UK headquarters of Corgi's worldwide diecast model vehicle enthusiasts club.

COTSWOLD ANTIQUE DEALERS ASSOCIATION, Barchedton Manor, Shipston-on-Stour CV36 5AY. Tel: (01608) 661268. Enquiries to: Sue Britton. Free members directory available.

ASSOCIATIONS

CRICKET MEMORABILIA SOCIETY, 29 Highclere Road, Crumpsall, Manchester M8 4WH. Tel: (0161) 740-3714. Enquiries to: Tony Sheldon. For collectors, quarterly magazine, meetings and auctions. Exclusive merchandise, most of all - friendship.

FOLLOWERS OF RUPERT, 31 Whiteley, Windsor, Berkshire SL4 5PJ. Tel: (01753) 865562. Sub. Secretary: Shirley Reeves. Est: 1983. Society for the growing interest in the Rupert Bear stories, books & collectables, past, present & future. Newsletters 4 times a year.

FRIENDS OF BLUE, Flat 3, 93 Landsdowne Place, Hove, East Sussex BN3 1PN. Tel: (01273) 733787. Enquiries to: Mr Mark Stacey. To promote interest and study and record patterns, marks, etc. of English underglazed blue transfer printed ware. Four bulletins issued, yearly membership £8 p.a. (£12 p.a. overseas).

THE GOSS AND CRESTED CHINA CLUB, 62 Murray Road, Horndean, Waterlooville, Hampshire PO8 9JL. Tel: (01705) 597440. Fax: 591975. Enquiries to: Mrs Withey. Proprietors: Lynda & Nicholas Pine.

THE GOSS COLLECTORS' CLUB, 31A The Crescent, Stanley Common, Derbyshire DE7 6GL. Tel: (0115) 930-0441. Est: 1970 by collectors for collectors. Monthly magazine containing details of postal auction. 2 major Goss and Crested China fairs per year, regular meetings for members. Not affiliated to any commercial organisations. Approx 1,000 members worldwide. Enquiries to: The Club Secretary.

GUILD OF ANTIQUE DEALERS & RESTORERS, 23 Belle Vue Road, Shrewsbury, Shropshire SY3 7LN. Tel: (01743) 271852. Secretary: Maureen Edmondson.

HORNBY RAILWAY COLLECTORS' ASSOCIATION, 2 Ravensmore Road, Sherwood, Nottingham NG5 2AH. Tel: (0115) 962-5693. Enquiries to: Bob Field. For collectors and operators of Hornby trains and their accessories, both O-gauge and Dublo, as manufactured by Meccano Ltd. up to 1964.

LAPADA (The Association of Art & Antique Dealers), 535 Kings Road, London SW10 0SZ. Tel: (0171) 823-3511. Fax: 823-3522. Email: lapada@lapada.co.uk. The UK's largest association of professional art and antiques dealers with over 700 members specialising in virtually every discipline from antiquities to contemporary fine art.

MAGICAL MOMENTS & MEMORIES, 31 Rowan Way, Exwick, Exeter EX4 2DT. Tel: & Fax: (01392) 431653. Enquiries to: Sue Langabeer. Club for Disney enthusiasts.

THE MILITARY HISTORICAL SOCIETY, c/o The National Army Museum, Royal Hospital Road, London. President: Field Marshal Sir John Chapple GCB CBE MA FZS FRGS. Hon. Secretary: David J. Hunter JP.

MUSICAL BOX SOCIETY OF GREAT BRITAIN, P.O. Box 299, Waterbeach, Cambridge CB4 4PJ. Enquiries to: The Secretary. A society interested in research, restoration and enjoyment of all types of mechanical musical instruments.

THE PEWTER SOCIETY, Hunter's Lodge, Paddock Close, St Mary's Platt, Sevenoaks, Kent TN15 8NN. Tel: (01732) 883314. Enquiries to: Dr J.F. Richardson. Est: 1918 for collectors and students of pewter, its makers, marks, repair and preservation.

PHOTOGRAPHIC COLLECTORS CLUB OF GREAT BRITAIN, 5 Station Industrial Estate, Low Prudoe, Northumberland NE42 6NP. Tel: & Fax: (0117) 983-1839. Enquiries to: The Hon. Secretary. For promoting the study and collection of photographic equipment and images.

THE SILVER SPOON CLUB OF GREAT BRITAIN, Glenleigh Park, Sticker, St. Austell, Cornwall PL26 7JD. Tel: (01726) 65269. Enquiries to: Terry and Mary Haines. International postal club for connoisseurs and collectors of antique and other fine silver spoons; with illustrated bi-monthly journal.

U.K. PERFUME BOTTLE COLLECTOR CLUB, 2,3,4 Great Western Antique Centre, Bartlett Street, Bath BA1 2QZ. Tel: (01225) 448488. Enquiries to: Lynda Brine.

WIRELESS PRESERVATION SOCIETY, 52 West Hill Road, Ryde, Isle of Wight PO33 1LN. Tel: (01983) 567665. Fax: 564708. Enquiries to: Douglas Byrne (Hon. Curator) at The National Wireless Museum, Arreton Manor, Newport, Isle of Wight PO30 3AA.

AUCTIONEERS

ACADEMY AUCTIONEERS & VALUERS, Northcote House, Northcote Avenue, Ealing, London W5 3UR. Tel: (0181) 579-7466. Fax: 579-0511. Monthly sales of antiques and fine art. Also monthly general household sales.

ALDRIDGES OF BATH, 130/2 Walcot Street, Bath BA1 5BG. Tel: (01225) 462830. Fax: 311319. Enquiries to: Ivan Street. Fortnightly general sales. Specialist antique sales & collectors' items at frequent intervals.

BEARNE'S, Rainbow, Avenue Road, Torquay TQ2 5TG. Tel: (01803) 296277. Fax: 291565 and Okehampton Street, Exeter. Tel: (01392) 422800. Regular sales of furniture, works of art, collectors' items, silver, jewellery, ceramics and pictures in either or both locations.

BIRMINGHAM RAILWAY AUCTIONS, 7 Ascot Road, Moseley, Birmingham B13 9EN. Tel: & Fax: (0121) 449-9707. Auctions at Sheffield, Kidlington, Nr. Oxford, Quorn, Matlock.

BONHAMS, 65-69 Lots Road, Chelsea, London SW10 0RN. Tel: (0171) 393-3951. Fax: 393-3906. Enquiries to: Tracie Vallis. Regular sales of dolls, dolls houses, miniatures, Disney, trains, diecast and tinplate toys, live steam, rocking horses, juvenilia and teddy bears.

PETER CHENEY, Western Road Auction Rooms, Western Road, Littlehampton, West Sussex BN17 5NP. Tel: (01903) 722264/713418. Fax: 713418. Auctions every 3 weeks. Antiques, furniture, collectables, silver & jewellery, ceramics, pictures etc.

CRANBROOK AUCTION ROOMS, Enquiries to: Raj and Sue Bisram, 15 High Street, Cranbrook, Kent. Tel: (01580) 712173.

CHRISTIE'S SOUTH KENSINGTON LTD., 85 Old Brompton Road, South Kensington, London SW7 3LD. Tel: (0171) 581-7611. Fax: 321-3321. Enquiries to: Julia Chinnery. Weekly sales of furniture and objects, fortnightly sales of silver, jewellery, pictures and ceramics and monthly sales of toys, dolls, teddy bears and cameras.

CRITERION AUCTIONEERS, 53-55 Essex Road, Islington, London N1. Tel: (0171) 359-5707. Fax: 354-9843. Antique auction held every Monday 6pm. 1st Monday of each month selective higher quality sale. Antique and decorative furniture, paintings, clocks, silver, rugs, mirrors, collectables and objets d'art. Viewing: Friday 4pm–8pm, Sat & Sun 11am–3pm & Monday 10am-6pm. Underground: Angel.

AUCTIONEERS

DOMINIC WINTER BOOK AUCTIONS, The Old School, Maxwell Street, Swindon, Wiltshire SN1 5DR. Tel: (01793) 611340. Fax: 491727. Enquiries to: Diane Hawke. Specialist Auctioneers. Aprox 20 sales per year including old and rare printed books, maps, prints, photographs, autographs, sporting memorabilia and all book-related items and bits of paper.

EDWARDS & ELLIOTT, 32 High Street, Ascot, Berkshire SL5 7HG. Tel: (01344) 872588. Fax: 24700. Enquiries to: F.M. Ogley. Monthly sales of general antiques at the Silver Ring Grandstands, Ascot Racecourse.

ROBIN A. FENNER & CO., The Stannary Gallery, Drake Road, Tavistock, Devon PL19 0AX. Tel: (01822) 617799. Fax: 617595. Enquiries to: R.A. or S.M. Fenner or D. Bates. Monthly sales of furniture, silver, jewellery, ceramics, objects, oil paintings, watercolours. Quarterly sales of collectors, vintage toys and models.

GEORGE STREET AUCTION GALLERIES, 66a George Street, Hastings, East Sussex. Tel: (01424) 438688. Fax: 423011. Enquiries to: R. Sladen. Monthly sales of antiques and collectables on 1st Saturday of the month.

HOBBS & CHAMBERS, Market Place, Cirencester GL7 1QQ. Tel: (01285) 642420. Fax: 885818. Monthly sales of furniture, small collectable items and effects, regular specialist sections of pictures, toys, silver, jewellery, glassware, etc. at Bingham Hall, Cirencester.

HOBBS & CHAMBERS, 15 Royal Crescent, Cheltenham GL50 3DA. Tel: (01242) 256363. Fax: 227175. Fortnightly sales of furniture, small collectable items and effects. Regular specialist sections of textiles, ceramics, silver, jewellery, collectables etc. at Chapel Walk Saleroom, Cheltenham.

HOGBEN AUCTIONEERS & VALUERS, St Johns Street, off Dover Road, Folkestone, Kent. Tel: (01303) 240808. Fax: 240809. Fortnightly antiques & collectable sales, Saturdays 10a.m., view Thursday & Friday prior.

HORNERS, North Walsham Salerooms, Midland Road, North Walsham, Norfolk NR28 9JR. Tel: (01692) 500603. Fax: 500975. Weekly sales of furniture and effects, periodic specialist sales. Sales every Friday commencing 10 a.m.

G.A. KEY, Aylsham Salerooms, Palmers Lane, Aylsham, Norwich NR11 6EH. Tel: (01263) 733195. Fax: 732410. Enquiries: Andrew Bullock. Bi-monthly auctions.

GLASGOW VINTAGE TOY AUCTION, 126 Maryhill Road, St Georges Cross, Glasgow G20 7QS. Tel: (0141) 331-1008. Fax: 509-1501. Enquiries to: Anne and Gordon Brown.

LADYBANK AUCTION ROOMS, 7 Kinloch Street, Ladybank, Fife KY7 7LE. Tel: (01337) 830488. Enquiries to: D. Campbell or F.I.A. Scot. Weekly sales of furniture and objects every Friday, 6p.m. Quarterly sales of antiques, fine art and collectables.

DAVID LAY, F.S.V.A. The Penzance Auction House, Alverton, Penzance, Cornwall TR18 4RE. Tel: (01736) 61414. Fax: 60035. Enquiries to: Barbara Kirk. Six sales of general antiques each year, two collectors' sales per year.

NORTH STAFFS RAILMANIA, 8 Hassall Road, Alsager, Stoke-on-Trent ST7 2HQ. Tel: (01270) 878519. Enquiries to: P.Hallam. Organisers of train and toy fairs in Chester and Stoke-on-Trent: 10 times per year.

ONSLOW'S, Metrostore, Townmead Road, London SW6 2RZ. Tel: (0171) 371-0505. Fax: 384-2682. Enquiries to: Patrick Bogue or John Jenkins. Sales held at different London venues.

PHILLIPS BAYSWATER, 10 Salem Road, London W2 4DL. Tel: (0171) 229-9090. Fax: 792-9201. Enquiries to: Emma Simpson. Weekly sales of furniture and objects, monthly picture sales and regular sales of collectors' items.

PHILLIPS INCORPORATING HENRY SPENCER & SONS, 20 The Square, Retford, Nottinghamshire DN22 6XE. Tel: (01777) 708633. Fax: 706724. Enquiries to: Simon Peck. Bi-weekly sales of furniture. Regular sales of silver, pictures, porcelain, clocks and collectors' items.

ROGERS JONES & CO., 33 Abergele Road, Colwyn Bay, Clwyd LL29 7RU. Tel: (01492) 532176. Fax: 533308. Modern/collectables auctions first 2 Tuesdays every month. Antiques/fine art every last Tuesday.

ROMSEY AUCTION ROOMS, 86 The Hundred, Romsey, Hampshire SO51 8BX. Tel: (01794) 513331. Fax: 511770. Enquiries to: Michael G. Baker. Monthly sales of general antiques, bi-monthly sales of silver, quarterly sales of silver and jewellery and quarterly sales of toys.

SAFFRON WALDEN AUCTIONS, 1 Market Street, Saffron Walden, Essex. (Tel: (01799) 513281. Fax: 513334. Enquiries to: Colin Bazley. Weekly sales of household furniture and bric-a-brac, bi-monthly sales of antiques, periodical sales of vintage toys and Rock n' Roll memorabilia.

SEMLEY AUCTIONEERS, Station Road, Semley, Shaftesbury, Dorset SP7 9AN. Tel: (01747) 855122. Fax: 855222. Enquiries to: Mr S.M.B. Pearce. Fortnightly sales of antiques and collectables, Saturdays 10 a.m.

G.E. SWORDER & SONS, Bishops Stortford Auction Rooms, Northgate End, Bishops Stortford, Hertfordshire CM23 2ET. Tel: (01279) 651388. Fax: 467467. Monthly fine art auctions, Thursdays 11 a.m. - Victorian, Edwardian and later furniture, china and collectables.

SOTHEBY'S, 34 New Bond Street, London W1A 2AA. Tel: (0171) 493-8080. Fax: 409-3100. Enquiries to: Collectors' Department. Regular sales of toys, dolls, teddy bears, rock & roll memorabilia, sporting & golf items, marine works of art, scientific instruments & mechanical music.

SOTHEBY'S, Summers Place, Billingshurst, West Sussex RH14 9AD. Tel: (01403) 783933. Fax: 785153. Enquiries to: Susan Duffield. Regular sales of toys, dolls, militaria and other collectors' items.

T.J. SPENSLEY & Co., Blyth Auction Centre, Quayside, Blyth, Northumberland. Tel: & Fax: (01670) 363777. Enquiries to: T.J.Spensley. Fortnightly sales and frequent special antique and collectables sales.

THOMSON, RODDICK & LAURIE, 19 Crosby Street, Carlisle CA1 1DQ. Tel: (01228) 28939. Fax: 592128. Regular sales in Carlisle, Wigton (Cumbria) and Dumfries. Furniture, antiques, ceramics and collectors' items. Specialist sales of books, pictures and toys.

TONY & SONS LTD., Lynwood House, 2–8 Lynwood Road, Blackburn, Lancashire BB2 6HP. Tel: (01254) 691748. Fax: 691750. Jewellery auctions held monthly, approx. 500 lots per sale to include antique & modern jewellery, pawnbrokers' unredeemed pledges and silver.

RUPERT TOOVEY & CO. LTD., Star Road, Partridge Green, West Sussex RH13 8RJ. Tel: (01403) 711744. Fax: 711919. Monthly two day sales of antiques, fine art and collectors' items, regular sales of antiquarian & modern books, stamps, cigarette cards, postcards and printed ephemera.

WALLIS & WALLIS, West Street Auction Galleries, Lewes, Sussex BN7 2NJ. Tel: (01273) 480208. Fax: 476562. Sales every six weeks - militaria, arms & armour, coins, medals, diecast & tinplate toys and collectors' items.

AUCTIONEERS

WILSON PEACOCK, 26 Newnham Street, Bedford MK40 3JR. Tel: (01234) 266366. Fax: 269082. Enquiries to: Sally Heard. Robert Room Antique sales on 1st Friday of each month including furniture, pictures, porcelain, silver, books, collectables etc.

WOOLLEY & WALLIS, Salisbury Salerooms Ltd., 51-61 Castle Street, Salisbury, Wiltshire SP1 3SU. Tel: (01722) 411422. Fax: 422192. Enquiries to: Jane Hurst. Regular sales of antique furniture; textiles, dolls, toys & collectables; Oriental rugs & carpets; silver & jewellery; oil paintings & watercolours; European & Oriental ceramics; books & prints; wine and general sales.

FAIR ORGANISERS

ANTIQUE FORUM GROUP, HEART OF ENGLAND Antiques, Collectors & Militaria fairs at Stoke-on-Trent (May, September & December), Birmingham (May, June, July, September, November & December) and Trentham Gardens - North Staffordshire (June, August, October and November). Enquiries to: C. Baskin, P.O. Box 465, Longton, Stoke-on-Trent ST3 7SE. Tel: (01782) 592805. Fax: 596133.

ATHENA FAYRES Regular Antique & Collectables fairs around Southampton and Fareham area nearly every weekend with venues at Minstead, Ocean Village, Sarisbury Green, Locks Heath and Wickham each month. Enquiries to: Athena Antiques, 31 Newtown Road, Warsash, Hampshire SO31 9FY. Tel: (01489) 584633/578093.

BIG SOUTHERN TOYFAIR Enquiries to: Cliff Maddock, P.O. Box 26, Mortimer, Nr. Reading, Berkshire RG7 3EE. Tel: & Fax: (01734) 833062.

BIG TEDDY BEAR SHOW (every April) incorporating the British Bear Artist awards, teddy bear shops, makers and artists from around the world. Enquiries to: Teddy Bear Times, Avalon Court, Star Road, Partridge Green, Horsham, West Sussex RH13 8RY. Tel: (01403) 711511. Fax: 711521.

JUDY BLACK FAIRS Antique dolls, teddy bears, doll's house miniatures & toy collectors fairs at: Abbey Hall, Abingdon, Oxfordshire (May, August, November). Enquiries to: Judy Black Fairs, Swiss Cottage, Shrivenham, Swindon SN6 8EY. Tel: (01793) 782541.

BRENTWOOD DECOR FAIRS Dolls house, miniature, doll and teddy fairs in Scotland and North of England (18 a year). Enquiries to: Sylvia Wood, 95 New Lane, Bolton, Lancashire BL2 5BY. Tel: (01204) 529930.

BRITISH BEAR FAIR (every December) The leading shops and artists all under one roof. Enquiries to : Teddy Bear Times, Avalon Court, Star Road, Partridge Green, Horsham, West Sussex RH13 8RY. Tel: (01403) 711511. Fax: 711521.

BRITISH TOY SOLDIER & FIGURE SHOWS Every June and December at Royal National Hotel, London. Enquiries to: Norman Joplin, 29 Greenlaw Road, Southfield Green, Cramlington, Northumberland NE23 6NP. Tel: (01670) 714522. Fax: 590683.

CAILE FAIRS 3 fairs a year (April, September, November) at Scotch Corner Hotel, Junction A6/A66 Nr. Darlington, North Yorkshire DL10 6NR. Enquiries to: Margaret & Arthur Hodge, 8 Arundel Way, Meadow Green, Meadowfield, Durham DH7 8UT. Tel: (0191) 378-1923.

COVENTRY FAIRS Saturday collectors markets (monthly) at The United Reform Church Hall, Stivichall, Coventry. Enquiries to: David Smith Tel: (01933) 225674.

EAST ANGLIAN DOLL, DOLLS HOUSE & MINIATURE FAIRS Braintree, Essex (Spring & Autumn) and Bury St. Edmunds, Suffolk (Summer). Enquiries to: Georgia Palmer, Bumby Hall, Kelvedon, Essex CO5 9DE. Tel: (01376) 583166.

E.W. SERVICES Antiques and Collectors Fairs at: Wellingborough, Peterborough, Ely, Northampton, Hemel Hempstead, Buckingham, Daventry, Desborough, Rushden, Huntingdon, Burton Latimer, Kettering and Brigstock. Enquiries to: David Smith, P.O. Box 90, Wellingborough, Northamptonshire NN8 1SU. Tel: (01933) 225674.

THE DECORATIVE ANTIQUES & TEXTILES FAIR in March and September at: The Marquee, Kings College, Chelsea. Enquiries to: Harvey Management Ltd., P.O. Box 149, London W9 1QN. Tel: (0171) 624-5173. Fax: (0171) 625-8326.

DOLL & TEDDY FAIRS (2 a year). A doll and teddy fair at the Penns Hall Hotel, Penns Lane, Walmley, Sutton Coldfield, West Midlands. Enquiries to: Mrs D.M. Woodhouse. Tel & Fax: (01203) 392284.

DOLLY DOMAIN FAIRS Leeds Doll & Teddy Fair, Pudsey (March and October). Tyneside Doll & Teddy Fair, Gateshead, (May and August). Tyneside Dolls House & Miniatures Fair, Gateshead, (February and July). Enquiries to: Dolly Domain Fairs, The Dolls' Hospital, 45 Henderson Road, South Shields, Tyne & Wear NE34 9QW. Tel: (0191) 427-6214. Fax: 424-0400.

EAST MIDLAND DOLL FAIRS (2 a year). Fairs at: Wakefield, Sutton Coldfield, Newark, Woburn, Derby, Stratford-upon-Avon, Huntingdon, Leicester, Cambridge, Northampton, Buxton (Derbyshire). Enquiries to: Bruce & Pam King, 1 The Hallards, Eaton Socon, St. Neots, Cambridgeshire PE19 3QW. Tel: & Fax: (01480) 216372.

FAIR AISLE PROMOTIONS fairs in Dublin (Ireland) (3-4 fairs monthly at various venues) and Irish International Collectables Fair (major annual event every May). Enquiries to: Joan Murray, P.O. Box 5057, Dublin 2, Ireland. Tel: & Fax: (00-353-1) 6708295.

FOUR SEASONS FAIRS (9 a year) at U.S.A.F. RAF Mildenhall, Suffolk in The Smoke House Inn, Beck Row. Est: 1982. Enquiries to: Lorna Quick, 6 Post Office Lane, Glemsford, Sudbury, Suffolk CO10 7RA. Tel: (01787) 281855.

GOLLY'S FRIENDS Organisers of dolls house, doll & teddy fairs at Tatton Park, Cheshire, Lancashire & Shropshire, 12 per annum. Enquiries to: P. Hallam, 8 Hassell Road, Alsager, Stoke-on-Trent ST7 2HQ. Tel: (01270) 878519.

GREAT NORTHERN INTERNATIONAL ANTIQUES & COLLECTORS FAIRS 6 large showground events per year, (Jan, March, May, July, Sept. & Nov.), exhibition halls & outdoor areas. Enquiries to: G.N.I. Ltd., P.O. Box 144, Darlington, Co. Durham DL1 3YZ. Tel: (01325) 380077. Fax: 360464.

GROWLIES Teddy Bears only fairs in Scotland (3 a year) in Glynhill Hotel, Renfrew Road, Paisley, Strathclyde. Enquiries to: Margaret McLean or Christine Gribbin, 15 Thorn Brae, Johnstone, Strathclyde, Scotland. Tel: (01505) 336551. Fax: 337373.

BRIAN HAUGHTON, Antique fairs. 3[B] Burlington Gardens, London W1X 1LE. Tel: (0171) 734-5491. Fax: 494-4604.

FAIR ORGANISERS

HERITAGE ANTIQUES FAIRS Locations in Central London every Sunday except Easter, Christmas and August. Enquiries to: Heritage Antiques Fairs, P.O. Box 149, London W9 1QN. Tel: (0171) 624-5173. Fax: 625-8326.

JAX FAIRS Antiques and Collectors Fairs held at Wembley Exhibition Centre and Lee Valley Leisure Centre. Enquiries to: Jacqui Greenland, P.O. Box 280, Haywards Heath, West Sussex RH17 6YA. Tel: (01444) 400570. Fax: 400754.

MELBA FAIRS Cheltenham Racecourse, monthly; Pittville Pump Room, Cheltenham; Weston-Super-Mare Winter Gardens, monthly; Newton Abbot Racecourse. Enquiries to: Melba Fairs, 96 Devonshire Road, Weston-Super-Mare BS23 4NX. Tel: (01934) 624854.

MIDLAND TEDDY BEAR FESTIVAL 1st Sunday in April and October each year in Telford. Enquiries to: 'Bears on the Square', 2 The Square, Ironbridge, Shropshire TF8 7AQ. Tel: (01952) 433924. Fax: 433926.

MINIATURA Est:1983. Dolls' house and miniatures only at N.E.C. Birmingham (March & September) and Royal Concert Hall, Glasgow (June). Bears and dolls at N.E.C. (April). Enquiries to: Bob & Muriel Hopwood, 41 Eastbourne Avenue, Hodge Hill, Birmingham B34 6AR. Tel: & Fax: (0121) 783-2070.

NEW FOREST FAIRS Dolls' houses and miniatures (2 per year) at Lyndhurst Park Hotel, Lyndhurst, Hampshire. April and October, 55 stands. Enquiries to E. Forder, P.O. Box 154, Cobham, Surrey KT11 2YE. Tel: (01932) 867938. Fax: 860607.

NORTH STAFFS RAILMANIA Toy fairs at Chester (6 times a year) and Stoke-on-Trent (3 times a year). Enquiries to: Peter Hallam, 8 Hassall Road, Alsager, Stoke-on-Trent ST7 2HQ. Tel: (01270) 878519.

PINK PIG PROMOTIONS Large indoor and outdoor events. Enquiries to: David Smith, P.O. Box 85, Wellingborough, Northamptonshire NN8 1ST. Tel: (01933) 225674.

POSSET FUNDRAISERS Dolls house and miniatures fairs, Portishead (2 a year). Enquiries to: Mrs R. Daniels, 10 Woodhill Avenue, Portishead, Bristol BS20 9EX. Tel: (01275) 847033.

THE RIGHT TIME CLOCK FAIRS Specialist clock, watch, barometer and scientific instrument fairs, 2 planned for 1996, 6 for 1997. Enquiries to David Smith, P.O. Box 56, Wellingborough, Northamptonshire NN8 1SF. Tel: (01933) 225674 or Ray Moorey (01536) 407776.

ROCHESTER DOLLS HOUSE FAIR once a year in Rochester, dolls house fair for the discerning collector. Enquiries to: Dolls House Shop, 68 High Street, Rochester, Kent. Tel: & Fax: (01634) 831615.

ROCHESTER TEDDY BEAR FAIR once a year in Rochester, teddy bear fair for the collector, free valuations, repairs & bear memorabilia. Enquiries to: Dolls House Shop, 68 High Street, Rochester, Kent. Tel: & Fax: (01634) 831615.

RON SPARKS MILITARIA FAIRS, P.O. Box 62, Sarisbury Green, Southampton SO31 5ZB. Tel: & Fax: (01703) 453418. Numerous fairs, list available.

TEDDY BEARS IN THE BORDERS Fairs in Melrose (3 a year). Enquiries to: The Linnet, 3 Tower View, Duddo, Berwick-upon-Tweed TD15 2PS. Tel: (01890) 820567.

THREE COUNTIES FAIRS dolls house and teddy fairs. Enquiries to: Joyce Boyask. Tel: (01279) 411002. Fax: (0171) 247-3710.

TOP HAT EXHIBITIONS LTD. National Art Deco Fairs at Town Hall, Loughborough, Leicestershire (4 times a year). Enquiries to: 70-72 Derby Road, Nottingham NG1 5FD. Tel: (0115) 941-9143.

TOYMAN FAIRS Promotors of vintage toy, doll, teddy bear, miniatures and specialist model collectors fairs around London. Enquiries to: Mike Ennis, P.O. Box 66, Waltham Cross, Hertfordshire EN7 6NA. Tel: (01992) 620376.

TUDOR ROSE MINIATURES Norwich's premier and only dolls house & miniatures fair (November). Enquiries to: Unit 5, Taverham Craft Centre, Fir Covert Road, Taverham, Norwich NR20 5HH. Tel: (01603) 260462. Fax: (01362) 668234.

JULIE and JOHN WEBB and D. & J. FAIRS (calender available). Enquiries to: John Webb, Rosebank House, Bardney, Lincolnshire LN3 5UF. Tel: (01526) 398198.

WESSEX MINIATURES FAIRS Dolls houses, dolls, teddys, miniatures fairs in Bath, Bristol, Salisbury, Sherborne and Winchester. (2 fairs each per venue). Enquiries to: Valerie Stevens, Jessamine Cottage, Peacemarsh, Gillingham, Dorset SP8 4HB. Tel: (01747) 824939. Mobile: (0589) 498517.

WEST MIDLAND ANTIQUES FAIRS at Prestwood Centre & Argyle Centre, County Showground, Stafford (A518) (6 a year). Enquiries to: P.O. Box 134, Shrewsbury SY1 1ZZ. Tel: (01743) 271444. Fax: 352353.

WEST OF ENGLAND FAIRS in Exmouth, Devon (3 a year). Mainly 1/12th miniatures. Enquiries to: Mrs J. Cogings, 24 Ganders Park, Edginswell Lane, Torquay, Devon TQ2 7JF. Tel: (01803) 875635.

WILTON HOUSE Antiques Fair held annually at the end of March in the Visitor Centre and Cloisters of Wilton House. Enquiries to: Alun Williams, The Estate Office, Wilton House, Wilton, Salisbury SP2 0BJ. Tel: (01722) 743115. Fax: 744447.

WORLD HERITAGE FAIRS 3 West Country Teddy Bear Fairs a year (Easter, Summer & Autumn). Held at Kingston Maurward House, Dorchester. All types of collectable teddy bears present. Enquiries to: Jackie Ridley, 25 High Street, Dorchester, Dorset DT1 1UW. Tel: (01300) 341639. Fax: (01305) 268885.

RESTORERS

A.K. MODELS, 45 Beacon Road, Wibsey, Bradford, West Yorkshire BD6 3ET. Tel: (01274) 690829. Fax: 685757. Model train repairs. Enquiries to: J. & P. Illingworth.

THE BAROMETER SHOP, New Street, Leominster, Herefordshire HR6 8BT. Tel: & Fax: (01568) 610200. Repairs to clocks and barometers. Enquiries to: R.C. Cookson or R.E. Worthington.

THE BARTLETT STREET ANTIQUES CENTRE, 5-10 Bartlett Street, Bath, Avon. Tel: (01225) 466689. Fax: 444146. Restoration workshops.

BONA ART DECO ORIGINALS, Princes Mead Shopping Centre, Farnborough, Hampshire GU14 6YB. Tel: & Fax: (01252) 372188. Repairs and restorations.

THE CAMERA HOUSE 65 Oakworth Hall, Colne Road, Oakworth, Keighley, West Yorkshire. Tel: & Fax: (01535) 642333. Repairs and video transfers.

CASQUE & GAUNTLET MILITARIA, 55-59 Badshot Lea Road, Badshot Lea, Farnham, Surrey GU9 9LP. Tel: (01252) 20745. Restoration of all metal work, cleaning and polishing copper and brass, re-silvering and re-gilding. Enquiries to: R.L. and A. Colt.

RESTORERS

CASTLE ANTIQUES CENTRE, 1 London Road, Westerham, Nr Sevenoaks, Kent TN16 1BB. Tel: (01959) 562492. Clock repairs.

CERAMICS RESCUE, Westerham, Kent. Tel: (01959) 564188. Specialist repair and restoration service for porcelain and glass. Enquiries to: K.W. Goodale.

CHILDRENS TREASURES, 17 George Street, Hastings, East Sussex TN34 3EG. Tel: & Fax: (01424) 444117. Dolls hospital. Enquiries to: Ann & Frank Strudwick.

THE CERAMIC RESTORATION WORKSHOP c/o 3 Bodtegwel Terrace, St. George, Abergele, Clwyd LL2 9BH. Tel: & Fax: (01745) 823774. Specialist in ceramic restoration and course tuition. Enquiries to: Mrs Susan Franks.

DOMINO RESTORATIONS, 129 Craig Walk, Windermere, Cumbria LA23 3AX. Tel: (01539) 445751. Restorers of china & porcelain, glass, jewellery and objet d'art. Enquiries to: Roy & June Hargreaves (appointment only).

DORKING GLASS, 98-102 South Street, Dorking, Surrey RH4 2EW. Tel: (01306) 682971. Chips ground out of glass, vases and paperweights. New glass for clocks and barometers.

G.B.E. TOY SOLDIERS, The Cedars, 97 High Street, Coningsby, Lincolnshire LN4 4RF. Tel: (01526) 342012. Restoration of old toy soldiers. Enquiries to: A.P.N. Humphries.

G.F.C. MODELS, 5 Coptfold Road, Brentwood, Essex CM14 5ED. Tel: (01277) 226999. Repairs to locos and scalextric cars. Enquiries to: Graham & Doris Cross.

GOLDCARE, 5 Bedford Street, Middlesborough, Cleveland TS1 2LL. Tel: (01642) 231343. Specialists in jewellery repairs and restoration.

JOSS GRAHAM ORIENTAL TEXTILES, 10 Eccleston Street, London SW1W 9LT. Tel: & Fax: (0171) 730-4370. Restoration and conservation of textiles.

GROWLIES, 15 Thorn Brae, Johnstone, Strathclyde, Scotland. Tel: (01505) 336551. Fax: 337373. Repairs to old bears. Enquiries to: Christine Gribbin or Margaret McLean.

KEITH HARDING'S WORLD OF MECHANICAL MUSIC, Oak House, High Street, Northleach, Gloucestershire GL54 3ET. Tel: (01451) 860181. Fax: 861133. Restoration of music boxes.

HAYBARN ANTIQUES The Bones Lane Antique Centre, Bones Lane, Battlesbridge, Essex SS11 7RE. Tel: (01268) 763500. Restoration of mechanical antiques, lamps and lighting.

LYMINGTON ANTIQUES CENTRE, 76 High Street, Lymington, Hampshire SO41 9AL. Tel: (01590) 675424. Jewellery repairs and oil lamp spares. Enquiries to Mr Hughes or Mr Stanley-Smith.

LYNTON DIALS 22 Norwich Street, Fakenham, Norfolk NR21 9AE. Tel: (01328) 863666. Fax: (01485) 518650. Re-enamelling and restoring clock and watch dials.

THE KEYHOLE, Dragonwyck, Far Back Lane, Farnsfield, Newark, Nottinghamshire NG22 8JX. Tel: & Fax: (01623) 882590. Repair, refurbishment and supply of antique locks and keys for use. Enquiries to: George & Valerie Olifent.

F.C. MANSER & SON LTD., 53/4 Wyle Cop, Shrewsbury, Shropshire S71 1XJ. Tel: (01743) 35112. Fax: 271047. Full restoration service.

PINOCCHIO, 79 High Street, Teddington, Middlesex TW11 8HG. Tel: (0181) 977-8995. Fax: 977-8890. Teddy and doll hospitals. Enquiries to: Mr & Mrs F.A. Langella.

RECOLLECT-DOLLS HOSPITAL, The Old School, London Road, Sayers Common, West Sussex BN6 9HX. Tel: (01273) 833314. Dolls hospital and supplies. Moulds for dolls and miniatures. Enquiries to: Paul Jago.

S. ROUSE Springfield House, 103 High Street, Clay Cross, Derbyshire S45 9DZ. Tel: (01246) 862241. Restoration of dolls and teddy bears.

STOCKBRIDGE ANTIQUES, 8 Deanhaugh Street, Edinburgh EH4 1LY. Tel: (0131) 332-1366. Repair, restoration and re-costuming of dolls and teddies. Enquiries to J. & D. Ross.

TINGEWICK ANTIQUES CENTRE, Main Street, Tingewick, Buckinghamshire. Tel: (01280) 848219. Restoration service available. Enquiries to: B.J. & R. Smith.

TOBILANE DESIGNS, Newton Holme Farm, Whittington, Nr Carnforth, Lancashire LA6 2NZ. Tel: (01524) 272662. Traditional toymakers and restorers. Enquiries to: Paul Commander.

DISPLAY MATERIALS AND EQUIPMENT

ALAN MORRIS 10 Coughton Lane, Coughton, Alcester, Warwickshire B49 5HN. Tel: (01789) 762800. Display stands, wire, plastic, acrylic, wood for ceramics etc.; plate hangers, wire & disc; brass easels, cleaning cloths, jewellery boxes, labels & tickets. Mail trade list. Enquiries to: Alan Morris Wholesale.

OLD FATHER TIME CLOCK CENTRE, 1st Floor Portobello Studios, 101 Portobello Road, London W11 2QB. Tel: & Fax: (0181) 546-6299. Mobile: (0836) 712088. Glass domes. Enquiries to: John Denvir.

PERIODICALS & REFERENCE BOOKS

BIGGLES & CO (the W.E. Johns quarterly magazine). 40 pages of articles and stories by and about W.E. Johns, the creator of Biggles. A non-profit making collectors' magazine in full colour covers. £12 per year UK subscription. Editor: J. Trendler, 4 Ashendene Road, Bayford, Hertfordshire. Tel: (01992) 511588. Fax: 511382.

COLLECTING – The Essential Guide, all you need to know about buying and selling antiques. Published by: Classic Books, P.O. Box 411, Longton, Stoke-on-Trent ST3 4SS. Tel: (01782) 314152. Fax: 315655.

COLLECTORS MART Collectors quarterly - articles and advertisements mainly items made for use and now collected - advertising material, beer trade items, transport ephemera. Published by: Collectors Mart Ltd., Parkgate House, 27 High Street, Hampton Hill, Middlesex TW12 1NG. Tel: (0181) 941-4512. Fax: 941-8630.

DOLLS HOUSE & MINIATURE SCENE The monthly definitive glossy magazine covering all aspects of the dolls house enthusiast. £2.75 per issue, £30.00 per year. Published by: EMF Publishing, 7 Ferringham Lane, Ferring, West Sussex BN12 5ND. Tel: (01903) 244900. Fax: 506626.

MODEL AUTO REVIEW published 10 times a year. Enquiries to: Model Auto, P.O. Box SM2, Leeds LS25 5XA.

PERIODICALS

MODEL COLLECTOR monthly magazine for collectors of die-cast, white metal or tin plate models of vehicles, whether old or new. Enquiries to: Link House, Dingwall Avenue, Croydon, Surrey CR9 2TA. Tel: (0181) 686-2599. Fax: 781-6044.

MODEL RAILWAY ENTHUSIAST monthly newstand colour magazine. £2 per month. Frequent articles on collecting old Hornby, Wrenn and other former model railway ranges. Editor: David Jinks. Published by: Link House Magazines, Link House, Dingwall Avenue, Croydon, Surrey CR9 2TA. Tel: (0181) 686-2599. Fax: 781-6044.

PICTURE POSTCARD MONTHLY Published by: Brian and Francis Mary Lund, 15 Debdale Lane, Keyworth, Nottingham NG12 5HT. Tel: (0115) 937-4079. Fax: 937-6197.

SHIRE ALBUMS a regular series of 32 page illustrated monographs on collectable subjects: bookmarkers, brassware, button hooks, cast iron, corkscrews, Copeland etc. Published by: Shire Publications, Cromwell House, Church Street, Princes Risborough, Buckinghamshire HP27 9AA. Tel: (01844) 344301. Fax: 347080.

TEDDY BEAR SCENE The definitive glossy magazine covering all aspects of the teddy bear enthusiast. £2.75 per issue, £15.00 per year. Published by: EMF Publishing, 7 Ferringham Lane, Ferring, West Sussex BN12 5ND. Tel: (01903) 244900. Fax: 506626.

TEDDY BEAR TIMES bi-monthly glossy colour magazine covering everything for you and your bear; antique, modern and artist bears. £21 per year (UK). (Overseas on request). Published by: Ashdown Publishing, Avalon Court, Star Road, Partridge Green, West Sussex RH13 8RY. Tel: (01403) 711511. Fax: 711521.

AN OVERVIEW by Nick Fletcher

The market for collectables is ever-changing, with new themes emerging almost every week. The time when items had to be at least 50 years old to attract the collector have long gone. There is now tremendous interest in collectables from as recent as the 1970s and 1980s – even the early 1990s!

The reason for this collecting-mania is partly due to people having more disposable income, and partly due to a growing nostalgia for the recent past. While collectors span all age groups, the vast majority are middle-aged and thus yearn for reminders of their youth, perhaps only 20 or 30 years ago. And younger collectors go for items of even more recent vintage because we live in a fast-changing world and possessions we had even in the early 1980s are now starting to look slightly quaint.

Modern sales and marketing techniques mean products have to constantly be re-invented, redesigned or merely re-packaged to attract more and more buyers. This means many products have short manufacturing runs and are then deleted to make way for new offerings. In many cases - toys in particular - the fact that the item is no longer in production provides an almost instant aura of collectability.

There is much evidence of this if you analyse some of the biggest collecting trends of recent years: rock & pop memorabilia, space toys, film spin-offs such as Batman, Swatch watches, pocket calculators, transistor radios.

And shrewd collectors with a keen eye on future investment are already homing-in on, among many, Fisher-Price nursery toys and TV spin-off material relating to characters such as Bart Simpson, Power Rangers and The Biker Mice from Mars.

Of course, there is always going to be a strong market for the well-established collectables, embracing everything from silver thimbles and cigarette cards, Victorian scent bottles, Clarice Cliff pottery, fine porcelain, exquisite glass, paintings, clocks and watches and so much more.

Whatever you may collect, it is important to look to the future, for while most collect for pleasure, future investment can be an important factor. Spotting emerging trends is the key to potential profit, and most experts have their own ideas on just where the next boom is coming from.

Personally, I feel there is still a big market ahead for TV-related toys, most of which have a very short shelf-life. And the market for sporting collectables still has much room to expand. For while golf and cricket items are in demand, many other sports, football for instance, are virtually ignored. This situation cannot last for long!

Collecting interest in the 1950s is also certain to escalate. One tip for a future price-boom is the tableware of the Midwinter company. Its Stylecraft products involved such great designers as Sir Hugh Casson and Sir Terence Conran, then struggling to make a name for themselves.

Yet whatever is, or becomes, collectable, part of the pleasure for the enthusiast is the hunt for the rarity and the bargain. Collectors trek around the country visiting antique shops and fairs, auctions, junk shops, and car-boot sales, hoping for a great 'find'.

The extensive specialist listings in this directory will be of tremendous help to all collectors, saving them an immense amount of time by pinpointing so many sources. And as every collector knows, saving time is saving money . . . .

INTRODUCTION

The first Sheppard Directory appeared in 1951 and in the following forty-five years, the name of Sheppard has become synonymous with reliable business information on antiquarian and secondhand book dealers. The first edition listed dealers in the British Isles but today, six directories list book dealers in fifty-eight countries around the world. To the list, we have added one directory listing print and map sellers and one specifically on ephemera dealers.

The publication of Sheppard's Dealers in Collectables marks another major achievement in the history of this imprint. The idea for it was conceived at a recent Frankfurt Book Fair and it has taken quite some time to produce this first edition. Now that we have reached this stage, we intend to publish a new edition annually.

The layout of this title follows that of other Sheppard titles. After the preliminary pages, the main section lists all dealers geographically and then alphabetically under town or city within each county. However, the present government has been hatching many changes to established counties, and last month saw nine counties disappear, to be replaced by seventy-two unitary authorities. As the geographical location of these authorities will be totally unknown to most people, we have retained the counties and the areas therein.

Indexes of Business Names, Proprietors and Specialities follow. The Speciality Index is in two parts, the first covering new and reproduction stock, the second old and antique stock. To our knowledge, this is the only directory to list dealers in this way. We hope that this will provide serious collectors with a single volume and unique reference book of unparalleled importance.

Within the one thousand, one hundred and forty-nine entries, there are a large number of 'antique centres' which house numerous dealers whose stock specialities vary enormously. It has not always been possible to list every major speciality due to the restrictions on space. We have contained these lists to twenty specialities at each centre.

Collectors may well find what they seek amongst these, but if they seek a specific item, then a visit to those dealers listed in the Speciality Index may prove more productive. There are over three-hundred headings in the 'new' section, and three-hundred in the 'old' section, and to our knowledge, no one has ever combined 'new' and 'old' in the one reference book on this subject.

Whether you are a serious collector, or just looking for some attractive ornaments for your home, this book will be invaluable. We wish every user a successful time visiting the dealers listed.

For those who acquire a copy of this book and wish to be included in the next edition, a free dealer entry form is included on page 343. This page may be photocopied. If any fair organiser, auctioneer, restorer or publisher of related magazines wishes to be included, please write in. Dealers who complete the form should send it to Alison Lake, at Richard Joseph Publishers Ltd, Unit 2 Monks Walk, Farnham, Surrey GU9 8HT.

R Joseph

USE OF THE DIRECTORY

This directory is divided into four sections. The first is the *Geographical Directory of Dealers*, in which full details, where supplied, are given for each business or private dealer. In each county these are listed alphabetically by town in which the shop or business premises are located. Where Unitary Authorities have been created, we have listed dealers within their original county for easy identification. The details, as supplied by dealers, are presented in the following manner:

Name of business.	As provided.
Postal address.	(∗) Indicates the dealer's preference for indexing or where we have imposed current county boundaries.
Prop:	Name of proprietor(s).
Tel:	Telephone number(s), together with the new codes followed by fax and/or telex number. NOTE: If the code for the fax number is the same as for the telephone, it has been omitted.
E-Mail:	Electronic mail numbers. Users should ignore the full point at the end of the entry.
Est:	Date at which business was established.
Type of premises occupied.	Shop, private, market stall or storeroom.
Opening times:	Of shop, or if premises are private, whether appointments to view stock may be made, or if postal business only.
NEW/OLD:	New & reproduction stock is listed as NEW, followed by old & antique stock listed as OLD.
Normal level of total stock:	Very small (less than 500), small (500–1,000), medium (1,000–5,000), large (5,000–10,000) or very large (more than 10,000).
Spec:	Subjects in which dealer specialises.
PR:	Price range of stock. This is intended as a guideline only.
CC:	Credit Cards eg. A – Access, AE – American Express, DC – Diners Club, EC – Eurocard, JCB – Japanese Credit Bureau, MC – Mastercard, V – VISA.
Important lines of business:	Other than collectables.
Cata:	Frequency and subject of catalogues, if issued.
Corresp:	Languages in which correspondence may be conducted.
Mem:	Membership of book trade organisations, eg. B.A.D.A. – British Antique Dealers Association B.N.T.A. – British Numismatic Trade Association

The next section is an alphabetical *Index of Businesses*, giving name and county.

This is followed by an alphabetical *Index of Proprietors*, giving their personal and trading names.

The fourth section is the *Speciality Index*. This is presented in two parts - New & Reproduction and Old & Antique. Entries are in alphabetical order by subject, giving the dealer's name, county and page reference.

GEOGRAPHICAL DIRECTORY OF DEALERS

INDEX OF CITIES AND TOWNS

Dealer locations listed alphabetically by country, city, town and village, as shown in the Geographical section.

INDEX OF TOWNS AND VILLAGES

INDEX OF TOWNS AND VILLAGES

AVON

Including the Unitary Authorities of Bath & North East Somerset, Bristol, North West Somerset and South Gloucestershire

BATH

Antique Linens & Lace, 11 Pulteney Bridge, Bath, Avon BA2 4AY. Prop: Rosalind Mellor. Tel: (01225) 465782. Fax: 754067. Est: c.1970. Shop; open Monday to Saturday 10–5.30, Sundays in Summer. OLD stock. Spec: antiques; bed linens; christening gowns; lace; fountain pens; beadwork; dolls/dolls clothes; embroideries; shawls. PR: £5–500. CC: V; MC; JCB; AE; DC. Corresp: French. Mem: Bradford-on-Avon and Bath Antiques Association.

The Bartlett Street Antiques Centre, 5-10 Bartlett Street, Bath, Avon. Manager: Richard Crowder. Tel: (01225) 466689. Fax: 444146. Est: 1983. Antique centre with 30 stands; open Monday to Saturday 9.30–5, Wednesday 8–5. OLD general stock - very large. PR: £1–3,000. CC: V; MC; JCB. Also, restorations workshop. Corresp: French, Spanish. Mem: Bath & Bradford Antiques Dealers Association.

Bath Stamp & Coin Shop, 12 Pulteney Bridge, Bath, Avon BA2 4AY. Prop: Michael Swindells. Tel: & Fax: (01225) 463073. Est: 1961. Shop; open Monday to Saturday 9.30–5.30, Sunday 10.30–4.30. OLD stock - small. Spec: coins (Roman - recent); stamps; medals; banknotes. PR: £1–250. CC: AE; V; MC. Corresp: Italian, Spanish, French. Mem: P.T.S.

Lynda Brine, 2,3,4, Great Western Antique Centre, Bartlett Street, Bath BA1 2QZ. Tel: (01225) 448488. Est: 1988. Market stand; open 10.30–4.30. Fairs: N.E.C. OLD stock - very large. Spec: scent bottles. PR: £15–1,500. CC: V. Cata: 4 a year. Also, the UK Perfume Bottle Collectors Club. Mem: I.P.B.A., U.K.P.B.C.C.

Peter & Sonia Cashman, Bartlett Street Antique Centre Bartlett Street, Bath, Avon. Tel: (01225) 469497. Est: 1972. Market stand; open Monday to Saturday 9.30–5. Fairs: N.E.C. OLD stock. Spec: embroideries; embroidered pictures; portrait miniatures; samplers; silhouettes.

Collectable Costume, The Great Western Antique Centre, Bartlett Street, Bath, Avon BA1 2QZ. Prop: M. Adams & K. Jones. Tel: (01225) 428731. Est: 1980. Market stand; open Monday to Saturday 10–5. OLD stock - large. Spec: Art Nouveau; Art Deco; binoculars; buckles & clasps; buttons; buttonhooks; china; costume; costume jewellery; cuff links; diecast toys; dolls/dolls clothes; fashion accessories; jewellery; luggage; samplers; shawls; shoes/shoe making; The Sixties; smocks; spectacles, lorgnettes & monacles; stanhopes; textiles. PR: £5–1,000.

Andrew Dando Antiques, 4 Wood Street, Bath, Avon BA1 2JQ. Prop: A. & J. Dando. Tel: (01225) 422702. Est: 1912. Shop; open Monday to Friday 9.30–5.30, Saturday 10–1. Fairs: NEC Birmingham (April & August). OLD stock (pre 1875) - medium. Spec: ceramics; china; pottery; Staffordshire. PR: £5–5,000. CC: A; V; AE. Mem: B.A.D.A.

31

AVON

Frank Dux Antiques, 33 Belvedere, Bath, Avon BA1 5HR. Prop: Frank Dux & Margaret Hopkins. Tel: & Fax: (01225) 312367. Est: 1976. Shop; open Monday to Saturday 10–6. Fairs: Little Chelsea, Shepton Mallett, Bath. OLD stock - medium. Spec: glass. PR: £10–1,500. CC: V; A; AE. Also, oak furniture and antique accessories. Corresp: French, Spanish, German, Greek. Mem: Bath & Bradford Antique Dealers Association (B.A.B.A.D.A.).

The English Teddy Bear Co., 8 Abbey Churchyard, Bath, Avon BA1 1LY. Prop: Alise & Jonty Crossick & Dominic Richards. Tel: (01225) 338655. Fax: 460128. Est: 1990. Shop; open during business hours. NEW stock - large. Spec: teddy bears, limited edition bears and related gifts. PR: £5–200 (bears). CC: V; M. Cata: quarterly. *Also shops in:* Canterbury, Cambridge, Carnaby Street (London), Meadowhall, Newcastle, Oxford, Regent Street (London), Stratford, Windsor, York.

T.J. Millard Antiques, Stand 10–11, Bartlett Street Antiques Centre, Bartlett Street, Bath BA1 2QZ. Tel: (01225) 469785. Market stand; open 9.30–5. Fairs: Newark, Western Burt. NEW stock - very small. Spec: boxes; chess sets. PR: £100–1,000. CC: V; MC; EC; D.

Nashers Music Store, 72 Walcot Street, Bath, Avon BA1 5BD. Prop: Paul Nachman. Tel: (01225) 332298. Fax: 425376. E-Mail: the-cafe@hub.co.uk. Est: 1991. Shop; open Monday to Saturday 10–5.30, Sunday 11–4. OLD stock - very large. Spec: musical - records, tapes, CD, memorabilia, autographs. PR: £1–1,500. CC: A; V; MC; EC. Cata: continuously updated on Internet.

Caroline Nevill Miniatures, 22A Broad Street, Bath, Avon BA1 5LN. Tel: & Fax: (01225) 443091. Est: 1995. Shop; open 10–5. NEW stock. Spec: dolls houses; British miniatures. PR: £3–10,000. CC: A; V.

Pennard House Antiques, 3/4 Piccadilly, London Road, Bath, Avon BA1 6PL. Prop: Martin Dearden. Tel: (01225) 313791. Fax: 448196. Est: 1978. Shop; open Monday to Saturday 9.30–5.30, Sunday 10–4. Fairs: Bath Decorative Fair. OLD stock - medium. Spec: arts & crafts; Art Deco; Art Nouveau; bamboo; barometers; birdcages; boxes; brass; chandeliers; decorative; French; inkstands; jardinières; mirrors; rocking horses; samplers; trays; treen. PR: £10–3,000. CC: V; AE; MC; JCB. Corresp: French, German, Italian. Mem: L.A.P.A.D.A., B.A.B.A.D.A.

Michael & Jo Saffell, 3 Walcot Buildings, London Road, Bath, Avon BA1 6AD. Tel: (01225) 315857. Est: 1975. Shop; appointment necessary. Fairs: Newark. OLD general stock - medium. Spec: tins, signs & advertising. PR: £5–1,500.

Walcot Reclamation Ltd., The Yard, 108 Walcot Street, Bath BA1 5BG. Prop: Mr Rick Knapp. Tel: (01225) 444404. Fax: 448163. Est: 1974. Shop and private premises; open Monday to Friday 8.30–5.30, Saturday 9–5. Fairs: Bath Decorative Antiques Fair, Country Living. NEW stock - medium. Spec: boot scrapers; brass; bronze; candles/candlesticks; chandeliers; doorstops; letter boxes; mirrors; sundials; weather vanes; kitchenalia; lighting. OLD stock. Spec: arts & crafts; Art Deco; bells; boot scrapers; bottles; brass; bronze; buckets; candlesticks; chandeliers; doorstops; Edwardian; Georgian; kitchenalia; letter boxes; lighting; metalware; mirrors; sculpture; sundials; tiles; Victorian; weather vanes. PR: £1–10,000. CC: A; V; MC. Cata: every other year. Also, a reproduction shop with quality replicas of fixtures and fittings and a depot dealing in reclaimed traditional building materials. Mem: Bath & Bradford Antique Dealers Association.

M. & R. Wellman Collectables, Stand 39, Great Western Antique Centre, Bartlett Street, Bath, Avon. Prop: Mark & Robert Wellman. Tel: (01225) 428731. Est: 1992. Market stand; open Monday to Saturday 9–5. Fairs: Shepton Toy Fair, Taunton, Devizes. OLD stock - medium. Spec: diecast toys; posters; tinplate toys; toys - general.

BRISTOL

Avon Miniatures (Bristol), 46 Forest Road, Fishponds, Bristol, Avon BS16 3XQ. Prop: Mrs Theresa Rich. Tel: (0117) 975-4673. Est: 1994. Private premises; appointment necessary. Fairs: Cardiff, Bristol, Portishead. NEW stock - very small. Spec: dolls houses, furniture and accessories. PR: 20p–£120. Cata: available at fairs 50p.

Militaria, 13/14 Lower Park Row, Bristol, Avon BS1 5BN. Prop: Christopher & Hazel Grimes. Tel: (0117) 929-8205. Est: 1968. Open Monday to Friday 11–6 and Saturday 11–5. Fairs: Shepton Mallet. OLD stock - medium. Spec: medals; medical and scientific instruments; militaria; aeronautica; automobilia; barometers; binoculars; cameras; drawing instruments; globes; gramophones; maritime/natuical; scales, weights and measures; sundials; swords; telescopes. PR: £1–3,500.

Gillian Richards, 27 North View, Westbury Park, Bristol, Avon BS6 7PT. Tel: & Fax: (0117) 973-1850. Est: 1985. Shop; open Wednesday to Saturday 10–5. NEW stock - large. Spec: dolls/dolls clothes; dolls houses; miniatures; teddy bears. OLD stock - very small. Spec: dolls/dolls clothes. PR: 25p–£750. Also, Bristol School of Dollmaking (5 dollmaking classes a week and 3 day courses). Mem: Global Doll Society.

M.A. Shipp, 21 High Street, Staple Hill, Bristol, Avon BS16 5HB. Tel: (0117) 956-9966. Est: 1946. Shop; open Tuesday and Thursday to Saturday 9.30–12 and 1.30–4. Fairs: 'Brunel' - Bristol, 'Timsbury' - Bath. OLD general stock - medium. PR: £1–250.

MIDSOMER NORTON

Somervale Antiques, 6 Radstock Road, Midsomer Norton, Bath, Avon BA3 2AJ. Prop: Wg Cdr R.G. Thomas. Tel: (01761) 412686. Fax: 417502. Modile: (0585) 088022. Shop; appointment necessary. Fairs: Chelsea. OLD stock - very large. Spec: glass; glass scent bottles. PR: £20–6,000. CC: V; A; MC; EC. Mem: B.A.D.A., L.A.P.A.D.A., C.I.N.O.A., B.A.B.A.D.A.

PORTISHEAD

Model Craft Woods, 42 Wetlands Lane, Portishead, Bristol BS20 8NF. Prop: R.G.W. Hathaway (Mr Royston Snr.). Tel: (01275) 818451. Est: 1756. Workshops; appointment necessary. Fairs: Bristol and Portishead. NEW stock - small. Spec: dolls houses; arts & crafts. PR: 25p–£1,000 (for commissions). Cata: 2 lists a year. Also, courses in miniature wood turning and carving. Corresp: French.

AVON

YATTON

Glenville Antiques, 120 High Street, Yatton, Avon BS19 4DH. Prop: Mrs S.E.M. Burgan. Tel: (01934) 832284. Est: 1969. Shop; open Monday to Saturday 10.30–1 and 2.15–5. Fairs: Westombirt School, Wilton House, Shepton Mallet, Westpoint, Exeter, Glass Fair (National Motorcycle Museum). NEW stock - small. Spec: jewellery; photograph frames. OLD stock - medium. Spec: boxes; buttonhooks; card cases; china; decanters; Edwardian; glass; jewellery; match boxes/books; Mauchline ware; pincushions; pottery; silver; spoons; Staffordshire; teapots; tiles; treen; vases; Victorian. PR: £1–2,500. CC: A; MC; AE. Mem: L.A.P.A.D.A.

BEDFORDSHIRE

AMPTHILL

Ampthill Antiques, 4 Market Square, Ampthill, Bedfordshire MK45. Prop: Alex Olney. Tel: (01525) 403344. Est: 1980. Shop; open Wednesday to Saturday 10–5, Sunday 2–5. OLD general stock - very large. PR: £1–1,500. CC: V; MC.

BIGGLESWADE

Shortmead Antiques, 46 Shortmead Street, Biggleswade, Bedfordshire SG18 0AP. Prop: Mr S.E. Sinfield. Tel: (01767) 601780. Est: 1988. Shop; open 10–4.30, closed Thursday and Sunday. Fairs: Haberdashers School, Elstree, Herts. OLD general stock - medium. Spec: boot scrapers; boxes; brass; bronze; buttonhooks; china; copper; cutlery; decanters; Edwardian; egg cups; hatpins & holders; oil lamps; pewter; pottery; silver; snuff boxes; vases; Victorian; walking sticks. PR: £1–1,000. CC: A; V. Also, Victorian and Edwardian furniture.

LUTON

Enstone Emergency Models, 36 Reedsdale, Luton, Bedfordshire, LU2 9TG. Tel: (01582) 483580. Fax: 413202. Est: 1994. Storeroom; appointment necessary. Fairs: many attended. NEW stock - very small. PR: £50–500. Cata: 1 a year.

WOBURN

Christopher Sykes Antiques, The Old Parsonage, Bedford Street, Woburn, Milton Keynes MK17 9QL. Tel: (01525) 290259. Fax: 290061. Est: 1967. Shop; open Monday to Saturday 9–5 and postal business. OLD stock - large. Spec: corkscrews and bottle openers; wine antiques; maritime/nautical; medical instruments; scales, weights and measures; scientific instruments; sundials. PR: £20–3,000. CC: V; MC; AE; DC. Cata: monthly, £3 each (US $15). Corresp: French. Mem: Canadian Corkscrew Collectors Club.

BERKSHIRE

ASCOT

Country Antiques, Country Gardens Garden Centre, London Road, Windlesham, Surrey. (•) Prop: Caroline Martin & Sue Sommers. Tel: (01344) 873404. Est: 1985. Shop; open Thursday to Tuesday 10–5. OLD general stock - large. Spec: chandeliers; Victorian; telephones; boxes; brass; candles/candlesticks; china; kitchenalia; copper; glass; mirrors; oil lamps; plates. PR: £2 upwards. CC: V; A. Mem: F.S.B.

BARKHAM

Barkham Antique Centre, Barkham Street, Barkham, Nr. Wokingham, Berkshire RG40 4PJ. Prop: Eileen Lowes & Ken Lowes A.R.C.M. Tel: & Fax: (01734) 761355. Est: 1990. Shop; open 7 days a week 10.30–5 (open Bank Holidays except Christmas and Boxing Day). NEW stock - small. Spec: model cars. OLD stock - small. Spec: porcelain. PR: £1–200. CC: V; A; AE; D. Corresp: French, Italian.

CROWTHORNE

Quality Coins & Antiques, 16 Bramley Grove, Crowthorne, Berkshire RG45 6EB. Prop: F.T. Kelly. Tel: & Fax: (01344) 771887. Est: 1993. Private premises; appointment necessary. Fairs: Crispin and Silhouette fairs. OLD stock - medium. Spec: coins and antiques from Roman to 20th century. PR: £1–300. Corresp: French.

ETON

Mostly Boxes, 92 & 93 High Street, Eton, Windsor, Berkshire SL4 6AF. Prop: Gary Munday. Tel: (01784) 256882. Fax: 240646. Est: 1982. Shops; open Monday to Saturday 9.45–6.45. Fairs: Park Lane Antique Fair, London W1. OLD stock - medium. Spec: wooden antique boxes. PR: £30–1,000. CC: V; MC; AE; DC. Cata: 1 a year.

Oriental Rug Gallery Limited, 115–116 High Street, Eton, Berkshire SL4 6AN. Tel: (01753) 623000. *For details see entry:* 42 Verulam Road, St. Albans, Hertfordshire (q.v.).

Times Past Antiques, 59 High Street, Eton, Berkshire SL4 6BL. Prop: Phillip Jackson. Tel: & Fax: (01753) 857018. Est: 1976. Shop; open 9.30–5. OLD stock. Spec: barometers; clocks. PR: £100–5,000. CC: all.

The Turks Head Antiques, 98 High Street, Eton, Berkshire SL4 6AF. Prop: Anthea Baillie, Margaret Wilcox, Andrew Reeve. Tel: (01753) 863939. Est: 1980. Shop; open Tuesday & Thursday to Saturday 10.15–5. OLD stock - medium. Spec: antique ceramics, commemorative ware, glass, jewellery, scent bottles, silver. PR: £1–1,000. CC: V; AE; A. Mem: Eton Traders Association.

HUNGERFORD

Dolls and Toys of Yesteryear, Bow House Antiques, 3-4 Faulknor Square, Charnham Street, Hungerford, Berkshire RG17 0ER. Prop: Dawn Herrington. Tel: (01488) 683198 and 684319. Est: 1973. Shop; open Monday to Wednesday, Friday and Saturday 10.30–4. Fairs: London Victoria International Doll Shows, Kensington Town Hall Doll Fairs. OLD stock - very large. Spec: dolls houses; miniatures; rocking horses. PR: £1–2,500.

Styles Silver, 12 Bridge Street, Hungerford, Berkshire RG17 0EH. Prop: Patsy & Derek Styles. Tel: (01488) 683922. Est: 1974. Shop; open Saturday and by appointment. NEW stock - medium Spec: silver. OLD stock - very large. Spec: silver. PR: £5–5,000. CC: V; A; D. Mem: L.A.P.A.D.A.

Walker & Walker, Halfway Manor, Halfway, Nr. Newbury, Berkshire RG20 8NR. (•) Prop: Alan & Kym Walker. Tel: & Fax: (01488) 658693. Est: 1984. Appointment necessary. Fairs: Olympia and many others. OLD stock. Spec: barometers; weather instruments. PR: £500–10,000. Also, restoration undertaken. Mem: T.V.A.D.A

MAIDENHEAD

The Model Store, Boundary Elms, Burchetts Green Lane, Maidenhead, Berkshire SL6 3QP. Director: R. Calcott. Tel: (01628) 822922. Fax: 823823. E-Mail: roncalcott@delphi.com. Est: 1993. Private premises; appointment necessary. Fairs: Matchbox conventions. NEW stock - very small. Spec: diecast toys. OLD stock - medium. Spec: diecast toys. PR: £1–1,000. CC: A; V; MC; D. Cata: 4 a year. Also, worldwide mail order of diecast models.

NEWBURY

Roberts, 6 Titan House, Calleva Park, Aldermaston, Berkshire RG7 4QW. Prop: T.J. Davies. Tel: (01734) 819973. Fax: 811176. Est: 1984. Storeroom; appointment necessary. Fairs: Britannia Medal Fairs. MEW stock - medium. Spec: militaria. OLD stock - small. Spec: militaria. PR: £5–1,000. CC: MC; V. Cata: 4 a year. Also, publishers of military reference books. Corresp: French. Mem: Federation of Small Businesses.

READING

Bits and Pieces, 11 Bridge street, Caversham, Reading, Berkshire RG4 8AA. Prop: Mrs Frances Munday. Tel: (01734) 463733. Est: 1992. Shop; open Tuesday to Saturday 10–5.30, some Sundays please telephone. NEW stock - medium. Spec: dolls houses; miniatures. PR: 50p–£500. Mem: F.P.B.

The Clock Workshop, 17 Prospect Street, Caversham, Nr Reading, Berkshire RG4 8JB. Prop: John M. Yealland F.B.H.I. Tel: (01734) 470741. Est: 1981. Shop; open Monday to Friday 9.30–5.30, Saturday 10–1. Fairs: L.A.P.A.D.A. Autumn, T.V.A.D.A., Olympia Spring. OLD stock - very large. Spec: barometer; clocks; musical boxes. PR: £300–50,000. CC: A; V. Also, restoration of clocks and barometers. Corresp: French, German. Mem: L.A.P.A.D., T.V.A.D.A.

BERKSHIRE

Footballana, 275 Overdown Road, Tilehurst, Reading, Berkshire RG31 6NX. Prop: Bryan Horsnell. Tel: (01734) 424448. Est: 1970. Private premises; postal business only. OLD stock - very small. Spec: association football including medals, caps, jerseys and postcards. PR: £2–100. Cata: occasionally.

Grant A. Healey Militaria, P.O. Box 86, Reading, Berkshire RG6 5FS. Tel: & Fax: (01734) 311634. Est: 1987. Private premises; appointment necessary or postal business. Fairs: all major South of England fairs. OLD stock - medium. Spec: medals; militaria. Cata: monthly (£8 for one years subscription).

Cliff Maddock Models, P.O. Box 26, Mortimer, Nr. Reading, Berkshire RG7 3EE. Tel: & Fax: (01734) 833062. Est: 1980. Private premises; postal business only. Fairs: major toyfairs in Southern Counties of England and Wales. OLD stock - small. Spec: constructional toys; diecast toys; model trains, cars and aircraft; railways; tinplate toys; toys - general; transport. PR: £1–2,000. CC: V; MC. Cata: 4 a year. Also, organiser of 'Big Southern' toyfair.

SLOUGH

K & G Collectibles, 33 Burroway Road, Langley, Slough, Berkshire SL3 8EH. Prop: Kath & Glyn Gilbert. Tel: (01753) 543258. Est: 1979. Shop at: Spectus Gallery, 298 Westbourne Grove, off Portobello Road, London W11; open Saturday 7–4. Fairs: Lee Valley Leisure Centre, Doulton fair. NEW stock - very small. Spec: teddy bears; Doulton; advertising memorabilia; pub jugs, tins & signs. OLD stock - very small. Spec: Doulton; advertising memorabilia; pub jugs, tins & signs; bottles & pot lids. PR: £1–250. Mem: Portobello Traders Association.

Edward Sanderson, 60A Upton Park, Slough, Berkshire SL1 2DE. Tel: (01753) 526601. Est: 1975. Private premises; appointment necessary. Fairs: London P.B.F.A., A.B.A., Ephemera Society Fairs. OLD stock - medium. Spec: bookmarkers; Edwardian; films & entertainment; fishing; London Transport; musical; Royal memorabilia; tobacco & associated; transport; Victorian; writing - general. PR: £5–500. Cata: irregularly. Corresp: French, German. Mem: A.B.A., P.B.F.A., E.S.

WINDSOR

The English Teddy Bear Co., 47 High Street, Windsor, Berkshire SL4 1LR. Prop: Alise & Jonty Crossick & Dominic Richards. Tel: (01753) 862524. Fax: 621594. Est: 1990. Shop; open during business hours. NEW stock - large. Spec: teddy bears, limited edition bears and related gifts. PR: £5–200 (bears). CC: V; M. Cata: quarterly. *Also shops in:* Bath, Canterbury, Cambridge, Carnaby Street (London), Meadowhall, Newcastle, Oxford, Regent Street (London), Stratford, York.

WOKINGHAM

China Search, Barkham Antique Centre, Barkham Street, Barkham, Nr Wokingham, Berkshire RG11 4PL. Prop: Susan Dawson. Tel: (01252) 877458. Fax: 875219. Est: 1994. Shop; open Monday to Sunday 10.30–5. Fairs: Eversley, Hartley Wintney (Hampshire). OLD stock - medium. Spec: Art Deco; bells; ceramics; china; commemorative ware; corkscrews and bottle openers; egg cups; games; glass; kitchenalia; plates; pottery; Royal memorabilia; teapots. PR: £1–100. CC: V. Also, Chinasearch - a china matching service. Corresp: French, Spanish.

BUCKINGHAMSHIRE

AMERSHAM

Amersham Antiques & Collectors Centre, 20–22 Whielden Street, Old Amersham, Buckinghamshire HP7 0HT. Prop: G. & G.F. Macaree. Tel: (01494) 431282. Est: 1988. Shop; open Monday to Saturday 9.30–5.30. Fairs: Ardingly. OLD general stock. PR: £1–1,000. CC: AE; DC; V; MC.

Buckingham Miniatures, 16 Clifton Road, Amersham, Buckinghamshire HP6 5PU. Prop: Lesley & Tony Cockrell. Tel: (01494) 434274. Fax: 725219. Private premises; appointment necessary. Fairs: dolls house fairs in South-East England. NEW stock - very small. Spec: dolls houses. PR: £1,000–2,000. Cata: annually.

BEACONSFIELD

RA Marketing International, 10 Wood Pond Close, Seer Green, Beaconsfield, Buckinghamshire HP9 2XG. Prop: Ronald Anlauf. Tel: (01494) 674872. Est: 1988. Private premises; appointment necessary. Fairs: Frankfurt Spring & Autumn, Nurenberg. NEW stock - small. Spec: Art Nouveau; Art Deco; boxes; china; glass; oil lamps; tea caddies; teapots; teddy bears; tools; toys - general; vases. PR: £5–15,000. Cata: 1 a year. Corresp: German. Mem: Independent Consultants Association.

BOURNE END

Model Motors, 21 The Parade, Bourne End, Buckinghamshire SL8 5SB. Prop: Michael Savage. Tel: (01628) 528617. Est: 1988. Shop; open Monday to Friday 10–5, Saturday 9–5. Fairs: Heathrow Toy Fair, Farnham Toy Fair. NEW stock - very large. Spec: diecast toys; model trains and cars; sci-fi. OLD stock - medium. PR: £1–100. CC: A; EC; MC; V. Also, scalextric and sci-fi plastic kits.

IVER

'Yester-year', 12 High Street, Iver, Buckinghamshire SL0 9NG. Prop: Peter J. Frost. Tel: (01753) 652072. Est: 1972. Shop; open Monday to Saturday 10–6. OLD general stock - very small. PR: £1–1,000. Also, picture framing and clock repairs. Corresp: German.

MARLOW

Coldstream Military Antiques, 55A High Street, Marlow, Buckinghamshire SL7 1BA. Prop: S. Bosley. Tel: & Fax: (01628) 822503. Est: 1978. Private premises; postal business only. Fairs: most major arms fairs. OLD stock - very large. Spec: antique military items including helmets, badges, swords etc. PR: £5–5,000. CC: V; A; MC. Also, valuations. Mem: L.A.P.A.D.A.

St. Ann's Dolls House, 44 West Street, Marlow, Buckinghamshire SL7 2NB. Prop: Ann & Alan Phyall. Tel: (01628) 487387. Est: 1995. Shop; open Monday to Saturday 9.30–5. NEW stock - medium. Spec: dolls/dolls clothes; dolls houses; miniatures; teddy bears. PR: £1–1,000. CC: all major cards. Also, toy restorations and doll valuations. Corresp: Braille.

BUCKINGHAMSHIRE

OLNEY

Market Square Antiques, 20 Market Place, Olney, Buckinghamshire MK46 4BA. Prop: Derek & Helen Vella. Tel: (01234) 712172. Est: 1988. Shop; open Monday to Saturday 10–5, Sunday 1–5. NEW general stock - small. OLD stock - medium. Spec: silver. CC: V; A; MC; D. Also, Georgian and Victorian furniture.

PRINCES RISBOROUGH

Well Cottage Antique Centre, 20/22 Bell Street, Princes Risborough, Buckinghamshire HP27 0AD. Tel: (01844) 342002. Est: 1985. Shop; open Monday to Saturday 9.30–5.30, Sundays and Bank Holidays 1–5. OLD general stock. Spec: barometers; boxes; brass; chandeliers; china; copper; costume jewellery; decanters; jewellery; miniatures; objets de vertu; pewter; portrait miniatures; pottery; silhouettes; silver; snuff boxes; tools; treen; writing. PR: £1–3,500. CC: V; MC; D; E; EC; JCB. Also, furniture. Corresp: French.

TINGEWICK

Tingewick Antiques Centre, Main Street, Tingewick, Buckinghamshire. Prop: B.J. & R. Smith. Tel: (01280) 848219. Est: 1982. Shop; open Monday to Thursday and Saturday 10–5.30, Sunday 11–5. OLD general stock. PR: £1–3,500. CC: V; MC; EC. Also, restoration service.

WENDOVER

Antiques at . . . Wendover, The Old Post Office, 25 High Street, Wendover, Buckinghamshire HP22 6DU. Prop: Mrs N.D. Gregory. Tel: (01296) 625335. Est: 1987. Shop with 30 dealers; open Monday to Saturday 10–5.30, Sundays and Bank Holidays 11–5.30. OLD (dateline 1940) general stock - very large. Spec: barometers; brass; ceramics; china; clocks; copper; Edwardian; Georgian; glass; jewellery; kitchenalia; lace; lighting; mirrors; plates; scientific instruments; silver; treen; Victorian; writing. PR: £1–4,000. CC: A; V; MC; D; AE. Also, architectural salvage and garden items and restoration workshops.

WINSLOW

Winslow Antique Centre, 15 Market Square, Winslow, Buckinghamshire MK18 3AB. Prop: Mr R.M. Taylor. Tel: (01296) 714540. Est: 1991. Shop; open Monday to Saturday 10–5 (closed Wednesday), Sunday 1–5. OLD general stock - very large. PR: £10–1,000. CC: A; BC.

CAMBRIDGESHIRE

CAMBRIDGE

The English Teddy Bear Co., 1 Kings Parade, Cambridge, Cambridgeshire CB2 1SJ. Prop: Alise & Jonty Crossick & Dominic Richards. Tel: (01223) 300908. Fax: 329248. Est: 1990. Shop; open during business hours. NEW stock - large. Spec: teddy bears, limited edition bears and related gifts. PR: £5–200 (bears). CC: V; M. Cata: quarterly. *Also shops in:* Bath, Canterbury, Carnaby Street (London), Meadowhall, Newcastle, Oxford, Regent Street (London), Stratford, Windsor, York.

David Kerr Toys, 16 Worts Causeway, Cambridge, Cambridgeshire CB1 4RL. Tel: (01223) 242581. Private premises; appointment necessary. OLD stock - medium. Spec: constructional toys; diecast toys; London Transport; tinplate toys; toys general; model cars; trains; transport. PR: 50p–£750. Cata: 4 monthly.

'Sarah's Bears' of Cambridge, 62 Mill Lane, Impington, Cambridge CB4 4HS. Prop: Sarah Cox. Tel: (01223) 566960. Est: 1990. Private premises; postal business only. Fairs: annual Teddy Bear Festival, Kensington, London. NEW stock - very small. Spec: teddy bears. PR: £35–150. Cata: 1 a year, new and limited editions details & price list.

Tom Stanley, P.O. Box 471, Cambridge CB5 8XF. Tel: (01223) 312503. Fax: 574766. Est: 1981. Private premises; appointment necessary. OLD stock - large. Spec: maritime/nautical. Corresp: Spanish, Catalan.

University Miniatures, 80 Crowland Way, Arbury North, Cambridge, Cambridgeshire. Prop: Ann Maltby. Tel: & Fax: (01223) 277677 or Tel: 364035. Est: 1993. Private premises; appointment necessary. Fairs: Northampton, Bar Hill - Cambridge, Waltham Abbey, Stevenage, Ely, Hertford, Woodford Green - London. NEW stock - small. Spec: miniatures. PR: £9. CC: A; V. Cata: 1 a year, of hand crafted items.

ELY

Old Bishop's Palace Antique Centre, Tower Farm, Little Downham, Ely, Cambridgeshire CB6 2TD. Prop: M.J. Stevens. Tel: (01353) 699177. Fax: 699501. Est: 1992. Shop; open Friday to Sunday and Bank Holidays 10–5.30. OLD general stock - medium. Spec: china; clocks; Edwardian; fishing; Georgian; jewellery; kitchenalia; silver; tools; Victorian; wrist watches. PR: £1–5,000. Also, antique furniture.

CAMBRIDGESHIRE

HUNTINGDON

T.W. Pawson – Clocks, 31A High Street, Somersham, Huntingdon, Cambridgeshire PE17 3JA. Tel: (01487) 841537. Est: 1987. Shop; open Monday to Friday 9.30–6, Saturday 10.30–1. OLD stock - very small. Spec: antique clocks and barometers. PR: £150–4,500. Also, repair and restoration of clocks and barometers. Mem: British Watch and Clockmakers Guild.

Warboys Antiques, High Street, Warboys, Huntingdon, Cambridgeshire PE17 2RH. Prop: John Lambden and Enid Godfrey. Tel: (01487) 823686. Fax: 496296. Est: 1986. Shop; Tuesday to Saturday 11–5. Fairs: Alexander Palace. NEW stock - very small. OLD stock - medium. Spec: buttonhooks; decorative; golf; gramophone needle tins; kitchenalia; leather; sports - general; tins, signs & advertising; Victorian. PR: 50p–£1,500. CC: AE.

PETERBOROUGH

T.V. Coles, 981 Lincoln Road, Peterborough, Cambridgeshire PE4 6AH. Tel: (01733) 577268. Est: 1980. Shop; open 9–4.30, closed Sunday. OLD stock - medium. Spec: badges; commemorative ware; medals; Royal memorabilia. PR: £1–75.

"Second Front", 265 Dogsthorpe Road, Peterborough, Cambridgeshire PE1 3PA. Prop: MR Peter S. Ferreday. Tel: & Fax: (01733) 68099. Est: 1987. Shop; open Monday to Saturday 9.30–5.30, closed Wednesday, and market stand at: Wisbech Market; every Sunday. NEW stock - large. Spec: badges; costume; medals; pen knives. OLD stock - very large. Spec: arms & armour; badges; buckles & clasps; buttons; costume; medals; militaria; pen knives. PR: 50p upwards. CC: all except AE. Also, dog tags and I.D. tags. Corresp: German.

Katy Williams Kollectables, The Collectors Corner, The Cresset, Bretton Centre, Peterborough, Cambridgeshire PE3 7DY. Tel: (01733) 262283. Est: 1995. Shop; open Monday to Saturday 9.30–4. NEW stock - large. Spec: dolls houses; miniatures; teddy bears. PR: 50p–£500. Also, dolls house furniture, dolls, DIY accessories in 1/12th scale.

RAMSEY (NR HUNTINGDON)

Abbey Antiques, 63 Great Whyte, Ramsey, Nr Huntingdon, Cambridgeshire PE17 1HL. Prop: John & Rita Smith. Tel: (01487) 814753. Shop; open Tuesday to Sunday. Fairs: Alexandra Palace, Wembley. NEW general stock - small. Spec: Mabel Lucie Attwell; Cherished teddies; Dandy & Beano; Rupert; Disney; Canterbury Bears; Bransgore Bears. OLD stock - medium. Spec: writing - general; Goss & Crested China; Beswick; Doulton; Sylvac glass. PR: £5–1,500. CC: V; A; MC. Cata: M.L.A. Collectors Newsletter, 2 a year. Also, Mabel Lucie Attwell Collectors' Club/Museum.

ST. IVES

B.R. Knight and Sons, Quay Court, Bull Lane, Bridge Street, St. Ives, Cambridgeshire PE17 Prop: Michael Knight. Tel: (01480) 468295 or 300042. Est: 1972. Shop; open Monday, Wednesday and Friday 11–2.30, Saturday 11–4.30. Fairs: Mencap Fair, Huntingdonshire. OLD stock - medium. Spec: arts & crafts; Art Deco; Art Nouveau; brass; bronze; ceramics; china; copper; costume; costume jewellery; fine art; glass; jardinières; jewellery; Oriental; pewter; plates; pottery; Staffordshire; teapots; textiles; vases. PR: £5–200.

CHESHIRE

AUDLEM

Les Wilson, 'South View', Coxbank, Audlem, Cheshire CW3 0EU. Tel: (01270) 812380. Fax: 812410. OLD stock - medium. Spec: automobilia. CC: all. Cata: 4 a year.

BRAMHALL

Daisies Miniatures, 3 Bramhall Lane South, Bramhall, Cheshire SK7 1AL. Prop: Mr A.R.F. & Mrs J.M. Forshaw. Tel: (0161) 439-9844. Fax: 439-7279. Est: 1982. Shop; open 6 days a week 9.30–5. NEW general stock - very large. Spec: dolls houses; teddy bears; dolls; furniture and accessories. CC: V; A. Also, gifts.

CHESTER

Aldersey Hall Ltd., Town Hall Square, 47 Northgate Street, Chester, Cheshire CH1 2HQ. Prop: Anthony Wilding. Tel: (01244) 324885. Est: 1933. Shop; open Monday to Saturday 8.30–5.30. Fairs: Alexandra Palace, Chester Northgate. OLD stock - medium. Spec: Art Deco; ceramics; commemorative ware. PR: £1–500. CC: all. Also, Interflora florist. Corresp: Dutch.

The Antique Shop, 40 Watergate Street, Chester, Cheshire CH1 2LA. Prop: Peter Thornber. Tel: (01244) 316286. Est: 1987. Shop; open Monday to Saturday 10–6 (Sunday from Easter to Christmas 11–5). OLD stock - brass; copper; pewter. PR: £5–350. CC: A; MC; V; EC. Also, metal polishing and repair/renovation.

Arts & Crafts Studio, 14,15,16 St. Michaels Row, Chester, Cheshire CH1 1EF. Prop: Michael Nicholas Hutcheson. Tel: (01244) 324900. Fax: 400135. Est: 1924. Shop; open Monday to Saturday 9–5.30. NEW stock - very large. Spec: arts & crafts; ceramics; china; constructional toys; crochet; diecast toys; dolls/dolls clothes; dolls houses; embroideries; embroidered pictures; model trains, cars and aircraft; playing cards; pottery; railways; tapestries; teddy bears; tinplate toys; toys - general; toy soldiers; traction/steam engines. PR: 2p–£600. CC: A. Mem: B.T.H.A.

Avalon Stamp & Postcard Shop, 1 City Walls/Rufus Court, Northgate Street, Chester, Cheshire CH1 2JG. Prop: Geoff Ellis. Tel: (01244) 318406. Est: 1982. Shop; open Monday to Saturday 10–5. Fairs: Chester and Llandudno Postcard Fair. NEW stock - medium and OLD stock - very large. Spec: stamps. PR: 50p–£1,000. CC: A; MC; V; EC.

Cameo Antiques, 19 Watergate Street, Chester, Cheshire CH1 2LB. Tel: & Fax: (01244) 311467. Shop; open Monday to Saturday 9–5. OLD stock - very large. Spec: jewellery; silver; china; Art Deco; automiobilia; decorative; teddy bears; Victorian. PR: £20–5,000. CC: A; V; AE.

Chester Toy Museum, 13a Lower Bridge Street, Chester, Cheshire CH1 1RS. Prop: S.A. Orr. Tel: (01244) 346297. Fax: 340437. Est: 1985. Shop; open 7 days a week 10–5. OLD stock - medium. Spec: model trains and cars; diecast toys; dolls/dolls clothes; dolls houses. PR: £1–500. CC: V; BC.

CHESHIRE

Collector's Corner (Tudor House), 29–31 Lower Bridge Street, Chester, Cheshire CH1 1RS. Prop: Mr David Fowell. Tel: (01244) 346736 (shop), (01260) 270429 (24hrs). Fax: (01260) 279113. Est: 1982. Shop; open Monday to Saturday 10.15–5.30. Fairs: Pop Memorabilia Road Shows, major record fairs, Beatles commemorations. NEW and OLD stock - medium. Spec: Rock & Pop; films & entertainment; icons; musical; posters; radio & television; the Seventies & Sixties. Also, a mail order service.

Farmhouse Antiques, 23 Christleton Road, Boughton, Chester, Cheshire CH3 5UF. Prop: Mr Keith Appleby. Tel: (01244) 322478. Est: 1974. Shop; open Monday to Saturday 9.30–5. OLD stock - medium. Spec: longcase and wall clocks; bottles; golf; gramophones; gramohphone needle tins; kitchenalia; musical boxes; pewter; samplers. PR: £1–5,000. Mem: Music Box Society of Great Britain.

House of Burlington, The Cross, 1A Eastgate Row, Chester, Cheshire CH1 1LQ. Manager: Mr D. Nield. Tel: (01244) 342034. Est: 1995. Shop; open Monday to Saturday 9.30–5.30. NEW general stock - small. PR: £10–2,500. CC: A; V; AE.

Made of Honour, 11 City Walls, Next to the Eastgate Clock, Wall Level, Chester CH1 1LD. Prop: Eric Jones. Tel: (01244) 314208. Est: 1976. Shop; open Monday to Saturday 10–5.30. OLD stock - medium. Spec: Staffordshire; ceramics; glass; pottery; Victorian; writing - general; brass; commemorative ware; copper; Edwardian; embroideries; embroidered pictures; glass; plates; samplers; tapestries; tea caddies; teapots; tiles; treen. PR: £1–1,000. CC: all. Also, export and lectures.

'On The Air', 42 Bridge Street Row, Chester, Cheshire CH1 1NN. Prop: S.R. Harris. Tel: & Fax: (01244) 348468. Est: 1990. Shop; open Monday to Saturday 10–5, Sunday 11–4.30. Fairs: specialist vintage radio/communications. NEW stock - very small. Spec: Art Deco; musical. OLD stock - medium. Spec: gramophones; radio & television; Art Deco; gramophone needle tins; musical; telephones; jukeboxes & slot machines. PR: £1–1,000. CC: A; V; JCB; MC. Cata: monthly (approx.). Also, museum of radio & TV on premises.

Tiffany Antiques, Chester Drawyers Antique Centr 26 Watergate Row, Watergate Street, Chester, Cheshire. Prop: A. Wilcox. Tel: (01270) 257425. Mobile: (0370) 380261. Est: 1989. Shop; open Monday to Saturday 10–5. OLD stock - very small. Spec: candles/candle sticks; china; copper; Georgian; glass; metalware; snuff boxes; stanhopes; Victorian; writing - general. PR: £20–500. Also, house clearance specialists.

Watergate Antiques, 56 Watergate Street, Chester, Cheshire CH1 2LD. Prop: Mr Alan L. Shindler. Tel: (01244) 344516. Fax: 320350. Est: 1966. Shop; open 6 days a week 9.30–5. Fairs: Newark. OLD stock - very large. Spec: militaria; porcelain; silver; silverplate; arms & armour; Art Deco; firearms; Georgian; inkstands; jewellery; photograph frames; plates; scent bottles; serviette rings; snuff boxes; spoons; Staffordshire; swords; tankards; tea caddies and many others. PR: £50–5,000. CC: V; A. Corresp: Italian.

Joyce & Rod Whitehead, 11 City Walls, Chester, Chesire CH1 1LD. Tel: (01244) 314208. Est: 1981. Shop; open Monday to Saturday 9.30–5.30. Fairs: Newark, Nottinghamshire (Crocker II Building). OLD stock - medium. Spec: beadwork; boxes; decorative; fine art; samplers; textiles; treen. PR: £1–1,000. CC: V; A; EC; MC. Corresp: French.

CREWE

Betley Court Gallery, Betley, Nr Crewe, Cheshire CW3 9BH. Prop: Professor G.N. & Dr F. Brown. Tel: (01270) 820652. Fax: 820165. Est: 1980. Shop; open Tuesday to Sunday 2–5 and other times by appointment. OLD stock - small. Spec: Edwardian; fine art; Georgian; vases; Victorian. Also, antique furniture and oils and watercolours. Corresp: French, Italian.

HELSBY

Sweetbriar Gallery, Sweetbriar House, Robin Hood Lane, Helsby, Cheshire WA6 9NH. Prop: Mrs Anne Metcalfe. Tel: (01928) 723851. Fax: 724153. Est: 1987. Private premises; appointment necessary. Fairs: Newark, Ardingly, NEC, Stafford (Bowmans), Glass Fair (MCM). NEW stock - very small. Spec: paperweights. OLD stock - small. Spec: paperweights. PR: £1–5,000. CC: A; V; MC. Cata: every 2 months. Mem: Paperweight Collectors Association Dealer-Member.

MACCLESFIELD

Hills Antiques, Unit 47, Grosvenor Centre, Indoor Market, Macclesfield, Cheshire. Prop: Derek Hill. Tel: (01625) 426777. Est: 1967. Market stand; open Monday to Saturday 9–5. OLD general stock - very small. PR: £1–300.

NANTWICH

Tim Armitage, 99 Welsh Row, Nantwich, Cheshire CW5 5ET. Tel: & Fax: (01270) 626608. Est: 1966. Appointment necessary. OLD stock. Spec: automobilia; bicycles; model trains and cars; motoring; tinplate toys; tins, signs & advertising; traction/steam engines; transport.

Nantwich Art Deco, 87 Welsh Row, Nantwich, Cheshire CW5 5ET. Prop: M.J. Poole. Tel: (01270) 624876. Est: 1989. Shop; open Thursday to Saturday 10–5. Fairs: Alexandra Palace, Warwick Deco, Loughborough Deco. OLD stock - medium. Spec: Deco pottery and accessories. PR: £1–200.

Weaver Models (1994), 54 Welsh Row, Nantwich, Cheshire CW5 5EJ. Prop: Mr R.F. Pearson. Tel: & Fax: (01270) 626962. Est: 1994. Shop; open Monday to Saturday 9.30–5.30, Wednesday 9.30–1. NEW stock - medium. Spec: constructional toys; Diecast toys; model trains, cars and aircraft; transport. OLD stock - medium. Spec: railways; Diecast toys; model trains, cars and aircraft; tinplate toys; transport. PR: £3–500. CC: JCB; A; MC; D; V. Corresp: German, Dutch. Mem: F.S.B.

NORTHWICH

Davenham Antique Centre, 461 London Road, Davenham, Northwich, Cheshire CW9 8NA. Prop: S. Dale. Tel: (01606) 44350. Est: 1984. Shop; open 10–5, Sunday 11–4. OLD general stock - large. Spec: boxes; brass; cameras; ceramics; china; copper; cutlery; decorative; Edwardian; embroidered pictures; games; jardinières; jewellery; kitchenalia; keys; lace; mirrors; papier mâché; pewter; rugs and many others. PR: £1–1,000. Also, furniture. Mem: Vale Royal Tourist Board.

Ted's Place, Unit 10, Blakemere Craft Centre, Chester Road, Sandiway, Nr. Northwich, Cheshire CW8 2EB. Prop: Helen Ives. Tel: (01606) 888600. Est: 1994. Shop; open Tuesday to Friday 10–5, Saturday and Sunday 10–5.30. NEW stock - medium. Spec: teddy bears and related items. PR: £1–200. CC: V; MC; EC.

POYNTON

Jane's Fine Arts, 3 & 3a Park Lane, Poynton, Nr. Stockport, Cheshire SK12 1RD. Prop: Jane A. Beeken & Michael Siodmok. Tel: (01625) 859178. Fax: 530938. Est: 1989. Shop; open during business hours. Fairs: Cheshire fairs - Bowden Rooms, Moat House, Park Royal, International. NEW stock - medium. Spec: teddy bears. OLD stock - medium. Spec: china; pottery; kitchenalia. CC: V; A. Also, pub refurbishment and bric-a-brac supply. Corresp: French.

TARPORLEY

Maria Hopwood Antiques, Hulgrave Hall, Tiverton, Tarporley, Cheshire CW6 9UQ. Tel: (01829) 733313. Fax: 733802. Est: 1991. Shop; open 7 days a week 9–5. OLD general stock - medium. Spec: bottles; horticultural and farm equipment; kitchenalia; metalware; street furniture; textiles; tins, signs & advertising; tools. PR: £5–2,000. CC: all major cards except AE. Also, supply interior designers and pub bric-a-brac.

Tarporley Antique Centre, 76 High Street, Tarporley, Cheshire CW6 0AT. Tel: (01829) 733919. Est: 1993. Shop; open Monday to Saturday 10–5, Sunday 11–4. NEW stock - very small. OLD stock - large. Spec: commemorative ware; glass; china; kitchenalia; copper; brass; cutlery. PR: £1–400. Also, small furniture, framing and caning chairs.

TILSTON

Well House Antiques, The Well House, Tilston, Malpas, Cheshire. Prop: Mrs S.H. French–Greenslade. Tel: (01829) 250332. Est: 1969. Shop; open Wednesday to Saturday (please ring first). OLD general stock - medium. Spec: sewing related. PR: £1–5,000.

WILMSLOW

Peter D. Bosson, 10B Swan Street, Wilmslow, Cheshire SK9 1HE. Tel: (01625) 525250. Est: 1967. Shop; open Tuesday and Thursday to Saturday 10–12.45 and 2.15–5. OLD stock - large. Spec: barometers; clocks; scientific instruments. PR: £50–5,000. CC: A; V.

CLEVELAND

*Including the Unitary Authorities of Hartlepool, Middlesbrough,
Redcar and Stockton-on-Tees*

STOCKTON-ON-TEES

Ingleby Promotions, P.O. Box 185, Stockton-on-Tees, Cleveland TS17 0LY. Prop: Anthony Byron Gowthorp. Tel: (01642) 765180. Est: 1995. Private premises; postal business only. Fairs: Doncaster Racecourse Toy Fair, Chester-le-Street and other Northern England Fairs. NEW stock - medium. Spec: diecast toys; Lledo series of bullnose Morris vans featuring 'British Pubs'. OLD stock - very small. Spec: diecast toys; Lledo 'Days Gone' and promotionals. PR: £4–50.

CORNWALL

CAMBORNE

Brigand Models, 59 Lower Pengegon, Camborne, Cornwall TR14 7UH. Prop: Brian & Anne Garstin. Tel: (01209) 716286. Est: 1983. Shop; open daily 9–9. NEW general stock - very large. Spec: diecast toys; model trains, cars and aircraft; tinplate toys. OLD stock - medium. Spec: diecast toys; model trains, cars and aircraft; tinplate toys. PR: £1–150. CC: A; EC; MC; V.

LAUNCESTON

Windmill Patchworks, 23 Westgate Street, Launceston, Cornwall PL15 7AD. Prop: L.G. & C.E. Daniel. Est: 1989. Shop; open 9–5.30. NEW stock. Spec: musical boxes; paperweights; teddy bears. PR: £1–500. CC: A. Also, fabrics & gifts. Mem: Chamber of Commerce.

MARAZION

Antiques, The Shambles, Market Place, Marazion, Cornwall TR17 0AR. Prop: Andrew S. Wood. Tel: (01736) 711381. Est: 1988. Shop; open Monday to Saturday 10–5.30, Sunday by appointment. OLD stock - medium. Spec: Art Deco; bottles; ceramics; china; commemorative ware; Edwardian; glass; kitchenalia; Mauchline ware; objets de vertu; Osborne Plaques; paperweights; plates; pottery; Royal memorabilia; Staffordshire; vases; Victorian; crested, souvenir and Devon ware. PR: £1–200.

Masterpiece Miniatures, The Old Print Works, The Market Place, Marazion, Cornwall TR17 0AR. Prop: James E. Hickling. Tel: (01736) 710860. Est: 1992. Shop; open 10–5.30. Fairs: Newquay, Nottingham, Exmouth. NEW stock - small. Spec: miniature copper, brass, silver wares; miniature furniture. PR: £1–100. Cata: 1 a year.

MEVAGISSEY

Curio Corner, River Street, Mevagissey, Cornwall PL26 6UE. Prop: Jonathan and Jane Barron. Tel: (01726) 843557. Est: 1961. Shop; open 7 days a week 10–10 June to September, 10–4 October to May. NEW stock - medium. Spec: dolls; dolls houses; 1/12th miniatures. PR: £1–150. CC: V; A: AE; DC. Also, general giftware. Mem: Mevagissey Chamber of Commerce.

MULLION

Atlantic Models, Atlantic Forge, Lender Lane, Mullion, Nr. Helston, Cornwall TR12 7HW. Prop: Mr Peter Wilkins. Tel: & Fax: (01326) 240294. Est: 1990. Shop; open normal business hours. NEW stock - large. Spec: Lledo diecast toys. OLD stock - medium. Spec: diecast toys. PR: £1–75. CC: A; V.

PENZANCE

Deeko Bears, Rydal, Long Rock, Penzance, Cornwall TR20 8LD. Prop: Mrs R. Deeko. Tel: (01736) 711998. Est: 1995. Private premises; postal business only. NEW stock - very small (20). Spec: handmade mohair teddy bears. PR: £32–160. Cata: brochure on request. Corresp: French.

Green Meadow Books, 2 Bellair House, Bellair Road, Madron, Cornwall TR20 8SP. Prop: Sue Bell. Tel: & Fax: (01736) 51708. Est: 1982. Private premises; appointment necessary. Fairs: West Cornwall. OLD stock - large. Spec: arts & crafts; Art Nouveau; Art Deco; badges; constructional toys; Diecast toys; Edwardian; games; playing cards; teddy bears; tinplate toys; toys - general; Victorian. PR: £1.50–600. Cata: 4 or 5 a year.

ST. IVES

Matchbox Labels Unlimited, Carnstabba House, St. Ives, Cornwall TR26 3LS. Prop: Rosemarie Van Der Plank. Tel: (01736) 793050. Est: 1949. Storeroom and private premises; appointment necessary. NEW and OLD stock - very large stock. Spec: match boxes/books; aeronautica; Anglo-Indian; bicycles; bottles; boxes; buckles & clasps; buttonhooks; golf; leather; luggage; militaria; railways; rocking horses; tins, signs & advertising; tobacco & associated; Scouts. PR: 10p–£1,000's. Cata: 4 a year. Corresp: French. Mem: British Matchbox Label and Booklet Society.

Mike Read Antique Sciences, Ayia Napa, Wheal Whidden, St. Ives, Cornwall TR26 2QX. Tel: & Fax: (01736) 798219. Fairs: International Scientific & Medical Instrument Fair, twice a year. OLD stock - small. Spec: barometers; bells; binoculars; calculating machines; drawing instruments; fossils, geology & prehistory; globes; maritime/nautical; medical instruments; optical toys; scales, weights & measures; science; scientific instruments; spectacles, lorgnettes & monacles; stanhopes; stereoscopes; sundials; telescopes. PR: £5–10,000. Mem: S.I.S.

TRURO

Allsorts Collectables, 8 Sunnyside, Perranporth, Cornwall TR6 0HN. Prop: N. Cockburn. Tel: (01872) 573102. Est: 1985. Private premises; appointment necessary. OLD stock - very small. Spec: Edwardian; Georgian; plates; Victorian; coins. PR: £5–1,500. Cata: quarterly.

Bric–a–Brac, 16A Walsingham Place, Truro, Cornwall. Prop: Richard & Lynne Bonehill. Tel: (01872) 225200. Est: 1989. Shop; open 9.30–5. Fairs: Lostwithiel Antiques. OLD stock - medium. Spec: aeronautica; arms & armour; bottles; china; commemorative ware; glass; gramophones; kitchenalia; maritime/nautical; medals; militaria; photograph frames; police memorabilia; swords; taxidermy; treen; writing - general. PR: 10p–£2,000.

CUMBRIA

CARLISLE

Second Sight, 4a Mary Street, Carlisle, Cumbria. Prop: B. Donowho. Tel: (01228) 591525. Est: 1991. Shop; open Monday, Tuesday, Wednesday, Friday and Saturday 10–5. OLD general stock - small. Spec: ceramics; china; costume jewellery; cutlery; decanters; fine art; inkstands; pen knives; pens; pewter; photograph frames; plates; pottery; scales, weights and measures; silver; snuff boxes; tankards; teapots; Toby Jugs; trays; vases; Victorian; walking sticks; wrist and chain watches; fountain pens. PR: £1–1,000. CC: V; A; AE. Mem: F.S.B.

Souvenir Antiques, Treasury Court, Fisher Street, Carlisle, Cumbria. Tel: (01228) 401281. Est: 1985. Shop; open Monday to Saturday 10–5. NEW stock - very small. Spec: spoons; thimbles; Toby Jugs. OLD stock - medium. Spec: ceramics; commomerative ware; costume jewellery; Oriental; plates; Royal memorabilia; spoons; thimbles; Toby Jugs; Victorian; Roman coins. PR: £1–300. CC: V; MC; AE. Corresp: French, Spanish, German.

Top Drawer, Fisher Street Galleries, 18 Fisher Street, Carlisle, Cumbria CA3 8RH. Prop: Bridin Kissane. Tel: (01228) 512560. Est: 1989. Shop; open Monday to Saturday 10.30–4.30, closed Wednesday. Fairs: Pudsey, Tyneside, Glasgow, Edinburgh, North-East. NEW stock - small. Spec: dolls houses; pre-school wooden toys. PR: 50p–£200.

COCKERMOUTH

Antique & Craft Market, Old Courthouse, Main Street, Cockermouth, Cumbria. Prop: Alan & Pauline Gilbert. Tel: (01900) 824346. Est: 1978. Shop; open Monday to Saturday 10–5. NEW stock - very small. OLD general stock - large. PR: £1–300. Also, pine stripping & antique furniture restoration.

The Printing House, 102 Main Street, Cockermouth, Cumbria CA13 9LX. Prop: D.R. Winkworth. Tel: (01900) 824984. Fax: 823124. Est: 1979. Shop; open 9–5. NEW stock - very small. OLD stock - small. Spec: printing and bookbinding. CC: A; V; MC. Cata: occasionally. Also, a museum of printing. Mem: B.A., Museums Association.

GRASMERE

The Stables, College Street, Grasmere, Ambleside, Cumbria LA22 9SW. Prop: Andrew & Kay Saalmans. Tel: (01539) 435453. Est: 1971. Shop; open daily 10–5 March to October, Saturday and Sunday 11–4 November to February. OLD stock - large. Spec: bottles; brass; copper; cutlery; Royal memorabilia; silver. PR: £1–200.

KENDAL

The Silver Thimble, 39 Allhallows Lane, Kendal, Cumbria. Prop: Mrs Valerie Ritchie. Tel: (01539) 731456. Est: 1980. Shop; open Monday to Saturday 10–4. OLD stock - medium. Spec: glass; silver; lace; jewellery; china; copper; brass; lighting. PR: £5–2,000. CC: V; MC; AE. Corresp: French, German.

KESWICK

Primrose Patch, 48 Main Street, Keswick, Cumbria CA12 5JJ. Prop: Roger & Margaret Purkiss. Tel: (01768) 775127. Fax: 775126. E-Mail: 100604.3012@ compuserve.com. Est: 1992. Shop; open Monday to Saturday 8.30–8, Sunday 10.30–5. NEW stock - medium. Spec: candles/candlesticks; decorative; doorstops; photograph frames; spoons; teddy bears; writing accessories. PR: £5–200. CC: AE; V; MC. Also, a copy centre. Mem: F.S.B.

KIRKBY LONSDALE

Tobilane Designs, Newton Holme Farm, Whittington, via Carnforth, Lancashire LA6 2NZ. (•) Prop: Paul Commander. Tel: (01524) 272662. Est: 1985. Shop; open Monday to Friday 10–5, and most weekends. NEW stock - medium. Spec: toys - general; teddy bears; rocking horses; dolls houses. OLD stock - very small. Spec: toys - general; rocking horses. PR: 75p–£1,300. CC: A; V. Also, traditional toymakers and restorers.

PENRITH

Antiques of Penrith, 4 Corney Square, Penrith, Cumbria CA11 7TT. Prop: L. Mildwurf, S. Tiffin & L. Cripps. Tel: (01768) 862801. Est: 1964. Shop; open 10–12 and 1.30–5, closed Wednesday, Saturday 10–12.30. OLD stock - very large. Spec: barometers; brass; buttons; candlesticks; china; clocks; commemorative ware; cutlery; Edwardian; embroidered pictures; glass; kitchenalia; luggage; metalware; pewter; pottery; Staffordshire; teapots; Toby Jugs; vases; Victoriana; writing - general. PR: £1–5,000. Corresp: French, German. Mem: Chamber of Trade.

Carol Black Miniatures, Sun Hill, Great Strickland, Penrith, Cumbria CA10 3DF. Tel: (01931) 712330. Fax: 712990 (24 hr). Est: 1963. Private premises; by appointment or postal business. Fairs: Miniatura - NEC Birmingham (March & September). NEW stock - large. Spec: miniatures (1/12 scale). PR: £1–200. CC: A; V; JCB etc. Cata: 1 a year (£2.50 - includes a £1 voucher). Also, export and mail order.

Jane Pollock Antiques, 4 Castlegate, Penrith, Cumbria. Tel: (01768) 867211. Shop; open 9.30–5, closed Wednesday. Fairs: West Kensington, Harrogate, Chester, Olympia. OLD stock - large. Spec: silver; snuff boxes; boxes; candles/candlesticks; card cases; ceramics; china; corkscrews & bottle openers; cutlery; inkstands; ivory; objets de vertu; plates; pottery; scent bottles; serviette rings; spoons; tea caddies; teapots; tortoiseshell; treen. CC: A; V. Mem: L.A.P.A.D.A.

Roadside Antiques, Watsons Farm, Greystoke Gill, Greystoke, Penrith, Cumbria CA11 0UQ. Prop: Richard & Kathleen Sealby. Tel: (01768) 483279. Est: 1988. Shop; open 7 days a week 10–6. OLD stock - medium. Spec: ceramics; Edwardian; Georgian; glass; Staffordshire; Victorian; writing - general. PR: £1–2,000.

Showcase Models, The Cornmarket, Penrith, Cumbria CA11 7HS. Prop: Mr & Mrs Nellis. Tel: & Fax: (01768) 891177. Est: 1990. Shop; open Monday to Saturday 10–5. NEW stock - medium. Spec: dolls/dolls clothes; dolls houses; miniatures; model cars. OLD stock - very small. Spec: model cars. PR: £1–500. CC: V; A; JCB; AE; MC; EC. Cata: 2 a year, on model cars. Also, white metal and resin model car kits. Mem: F.S.B.

CUMBRIA

SEDBERGH

Stable Antiques, 15 Back Lane, Sedbergh, Cumbria LA10 5AQ. Prop: Miss Suzy Thurlby. Tel: (01539) 620251. Est: 1960. Shop; open Monday to Saturday 9–6 and by appointment. OLD general stock. PR: £1–500. CC: V; A; D; AE. Also, Bed & Breakfast and buys at auction.

WINDERMERE

The Birdcage Antiques, College Road, Windermere, Cumbria CA23 1BX. Prop: Mrs Tracy Griffiths. Tel: (01539) 445063. Est: 1983. Shop; open Wednesday, Friday & Saturday 10–1 and 2–5. OLD stock - small. Spec: brass; copper; candles/candlesticks; chandeliers; glass; kitchenalia; lighting; oil lamps; silhouettes; Staffordshire; tapestries; treen; writing - general. PR: £25–1,000.

DERBYSHIRE

ASHBOURNE

Spurrier-Smith Antiques, 28, 29, 39 & 41 Church Street, Ashbourne, Derbyshire. Prop: Ivan Spurrier–Smith. Tel: (01335) 343669. Tel: & Fax: 342198. Est: 1974. Shop and storeroom; open Monday, Tuesday and Thursday to Saturday 10–5.30 and other times by appointment. OLD stock - very large. Spec: 16th–19th Century antiques including china, glass, pictures, sculpture and decorative items; corkscrews & bottle openers; fishing; Georgian; kitchenalia; mirrors; motor car mascots; objets de vertu; Oriental; paperweights; pewter; pottery; rocking horses; tortoiseshell; treen; wine antiques. PR: £10–30,000. CC: all major cards. Also, valuations, commissions and interior decoration. Mem: L.A.P.A.D.A.

BUXTON

What Now Antiques, Cavendish Arcade, The Crescent, Buxton, Derbyshire SK17 8XA. Prop: Mrs Lindsay Carruthers. Tel: (01298) 27178. Est: 1987. Shop; open Tuesday to Saturday 10–5, Sunday 2–5. OLD stock - small. Spec: Art Deco; bottles; clocks; cutlery; diecast toys; Edwardian; golf; jewellery; lighting; pottery; rugs; samplers; silver; Victorian. PR: £1–1,500. CC: V; MC; AE; A; DC. Also, valuations and a courier service to foreign trade.

CHESTERFIELD

Chasing Rainbows, 78 Wellington Street, New Whittington, Chesterfield, Derbyshire S43 2BQ. Prop: Miss C.M. While. Tel: (01246) 453269. Est: 1990. Private premises; appointment necessary. Fairs: Kelham Hall (Newark), Buxton, occasionally Harrogate. NEW stock - very small. Spec: teddy bears mostly miniature made of mohair. PR: £25–60. Cata: photographs available. Also, porcelain dolls (kits).

The Old Bear Company, P.O. Box 29, Chesterfield, Derbyshire S42 5YY. Prop: Marilyn & Fiona Miller. Tel: (01246) 850446. Est: 1993. Private premises; appointment necessary. Fairs: all major teddy bear fairs. OLD stock - very small. Spec: antique teddy bears. PR: £20–1,000. Cata: every 8 weeks (cost £3). Also, help and advice on antique teddy bears available.

Sue Rouse, Springfield House, 103 High Street, Clay Cross, Derbyshire S45 9DZ. Tel: (01246) 862241. E-Mail: sue@timewarp.demon.co.uk. Est: 1987. Private premises; appointment necessary. NEW stock - very small. Spec: dolls/dolls clothes. OLD stock - very small. Spec: dolls/dolls clothes; teddy bears. PR: £1–300. Also, restoration of dolls and teddy bears.

DERBYSHIRE

DERBY

The Dolls House Emporium, Victoria Road, Ripley, Derbyshire DE5 3YD. Tel: (01773) 513773. Fax: 513772. Est: 1979. Shop; open 7 days a week 10–4. NEW stock - very large. Spec: dolls houses; miniatures. PR: £1–125. CC: A; V. Cata: monthly and annual catalogue.

Etwall Crafts & Models, 3 Eggington Road, Etwall, Derbyshire DE65 6NB. Prop: G.A.N. & S. Wagg. Tel: (01283) 734448. Est: 1989. Shop; open Tuesday to Saturday 9–dusk, and most Sundays. Fairs: Donington and NEC Toy & Train Fairs, Elvaston, Belfry & Buxton Doll Fairs. NEW stock - medium Spec: diecast toys; model cars; 1/12th scale dolls house furniture, accessories and dolls. PR: £1–50. Cata: updated annually. Also, ribbons and lace.

Shirley White Antique Dolls & Teddies, Abbey House, 115 Woods Lane, Derby DE22 3UE. Tel: & Fax: (01332) 723251. Est: 1960. Private premises; appointment necessary. Fairs: Donington 4 in one. OLD stock - medium. Spec: antique dolls; teddies; juvenilia. Also, antique furniture restoration and quality pine made to order.

HOPE

Itsybitsy World, Underleigh, off Edale Road, Hope, Derbyshire S30 2RF. Prop: Mrs Barbara Singleton. Tel: & Fax: (01433) 621372. Est: 1990. Private premises; appointment necessary. NEW stock - small. Spec: dolls houses; miniatures; walking sticks. OLD stock - very small. Spec: dolls houses; dolls/dolls clothes; miniatures. PR: £2–600. CC: A; V; D. Cata: 2 a year. mem: British Toymaker Guild.

MATLOCK

Valerie Claire Miniatures, 42 Highfield Drive, Matlock, Derbyshire DE4 3FZ. Prop: Angela Sinnott. Tel: (01629) 580759. Est: 1993. Private premises; postal business only. Fairs: Tatton Park, Cheshire and dolls house and miniatures fairs. NEW stock - medium. Spec: miniatures. PR: £1–40. Cata: 3 a year. Corresp: French, German. Mem: M.I.N.T.A.

OCKBROOK

The Good Olde Days, 6 Flood Street, Ockbrook, Derbyshire. Prop: Mr & Mrs S. Potter. Tel: (01332) 544244 or 663586. Est: 1996. Shop; open Tuesday to Saturday 10–6. Fairs: various. OLD antique stock - small. Spec: Art Deco; Art Nouveau; candles/candlesticks; ceramics; china; Edwardian; kitchenalia; mirrors; pottery; writing - general. PR: £5–500. Also, furniture.

SWADLINCOTE

G.K. Hadfield, Rock Farm, Chilcote, Swadlincote, Derbyshire DE12 8DQ. Prop: G.K. Hadfield, J.V. Hadfield, D.W. Hadfield–Tilly. Tel: (01827) 373466. Fax: 373699. Est: 1972. Shop; open Tuesday to Saturday 9–5 or by appointment. Fairs: British Horological Institute, Brunel, Birmingham clock fairs. NEW stock - small. OLD stock - medium. Spec: barometers; bells; clocks; drawing instruments; globes; keys; musical boxes; musical instruments; scales, weights & measures; scientific instruments; sundials; telescopes; wrist and chain watches. PR: 50p–£8,000. CC: V; MC; AE. Cata: 2 or 3 a year. Also, restoration materials. Corresp: French. Mem: British Horological Institute.

TIBSHELF

Brock Miniatures/Spacroft Models, 98 High Street, Tibshelf, Derbyshire DE55 5NU.
Prop: Michael Coupe. Tel: & Fax: (01773) 872780. Est: 1984. Private premises;
appointment necessary. Fairs: NEC, Donington, Mansfield, Doncaster
Racecourse, Beverley. NEW stock - very small. Spec: model cars (white metal).
PR: £35–90. CC: A; V; MC; EC. *Note:* Spacroft Models is production of own
model range.

DEVON

ASHBURTON

Moor Antiques, 19a North Street, Ashburton, South Devon TQ13 7QH. Prop: Mr T. & Mrs E. Gatland. Tel: (01364) 653767. Est: 1987. Shop; open Monday to Saturday 9.30–5, closed Wednesday afternoon. OLD stock - medium. Spec: china; clocks; Georgian; glass; lighting; plates; silver; spoons; Victorian; writing. PR: £20–2,500. Also, valuations (insurance & probate).

BAMPTON

Bampton Antiques, 9 Castle Street, Bampton, Devon EX16 9NS. Prop: Jill M. Yendell. Tel: (01398) 331197. Est: 1980. Shop; open Monday to Saturday 10.30–5. OLD stock - very small. Spec: Edwardian; glass; Victorian; country antiques. PR: £1–1,000. Also, pictures. Corresp: French, German.

BIDEFORD

Cottonwood Doll's Houses, Byways, Chope Road, Northam, Bideford, Devon EX39 3QE. Prop: Mr B. Cox. Tel: (01237) 474712. Est: 1992. Private premises; appointment necessary. Fairs: various in the South & South West. NEW stock - very small (approx. 12 at one time). Spec: dolls houses of individual design. PR: £100 upwards.

Nicholas Nickleby, 6 Grenville Street, Bideford, North Devon EX39 2EA. Prop: E. Gaskell & J.P. Simpson O'Gara. Tel: & Fax: (01237) 421195. Est: 1984. Shop; open 9–5.30 and market stand at: P 23, Butcher's Row, Bideford Pannier Market. OLD stock - medium. Spec: aeronautica; railways. PR: £1.50–200. Also, publishing.

BRIXHAM

The Shell Shop, 9 The Quay, Brixham, Devon TQ5 8AW. Prop: Mr P.C.D. Sturrock. Tel: (01803) 852039. Est: 1961. Shop; open 7 days a week 10.30–5 March to December. NEW stock - very large. Spec: shells; shell craft; brass; costume jewellery; fossils, geology & prehistory; jewellery; mother-of-pearl. PR: 50p–£100. CC: V; MC; A; EC.

BUCKFAST

Hembury Bears, Hockmore Lodge, Buckfast, West Buckfastleigh, Devon TQ11 0HN. Prop: Sue Tolcher. Tel: (01364) 643758. Fax: 643835. Private premises; appointment necessary. Fairs: major teddy bear fairs, schedule available. NEW stock - very small. Spec: teddy bears. PR: £100–500. Cata: photos available on request. Corresp: French. Mem: British Toymakers Guild.

EXETER

Micawber Antiques, New Buildings Lane, 25-26 Gandy Street, Exeter, Devon. Prop: Penny Standing. Tel: (01392) 52200. Est: 1985. Shop; open Monday to Saturday 10–5. OLD stock - small. Spec: Art Deco; barometers; china; clocks; costume jewellery; Edwardian; metalware; oil lamps; Staffordshire; Victorian. PR: £1–400. *Shop located:* behind 'C&A's' in city centre.

EXMOUTH

Boase Antiques, 5 High Street, Exmouth, Devon EX8 1NN. Prop: David Boase. Tel: (01395) 271528. Est: 1982. Shop; open 6 days a week 10–5. OLD stock - large. Spec: jewellery. PR: £1–1,000. CC: A.

Omega House, 4 Queen Street, Exmouth, Devon EX8 1NU. Prop: Z. Clatworthy. Tel: (01395) 223084. Est: 1990. Shop; open Monday to Saturday 9.30–5, closed Wednesday. NEW stock - medium. Spec: dolls/dolls clothes; dolls houses; miniatures; musical boxes. PR: 10p–£700 plus. Also, hand made miniature period furniture. Corresp: French, German.

Tucketts, 20 High Street, Exmouth, Devon EX8 1NP. Prop: Alan & Mary Tuckett. Tel: (01395) 270052. Est: 1935. Shop; open Monday to Saturday 6.30–5.30, Wednesday 6.30–1. NEW stock - medium. Spec: diecast toys; model cars; tankards; tobacco & associated; toy soldiers; fountain pens. PR: £5–150. Mem: National Federation of Newsagents.

HOLSWORTHY

The Pixie Kiln, Gnome Reserve & Wildflower Gar West Putford, Nr Bradworthy, Devon EX22 7XE. Prop: Ann Atkin. Tel: & Fax: (01409) 241435. Est: 1979. Shop; open 21 March–31 October Monday to Saturday 10–6, 1 November–20 March Monday to Friday 10–4. NEW stock - small. OLD stock - very small. Spec: gnomes. PR: £2–100. Mem: National Federation of Small Businesses.

HONITON

Honiton Antique Centre, Abingdon House, 136 High Street, Honiton, Devon EX14 8JP. Prop: J.J. Butler & M.V. Melliar–Smith. Tel: (01404) 42108. Est: 1985. Shop; open Monday to Saturday 10–5. OLD stock- very large. Spec: arts & crafts; clocks; fine art; horsebrasses and harnesses; luggage; musical boxes; pewter. PR: £1–2,000. CC: V; MC; AE. Corresp: French, German, Italian, Spanish.

Honiton Antique Toys, 38 High Street, Honiton, Devon EX14 8PJ. Prop: L. & S. Saunders. Tel: (01404) 41194. Est: 1976. Shop; open Tuesday, Wednesday, Friday and Saturday 10.30–5. Fairs: Sandown Toy Show. NEW stock - very small. Spec: teddy bears. OLD stock - large. Spec: constructional toys; diecast toys; dolls/dolls clothes; dolls houses; games; model trains, cars and aircraft; money boxes; teddy bears; tinplate toys; toys - general; toy soldiers; traction/steam engines. PR: 10p–£1,000. CC: A; V.

The Honiton Lace Shop, 44 High Street, Honiton, Devon EX14 8PJ. Prop: Jonathan Page. Tel: (01404) 42416. Fax: 47797. Est: 1984. Shop; open Monday to Saturday 9.30–1 and 2–5. NEW stock - very small. OLD stock - large. Spec: lace; textiles; samplers; costume; embroidered pictures; shawls. PR: £5–2,000. CC: V; MC; EC; A. Also, lace making equipment. Corresp: French, Dutch, German. Mem: O.I.D.F.A., Lace Guild, Antique Textile Society.

ILFRACOMBE

Relics, 113 High Street, Ilfracombe, Devon EX34 9ET. Prop: Nicola Bradshaw. Tel: (01271) 865486. Est: 1976. Shop; open Monday to Saturday 10–5, Thursday ½ day. NEW general stock - very small. OLD general stock - very small. PR: 50p–£250.

DEVON

MODBURY

Antiques & Restoration, Ye Little Shoppe, 1b Broad Street, Modbury, Devon PL21
0PS. Prop: Eric W. Ridsdill. Tel: (01548) 830732. Est: 1990. Shop; open Monday
to Saturday 10–5, closed Wednesday. Fairs: Ardingly. OLD stock - small. Spec:
boxes; oil lamps; scales, weights & measures; tea caddies; 19th Century wood
working tools; writing. PR: £5–500. CC: A; V. Also, restoration.

NEWTON ABBOT

Newton Abbot Antiques Centre, 55 East Street, Newton Abbot, South Devon TQ12 2JP.
Prop: Paul Stockman. Tel: (01626) 54074. Est: 1972. Market of 50 dealers; open
Tuesday 9–3. OLD general stock - very large. PR: £1–2,500.

OKEHAMPTON

Barometer World & Museum, Quicksilver Barn, Merton, Okehampton, Devon EX20
3DS. Prop: Philip R. Collins. Tel: (01805) 603443. Fax: 603344. Est: 1979. Shop;
open Monday to Saturday 9–5. NEW and OLD stock - very small. Spec:
barometers. PR: £30–900. CC: V; MC. Cata: available on application. Also, repair
and restoration of barometers and barographs, and a museum of barometers.

PLYMOUTH

Barbican Antiques Centre, 82–84 Vauxhall Street, Barbican, Plymouth, Devon. Prop:
Tony Cremer–Price. Tel: (01752) 266220. Est: 1971. Shop; open 7 days a week 10–
5. NEW and OLD stock - very large. Spec: jewellery; silver. PR: £5 plus. CC: V; A.

Paul Boulden Antiques, Parade Antiques Market, 17 The Parade, The Barbican,
Plymouth, Devon PL1 2JW. Tel: (01752) 221443. Fax: (01548) 521203. Est: 1984.
Market stand; open 7 days a week 10–5. Fairs: Bristol, Gloucester, Aldershot
Militaria fairs. OLD stock - medium. Spec: arms & armour; badges; firearms;
medals; militaria; police memorabilia; swords. PR: £1–1,000. CC: V; MC.

Boy Scout & Baden–Powell Collectables, 28 Rawlin Close, Eggbuckland, Plymouth,
Devon PL6 5TF. Prop: Graham Brooks. Tel: & Fax: (01752) 774467. Est: 1989.
Private premises; appointment necessary. OLD stock - small. Spec: Boy Scout &
Baden–Powell memorabilia including badges, commemorative ware, Edwardian,
Staffordshire, tea caddies, Mafeking items, Jamborees etc. PR: £1–300. Cata: 2 a
year, postal auctions and Scout badge sale lists.

Peregrine Model Cars, 1 Bowers Road, Milehouse, Plymouth, Devon PL2 3DT. Prop:
Peter Stoyle. Tel: & Fax: (01752) 563093. Est: 1986. Private premises;
appointment necessary. Fairs: N.E.C., Donington, Farnham, Sandown Park.
NEW stock - medium. OLD stock - very small. PR: £2–7,000. CC: V; MC; JCB;
AE.

Brian Taylor Antiques, 24 Molesworth Road, Plymouth, Devon PL1 5LZ. Tel: (01752)
569061. Fax: 605964. Est: 1978. Shop; open Monday to Saturday 10–5. OLD
stock - small. Spec: Art Nouveau; Art Deco; clocks; gramophones; gramophone
needle tins; lighting; musical boxes; radio & television; telephones. PR: £5–5,000.
CC: V; MC; EC; JCB. Cata: 1 a year. Also, repairs and valuations. Corresp:
French, Thai. Mem: F.S.B.

Toad Hall Medals, Toad Hall, Court Road, Newton Ferrers, Plymouth, Devon PL8 1DM. Prop: Malcolm Hitchings & Chrissy Maxey. Tel: (01752) 872672. Fax: 872723. Est: 1978. Private premises; postal business only. Fairs: Britannia Medal Fair, Marble Arch, London. NEW and OLD stock - very large. Spec: medals. CC: V; MC. Cata: 4 a year.

L.G. Wootton, 2 Church Street, South Brent, Devon TQ10 9AB. Tel: (01364) 72553. Est: 1938. Private premises; appointment necessary. NEW stock - medium. Spec: clocks; wrist watches. OLD general stock - medium. Spec: stamps. PR: £1–5,000. Mem: The British Watch & Clock Makers Guild.

SIDMOUTH

Bits and Pieces, The Sidmouth Shopping Centre, 91 High Street, Sidmouth, Devon EX10 8LD. Prop: Mrs P. Newland. Tel: (01395) 579048. Market stand; open Monday to Saturday 9–5. NEW stock - large. Spec: candles/candlesticks; ceramics; costume jewellery; teddy bears. PR: £2–150. CC: A; EC; MC; V.

Gainsborough House Antiques, Libra Court, Fore Street, Sidmouth, Devon EX10 8AJ. Prop: Mr Kim S. Scratchley. Tel: (01395) 514394. Est: 1935. Shop; open Monday to Saturday 9.15–5, early closing Thursday and Saturday. OLD stock. Spec: arms & armour; badges; buttons; candle extinguishers; ceramics; china; dolls/dolls clothes; firearms; ivory; maritime/nautical; militaria; police memorabilia; pottery; railways; swords; Victorian. PR: £1–1,000. Also, valuations.

Puddleducks, Old Fore Street, Sidmouth, Devon EX10 8LP. Prop: Mrs Tereza Jarvis. Tel: (01395) 515999. Est: 1988. Shop; open 10–5. NEW stock - small. Spec: dolls houses; miniatures; teddy bear; wooden toys. PR: £1–650. CC: A; V. Cata: 1 a year.

Vintage Toy Shop, Market Place, Sidmouth, Devon EX10 8LU. Prop: Mr J.W. Salisbury. Tel: (01395) 515124 ext. 208. Est: 1982. Shop; open Easter to October daily 10–5, closed Sundays and Bank Holidays. Fairs: Shepton Mallet, Bristol, Gloucester, Malvern, Newton Abbot, Exeter. NEW stock - very small. Spec: diecast toys; tinplate toys; toy soldiers. OLD stock - medium. Spec: constructional toys; diecast toys; model trains; tinplate toys; toy soldiers. PR: £1–500. Corresp: French.

SOUTH MOLTON

Cobbs Curiosity Shop, 24 East Street, South Molton, Devon. Prop: Hazel J. MacKay. Tel: (01769) 574104. Est: 1985. Shop; open Monday to Saturday 10–2. NEW stock - very small. OLD stock - large. Spec: cutlery; egg cups; hatpins & holders; kitchenalia; pottery; Royal memorabilia; walking sticks; scent bottles. PR: £5–500.

Treasure Trove Antiques, 101 East Street, South Molton, North Devon EX36 3DF. Prop: Diane E. Mason. Tel: (01769) 574288. Fax: 574964. Est: 1994. Shop; open 10–5. Fairs: Shepton Mallet, Exeter, Newark. NEW stock - very small. OLD general stock - medium. PR: £1–1,000. CC: V; A; MC. Also, cutlery, lampshades, glass, tea & dinner services. Mem: F.S.B., Chamber of Trade.

DEVON

TAVISTOCK

King Street Curios, 5 King Street, Tavistock, Devon PL19 0DS. Prop: Tony & Pat Bates. Tel: (01822) 615193. Est: 1977. Shop; open Monday to Saturday 9–5. NEW stock - very small. OLD general stock - very large. Spec: china. PR: up to £300. Also, country furniture.

TEIGNMOUTH

Charterhouse Antiques, 1B Northumberland Place, Teignmouth, South Devon TQ14 8DD. Prop: A.J. & S.N. Webster. Tel: (01626) 54592. Est: 1974. Shop; open Tuesday, Wednesday, Friday and Saturday 11–1 and 2.30–4. Fairs: Shepton Mallet, Somerset (County fairs). OLD stock - medium. Spec: commemorative china; Art Deco; buttonhooks; embroidered pictures; fairground relics; jewellery; portrait miniatures; silver. PR: £1–500. CC: A; MC; BC. Corresp: some French.

TORQUAY

Dolly Mixtures of Devon, Torquay, Devon. Prop: Ms Sylvia Harvey. Tel: (01803) 215667. Est: 1988. Private premises; appointment necessary. Fairs: Newark, Shepton Mallet, Westpoint Exeter. NEW stock - very small. Spec: writing accessories; dolls/dolls clothes; teddy bears; Steiff animals. PR: £2–1,500.

TOTNES

Bear Shop, 75 High Street, The Narrows, Totnes, Devon TQ9 5PB. Prop: James & Norissa Sturges. Tel: (01803) 866868. Est: 1992. Shop; open 9–5. Fairs: 2 or 3 a year. NEW stock - medium. Spec: Steiff Club, Hermann, Deans Club, Merrythought, North American and artists bears. OLD stock - very small. PR: £3–500. CC: V; A. Also, bear outfits and a leather boutique. Corresp: French, German. Mem: B.T.B.A.

Geoff Cox, East Wing, Tristford House, Harberton, Totnes, Devon TQ9 7RZ. Tel: (01803) 866181. Est: 1976. Private premises; appointment necessary. Fairs: Bristol, Dorchester, Sherborne, Wells, Tiverton and Monmouth book fairs. OLD stock - medium. Spec: aeronautica; Anglo-Indian; arts & crafts; automobilia; bookmarkers; canal memorabilia; fire fighting equipment; London Transport; militaria; motoring; photographic pictures; posters; railways; stationery; tins, signs & advertising; traction/steam engines; transport; tugs & towage. PR: £1–500. Cata: 1 a year. Corresp: French, German, Dutch. Mem: P.B.F.A.

The Magpie, Rotherfold Square, Totnes, Devon TQ9 5ST. Prop: Henry & Eileen Helmer. Tel: (01803) 556501. Est: 1990. Shop; open 10–5, closed Wednesday and Thursday. OLD stock - medium. Spec: badges; bookmarkers; bottles; buckles and clasps; buttons; crochet; early plastics; golf; gramophone needle tins; keys; lace; match boxes/books; money boxes; Mother-of-Pearl; photograph frames; playing cards; teapots; phonecards; Royal memorabilia; fountain pens. PR: £1–50.

DORSET

ABBOTSBURY

Abbotsbury Bears and Friends, 10 Rodden Row, Abbotsbury, Dorset DT3 4JL. Prop: Mr C. Dawson. Tel: (01305) 871199 (Shop) and Tel: & Fax: 871808 (Office). Est: 1995. Shop; open 7 days a week 11–4 Winter, 10–5 Summer, closed January 3rd to February 16th. NEW stock - large. Spec: teddy bears. PR: 99p–£295. CC: BC; A.

BEAMINSTER

Beaminster Antiques, 4 Church Street, Beaminster, Dorset DT8 3AZ. Prop: Trixie Frampton. Tel: (01308) 862591. Est: 1976. Shop and market stand; open 10–4.30. Fairs: county fairs Shepton Mallett, West of England, Westpoint, Exeter. OLD general stock - very small. Spec: brass; buttonhooks; card cases; ceramics; copper; decorative; Edwardian; Georgian; glass; hatpins & holders; inkstands; miniatures; thimbles; treen; Victorian; wine antiques; objets de vertu; silver; frames. PR: £1–100. CC: A; V.

BOURNEMOUTH

Arcade Antiques, 6 Westbourne Arcade, Westbourne, Bournemouth, Dorset BH4 9AY. Prop: Richard Samuel. Tel: (01202) 764800. Fax: 769537. Est: 1981. Shop; open Monday to Saturday 10–4.30, half day Wednesday. OLD stock - medium. Spec: arts & crafts; Art Deco; Art Nouveau; automobilia; cameras; ceramics; gramophones; jewellery; tools; Victorian. PR: £10–1,000. CC: V; MC; D.

Boscombe Militaria, 86 Palmerston Road, Boscombe, Bournemouth, Dorset BH1 4HU. Prop: Mr E.A. Browne. Tel: (01202) 304250. Fax: 733696. Est: 1982. Shop; open 10–5, but closed Tuesday from 1.30 and all day Wednesday. Fairs: Aldershot, Cheshunt, Farnham, Didcot, Tolworth, Warnham. OLD stock - medium. Spec: militaria - German and British; World War I & II. PR: £1–1,000. CC: A; V; MC. Also, de-activated arms.

Boscombe Models and Collectors Shop, 802C Christchurch Road, Boscombe, Bournemouth, Dorset BH7 6DD. Prop: Sylvia Hart. Tel: (01202) 398884. Est: 1981. Shop; open 10–1 and 2–4.30, excluding Wednesday. Fairs: Sandown Toy Fair, Farnham Maltings Toy Fair. OLD stock - large. Spec: toy collectables – diecats toys, dolls, model trains, cars and aircraft, railways, teddy bears, tinplate toys, toy soldiers, traction/steam engines. PR: £1–1,000.

Bournemouth Bears, J.J. Allen Centre, Old Christchurch Lane, Bournemouth, Dorset BH1. Prop: Jackie Ridley. Tel: (01202) 315350. Fax: (01305) 269741. Est: 1995. Shop; open Monday to Saturday 9.30–5. Fairs: West Country Teddy Bear Fairs. NEW general stock - small. Spec: teddy bears. OLD general stock - very small. Spec: teddy bears. PR: £5–400. CC: A; V; MC.

H.L.B. Antiques, 139 Barrack Road, Christchurch, Dorset BH23 2AW. Prop: H.L. Blechman. Tel: (01202) 482388 and 429252. Est: 1966. Shop; appointment necessary. NEW and OLD stock - very small. Spec: Art Deco; bronze; clocks; commemorative ware; dolls; walking sticks; watches. PR: up to £100.

DORSET

Smurf Collectors Club, P.O. Box 2326, Bournemouth, Dorset BH11 8ZA. Prop: T. & I.J. Anderson. Tel: (01202) 580666. Fax: 590333. Est: 1995. Postal business only. Fairs: NEC Birmingham, Olympia toy fairs. NEW stock - very large. Spec: entire range of Smurf figures & accessories. PR: £1–50. Cata: 1 a year.

Yesterday Tackle and Books, 42 Clingan Road, Boscombe East, Bournemouth, Dorset BH6 5PZ. Prop: David & Alba Dobbyn. Tel: (01202) 476586. Est: 1983. Storeroom and private premises; appointment necessary. NEW stock - very small. Spec: fishing tackle. OLD stock - medium. Spec: fishing tackle, reels, lures, collectables; taxidermy. PR: £1 plus. Cata: available. Corresp: Spanish.

DORCHESTER

Box of Porcelain, 51d Icen Way, Dorchester, Dorset DT1 1EW. Prop: R. Lunn. Tel: (01305) 250856. Est: 1988. Shop; open Monday to Saturday 10.30–5. NEW and OLD stock - medium. Spec: ceramics; china; Worcester; Beswick; Doulton. PR: £1–150.

Florianas Dolls House, 47 Charles Street, Dorchester, Dorset DT1 1EE. Prop: Carol Matthews and Anne Holloway. Tel: & Fax: (01305) 250881. Est: 1991. Shop; open Monday to Saturday 10–5. NEW stock - very large. Spec: dolls houses and accessories. PR: 20p–£650. CC: A; V. Cata: 2 a year.

Teddy Bear House, Antelope Walk, Dorchester, Dorset DT1 1BE. Prop: Jackie Ridley. Tel: (01305) 263200. Fax: 268885. Est: 1995. Shop; open 7 days a week 9.30–5.30 (phone for winter hours). Fairs: West Country Teddy bear Fairs (Easter, Summer & Autumn). NEW stock - small. Spec: teddy bears. OLD stock - very small. Spec: teddy bears. PR: £1–300. CC: A; V; D. Also, teddy bear repairs identification and valuations.

Teddy 'n Friends, Bruins, Church Lane, Piddletrenthide, Dorset DT2 7QY. (•)Prop: Jane Clayton. Tel: (01300) 348483. Est: 1986. Private premises; appointment necessary. Fairs: Surrey and Dorset. NEW stock - very small. Spec: artists dolls and bears. PR: £20–500.

POOLE

Button Shop Antiques, The Old Button Shop, Lytchett Minster, Poole, Dorset BH16 6JF. Prop: Thelma & Paul Johns. Tel: (01202) 622169. Est: 1970. Shop; open Tuesday to Friday 2–5, Saturday 11–1 or by appointment. NEW general stock - very small. OLD general stock - medium. Spec: Dorset and antique buttons. PR: 50p–£500. Also, shop was connected with 300 year old Dorset button industry.

Emporium Collectors Shop, The Emporium, Mansfield Road, Upper Parkstone, Poole, Dorset BH14 0DD. Prop: L. Saunders. Tel: (01202) 743742. Est: 1990. Shop; open Tuesday to Friday 10–5. NEW general stock. OLD general stock - small. Spec: stamps; diecast toys; maritime/nautical; model trains and cars; motoring; railways; Royal memorabilia; street furniture; phonecards; tins, signs & advertising; toys - general; transport. PR: 50p upwards. Also, Charminster Collectors Auction (10 a year) and toy, train and collectors fairs in Dorset. Corresp: French, German.

D.J. Jewellery Ltd., 166-168 Ashley Road, Parkstone, Poole, Dorset BH14 9BY. Tel: (01202) 381506. Fax: 745148. Est: 1979. Shop; open Monday to Saturday 9.30–5. NEW general stock - medium. Spec: jewellery; small silver items. OLD general stock - medium. PR: £5–1,000. CC: AE; DC; V; A; JCB. Also, repairs to clocks, jewellery and silverware. Mem: The British Watch and Clockmakers Guild.

The Queen's Shilling, 56a Sandbanks Road, Poole, Dorset BH14 8BS. Prop: A. Wolf. Tel: (01202) 723335. Est: 1990. Shop; open during normal shop hours, closed Wednesday afternoons. NEW stock - small. Spec: aeronautica; maritime/nautical; medals; militaria. OLD stock - small. Spec: aeronautica; maritime/nautical; medals; militaria; taxidermy; tribal. PR: £1–500. Also, medal sewing service. Corresp: German.

STURMINSTER NEWTON

Quarter Jack Antiques, Bridge Street, Sturminster Newton, Dorset DT10 1BZ. Prop: A.J. Neilson. Tel: (01258) 472558. Est: 1969. Shop; open Monday to Saturday 9–5.30. NEW stock - very small. Spec: glass; walking sticks; corkscrews & bottle openers; horsebrasses & harnesses. OLD stock - small. PR: £1–500.

SWANAGE

Georgian Gems, 28 High Street, Swanage, Dorset BH19 2NU. Prop: Mr Brian Barker. Tel: (01929) 424697. Fax: 426200. Est: 1970. Shop; open 9.30–12.30 and 2.30–5 or by appointment. NEW stock - very small. Spec: small silver; Georgian; Victorian. OLD stock - medium. Spec: Georgian and Victorian interesting and investment pieces; small silver. PR: £2–6,000. CC: V; MC; JCB; DC; AE. Also, valuations, special pieces made and a search service. Corresp: Italian, French, German. Mem: N.A.G., Gemmological Association Society, Jewellery Historians.

Teddies Corner, 11 Institute Road, Swanage, Dorset BH19 1BT. Prop: Mrs Jennifer Bulbeck. Tel: (01929) 422264. Est: 1986. Shop; open Monday to Saturday 10–4 (Winter), Monday to Sunday 9–6 (Summer), July & August evenings 8–10, and by appointment. Fairs: major teddy bear fairs. NEW stock - medium. Spec: teddy bears and related items. OLD stock - medium. Spec: teddy bears. PR: £1–500. CC: all except AE. Mem: Swanage Chamber trade.

WEYMOUTH

Books Afloat, 66 Park Street, Weymouth, Dorset DT4 7DE. Prop: John Ritchie. Tel: (01305) 779774. Est: 1983. Shop; open Monday to Saturday 9.30–5.30. OLD stock - small. Spec: diecast toys; maritime/nautical; tugs & towage.

Books and Bygones, 13 Great George Street, Weymouth, Dorset DT4 7AR. Prop: Mrs D. Nash. Tel: (01305) 777231. Est: 1992. Shop; open 7 days a week 10.30–5.30. OLD general stock - medium. PR: £1–1,000.

Nautical Antique Centre, Old Harbour Passage, 3a Hope Square, Weymouth, Dorset DT4 8TR. Prop: Mr D.C. Warwick. Tel: (01305) 777838 (day), 783180 (evening). Est: 1990. Shop; open Tuesday to Friday 10–1 and 2–5 or by appointment. Fairs: Beaulieu Boat Jumble (April). OLD stock - large. Spec: maritime/nautical; badges; barometers; binoculars; canal memorabilia; clocks; militaria; swords; telescopes; transport; model ships. PR: £5–1,000. CC: BC; V; A; MC. Cata: specific list available on request.

DORSET

Pat Venning Porcelain, Pineways, Faircross Avenue, Weymouth, Dorset DT4 0DD. Tel: (01305) 773325. Est: 1990. Private premises; appointment necessary. Fairs: Lyndhurst, N.E.C. Birmingham, London. NEW stock - very small. Spec: miniatures. PR: £1–75. Cata: lists free with S.A.E. Mem: M.I.N.T.A.

WIMBORNE MINSTER

Merley House Model Museum, Merley Park, Wimborne, Dorset BH21 3AA. Prop: J. Hammick. Tel: (01202) 886533. Fax: 881415. Est: 1987. Shop; open 10.30–4.30 Easter to end October. NEW stock - medium. OLD stock - very small. Spec: model cars and aircraft. PR: £1–250. CC: V; MC.

DURHAM

DARLINGTON

Robin Finnegan Jeweller, 83 Skinnergate, Darlington, Co. Durham DL3 7LX. Prop: Robin & Sandy Finnegan. Tel: (01325) 489820. Fax: 357674. Est: 1974. Shop; open 6 days a week 10–5.30. NEW stock - very large. Spec: jewellery; badges; cuff links; fine art; silver; medals; thimbles; chain watches; looms & weaving. OLD stock - very large. Spec: jewellery; silver; medals; militaria; badges; ivory; miniatures; Oriental; paper money; portrait miniatures; watches - wrist and chain; coins; stamps. PR: £1–20,000. CC: A; V; AE; D. Mem: N.A.G., G.A.G.J.L.

DURHAM

The Squirrel Collection, Unit B15, Lake Road, Houghton-Le-Spring, Tyne & Wear DH5 8BJ. (•) Prop: Jeff Barwick. Tel: (0191) 584-0840. Fax: 584-5057. Est: 1994. Storeroom; appointment necessary. Fairs: dolls house & miniature fairs throughout UK. NEW stock - very small. Spec: dolls houses. PR: £50–1,000. CC: V; MC. Cata: on request. Also, light fittings and trims.

EAST SUSSEX

BEXHILL-ON-SEA

Busy Beeze Miniatures, Bexhill Antique & Craft Centre 29-31 Sea Road, Bexhill-on-Sea, East Sussex TN40 1EE. Prop: Mrs Stella Wilson. Tel: (01424) 731224. Est: 1995. Shop; open 7 days a week 10–5.30. NEW stock - medium. Spec: dolls houses; miniatures. OLD stock - very small. PR: 50p–£1,500. Corresp: French, Spanish.

Val and Tyme, 107 London Road, Bexhill-on-Sea, East Sussex TN39 3LB. Prop: A. Seymour. Tel: (01424) 731268. Est: 1991. Shop; open 10–4.30. Fairs: Battle Antiques Fair. NEW stock - very small. OLD stock - small. Spec: militaria. PR: £35 (average).

BRIGHTON

Art Deco Etc., 73 Upper Gloucester Road, Brighton, East Sussex BN1 2LQ. Prop: John C. Clark. Tel: & Fax: (01273) 329268. Est: 1979. Shop; appointment necessary. Fairs: Newark, Ardingly, Kensington Deco Fair, Battersea Deco Fair, Alexandra Palace. OLD stock - medium. Spec: Poole Pottery; arts & crafts; Art Deco; Art Nouveau; ceramics; china; clocks; early plastics; fine art; glass; jardinières; lighting; metalware; mirrors; photograph frames; pottery; radio & television; rugs; scent bottles; the Sixties. PR: £5–3,000. CC: V; MC.

Bears & Friends, 41 Meeting House Lane, Brighton, East Sussex BN1 1HB. Prop: Paul Goble. Tel: (01273) 208940. Fax: 202736. Est: 1989. Shop; open Monday to Friday 9–5.30, Saturday 9–6, Sunday 10–6. Fairs: Kensington Town Hall. NEW general stock - medium. Spec: teddy bears; dolls/dolls clothes. OLD general stock - very small. Spec: teddy bears; dolls/dolls clothes. PR: £1–1,500. CC: A; V; AE; JCB. Cata: 1 a year. *At same premises:* Paul Goble Jewellers (q.v.).

C.A.R.S., 4/4a Chapel Terrace Mews, Kemp Town, Brighton, East Sussex BN2 1HU. Prop: G.G. Weiner & A.P.Gayler. Tel: (01273) 601960. Fax: 623846. Showroom; open 10–6 and weekends by appointment. Fairs: Ally Pally (March), Brighton Centre (April), Kempton Park (September). NEW and OLD stock - medium. Spec: automobilia; badges; bicycles; children's sit & ride vehicles; diecast toys; model cars; motor car mascots; pedal cars; powered vehicles for children; tinplate toys; transport. PR: £35–1,500. CC: V; AE. Cata: 4 a year. Corresp: German. Mem: I.A.M., O. & R.

Fisher Nautical, Huntswood House, St Helena Lane, Streat, Hassocks, West Sussex BN6 8SD. (•) Tel: & Fax: (01273) 890273. Storeroom; postal business only. OLD stock - very large. Spec: maritime and nautical. PR: £5–2,500. CC: all except AE. Cata: 1 a month.

Paul Goble Jewellers, 44 Meeting House Lane, Brighton, East Sussex BN1 1HB. Tel: (01273) 202801. Fax: 202736. Est: 1978. Shop; open 7 days a week 9–5.30. Fairs: Newark, Sandown, Ardingly. NEW stock - very small. Spec: jewellery; silver. OLD stock - medium. Spec: jewellery; silver; teddy bears; dolls/dolls clothes. PR: £9–25,000. CC: V; A; AE; JCB. Mem: N.A.G., Pawnbrokers Association. *At same premises:* Bears & Friends (q.v.).

Hyndford Antiques, 143 Edward Street, Brighton, East Sussex BN2 1JG. Prop: Mrs McSkelson. Tel: (01273) 679936. Est: 1983. Shop; open Thursday to Saturday 10.30–1.30 and 2.30–4.30 or by appointment. Fairs: Hove Town Hall. NEW stock - very small. Spec: boxes; china; decorative. OLD stock - small. Spec: Anglo-Indian; boxes; brass; bronze; china; decorative; Diecast toys; eccentrics; ivory; Oriental; photograph frames; toys - general, soldiers; Victorian; writing. PR: £1–250.

The Lanes Armoury, 27 Meeting House Lane, The Lanes, Brighton, East Sussex BN1 1HD. Prop: M. & D. Hawkins. Tel: & Fax: (01273) 321357. Est: 1972. Shop; open Monday to Saturday 9.30–5.15, some Sundays 12–4. OLD stock - medium. Spec: arms & armour; militaria; bronze; fine art; scientific instruments. PR: £1–5,000. CC: A; V; MC; AE. Also, new and secondhand books (military reference).

Patrick Moorhead, 22B Ship Street, Brighton, East Sussex. Tel: (01273) 326062. Fax: 774227. Shop; open 10–5. OLD stock - large. Spec: porcelain; bronzes. PR: £300–10,000. Also, Georgian, Victorian and continental furniture and overseas dealings in Australia, Europe and USA, and interior decorators. *Showroom also at:* 15B Prince Albert Street, Brighton.

Oasis Antiques, 39 Kensington Gardens, Brighton, East Sussex. Prop: I. & A. Stevenson. Tel: (01273) 683885. Est: 1969. Shop; open 10.30–5.30, Saturday 9–6. OLD stock - medium. Spec: arts & crafts; Art Deco; Art Nouveau; boxes; bronze; costume; costume jewellery; diecast toys; early plastics; fashion accessories; glass; jewellery; lighting; pottery; radio & television; rock & pop; telephones; tools; wrist watches; writing - general. PR: £1–5,000. Also, furniture and metal restoration.

Recollections, 1A Sydney Street, Brighton, East Sussex BN1 4EN. Prop: Bruce Bagley. Tel: (01273) 681517. Est: 1973. Shop; open Tuesday and Thursday to Saturday 10.30–5. NEW stock - very small. Spec: reproduction brass fire items. OLD stock - medium. Spec: brass, copper and iron items; oil lamps; gold & silver; glassware; porcelain; clocks; boxes. PR: £1–250. Also, fireplace furniture, door furniture, small architectural and salvage items. Mem: Brighton North Lanes Traders Association.

Rin-Tin-Tin, 34 North Road, Brighton, East Sussex BN1 1YB. Prop: Rick Irvine. Tel: & Fax: (01273) 672424. Est: 1983. Shop; open Monday to Saturday 11–5.30. Fairs: Alexandra Palace Antiques & Collectors Fair. NEW stock - very small. Spec: Art Deco; lighting. OLD stock - medium. Spec: tins, signs & advertising; tobacco & associated; early plastics; radio & television; games; jukeboxes & slot machines; playing cards. PR: £1–150. CC: A; V; EC; MC. Also, picture framing.

Snoopers Paradise, 7/8 Kensington Gardens, Brighton, East Sussex BN1 4AL. Prop: F.G. & J.G. Thompson. Tel: (01273) 602558. Est: 1990. Open Monday to Saturday 9.30–5.30. OLD stock. PR: £1–2,000.

Timewarp, 6 Sydney Street, Brighton, East Sussex BN1 4EN. Prop: Miss J. Whiskin. Tel: (01273) 607527. Est: 1991. Shop; open during normal business hours. Fairs: Battersea/Greenwich Art Deco. NEW stock - very small. OLD stock - small. Spec: Art Deco; lighting; oil lamps. PR: £50–100. CC: MC; A; V; EC.

CROWBOROUGH

Squirrels Place, Ashdown Parade, The Broadway, Crowborough, East Sussex. Prop: Paul & Janice Harding–Mabbs. Tel: (01892) 653509. Est: 1995. Shop; open Monday to Friday 9.30–4.30, Saturday 9.30–5. NEW stock - medium. Spec: dolls/dolls clothes; dolls houses. PR: £1–500.

DITCHLING

Keiron James Designs, St. Dominic's Gallery, 4 South Street, Ditchling, East Sussex BN6 8UQ. Tel: (01273) 846411. Est: 1989. Shop; open Monday to Saturday 10.30–5, Wednesday 10.30–3. Fairs: British Bear Fair, Hove, Sussex (December). NEW stock. Spec: teddy bears; doll houses; miniatures. PR: £3–400 plus. CC: V; MC; EC; AE. Mem: Guild of British Toy Makers.

EASTBOURNE

Eastbourne Models, 37 Seaside, Eastbourne, East Sussex BN22 7NB. Prop: Mr Paul Simmons. Tel: (01323) 722026. Shop; open Monday to Saturday 9.30–5.30. Fairs: in the local area. NEW stock - very large. Spec: diecast toys; model trains and cars; railways; toy soldiers; traction/steam engines. OLD stock - medium. Spec: tinplate toys; diecast toys; model trains and cars. PR: £8 plus. CC: MC; V. Corresp: French.

Enterprise Collectors Market, Enterprise Shopping Centre, Station Parade, Eastbourne, East Sussex. Prop: c/o J. Prysor. Tel: (01323) 732690. Est: 1989. Shop; open Monday to Saturday 9.30–5. Fairs: Folkestone, Dorking, Chichester, Croydon, Bexhill etc. NEW general stock - very small. OLD stock - large. Spec: ceramics; commemorative ware; costume jewellery; diecast toys; dolls/dolls clothes; jewellery; medals; model cars; Toby Jugs; wrist watches; Wade; Sylvac; Beswick; gold; silver. CC: V; A. Corresp: French. Mem: Eastbourne Chamber of Commerce.

Pharoahs Antiques, 28 South Street, Eastbourne, East Sussex BN21 4XB. Prop: W. & J. Pharoah. Tel: (01323) 738655. Est: 1987. Shop; open Monday to Saturday 10–5. Fairs: International Antique & Collectors Fair, Ardingly. OLD stock - medium. Spec: brass; lighting; costume jewellery; lace; copper; decorative; eccentrics; kitchenalia; games; oil lamps; textiles; treen; writing - general. PR: £1–800. Corresp: French.

Southern Miniature Models, Boyne House, 12 St. Aubyns Road, Eastbourne, East Sussex BN22 7AS. Prop: Alexander Mitchell and Janet Harper. Tel: & Fax: (01323) 728494. Est: 1991. Storeroom and private premises; appointment necessary. Fairs: London International, Brighton, Maidstone. NEW stock - medium. Spec: diecast models - buses and commercials including Code 3, and enhanced/modified models. OLD stock - medium. Spec: Dinky, Corgi, Yesteryear etc. PR: £1–50. Cata: colour pamphlets available (please send SAE). Also, worldwide mail order business.

FOREST ROW

South Eastern Finecast, Glenn House, Hartfield Road, Forest Row, East Sussex RH18 5DZ. Prop: C.A. & D.P. Ellis. Tel: (01342) 824711. Fax: 822270. Est: 1986. Storeroom and factory; appointment necessary. NEW stock - medium. Spec: white metal model train and car kits. CC: V; A. Cata: annually. Corresp: Spanish. Mem: F.S.B.

HASTINGS

Childrens Treasures, 17 George Street, Hastings, East Sussex TN34 3EG. Prop: Ann & Frank Strudwick. Tel: & Fax: (01424) 444117. Est: 1972. Shop; open Monday, Tuesday, Thursday & Friday 9.30–5, Saturday 10.30–5.30. Fairs: Victoria Doll Fair, London. NEW stock - small. Spec: diecast toys; dolls/dolls clothes; teddy bears; dolls houses; toy soldiers. OLD stock - very small. Spec: diecast toys; dolls/ dolls clothes; toy soldiers. PR: £1–500. CC: all major. Cata: 1 a year. Also, a dolls hospital and wholesale business.

Coach House Antiques, 48 George Street, Old Town, Hastings, East Sussex. Prop: R.J. Luck. Tel: (01424) 461849. Est: 1980. Shop; open 7 days a week 10–5. OLD stock - very large. Spec: barometers; clocks; commemorative ware; diecast toys; jukeboxes & slot machines; model trains and aircraft; money boxes; musical instruments; paper money; plates; railways; Staffordshire; teapots; tins, signs & advertising; Toby Jugs; toys - general. PR: £100–2,000. CC: V; MC.

Courthouse Mews, 8 Courthouse Street, Hastings, East Sussex. Prop: I.R. Porter. Tel: (01424) 461834. Fax: 423011. Est: 1990. Shop; open 7 days a week 10–5. NEW and OLD general stock - medium. PR: £1–100. CC: V; MC.

George Street Antique Centre, 47 George Street, Old Town, Hastings, East Sussex. Prop: Mrs F. Stanley & Mr P. Heuduk. Tel: (01424) 429339. Est: 1986. Shop; open Monday to Friday 9–5, Saturday 10–5, Sunday 11–4. OLD stock - medium. Spec: Art Nouveau; Art Deco; jewellery; writing - general; coins; stamps. PR: £1–500.

Hastings Antique Centre, 59-61 Norman Road, St. Leonards on Sea, Hastings, Sussex TN38 0EG. Prop: Mr Robert Amstad. Tel: (01424) 428561. Est: 1971. Shop; open Monday to Saturday 9–5.30. Fairs: frequently attended. OLD general stock - large. Spec: sporting; fishing. PR: £5–1,000 plus. Corresp: French.

HOVE

Sussex Commemorative Ware Centre, 88 Western Road, Hove, East Sussex BN3 1JB. Prop: Mrs R. Prior. Tel: (01273) 773911. Fax: 747866. Est: 1976. Shop; erratic please ring first. OLD stock. Spec: commemorative ware; Royal memorabilia. PR: £1–1,000. CC: V; A; MC; BC. Cata: 6 a year in alternate months £3 each.

HURST GREEN

Libra Antiques, 81 London Road, Hurst Green, Etchingham, East Sussex TN19 7PN. Prop: Janice P. Herbert. Tel: (01580) 860569. Est: 1985. Shop; open Tuesday to Saturday 9.30–6, Sunday and Monday by appointment only. OLD stock - medium. Spec: brass; iron working; kitchenalia; oil lamps; scales, weights & measures; treen; Victorian; copper. PR: £10–500. CC: V; AE.

LEWES

Church House Bears, 171 High Street, Lewes, East Sussex BN7 1YE. Prop: Anne F. Walpole. Tel: (01273) 476002. Est: 1994. Shop; open Monday to Saturday 10–5.30, except Wednesday 10–2.30. NEW stock - medium. Spec: teddy bears and related china and jewellery. OLD stock - small. PR: £5–1,000. CC: V; MC. Mem: Toymakers Guild.

EAST SUSSEX

Cliffe Gallery Antiques, 39 Cliffe High Street, Lewes, East Sussex. Prop: Dee Grimes & Robert Hayward. Tel: (01273) 471877. Est: 1985. Shop; open 10–5. OLD general stock - small. Spec: lighting; luggage; music; sports. PR: £1–1,500. Also, antique pine. Corresp: Italian, French.

ROTHERFIELD

Square Wheels, The Square, Rotherfield, East Sussex TN6 3LG. Prop: Martin Wright & David Lambert. Tel: (01892) 852286. Fax: 852357. Est: 1994. Shop; open Tuesday & Thursday 10–5, Saturday 9–5. OLD stock - large. Spec: constructional toys; diecast toys; model trains, cars and aircraft; tinplate toys; toys - general; toy soldiers; traction/steam engines. PR: £1–250. CC: A; BC; V; MC.

RYE

The Dolls House (Rye), 113 High Street, Rye, East Sussex TN31 7JE. Prop: Bernard & Sandra Jerome. Tel: (01797) 224634. Est: 1995. Shop; open Monday to Saturday 10–5, Sunday 11–4, closed Tuesdays. NEW stock - large. Spec: dolls houses; miniatures. PR: 50p–£500 plus. CC: V; A; MC. Also, full range of furnishings and DIY materials. Mem: M.I.N.T.A.

Herbert G. Gasson, The Lion Galleries, Lion Street, Rye, East Sussex TN31 7LB. Prop: T.J. Booth. Tel: (01797) 222208. Est: 1909. Shop; open Monday to Saturday 9–5.30. OLD stock - very small. Spec: brass; candles/candlesticks; china; mirrors; pewter; tea caddies; treen. PR: £20–3,000. Also, 17th to 19th Century furniture.

Ann Lingard Antiques, 18–22 Rope Walk, Rye, East Sussex TN31 7NA. Prop: M.A. & J.F. Lingard. Tel: (01797) 223486. Fax: 224700. Shop; open Monday to Friday 9–5.30, Saturday 10–1 and 2–5. OLD stock - medium. Spec: ceramics; copper; glass; horticultural & farm equipment; kitchenalia; metalware; scales, weights & measures. PR: £1–5,000. CC: V; MC. Mem: L.A.P.A.D.A.

SEAFORD

Barn Collectors Market & Studio Bookshop, Church Lane, Seaford, East Sussex BN25 1HL. Prop: Lynn S. Price & D.M. Hollyer. Tel: (01323) 890010. Est: 1967. Shop; open Tuesday, Thursday and Saturday 10–4.30. OLD stock - medium. Spec: buckles & clasps; buttons. PR: 25p–£25.

UCKFIELD

The Hobby Box, 8 Framfield Road, Uckfield, East Sussex TN22 5AG. Prop: K.G. & J.E. Nock. Tel: (01825) 765296. Est: 1979. Shop; open Monday to Saturday 9–5.30, Wednesday 9–1. NEW stock - medium. Spec: constructional toys; diecast toys; model trains, cars and aircraft. PR: £3–75. CC: V; A; AE.

ESSEX

AVELEY

Ray Bygate Models, 31A High Street, Aveley, Essex RM15 4BE.

BASILDON

Animal Magic, c/o Richard Joseph Publishers, Unit 2, Monks Walk, Farnham, Surrey GU9 8HT. Prop: Diane Raggett. Tel: (01268) 414866. Est: 1994. Private premises; appointment necessary. Fairs: Brentwood, Wembley, Woking, Pakefield. OLD stock - medium. Spec: Beswick horses & animals; Royal Doulton ladys. PR: £5–1,000.

Patricia's Dollshouses, 119 Eastgate, Basildon, Essex SS14 1AG. Prop: P. Mann. Tel: (01268) 293169. Est: 1986. Shop; open 6 days a week 10–6. NEW stock - large. Spec: dolls houses and accessories. PR: £1–400. CC: BC; A. Mem: Guild of Toymakers, M.I.N.T.A.

BATTLESBRIDGE

The Antique & Unique Emporium, at: The Haybarn Building, Bones Lane, Battlesbridge, Essex. Prop: Brian Riley. Tel: (01268) 571770. Est: 1968. Shop; open Saturday & Sunday 11–5. OLD stock - very large. Spec: Georgian; Victorian; porcelain; glass; jewellery. PR: £15–5,000. Also, furniture restoration and upholstery.

Arthurs Antiques, Bridgebarn Antiques Centre, The Green, Bones Lane, Battlesbridge, Essex SS11 7RE. Prop: Arthur Deller. Tel: (01268) 769755. Est: 1988. Shop; open Tuesday to Sunday 10.30–5. Fairs: Kempton. OLD stock - medium. Spec: Art Nouveau; boxes; ceramics; china; clocks; costume jewellery; decanters; glass; teapots; vases; Victorian; wrist and chain watches. PR: £1–600. CC: V.

Haybarn Antiques, The Bones Lane Antiques Centre, Bones Lane, Battlesbridge, Essex SS11 7RE. Prop: J.P. Pettitt. Tel: (01268) 763500. Est: 1956. Shop; open Tuesday to Sunday 10–5. OLD stock - very large. Spec: amusement machines; automata; fairground relics; gramophones; gramophone needle tins; jukeboxes & slot machines; lighting; musical boxes; oil lamps; scientific instruments. PR: £5–2,000. CC: V; MC; EC. Also, restorations of mechanical antiques and lamps & lighting.

Klas Cameras, Bridgebarn Antiques Centre, The Green, Bones Lane, Battlesbridge, Essex SS11 7RE. Prop: Keith Shepherd. Tel: (01268) 763500. Shop; open Tuesday to Sunday 10–5. OLD stock - very small. Spec: binoculars; cameras; optical toys; photograph frames and pictures; scientific instruments; stanhopes; stereoscopes; telescopes; traction/steam engines; trains. PR: £15–1,500. CC: V.

Minnie's Antiques, Haybarn Antiques Centre, The Green, Bones Lane, Battlesbridge, Essex SS11 7RE. Prop: M.V. Snelling. Tel: (01268) 571770. Est: 1971. Shop; open Wednesday 11.30–4.30, Saturday & Sunday 11–5. NEW stock - very small. OLD stock - small. Spec: horticultural & farm equipment; kitchenalia; laundry bygones; medical instruments. PR: £5–1,200.

ESSEX

The Old Telephone Company, The Old Granary, Battlesbridge Antiques Centre, Wickford, Essex SS11 7RF. Prop: G.J. Payne. Tel: & Fax: (01245) 400601. E-Mail: gf54@dial.pipex.com. Est: 1987. Shop; open 7 days a week 10–5.30. OLD stock - very small. Spec: telephones. PR: £80–1,000. CC: V; MC. Also, restoration service and technical and historical information about telephones available.

Rich Finds Antiques, Bridgebarn Antiques Centre, The Green, Bones Lane, Battlesbridge, Essex SS11 7RE. Prop: Stuart Fitch. Tel: (01268) 769755, workshop (0181) 221-1140, mobile (0585) 783344. Open Tuesday to Sunday 10–5. OLD stock - very small. Spec: kitchenalia; advertising material. CC: V. Also, pine furniture and pine stripping.

Rosina's, Haybarn Courtyard, Battlesbridge Antiques Centre, The Green, Chelmsford Road, Battlesbridge, Essex SS11 7RE. Prop: R. Pettitt. Tel: (01268) 763500. Est: 1993. Shop; open Saturday & Sunday 10.30–5. OLD general stock - very small. PR: £1–200.

Tinkers Antiques, The Haybarn, Bones Lane Antiques Centre, Battlesbridge, Essex SS11 7RE. Prop: Mr P. Butts. Tel: (0181) 472-9633. Est: 1995. Shop; open Tuesday to Sunday 9–5.30. Fairs: Ardingly, Newark, Kempton. OLD general stock - small. PR: £1–200.

BENFLEET

Granny's Attic, 47 New Park Road, Benfleet, Essex SS7 5YR. Prop: Rose Andrews. Tel: & Fax: (01268) 793382. Est: 1982. Private premises; appointment necessary. Fairs: East Anglia, Kent. NEW stock - medium. Spec: dolls houses; miniatures. PR: £1–20. Cata: mail order list £1 with S.A.E. Also, miniature curtain maker tools.

BRAINTREE

Hedingham Models, 7 Market Street, Phoenix Shopping Centre, Braintree, Essex CM7 3YA. Prop: Mrs S.V. Thorogood. Tel: (01376) 320522. Fax: (01787) 462527. Shop; open Monday to Wednesday 10–5, Friday 10–6 and Saturday 9–5. Fairs: Kempton Park (Heathrow), London International Picketts Lock, Norwich. NEW stock - very large. Spec: diecast toys; teddy bears; model cars; toy soldiers; Coca-Cola; Star Trek; X-Files. CC: V; A; D. Also, a games workshop.

BRENTWOOD

G.F.C. Models, 5 Coptfold Road, Brentwood, Essex CM14 5ED. Prop: Graham and Doris Cross. Tel: (01277) 226999. Est: 1994. Shop; open Monday to Saturday 9–5.30, closed Wednesday. Fairs: Brentwood Centre, Picketts Lock, venues in Essex. NEW stock - very large. Spec: dolls houses; diecast toys; miniatures; model trains and cars; scalextric cars; railways; traction/steam engines; writing. OLD stock - small. Spec: diecast toys; railways. PR: £1–300. CC: V; D; BC; A. Also, repairs to loco's and scalextric cars.

CHELMSFORD

Heirloom Tudor Dollshouses, 24 Collingwood Road, South Woodham Ferrers, Chelmsford, Essex CM3 5YB. Prop: Simon & Emma Milner. Tel: (01245) 328309. Est: 1992. Private premises; appointment necessary. Fairs: Miniatura (trade section), phone for details of others. NEW stock - very small. Spec: dolls houses. PR: £350–1,500. Cata: 1 a year. Mem: M.I.N.T.A.

CHIGWELL

Fairview Designs, 18 Fairview Road, Chigwell, Essex IG7 6HN. Prop: W.J. Craske. Tel: (0181) 500-1012. Est: 1982. Private premises; appointment necessary. Fairs: British Toy Soldier & Model Show. NEW stock - very small. Spec: corkscrews & bottle openers; maritime/nautical; militaria; miniatures; toy soldiers; writing accessories. PR: £6–12. CC: AE. Cata: on request.

COGGESHALL

Goodies, 11 East Street, Coggeshall, Essex CO6 1SH. Prop: Belinda Opie. Tel: (01376) 562885. Fax: 563885. Est: 1985. Shop; open Monday to Saturday 9.30–5.30, Sunday and Bank Holidays 12.30–5.30. NEW stock - very large. Spec: dolls houses; miniatures; boot scrapers; brass. PR: 50p–£1,500. CC: V; MC; D. Also, minature lighting and tools. Mem: Chamber of Trade.

ESSEX

COLCHESTER

Auto in Print, Mill Lodge, Mille Lane, Birch, Colchester, Essex CO2 ONG. Tel: (01206) 331052. Fax: 330438. Est: 1975. Private premises; postal business only. Fairs: Beaulieu Autojumble. NEW stock - very small. Spec: automobilia; transport. OLD stock - very large. Spec: automobilia; transport. PR: £2–40. Cata: lists sent on demand with S.A.E.

The Bear Shop, 3 Sir Isaac's Walk, Colchester, Essex CO1 1JJ. Prop: R.J. Stone. Tel: (01206) 577345. Est: 1990. Shop; open Monday to Saturday 10–5. NEW stock - large. Spec: teddy bears collectors bears and associated merchandise. PR: £1–500. CC: V; A; MC. Cata: 1 a year.

Elizabeth Cannon Antiques, 85 Crouch Street, Colchester, Essex CO3 3EZ. Prop: Elizabeth & Brian Cooksey. Tel: (01206) 575817. Est: 1979. Shop; open Monday to Saturday 9–5.30. OLD general stock - large. Spec: boxes; china; cuff links; cutlery; glass; jewellery; silver; spoons. PR: £10–5,000. Also, furniture.

Mankim (Colchester) Ltd, 213 Shrub End Road, Colchester, Essex CO3 4RN. Directors: V.S.G., P.M. & K.J. Manning. Tel: (01206) 574929. Fax: 563171. Est: 1976. Shop; open 6 days a week 9–5.30 (closed Bank Holidays). Fairs: Colchester, Ipswich, Brentwood. NEW stock - large. Spec: diecast toys; model cars, trains and aircraft. OLD stock - medium. Spec: diecast toys; model cars and trains. CC: all. Mem: F.S.B.

Times Past, 110 High Street, Kelvedon, Colchester, Essex CO5 9AA. Prop: Mrs Victoria Waine. Tel: (01376) 571858. Est: 1984. Shop; open Tuesday, Thursday to Saturday 10–5. OLD stock - small. Spec: vases; Art Nouveau; Art Deco; ceramics; china; costume jewellery; early plastics; glass; lighting; metalware; pewter; pottery; scent bottles; sculpture; serviette rings; stationery. PR: £5–3,000.

Trinity Antiques Centre, 7 Trinity Street, Colchester, Essex CO1 1JN. Prop: Mrs J.H. Last. Tel: (01206) 577775. Est: 1976. Shop; open Monday to Saturday 9.30–5. OLD general stock - medium. Spec: Art Deco; Art Nouveau; badges; bookmarkers; buttonhooks; candles/candlesticks; china; commemorative ware; copper; corkscrews & bottle openers; costume jewellery; cuff links; decanters; Edwardian; embroideries; fans; mirrors; jewellery; serviette rings; tiles. PR: 50p–£350.

GRAYS

Kendons, 10 London Road, Grays, Essex RM17 5XY. Prop: Mrs Hilary A. O'Connor. Tel: (01375) 371200. Est: 1978. Shop; open Monday & Thursday to Saturday 9.30–5. Fairs: Alexandra Palace (Stall E37). NEW general stock - very small. OLD stock - medium. Spec: cameras; clocks; jewellery; medals; chain watches. PR: £5–150. Also, stamp auctions. Mem: British Watch & Clock Makers Guild.

Terran, 6 London Road, Grays, Essex RM17 5XY. Prop: D.J.R. Hill & J.A. Reynolds. Tel: & Fax: (01375) 393133 (for fax ring first). Est: 1994. Shop; open Monday to Saturday 9–5.30. Fairs: East Anglian and London toy fairs, Farnham Maltings, Salisbury etc. NEW stock - medium and OLD stock - very small. Spec: diecast toys; model trains and aircraft occasionally. PR: £3–50. CC: V; MC. Also, printing. Mem: F.S.B., Association of Hot Foil Printers.

GREAT BADDOW

Baddow Antiques Centre, Church Street, Great Baddow, Nr. Chelmsford, Essex CM2 7JW. Prop: J.A.D. McEntire. Tel: (01245) 476159. Est: 1976. Warehouse; open Monday to Saturday 10–5, Sunday 11–5. NEW and OLD general stock - medium. PR: £10–10,000. Also, antique brass beds.

HARWICH

Mayflower Antiques, 105 High Street, Dovercourt, Harwich, Essex CO12 3AP. Prop: John, Sue & Kevin Odgers. Tel: & Fax: (01255) 504079. Est: 1970. Shop; open Monday to Friday 10–5. Fairs: Scientific fairs - London. OLD stock - very small. Spec: barometers; calculating machines; cameras; dolls/dolls clothes; drawing instruments; gramophones; ivory; maritime/nautical; medical instruments; model trains; musical boxes; scientific instruments; sewing machines; stereoscopes; sundials; telescopes; tinplate toys; traction/steam engines; trains; typewriters. PR: £5–5,000. CC: V; MC; EC; JCB. *See also:* Mayflower Antiques, 117 Portobello Road, London W11 (q.v.).

LEIGH-ON-SEA

Collectors Paradise, 993 London Road, Leigh-on-Sea, Essex SS9 3LB. Prop: Mr & Mrs H.W. & P.E. Smith. Tel: (01702) 73077. Shop; open 10–5.30, closed Friday and Sunday. OLD stock - medium. Spec: barometers; china; clocks; costume jewellery; diecast toys; model cars and aircraft; tobacco & associated; toy soldiers. PR: £1–850. CC: V.

Mister Bear, 17 Lord Roberts Avenue, Leigh-on-Sea, Essex SS9 1ND. Prop: Jennie Sharman–Cox. Tel: & Fax: (01702) 710733. Est: 1990. Private premises; postal business only. Fairs: Teddies '96 Kensington (August). Spec: teddy bears. PR: £150–250. CC: V; MC. Cata: photos 2 or 3 times a year.

MALDON

Abacus Antiques, 105 High Street, Maldon, Essex CM9 5EP. Prop: Mrs Joan Davidson. Tel: (01621) 850528. Est: 1986. Shop; open Tuesday, Thursday, Friday and Saturday 10–4.30. OLD general stock - small. Spec: Art Nouveau; boxes; buttons; ceramics; china; costume jewellery; cuff links; decanters; Edwardian; fans; Georgian; glass; hatpins & holders; jewellery; scent bottles; serviette rings; silver; thimbles; Victorian; writing - general. PR: £1–1,500. CC: V; MC; A. Also, valuations and jewellery repairs.

Heritage Models, 179 High Street, Maldon, Essex CM9 7BS. Prop: Mr R. De'Ath. Tel: (01621) 855420. Est: 1992. Shop; open during business hours. NEW general stock - medium and OLD general stock - small. Spec: diecast toys; firearms; toy soldiers; model trains, cars and aircraft; tinplate toys. PR: £1–250.

ONGAR

Carr Collectables, Central House, High Street, Ongar, Essex CM5 9AA. Prop: Paul Carr. Tel: (01277) 364970. Est: 1991. Shop; open Tuesday to Saturday 10–5. Fairs: toy shows around the UK. NEW and OLD stock - medium. Spec: diecast toys; model cars and aircraft. PR: £3–200. CC: V; MC. Cata: updated quarterly. Also, one of the 8 Matchbox collectible centres in UK. Mem: M.I.C.A.

SAFFRON WALDEN

Lankester Antiques & Books, The Old Sun Inn, Church Street and Market Hill, Saffron Walden, Essex CB10 1HQ. Prop: Paul Lankester. Tel: (01799) 522685. Est: 1967. Shop; open Monday to Saturday 9.30–5.30. NEW stock - medium. OLD general stock - large. PR: £1–500.

SOUTHEND-ON-SEA

David and John Antiques, 587 London Road, Westcliff-on-Sea, Essex SS0 9PQ. (•) Tel: (01702) 339106. Fax: 560536. Est: 1965. Shop; open Monday, Tuesday and Thursday to Saturday 10–4.30. OLD general stock - medium. Spec: clocks; barometers; jewellery; watches; silver. PR: £1–1,000. Also, clock repairs, furniture and paintings. Corresp: French, German.

Dolls Designs, 311 Bournemouth Park Road, Southend-on-Sea, Essex SS2 5LQ. Prop: Jane Woodbridge. Tel: (01702) 460506. Est: 1988. Private premises; postal business only. Fairs: toy doll & miniature fairs. NEW stock - medium. Spec: dolls/dolls clothes. PR: £1–15. Cata: 1 a year.

Essex Models, 210 Woodgrange Drive, Southend-on-Sea, Essex SS1 2SJ. Prop: E.L. Archer. Tel: (01702) 615921. Fax: 601177. Est: 1989. Shop; open Monday to Saturday 9–5.30 and postal business. NEW stock - very large. Spec: Lledo. OLD stock - very large. Spec: Lledo (collections bought & sold). PR: £1.99–600. CC: A; AE; DC; MC; V. Cata: every 6 to 8 weeks. Mem: F.S.B.

It's About Time, 863 London Road, Westcliff-on-Sea, Essex SS0 9SZ. (•) Prop: R. & V. Alps. Tel: & Fax: (01702) 72574. Est: 1980. Shop; open Monday to Saturday 8.30–5.30. OLD stock - large. Spec: clocks; Victoriana. PR: £300–5,000. CC: A; V. Also, export business.

Pall Mall Antiques, 104c & 104d Elm Road, Leigh-on-Sea, Essex. (•) Prop: Maurice Sherman. Tel: (01702) 77235. Est: 1975. Two shops with storerooms; open Monday to Saturday 10–5. OLD stock - very large. Spec: Art Deco; barometers; boot scrapers; boxes; buttonhooks; candles/candelsticks; ceramics; commemorative ware; cutlery; glass; hatpins & holders; jardinières; kitchenalia; Mauchline ware; metalware; paperweights; serviette rings; tankards; Toby jugs; walking sticks. PR: £1–500. CC: all except AE; DC.

Selecteds, 124 Hamlet Court Road, Westcliff-on-Sea, Southend, Essex SS0 7LP. (•) Prop: Mrs Josée Lewis. Tel: (01702) 390097. Est: 1995. Shop; open Monday to Saturday 9.30–5.30, Sundays by appointment. Fairs: some in Essex. NEW stock - small. Spec: teddy bears. PR: £5–500 plus. CC: V; A; AE. Cata: occasional photographs on request. Also, gifts with a teddy bear theme and expanding to stock old bears. Mem: B.T.B.A.

STANSTED

Auto & Miniature, 15 Cambridge Road, Stansted, Essex CM24 8BX. Director: K.A. Bayford. Tel: (01279) 815723. Fax: 815648. Est: 1982. Shop; open Monday to Saturday 9–5.30 (closed 12.30–2). NEW stock - large. Spec: diecast toys; model cars, buses & lorries; tins, signs & advertising; traction/steam engines; Corgi Gold Star. OLD stock - very small. Spec: diecast toys; model cars, buses & lorries; tins, signs & advertising; traction/steam engines; Corgi Gold Star. PR: £1–50. CC: AE; EC; MC; V. Cata: 4 a year.

Little Bears at Auto & Miniature, 15 Cambridge Road, Stansted, Essex CM24 8BX. Prop: K.A. Bayford. Tel: (01279) 815723. Fax: 815648. Est: 1993. Shop; open Monday to Saturday 9–5.30 (closed 12.00–2). NEW stock - large. Spec: teddy bears. OLD stock - small. Spec: teddy bears. PR: £5–400. CC: EC; MC; V. Cata: 4 a year.

THURROCK

Dolls House Trading Post, Lakeside Pavilion, 612 Lakeside Shopping Centre, West Thurrock, Essex RM16 1ZN. Prop: W. Cowling. Tel: (01708) 866881. Fax: (01375) 678779. Est: 1984. Shop; open 7 days a week, open until 8 weekdays. NEW stock - very large. Spec: dolls houses; miniatures. PR: 20p–£850. CC: AE; A; V.

WALTON-ON-THE-NAZE

Crispin's Day Antiquarian and Out-of-Print Military Books, 43 Woodside, Walton-on-the-Naze, Essex CO14 8NR. Prop: Ian Capper. Tel: (01255) 672646. Fax: 674646. Est: 1990. Private premises; by appointment or postal business. Fairs: occasionally. OLD stock of fine and rare antique arms and armour from 15th–19th Century. Spec: ordnance of same period.

WESTCLIFF-ON-SEA

Frontline Figures UK, 1 Holmsdale Close, Westcliff-on-Sea, Essex SS0 0QW. Prop: Gerard Prime. Tel: (01702) 352060. Fax: 431797. Est: 1982. Private premises; appointment necessary. Fairs: toy soldier fairs. NEW stock - small. Spec: toy soldiers. PR: £30–70. Cata: listings 6 monthly.

GLOUCESTERSHIRE

ANDOVERSFORD

Tatham-Losh Antiques, Brereton House, Stow Road, Andoversford, Cheltenham, Gloucestershire GL54 4JN. Prop: Julian Tatham-Losh. Tel: & Fax: (01242) 820646. Est: 1980. Storeroom and private premises; open Monday to Friday 8–6 or by appointment. Fairs: Newark, N.E.C. OLD stock - medium. Spec: bamboo; boxes; brass; candles/candlesticks; ceramics; china; decorative; doorstops; embroidered pictures; glass; inkstands; kitchenalia; luggage; lighting; mirrors; papier mâché; Staffordshire; tortoiseshell; trays; writing. PR: £5–4,000.

BOURTON-ON-THE-WATER

Model Garage, 4 The Old Forge, Moore Road, Bourton-on-the-Water, Gloucestershire GL54 2AZ. Prop: R.C. Hunt. Tel: & Fax: (01451) 810308. Est: 1992. Shop; open Tuesday to Friday 10–5, Saturday and Sunday 10–5 (please phone first). Fairs: toy fairs at NEC, Kempton Park, Shepton Mallet and classic car shows. NEW stock - very large. Spec: model cars; diecast toys. OLD stock - medium. Spec: model cars; diecast toys. PR: £10–90. CC: V; MC; EC; AE. Cata: 4 a year. Corresp: French, German.

CHELTENHAM

Bottles and Bygones, 96 Horsefair Street, Charlton Kings, Cheltenham, Gloucestershire GL53 8JS. Prop: John H. Brown. Tel: (01242) 236393. Est: 1978. Shop; open Wednesday to Saturday 10–5. NEW stock - very small. OLD stock - large. Spec: badges; bottles & bottle tops; boxes; brass; cameras; china; commemorative ware; copper; decanters; gramophone needle tins; horsebrasses and harnesses; kitchenalia; medals; metalware; militaria; paperweights; pen knives; pottery; spoons; pot lids. PR: 50p–£250. Corresp: Welsh, Spanish.

The Dolls House, Market Place, Northleach, Nr Cheltenham, Gloucestershire GL5U 3EJ. Prop: Miss Michal Morse. Tel: & Fax: (01451) 860431. Est: 1971. Shop; open Thursday to Saturday 10–5, some Sundays 11–4, other times by appointment. NEW stock - large. Spec: dolls houses. OLD stock - very small (2 or 3). Spec: dolls houses. PR: 20p–£1,500. CC: MC; A; BC; V; AE. Cata: 1 every 2 years, full colour, £3.50 incl. UK postage. Mem: MINTA.

Heydens, 420 High Street, Cheltenham, Gloucestershire GL50 3JA. Prop: Rhys E.J. Heyden. Tel: (01242) 690909. Est: 1980. Shop; open 6 days a week 10–1 and 3–5.30. NEW general stock - very small. OLD stock - small. Spec: aeronautica; arms & armour; badges; buttons; commemorative ware; firearms; medals; militaria; swords; writing - general. PR: £1–200.

Showcase, 13 Montpellier Arcade, Cheltenham, Gloucestershire GL50 1SU. Prop: Mr & Mrs J. Pannett. Tel: (01242) 224144. Est: 1992. Shop; open Monday to Saturday 9.30–5.30, closed Wednesday. NEW stock - very large. Spec: teddy bears; porcelain dolls. PR: £1–400. CC: V; BC. Also, fancy dress and dancewear. Mem: Fancy Dress Association.

Telephone Lines Ltd., 339 High Street, Cheltenham, Gloucestershire GL50 3HS. Tel: (01242) 583699. Fax: 690033. Est: 1992. Shop; open Monday to Saturday 9–5.30. Fairs: N.E.C., N.U.C.F. NEW stock - small. Spec: telephones. OLD stock - very large. Spec: telephones. PR: £40 plus. Cata: long standing brochure. Corresp: German, French, Italian, Spanish. Mem: Independent Telecommunications Supplies Association.

CIRENCESTER

Silver Street Antiques and Things, 9 Silver Street, Cirencester, Gloucestershire GL7 2BJ. Prop: Mr S. Tarrant. Tel: (01285) 641600. Est: 1994. Shop; open 7 days a week 10–5.30. OLD stock - medium. Spec: Art Deco; boot scrapers; bottles; boxes; brass; candles/candlesticks; ceramics; china; commemorative ware; costume jewellery; Diecast toys; Edwardian; jewellery; kitchenalia; pens; pottery; scales, weights & measures; silver; tinplate toys; tins, signs & advertising; toys - general, soldiers; treen; vases; fountain pens. PR: £50–200.

EBRINGTON

Natural Craft Taxidermy, 21 Main Street, Ebrington, Nr Chipping Campden, Gloucestershire GL55 6NL. Prop: John Burton. Tel: (01386) 593231. Est: 1973. Private premises and showrooms; appointment necessary. NEW stock. Spec: taxidermy. OLD (Victorian and Edwardian) stock. Spec: taxidermy; sport. PR: £25–2,000. CC: A; V. Mem: Guild of Taxidermy; British Field Sport Society.

GLOUCESTER

K. & D. Antique Clocks, Unit 57, Gloucester Antiques Centre, Severn Road, Gloucester, Gloucestershire GL1 2LE. Prop: Paul Kembery. Tel: & Fax: (0117) 956-5281. Est: 1988. Shop; open Monday to Saturday 9.30–5, Sunday 1–5, appointment advisable. Fairs: NEC (April & August). OLD stock. Spec: antique clocks and barometers. PR: £100–5,000. CC: A; V. Cata: photos available on request. Also, restoration service. Also, worldwide delivery. Mem: Guild of Master Craftsman.

Gloucester Toy Mart, Shop 23, Antique Centre, Severn Road, Gloucester, Gloucestershire GL1 2LE. Prop: C. Davies. Est: 1988. Shop; open 9.30–5, closed Sunday. Fairs: NEC, Donington, Sandown Park. NEW stock - very small. Spec: diecast toys; model trains and cars. OLD stock - small. Spec: diecast toys; model trains and cars; tinplate toys; toys - general. PR: £1–500. CC: V; A. Mem: H.R.C.A.

HQ84, The Curiosity Shop, 84 Southgate, Gloucester, Gloucestershire GL1 2DX. Prop: Mrs B. Williams. Tel: & Fax: (01452) 527716. Est: 1964. Shop; open every day 9.30–5.30 (closed Christmas day). NEW stock - medium. Spec: arms & armour; badges; brass; replica & air firearms; medals; militaria; miniatures; paper money; tinplate toys. OLD stock - large. Spec: arms & armour; badges; brass; replica & air firearms; medals; militaria; miniatures; motor car mascots; pen knives; Victorian. PR: £1–250. Cata: annually. Also, makers of blazers, badges, bullion etc. Corresp: French, German, Italian, Esperanto.

GLOUCESTERSHIRE

LECHLADE

Antiques Etcetera, High Street, Lechlade, Gloucestershire GL7 3AD. Prop: Caroline Haillay. Tel: (01367) 252567. Est: 1968. Shop; open Monday to Saturday 10–6, Sunday 12–6. OLD general stock. Spec: antiques. Corresp: French. Mem: L.A.D.A.

Bridge House Gallery, Fairford Road, Lechlade on Thames, Gloucestershire GL7 3DL. Prop: Gill and Keith Newson. Tel: (01367) 252457. Est: 1988. Shop; open 2–6 except Thursday and Sunday, 1 March to 23 December or by appointment. NEW stock - large. Spec: dolls houses; jewellery; marbles; miniatures; pottery; rocking horses; toys - general. PR: 3p–£1,800. CC: A; EC; MC; V. Also, kites, cards and giftwrap. Mem: Lechdale & District Chamber of Commerce.

Mark A. Serle Antiques, 6 Burford Street, Lechlade, Gloucestershire GL7 3AP. Tel: (01367) 253145. Est: 1978. Shop; open Monday to Friday 9.30–5, Saturday 9–12.30. Fairs: Lechdale Antiques Fair (1st Sunday each month), Stonleigh. OLD stock - medium. Spec: horticultural and farm equipment; metalware; militaria; tools; toys - general; writing. PR: £1–500. Also, restoration of antique furniture. Mem: Lechdale Antique Dealers Association.

LYDNEY

Simon Lewis Transport Bookshop, 11 The Marina, Harbour Road, Lydney, Gloucestershire GL15 4EJ. Tel: (01594) 843151. Fax: 843158. Est: 1986. Shop; open Monday to Friday 9–4.30, Saturday 10–1. NEW stock - very small. Spec: motoring. OLD stock - very large. Spec: motoring; model cars; automobilia; transport; photographs; posters. PR: £1–750. CC: A; V; MC; EC. Cata: 4 a year.

MINCHINHAMPTON

Mick & Fanny Wright, The Trumpet, West End, Minchinhampton, Stroud, Gloucestershire GL6 9JA. Tel: (01453) 883027. Est: 1979. Shop; open Wednesday to Saturday 10.30–5.30. Fairs: Newark. OLD stock - medium. Spec: ceramics; clocks; commemorative ware; corkscrews & bottle openers; cutlery; diecast toys; Edwardian; glass; gramophones; jewellery; kitchenalia; model cars; musical boxes; silver; stereoscopes; toys - general; Victorian; wrist and pocket watches. PR: 50p–£1,000. Also, pine furniture. Corresp: German.

NORTHLEACH

Keith Harding's World of Mechanical Music, Oak House, High Street, Northleach, Gloucestershire GL54 3ET. Prop: Keith Harding & Cliff Burnett. Tel: (01451) 860181. Fax: 861133. Est: 1961. Shop; open 7 days a week 10–6. NEW stock - medium. Spec: music boxes. OLD stock. Spec: music boxes; clocks. PR: £2–35,000. CC: A; V. Also, restoration of music boxes and a musical museum. Mem: British Horological Institute.

PAINSWICK

Antiques & Craft Centre, New Street, Painswick, Gloucestershire GL6 6XH. Prop: Mr R. Short. Tel: (01452) 812431. Est: 1986. Shop; open Monday to Friday 10–5, Saturday and Sunday 10.30–5.30. OLD stock - large. Spec: jewellery; silver; china. PR: £2–3,000. CC: V; A; AE. Also, furniture and crafts.

STOW-ON-THE-WOLD

Acorn Antiques, Sheep Street, Stow-on-the-Wold, Gloucestershire GL54 1AA. Prop: Maggie Masters. Tel: (01451) 831519. Est: 1987. Shop; open Monday to Saturday 10–1 and 2.15–5. OLD stock - medium. Spec: Staffordshire; ceramics; china; commemorative ware; egg cups; glass; portrait miniatures; Victorian. PR: £5–1,500. CC: V; A; MC; EC.

Durham House Antiques Centre, Sheep Street, Stow-on-the-Wold, Gloucestershire GL54 1AA. Prop: Alan Durham–Smith. Tel: & Fax: (01451) 870404. Shop with over 30 dealers; open Monday to Saturday 10–5, Sunday 11–5. OLD antique stock - medium. Spec: arms & armour; arts & crafts; Art Deco; Art Nouveau; bamboo; birdcages; bottles; boxes; brass; bronze; buckets; candle extinguishers; candles/candlesticks; card cases; ceramics; chandeliers; china; clocks; commemorative ware; copper and many others. PR: £4–3,000. CC: MC; V.

Roger Lamb Antiques & Works of Art, 5 Church Street, Stow-on-the-Wold, Gloucestershire GL54 1BB. Tel: (01451) 831371. Est: 1993. Shop; open Monday to Saturday 10–5. Fairs: Westonbirt (South Cotswold), NEC. OLD stock - very small. Spec: Georgian; French; fine art; objets de vertu; papier mâché; decorative; tea caddies; boxes. PR: £50–5,000. Also, interior design and search service. Corresp: most European. Mem: C.A.D.A., L.A.P.A.D.A.

Peter Norden Antiques, Durham House Antique Centre, Sheep Street, Stow-on-the-Wold, Gloucestershire. Prop: Peter & Jenny Norden. Tel: (01993) 831607. Est: 1960. Market stand; open 7 days a week 9.30–5. Fairs: N.E.C., Kensington (Penman Fairs) and 12 Bailey Fairs. OLD general stock - very small. Spec: arms & armour; boxes; brass; bronze; candles/candlesticks; ceramics; copper; glass; kitchenalia; keys; metalware; Oriental; pewter; pottery; samplers; snuff boxes; taxidermy; treen. PR: £5–3,000. CC: all major. Also, advisory on all aspects of antiques.

Park House Antiques, 8 Park Street, Stow-on-the-Wold, Gloucestershire GL54 1AQ. Prop: George & Barbara Sutton. Tel: & Fax: (01451) 830159. Est: 1985. Shop (6 showrooms); open Monday to Saturday 10–1 and 2–5. NEW stock - very small. OLD general stock - medium. Spec: dolls/dolls clothes; teddy bears; toys - general; lace. PR: £5–1,000. CC: V; MC; AE; DC. Also, brass fenders.

Ruskin Decorative Arts, 5 Talbot Court, Stow-on-the-Wold, Cheltenham, Gloucestershire GL54 1DP. Prop: Anne & William Morris. Tel: (01451) 832254. Est: 1989. Shop; open 7 days a week 10–1 and 2–5.30. OLD stock - very large. Spec: arts & crafts; Art Deco; Art Nouveau; ceramics; copper; glass; pottery; silver; photograph frames. PR: £50–750. CC: MC; A; V; AE; DC.

Samarkand Galleries, 8 Brewery Yard, Sheep Street, Stow-on-the-Wold, Gloucestershire GL54 1AA. Prop: Brian MacDonald. Tel: & Fax: (01451) 832322. Est: 1989. Shop; open Monday to Saturday 10–5.30. NEW and OLD stock - very small. Spec: rugs; tribal; Oriental. PR: £50–5,000. CC: AE; V; A; MC. Mem: L.A.P.A.D.A., C.A.D.A.

STROUD

Shabby Tiger Antiques, 18 Nelson Street, Stroud, Gloucestershire GL5 2HN. Prop: Stephen Krucker. Tel: (01453) 759175. Est: 1975. Shop; open Monday to Saturday 10.30–5.30. OLD stock - small. Spec: jewellery; silver. PR: £5–1,000. Corresp: French, German.

GLOUCESTERSHIRE

TETBURY

The Antiques Emporium, The Old Chapel, Long Street, Tetbury, Gloucestershire GL8 8AA. Prop: Mrs Debbie Sayers. Tel: (01666) 505281. Est: 1993. Shop; open Monday to Saturday 10–5, Sunday 1–5. OLD stock - large. Spec: boxes; brass; candles/candlesticks; ceramics; china; cutlery; decorative; French; glass; jewellery; kitchenalia; militaria; objets de vertu; Oriental; plates; pottery; scent bottles; silver; Victorian; fountain pens. PR: £1–1,000. CC: AE; V; D; MC; A. Corresp: French. Mem: Chamber of Commerce.

TEWKESBURY

Tewkesbury Antique Centre, Tolsey Hall, Tolsey Lane, Tewkesbury, Gloucestershire. Manager: R.L. Hawker. Tel: (01684) 294091. Est: 1991. Old Chapel; open Monday to Saturday 10–5, Sunday 11–5. OLD general stock. Spec: Art Deco; boxes; ceramics; china; clocks; commemorative ware; costume jewellery; Edwardian; egg cups; glass; gramophone needle tins; lace; pewter; pottery; silver; teapots; Toby jugs. PR: £1–1,000. Also, antique and pine furniture.

WINCHCOMBE

Muriel Lindsay, Queen Anne House, Winchcombe, Gloucestershire. Prop: Douglas John & Muriel Lindsay. Tel: & Fax: (01242) 602319. Est: 1965. Shop; open Tuesday to Saturday 10–1 and 2.15–5. NEW stock - small. Spec: silver. OLD stock - very large. Spec: brass; candles/candlesticks; copper; glass; horsebrasses & harnesses; keys; metalware; scales, weights & measures; Staffordshire; trays. PR: £3–500. CC: A; V; AE. Corresp: French.

GREATER MANCHESTER

Including the Unitary Authorities of Bolton, Bury, Manchester, Oldham, Rochdale, Salford, Stockport Tameside, Trafford and Wigan

ALTRINCHAM

Toto's, Grafton Street, Altrincham, Cheshire WA14 1DU. (•) Prop: W.B. Wright. Tel: (0161) 928-7657. Est: 1980. Shop; open Monday to Saturday 9.30–5. NEW stock - very small. Spec: dolls/dolls clothes; miniatures; teddy bears. CC: V; MC; AE. Mem: N.C.W.A., B.S.S.A.

BOLTON

Bolton Antique Centre, Central Street, Bolton, Lancashire BL1 2AB. (•) Prop: Mr Roberts & Mr Owen. Tel: (01204) 362694. Est: 1991. Shop; open Monday to Saturday 10–5, Sunday 11–4. OLD general stock. Spec: jewellery. PR: £1–2,000. *Note:* 20 dealers selling varied antiques and collectables.

Ironchurch Antiques Centre, The Iron Church, Blackburn Road, Bolton, Lancashire BL1 8DR. (•) Prop: Peter Wilkinson. Tel: (01204) 383616. Est: 1993. Open 7 days a week 10–5. OLD general stock - very large. Spec: arts & crafts; Art Nouveau; barometers; cameras; ceramics; china; clocks; costume jewellery; fashion accessories; Georgian; glass; jewellery; kitchenalia; lighting; metalware; musical instruments; pens; photographic pictures; pottery; Victorian. PR: 50p–£5,000. CC: V; A; D.

HAZEL GROVE

The Clock House, 14 Buxton Road, Hazel Grove, Stockport, Greater Manchester. Prop: Alan W. Thom. Tel: & Fax: (01298) 815174. Est: 1974. Shop; open 7 days a week 10–6. OLD stock - very large. Spec: Rolex and vintage watches; jewellery; clocks. PR: £1–5,000. CC: all. Cata: monthly, on watches. Also, repairs. Mem: N.A.W.C.C.C., B.H.I.

MANCHESTER

AS Antique Galleries, 26 Broad Street, Pendleton Salford, Manchester M6 5BY. Prop: A. Sternshine. Tel: (0161) 737-5938. Fax: 737-6626. Est: 1973. Shop; open Monday & Wednesday to Saturday 10–5.30. OLD stock - very large. Spec: Art Deco; Art Nouveau; bronze; clocks; jarnidières; lighting; sculpture; silver. PR: £100–10,000. CC: MC; A.

Britannia Models, 86 Bury Old Road, Whitefield, Manchester M45 6TQ. Prop: Mr J.H. Pye and Mr C.J. Stephens. Tel: & Fax: (0161) 773-0611 or Tel: 773-0023. Est: 1990. Shop; open Monday, Tuesday and Thursday to Saturday 9–5. Fairs: N.E.C., Donington, Buxton, Chester, Manchester, Heywood. NEW stock - large. Spec: arms & armour; arts & crafts; bicycles; constructional toys; diecast toys; firearms; fire fighting equipment; London Transport; militaria; model cars and aircraft; motoring; radio & television; tinplate toys; traction/steam engines; transport. OLD stock - medium. Spec: diecast vehicles. PR: £1–600. CC: A; V; MC; AE. Cata: monthly. Also, Tekno trucks. Corresp: German, French. Mem: Federation of Small Businesses.

British Heritage Telephones, 11 Rhodes Drive, Unsworth, Bury, Lancashire. Tel: & Fax: (0161) 767-9259. Est: 1989. Private premises; appointment necessary. NEW and OLD stock - large. Spec: telephones; telephone boxes; Victorian; letter boxes; lighting; police memorabilia; tins, signs & advertising; street furniture. PR: £150–10,000. Cata: available on request. Corresp: French, Italian, German.

P. Christian Decorative Arts, 402 Waterloo Road, Blackpool, Lancashire PY4 4BL. (•) Tel: (0161) 833-9037. Market stand at: The Ginnel Gallery, 18-22 Lloyd Street, Manchester; open Monday to Saturday 9.30–5.30. OLD stock - medium. Spec: arts & crafts; Art Nouveau; Art Deco; The Seventies; The Sixties. PR: £5–500.

The Ginnel Gallery Antique Centre, Basement, 18–22 Lloyd Street, Manchester M2 5WA. Prop: Keith & Irene Mottershead. Tel: (0161) 833-9037. Est: 1982. Shop; open Monday to Saturday 9.30–5.30 or by appointment. OLD stock - large. Spec: arts & crafts; Art Nouveau; Art Deco; badges; boxes; brass; cameras; ceramics; china; early plastics; fine art; glass; jewellery; kitchenalia; The Fifties; The Sixties. PR: £1–1,000. CC: AE; BC; DC; D; JCB. Also, a recognised leader in the 1950's and 1960's.

Imperial Antiques, 295 Buxton Road, Great Moor, Stockport, Cheshire SK2 7NR. Prop: Mr Alfred Todd. Tel: (0161) 483-3322. Fax: 483-3376. Est: 1981. Shop; open 9.30–5, 6 days a week. OLD stock - very large. Spec: Art Nouveau; Art Deco; bronze; chandeliers; ivory; oil lamps; Oriental; silver. PR: £5–10,000. CC: V; MC. Also, export. Mem: L.A.P.A.D.A.

Stewart Diecast Model Vehicles, 10 Normanby Road, Worsley, Manchester M28 7TR. Prop: Stewart T. Booth. Tel: (0161) 799-2621. Est: 1992. Private premises; appointment necessary. NEW stock - small. Spec: model cars; commercial vehicles; Lledo; Corgi; EFE. PR: £3–50. Cata: on request and with orders.

Toystore Collectables, Unit 32, 33 & 34, Corn Exchang Manchester City Centre, M4 3BW. Prop: G. Maguire & T. Sanders. Tel: (0161) 839-6882. Fax: 281-0815. Est: 1994. Shop; open Monday to Saturday 10.30–5. Fairs: Sandown, N.E.C. NEW stock - large. Spec: toys - Star Wars, Star Trek, X-Men, Spawn, Batman and Aliens. OLD stock - large. Spec: toys - Star Wars, Action Man, Robots, Daleks, TV/film, diecast. PR: £1–1,000.

Underhill Crafts, 14 High Street East, Glossop, Derbyshire SK14 6DR. (•) Prop: Deborah J. Nelson. Tel: (01457) 857500. Shop; open Monday and Wednesday to Saturday 10.30–5, Sunday 1–4. NEW stock - medium. Spec: dolls houses; miniatures; porcelain dolls. PR: 90p–£500. CC: A; V; AE. Cata: annually. Also, some exclusive items made by us. Mem: North Derbyshire Chamber of Commerce.

OLDHAM

Papersafe, 11A Printer Street, Oldham, Greater Manchester OL1 1PN. Prop: Graham Moss. Tel: (0161) 627-1966. Est: 1986. Storeroom; appointment necessary. Fairs: Pudsey, Buxton. OLD stock - small. PR: £3.50–50. Cata: rarely. Also, letterpress printing. Corresp: German, Swedish.

STOCKPORT

Abbatt Toys, 45 St. Petersgate, Stockport, Cheshire SK1 1DH. Prop: Marion Rigby. Tel: (0161) 480-7665. Est: 1980's. Shop; open 9.30–5.30. Fairs: Olympia. NEW general stock - medium. Spec: arts & crafts; dolls/dolls clothes; dolls houses; model cars; teddy bears; toys - general and soldiers. PR: 1p plus (toys) £20–300 (bears). CC: D; V; A; MC. Also, traditional wooden toys. Mem: B.A.T.R.

Brabyns Browse, at 'Lovin Givin', 86 Lower Fold, Marple Bridge, Stockport, Cheshire SK6 5DU. Prop: Alison L. Barstow. Tel: (0161) 427-7460. Shop; open Tuesday, Thursday to Saturday 9.30–5. NEW stock - medium. Spec: teddy bears; toys - general. OLD stock - medium. Spec: costume jewellery; teddy bears; toys - general. Corresp: German.

E.R. Antiques Centre, 122 Wellington Street, off Wellington Road South, Stockport, Cheshire SK1 1YH. Prop: Eunice Ruth Warburton. Tel: (0161) 429-6646. Fax: 480-5598. Est: 1980. Shop; open Monday to Saturday 12–5.30. Fairs: Deanwater Hotel - Wilmslow, Alderley Edge Assembley Rooms, Bowden Assembley Rooms. NEW stock - medium. Spec: Winstanley pottery cats. OLD stock. Spec: ceramics; costume jewellery; decorative; glass; clocks; Edwardian; pens; vases; Victorian; writing - general. CC: all. Also lecturer on antiques & collectables. Corresp: French, Italian.

Highland Antiques Export, 67 Wellington Road North, Stockport, Cheshire SK4 2LP. Prop: Mr E. Todd. Tel: (0161) 476-6660 Fax: 476-6669. Shop; open Monday to Friday 9–5.30, Saturday by appointment. Fairs: Newark, N.E.C. NEW stock - very small. Spec: silver plate. OLD stock - medium. Spec: arts & crafts; Art Deco; Art Nouveau; bronze; candle extinguishers; candles and candlesticks; card cases; ceramics; chandeliers; china; clocks; cutlery; decanters; egg cups; fine art; French; inkstands; ivory; jardinières; lighting; mirrors; paperweights; pewter; Japanese antiques; Chinese & Japanese porcelain. PR: £20–6,500. CC: V; A etc.

"Lovin' Givin'", 86 Lower Fold, Marple Bridge, Stockport, Cheshire SK6 5DU. Prop: Robert & Audrey Barstow. Tel: (0161) 427-7460. Est: 1972. Shop; open Tuesday, Thursday to Saturday 9.30–5. NEW stock - large. Spec: Folk Art from Russia & Germany (Erzgebirge); dolls house miniatures. PR: 30p–£450. Corresp: German. Mem: MinTA.

《Lovin' Givin'》, Marple Bridge, Cheshire.
Tel: 0161.427.7460   Specialists in:

DOLLS' HOUSE MINIATURES
and
FOLK ART
FROM RUSSIA & GERMANY

Russia: Matryoshkas, Lacquer Boxes, Decorated Eggs, Character Dolls, Tea Cosy Dolls, Bogorodsk 'Toys' etc.
Germany (Erzgebirge): Nutcrackers, Smokers, Pyramids, Schwibbogen, Chip Box Ornaments, Matchbox Scenes, Teddies etc.

GREATER MANCHESTER

Roads and Rails, The Sidings, 7 Lynwood Grove, Heaton Chapel, Stockport, Cheshire SK4 5DP. Prop: Roy & Julie Chapman. Tel: & Fax: (0161) 442-5953. Est: 1989. Private premises; appointment necessary. NEW and OLD stock - very small. Spec: railways; trains; transport; buses & tramways. PR: £1–500. Cata: 4 a year. Corresp: German.

HAMPSHIRE

ALDERSHOT

Concorde Models, 179 Victoria Road, Aldershot, Hampshire GU11 1JU. Prop: Brian & Dennis Ballard. Tel: & Fax: (01252) 26825. Est: 1969. Shop; open Monday, Tuesday and Thursday to Saturday 9.15–6, Wednesday 9.15–1. NEW stock - large. Spec: diecast toys; model trains, cars and aircraft; toy soldiers. OLD stock - very small. Spec: diecast toys; model aircraft; toy soldiers. PR: £1–100. CC: V; MC; AE; DC; D; EC; E; JCB. Also, plastic construction kits.

Stewart Davis, c/o Richard Joseph Publishers Ltd., Unit 2, Monks Walk, Farnham, Surrey GU9 8HT. Private premises; postal business only. OLD stock - small. Spec: rifle shooting memorabilia.

ALRESFORD

Alresford Antiques, 49 West Street, Alresford, Hampshire SO24 9AB. Prop: Mr & Mrs C. Carpenter. Tel: Shop (01962) 735959, Home: 733160, Mobile: (0860) 590647. Est: 1993. Shop; open variable hours. Fairs: Sandown, Alexandra Palace. OLD general stock. PR: £1–200.

Evans and Evans, 40 West Street, Alresford, Hampshire SO24 9AU. Prop: Noel & David Evans. Tel: & Fax: (01962) 732170. Email: evans and evans@ compuserve.com. Est: 1968. Shop; open Friday and Saturday 9–1 and 2–5 or by appointment. NEW stock - medium. Spec: barometers; clocks; watches - wrist and chain. OLD stock - very large. Spec: barometers; clocks; gramophones; musical boxes; watches - wrist and chain. PR: £300–25,000. CC: MC; V; JCB; EC. Mem: L.A.P.A.D.A.

ALTON

Wey Valley Promotionals International, P.O. Box 48, Alton, Hants GU34 1YD. Prop: David Sumner. Tel: (01420) 84074, evenings (01428) 653660, mobile (0378) 423405. Est: 1994. Private premises; postal business only. Fairs: frequently attended. NEW and OLD stock - medium. Spec: Lledo models promotional diecast vehicles. PR: £5.95–750. Cata: lists sent bi-monthly. Corresp: Tagalo.

ANDOVER

G M Services, 98 Junction Road, Andover, Hampshire SP10 3JA. Prop: George Murdoch. Tel: & Fax: (01264) 362048. Est: 1990. Private premises; postal business only. NEW stock - very small. Spec: aeronautica, militaria, medals relative to 1914-18 Great War. OLD stock - small. Spec: aeronautica, militaria, medals relative to Great War. Cata: monthly.

BASINGSTOKE

Caroline French – Wedgwood, c/o Richard Joseph Publishers, Unit 2, Monks Walk, Farnham, Surrey GU9 8HT. Tel: (01256) 819617. Est: 1995. Private premises. Fairs: Winchester (Magnums), Woking (Take Five Fairs) and Benson (County Fairs). OLD stock - medium. Spec: Wedgwood - commemorative ware, jewellery, plates, Royal memorabilia, teapots, thimbles. PR: £5–500.

This and That, Beech Hill, Woods Lane, Cliddesden, Basingstoke RG25 2JF. Est: 1990. Private premises; postal business only. OLD stock - small. Spec: teddy bears, thimbles. PR: £1–100. Cata: occasional.

FARNBOROUGH

Bona Art Deco Originals, Princes Mead Shopping Centre, Farnborough, Hampshire GU14 6YB. Tel: & Fax: (01252) 372188. Est: 1989. Shop; open Monday to Saturday 9.30–5.30 (closed Bank Holidays). NEW stock - very small. Spec: Art Deco. OLD stock - very large. Spec: Art Deco; china; ceramics; clocks; costume jewellery; decanters; decorative; early plastics; egg cups; glass; gramophones; jewellery; lighting; mirrors; motor car mascots; posters; pottery; radio & television; vases. PR: 50p–£20,000. CC: A; AE; DC; V. Also, valuations, repairs/restorations and auctions. Mem: Art Deco Dealers Association.

FLEET

BFM Collectables, P.O. Box 69, Fleet, Hampshire GU13 9YN. Prop: Gerald & Barbara Ford. Est: 1982. Private premises; postal business only. NEW stock - small. Spec: railway, ambulance and Automobile Association model vehicles. OLD stock - very small. Spec: AA memorabilia. PR: £5–50. CC: V; MC; A; EC. Cata: quarterly.

HARTLEY WINTNEY

A.W. Porter & Son, High Street, Hartley Wintney, Hook, Hampshire RG27 8NY. Prop: M.A. & S.J. Porter. Est: 1844. Shop; open Monday to Saturday 9–5.30. NEW stock - medium. Spec: jewellery; silver; clocks; barometers; china; leather. OLD stock - medium. Spec: jewellery; silver; clocks. PR: £10–1,000. CC: A; V. Also, restoration of clocks. Mem: N.A.G., B.N.I.

LYMINGTON

Lymington Antiques Centre, 76 High Street, Lymington, Hampshire SO41 9AL. Prop: Mr Hughes & Mr Stanley–Smith. Tel: (01590) 675424. Est: 1990. Shop; open Monday to Friday 10–5, Saturday 9–5. Fairs: Sandown Park, Kempton Park, Alexandra Palace. NEW stock - very small. Spec: oil lamps; jewellery; silver plated frames. OLD stock - medium. Spec: ceramcis; kitchenalia. PR: £1–1,000. CC: taken by some stallholders. Also, jewellery repair and oil lamp spares.

Barry Papworth, 28 St. Thomas Street, Lymington, Hampshire SO41 9NE. Prop: Barry Papworth. Tel: (01590) 676422. Est: 1976. Shop; open 9–5. NEW stock - small. Spec: barometers; candle extinguishers; clocks; cuff links; egg cups; jewellery; photograph frames; pincushions; thimbles; wrist and chain watches; silver; tankards. OLD stock - small. Spec: antique diamond rings; jewellery; buttonhooks; cuff links; decanters; pen knives; silver; wrist chain watches. PR: £1–5,000. CC: all major. Mem: N.A.G.

PETERSFIELD

Folly Antiques Centre, College Street, Petersfield, Hampshire. Prop: Pemas Limited. Tel: (01730) 266131. Fax: 269370. Est: 1978. Shop at: Causeway House, The Casueway, Petersfield; open Monday to Saturday 9.30–5.30. NEW stock - small. Spec: model cars and trains. OLD general stock - medium. Spec: china; clocks; jewellery; commemorative ware; pottery. PR: £1–1,000. CC: V; A; MC; D.

PORTSMOUTH

A. Fleming (Southsea) Ltd., The Clock Tower, Castle Road, Southsea, Portsmouth, Hampshire PO5 3DE. Prop: Mr A.J. and Mrs C.E. Fleming. Tel: (01705) 822934. Fax: 293501. Est: 1908. Shop; open Monday to Friday 9.30–5.30, Saturday 9.30–1. Fairs: Goodwood House (Soper Exhibitions), Petworth Antiques Fair (Bailey). NEW stock - small. Spec: silver; decanters; cutlery. OLD general stock - very large. Spec: silver; decorative; nautical items. PR: £25–5,000. CC: MC; V; A. Corresp: German.

RINGWOOD

Millers Antiques, Netherbrook House, 86 Christchurch Road, Ringwood, Hampshire BH24 1DR. Prop: Alan J. & Carole M.G. Miller. Tel: (01425) 472062. Fax: 472727. Est: 1897. Shop; open Monday to Friday 9–5, Saturday 10–4. Fairs: Decorative Antiques Fair - London (Harvey Management January, March & September), Wilton House Antiques Fair (March), Chelsea Brocante (February, April & October). OLD stock - large. Spec: decorative; French; pottery; majolica; faience. PR: £10–4,000. CC: V; A; AE. Corresp: French, German, Spanish. Mem: L.A.P.A.D.A.

Wendy F. Pegler, 4 College Road, Ringwood, Hampshire BH24 1NX. Tel: (01425) 473534. Est: 1979. Private premises; postal business only. Fairs: Ephemera Society Fairs (2 a year). OLD stock - small. Spec: bookmarkers; chocolate; games; gramophone needle tins; match boxes/books; optical toys; playing cards; posters; Royal memorabilia; tins, signs & advertising; tobacco & associated; toys - general. PR: £1–250. Cata: 4 a year. Mem: E.S.

Lorraine Tarrant Antiques, 23 Market Place, Ringwood, Hampshire BH24 1BL. Tel: (01425) 461123. Est: 1991. Shop; open Tuesday to Saturday 10–5. NEW stock - very small. Spec: candle extinguishers; candles/candlesticks; egg cups; glass; hatpins & holders; lighting; mirrors; photograph frames; serveitte rings; stationery; tapestries; teddy bears; textiles. OLD stock - medium. Spec: arts & crafts; automobilia; bottles; brass; candles/candlesticks; chandeliers; china; copper; decorative; embroideries; embroidered pictures; Georgian; motor car mascots; objets de vertu; samplers; tapestries; teddy bears; tins, signs & advertising; toys; Victorian. PR: £4–2,500. CC: A: MC; V; EC. Also, furniture.

The Tennis Bookshop, West Gate, Moyles Court, Nr Ringwood, Hampshire BH24 3NF. Prop: Alan P.H. Chalmers. Tel: & Fax: (01425) 480518. Est: 1988. Private premises; appointment necessary. NEW stock - medium and OLD stock - small. Spec: lawn tennis; Royal tennis; croquet. PR: £10–100 (occasionally upto £10,000). CC: A; V; EC; MC. Corresp: French. Mem: P.B.F.A.

ROMSEY

Romsey Medals, 5 Bell Street, Romsey, Hampshire SO51 8GY. Prop: Trevor & Mary Cambridge. Tel: (01794) 512069. Fax: 830332. Est: 1973. Shop; open Monday to Saturday 8.30–5. Fairs: 3 or 4 big medal fairs a year. OLD stock - very large. Spec: medals. PR: £2–10,000 plus. Mem: O.M.R.S., L.A.P.A.D.A.

SOUTHAMPTON

Athena Antiques, 31 Newtown Road, Warsash, Nr. Southampton, Hampshire SO31 9FY. Tel: (01489) 584633 and 578093. Est: 1980. Shop; open most days, but ring for opening hours. Fairs: Minstead, Wickham, Ardingly and Newark. NEW stock - very small. Spec: stamps, first day covers and accessories. OLD stock - large. Spec: ceramics; chandeliers; china; glass; lighting; stamps. PR: £1–500. CC: AE. Cata: 2 a year, for railwayana auctions. Also, 2 railwayana auctions and 40 Athena fairs a year. *At same premises:* Solent Railwayana (q.v.).

Cobwebs (Ocean Liner Memorabilia), 78 Northam Road, Southampton, Hampshire SO14 0PB. Prop: P.R. Boyd–Smith. Tel: & Fax: (01703) 227458. Est: 1976. Shop; open Monday to Saturday 10.30–4, closed Wednesday. Fairs: Alexandra Palace, London. OLD stock - large. Spec: Ocean liner memorabilia; aeronautica; automobilia; maritime/nautical; motor car mascots; police memorabilia; posters; railways; telescopes; transport. PR: £2 upwards. CC: V; MC. Corresp: French.

Ducal Models, Fort Ducal, 5 Weavills Road, Eastleigh, Hampshire SO5 8HQ. (•) Prop: Jack & Thelma Duke. Tel: (01703) 692119. Fax: 602456. Est: 1975. Private premises; open Monday to Friday 9.30–4.30 or by appointment. Fairs: D & J Fairs - Picketts Lock and NEC, Toy & Model Soldier Show - Royal National, London. NEW stock - large. Spec: toy soldiers; badges. OLD stock - very small. PR: £5–150. CC: MC; V. Cata: 1 a year. Also, LP records, military only.

Langlass, 198 Falkland Road, Chandlers Ford, Southampton, Hampshire SO53 3HX. Prop: J.E. Lang. Tel: (01703) 260787. Est: 1987. Private premises; appointment necessary. Fairs: dolls house & miniature - Lyndhurst, Bournemouth etc. NEW stock - small. Spec: miniatures. PR: £1.50–50.

Bob May, 25 Oakwood Way, Hamble Le Rice, Southampton, Hampshire SO31 4HJ. Tel: & Fax: (01703) 453318. Est: 1989. Private premises; appointment necessary. Fairs: Farnham, Sandown, Windsor, Kempton Park. NEW stock - very small. Spec: model cars (Matchbox toys and Corgi classics); diecast toys. OLD stock - medium. Spec: model cars; diecast toys (old Matchbox toys). PR: £25–250. CC: A; EC; MC; V. Cata: 4 a year.

S.P.M. Jewellers, 9 Bedford Place, Southampton, Hampshire. Prop: A. Payne & A. Adams. Tel: (01703) 223255. Fax: 335634. Est: 1975. Shop; open Tuesday to Saturday 9–5. NEW stock - small. Spec: jewellery, silver. OLD stock - medium. Spec: jewellery; silver; snuff boxes; sovereign holders; spoons; wrist and chain watches. PR: £20–1,000. CC: A; V; DC. Mem: N.A.G., B.N.T.A.

Solent Railwayana, 31 Newtown Road, Warsash, Hampshire SO31 9FY. (•) Prop: Alan R. Tonks. Tel: (01489) 584633 and 578093. Est: 1992. Shop; open most days, but ring for opening hours. Fairs: Athena Fayres, I.A.C.F. Newark, Ardingly. NEW stock - very small. Spec: model trains; railways; tins, signs & advertising. OLD stock - medium. Spec: badges; London Transport; model trains; railways. PR: £1–500. CC: AE. Cata: 2 a year for Railwayana auctions. *At same premises:* Athena Antiques (q.v.).

Toy Exchange (Southampton Model Car Centre), 9 Romsey Road, Shirley, Southampton SO16 4BY. Prop: G. Hames & A. Frampton. Tel: (01703) 787913. Est: 1979. Shop; open 10–5 (closed Wednesday and Sunday). Fairs: major English and West European. NEW stock - medium. Spec: diecast toys; Corgi; EFE; Solido; Verem; Eligor; Vitesse; Gama; Onyx; Trofeu. OLD stock - large. Spec: diecast toys; tinplate toys; railways; toys - general; toy soldiers; traction/steam engines; trains; Hornby; Dinky; Matchbox; Corgi; Triang; most diecast manufacturers. CC: all major. Also, insurance valuations.

Western Antique Arms, Station House, Macnaghton Road, Bitterne, Southampton SO18 1GG. Prop: G. Pearson & J. Porter. Tel: (01703) 363727. Fax: 341728. Shop; appointment necessary. Fairs: all large European shows. OLD stock - medium. Spec: arms & armour; swords; beadwork; North American Indian items; guns from cowboy era and American Civil War. PR: £50–3,000. CC: V; MC. Cata: every 6 weeks.

SOUTHSEA

Sabre Sales, 85–87 Castle Road, Southsea, Hampshire PO5 3AY. Prop: Nick Hall. Tel: (01705) 833394. Fax: 837394. Est: 1986. Shop; open Monday to Friday 9–5, Saturday 10–4.30. Fairs: many attended. NEW stock - very large. Spec: conflicts of the 20th Century. OLD stock - very large. Spec: military clothing, helmets, insignia, camo nets, uniforms, caps; de-activated guns. PR: £1–50. CC: all. Cata: 1 a year. Corresp: French, German.

WATERLOOVILLE

Thistledown, 22 London Road, Purbrook, Waterlooville, Hampshire PO7 5LJ. Prop: Mr & Mrs C.H. Cairns. Tel: (01705) 255669. Est: 1994. Shop; open Tuesday & Thursday to Saturday 10–5.30. NEW general stock - medium. Spec: china; dolls/dolls clothes; dolls houses; embroideries; miniatures; teddy bears. PR: £1–600. CC: V; A; MC.

HEREFORD AND WORCESTER

BROADWAY

Broadway Bears & Dolls, 76 High Street, Broadway, Worcestershire WR12 7AJ. Prop: Ms Janice Longhi & Mr Brian Davis. Tel: & Fax: (01386) 858323. Est: 1995. Shop; open in normal business hours. NEW stock - medium. Spec: teddy bears; dolls/dolls clothes. OLD stock - very small. Spec: teddy bears; dolls/dolls clothes. PR: £1–500. CC: all except AE. Also, a teddy bear museum. Corresp: Spanish, Danish.

Fenwick and Fenwick Antiques, 88–90 High Street, Broadway, Worcestershire WR12 7AL. Tel: (01386) 853227. Fax: 858504. Shop; open Monday to Saturday 10–6. OLD stock - very large. Spec: barometers; beadwork; bells; boot scrapers; bottles; boxes; brass; bronze; buttons; buttonhooks; candle extinguishers; candles/candlesticks; card cases; ceramics; china; clocks; copper; corkscrews & bottle openers; cutlery; decanters and many others. PR: £2.50–8,000. CC: V; MC. Corresp: French, German. Mem: C.A.D.A.

CLEOBURY MORTIMER

Antique Centre, Childe Road, Cleobury Mortimer, Kidderminster, Hereford & Worcester. Prop: Mr P.A. & Mrs H. Rust. Tel: (01299) 270513. Est: 1977. Open 7 days a week 10–5. NEW stock - very small. Spec: boot scrapers; bottles; boxes; brass; buckles & clasps; buttons; ceramics; mirrors; silver; walking sticks; sundials; teapots; Staffordshire; spoons. OLD general stock - medium. Spec: arts & crafts; buttons; candles/candlesticks; china; cutlery; decanters; dolls/dolls clothes; Edwardian; egg cups; Georgian; gramophone needle tins; hatpins and holders; horsebrasses & harnesses; kitchenalia; lace; laundry bygones; luggage; scales, weights & measures; thimbles; writing. Also, antique furniture.

DROITWICH

Grant Books, The Coach House, New Road, Cutnall Green, Droitwich WR9 OPQ. Prop: H.R.J. & S.J. Grant. Tel: (01299) 851588. Fax: 851446. Est: 1971. Office; open 9–5, Saturday by appointment. Fairs: NEC Eurogolf Trade Exhibition. NEW and OLD stock - very small. Spec: golf only. PR: £1–500. CC: all major. Mem: P.B.F.A., British Golf Collectors Society, Golf Collectors Society (U.S.A.).

HEREFORD

Hereford Antique Centre, 128 Widemarsh Street, Hereford, Hereford & Worcester. Prop: Mrs L.F. Mitchell. Tel: (01432) 266242. Est: 1991. Shop (covering 6,000 sq ft); open Monday to Saturday 9–5, Sunday 1–5. OLD general stock - large. PR: £1–800. CC: A; V. Also, furniture. Corresp: French.

KIDDERMINSTER

The Antique Centre, 5 to 8 Lion Street, Kidderminster, Worcestershire DY10 1PT. Prop: Mrs V. Bentley. Tel: (01562) 740389. Est: 1980. Shop; open Tuesday to Saturday 10–5.30. OLD general stock - very large. Spec: ceramics; china; fine art; jewellery; silver. PR: £1–1,000. Also, furniture, stripped pine and antique fireplaces.

BBM Jewellery, 8–9 Lion Street, Kidderminster, Worcestershire DY10 1PT. Prop: W.V. Crook. Tel: (01562) 744118. Fax: 825954. Est: 1980. Shop; open Monday and Wednesday to Saturday 10–5. NEW stock - large. Spec: silver. OLD stock - large. Spec: buttonhooks; ceramics; coins; jewellery; silver; Victorian. PR: £1–5,000. CC: all except DC. Mem: B.J.A.

Chris-A-Liz, 85-86 New Road, Kidderminster, Worcestershire DY10 1AE. Prop: Elizabeth and Christopher Lawrence. Tel: (01562) 825466. Fax: 755058 (24 hour). Est: 1990. Shop; open Monday to Saturday 10–5, closed Wednesday. Fairs: all major dolls house fairs, full list on application. NEW stock - large. Spec: dolls houses; figures, accessories, lighting and tools for 1/12th scale. PR: houses £80–750, accessories 50p–£100. CC: all major cards. Cata: monthly. Mem: F.S.B.

Hoo Bears, 15 Pochard Close, Kidderminster, Worcestershire DY10 4UB. Prop: Helen & Steve Oliver. Tel: (01562) 746116. Fax: by arrangement. E-Mail: 101517.3417@compuserve.com. Est: 1994. Private premises; appointment necessary. Fairs: major teddy fairs. NEW stock - very small. Spec: teddy bears. PR: £40–200. Cata: approximately 6 monthly.

LEOMINSTER

The Barometer Shop, New Street, Leominster, Herefordshire HR6 8BT. Prop: R.C. Cookson & R.E. Worthington. Tel: & Fax: (01568) 610200 or Tel: 613652. Est: 1963. Shop; open 9–5 or by appointment. NEW stock - medium. OLD stock - very large. Spec: barometers; clocks; sundials. PR: £60–5,000. CC: V; A. Cata: 3 to 5 a year. Also, repairs to clocks and barometers. Mem: British Horological Institute.

Courts Miscellany, 48A Bridge Street, Leominster, Herefordshire HR6 8DZ. Prop: George Court. Tel: (01568) 612995. Est: 1983. Shop; open Monday to Saturday 10–5 or by appointment. OLD general stock. Spec: aeronautica; corkscrews and bottle openers; fire fighting equipment; horsebrasses and harnesses; militaria; police memorabilia; pottery; sports; tools. PR: £1–2,000.

MALVERN

Gandolfi House, 211–213 Wells Road, Malvern, Worcestershire WR14 4HF. Prop: P.A. & Mrs R.E. Weller. Tel: (01684) 569747. Est: 1988. Shop; open Tuesday to Saturday 10–5.30. NEW stock - very large. Spec: dolls houses; lighting; mirrors; rocking horses. OLD stock - very large. Spec: fine art; Art Nouveau; Art Deco; brass; china; copper; decanters; glass; pottery. PR: £50–3,000 (dolls house related 20p–£1,200). CC: A; BC. Also, garden ornaments and furniture. Corresp: German. Mem: British Shops and Stores Association (B.S.S.A.).

Whitmore, Teynham Lodge, Chase Road, Upper Colwall, Malvern WR13 6DT. Prop: J.A. & S. Whitmore. Tel: & Fax: (01684) 540651. Est: 1965. Private premises; appointment necessary. OLD stock - large. Spec: paper money; Royal memorabilia; phonecards; coins; tokens; medallions. PR: £1–500. Cata: 2 a year. Mem: B.N.T.A.

HEREFORD AND WORCESTER

ROSS-ON-WYE

Fritz Fryer Decorative Antique Lighting, 12 Brookend Street, Ross-on-Wye, Herefordshire HR9 7EG. Prop: Fritz Fryer & Joan Graham. Tel: (01989) 567416. Fax: 566742. Est: 1982. Shop; open Monday to Saturday 10–5.30. NEW stock - very small. OLD stock - medium. Spec: lighting. PR: £50–5,000. CC: V; MC; D.

WORCESTER

'Abookortwo', No. 6 Tything, Worcester, Hereford & Worcester WR1 1NH. Prop: Colin Clarke. Tel: (01905) 20816. Shop and storeroom; open 9.30–5. OLD stock - medium. Spec: small collectables.

HERTFORDSHIRE

BALDOCK

The Attic, 20 Whitehorse Street, Baldock, Hertfordshire. Prop: Pat Sheppard. Tel: (01462) 893880. Est: 1985. Shop; open Monday to Wednesday, Friday and Saturday 10–4.30. OLD general stock. Spec: brass; ceramics; china; copper; lighting; radio & television; teddy bears; general toys.

Howards, 33 Whitehorse Street, Baldock, Hertfordshire SG7 6QF. Prop: D.N. Howard. Tel: (01462) 892385. Est: 1976. Shop; open Tuesday to Saturday. OLD stock. Spec: antique clocks. PR: £250–3,500. CC: V; A.

HEMEL HEMPSTEAD

Beatties of London Ltd., Enterprise House, Maxted Road, Hemel Hempstead, Hertfordshire HP2 7BT. Tel: (01923) 238298. Est: 1954. 70 shops nationwide; open Monday to Saturday 9–5.30 please telephone for your nearest store. NEW stock - large. Spec: diecast toys; model trains, cars and aircraft; toy soldiers; models; toys; games. PR: £1–500. CC: most major cards.

Cherry Antiques, 101-103 High Street, Hemel Hempstead, Hertfordshire HP1 3AH. Prop: Mrs A.I.M. & Mr R.S. Cullen. Tel: (01442) 64358. Est: 1981. Shop; open Monday to Saturday 9.30–4.30, except Wednesday 9.30–1. NEW stock - medium. OLD general stock - very small. PR: £1–5,000. CC: V; AE; DC.

HERTFORD

Beckwith and Son, St. Nicholas Hall, St. Andrew Street, Hertford, Hertfordshire SG14 1HZ. Prop: G.C.M. Gray. Tel: (01992) 582079. Est: 1904. Shop; open Monday to Saturday 9–1 and 2–5.30. NEW stock - very small. Spec: brass; copper; horsebrasses and harnesses; silver. OLD general stock - large. PR: £10–10,000. Also, period furniture, restoration and French polishing.

Robert Horton Antiques, 13 Castle Street, Hertford, Hertfordshire SG14 1ER. Tel: (01992) 587546. Est: 1972. Shop; open Monday to Wednesday, Friday & Saturday 9–5. OLD stock - very small. Spec: barometers; clocks. PR: £200–5,000. Also, clock repairs. Mem: British Watch & Clockmakers Guild.

Oxfam, 8 Railway Street, Hertford, Hertfordshire SG14 1BG. Tel: (01992) 583221. Est: 1985. Shop; open Monday to Saturday 9.30–5. OLD general stock - medium. Spec: records. PR: £3–50.

PUCKERIDGE

St. Ouen Antiques, Vintage Corner, Old Cambridge Road, Puckeridge, Hertfordshire. Prop: John & Tim Blake. Tel: (01920) 821336. Fax: 822877. Est: 1967. Shop and storeroom; open Monday to Saturday 10–5. OLD stock - very large. Mem: L.A.P.A.D.A.

RICKMANSWORTH

David Harriman, 25 Nightingale Road, Rickmansworth, Hertfordshire WD3 2DE. Tel: (01923) 776919. Fax: 773995. Est: 1960. Private premises; appointment necessary. OLD stock - medium. Spec: Art Nouveau; Art Deco; bronze; clocks. PR: £25–5,000. CC: V. Cata: 2 or 3 a year. Corresp: French.

ST. ALBANS

Magic Lanterns Antique Lighting, at By George, 23 George Street, St. Albans, Hertfordshire AL3 4ES. Prop: Ms Josie A. Marsden. Tel: (01727) 865680 or 853032. Mobile: (0802) 876335. Est: 1986. Shop; open Monday to Friday 10–5, Thursday 11–5, Saturday 10–5.30, Sunday 1–5, appointment necessary to see proprietor. OLD stock - large. Spec: antique gas & electric lighting; candlesticks; antique boxes; brass knockers. PR: £35–350. Also, lighting consultancy.

Graham O'Hara, P.O. Box 182, St. Albans, Hertfordshire AL3 5QR. Tel: (01727) 832963. Market stand; open Monday to Friday 9–5.30. Fairs: St. Albans Antique Fair, St. Albans Stamp Fair, Hertford Stamp Fair. NEW stock - small. Spec: stamps; philatelic accessories. OLD stock - very large. Spec: stamps; postal history - modern covers; phonecards; philatelic accessories. PR: 25p–£500. Also, anything related to Marilyn Monroe. Mem: Philatelic Traders Society Ltd., American Philatelic Society.

Oriental Rug Gallery Limited, 42 Verulam Road, St Albans, Hertfordshire AL3 4DQ. Prop: Richard Mathias & Julian Blair. Tel: & Fax: (01727) 841046. Est: 1988. Shop; open Monday to Saturday 9–6, Sunday 10.30–4. Fairs: Thames Valley Antique Dealers Association - Eton and Oxford. NEW stock - medium. Spec: Persian rugs. OLD stock - small. Spec: rugs. PR: £100–5,000. CC: A; V. Also, import directly and manufacture. Corresp: French. Mem: T.V.A.D.A., I.D.D.A., B.O.N.D.A. *Also at:* High Street, Eton, Berkshire (q.v.).

Stuart Wharton, 1 George Street, St. Albans, Hertfordshire AL3 4ER. Tel: (01727) 859489. Fax: 855474. Est: 1967. Shop; open Monday to Saturday 9–5.30. NEW stock - very large. Spec: glass; jewellery; bookmarkers; buckles & clasps; tankards. OLD stock - medium. Spec: Victorian; spoons; Edwardian; inkstands; Georgian; jewellery; glass; tankards; silver. PR: £25–3,000. Also, registered valuers and a gemmologist. Corresp: French, German. Mem: N.A.G., F.G.A., D.G.A.

SAWBRIDGEWORTH

Herts & Essex Antiques Centre, Unit 1, The Maltings, Station Road, Sawbridgeworth, Hertfordshire CM21 9JX. Prop: Morton Stuart M.B.E. & Melanie Stuart. Tel: (01279) 722044. Est: 1980. Shop; open Tuesday to Friday 10–5, Saturday & Sunday 10.30–6. OLD general stock - large. Spec: Art Nouveau; Art Deco; badges; china; costume jewellery; dolls/dolls clothes; dolls houses; Edwardian. PR: £1–2,000. CC: all except AE; DC. Corresp: French, German. Mem: Small Business Organisation.

STEVENAGE

Pet–Away Bears, 166 Broadwater Crescent, Stevenage, Hertfordshire, SG2 8EP. Prop: Mr P. and Mrs J.E. Hunter. Tel: (01438) 369482. Est: 1995. Private premises; appointment necessary. Fairs: major bear fairs. NEW and OLD stock - very small. Spec: teddy bears. PR: £1–450. Cata: monthly.

WATFORD

Network, 5 Temple Close, Watford, Hertfordshire WD1 3DR. Prop: S. & V.M. Friedman. Tel: (01923) 233706. Fax: 226095. Est: 1972. Private premises; postal business only. OLD stock - medium. Spec: London Transport; maritime/nautical; railways; trains; transport. Cata: 2 a year.

Norman Wright, 60 Eastbury Road, Watford, Hertfordshire WD1 4JL. Tel: (01923) 232383. Est: 1985. Private premises; postal business only. Fairs: Pulp & Paperback Fair - Victoria, London, Cartoon Arts Trust - London. NEW stock - very small. OLD stock - medium. Spec: badges; games; films & entertainment; playing cards. PR: £10–100. Cata: 4 a year.

HUMBERSIDE

Including the Unitary Authorities of East Riding of Yorkshire, North East Lincolnshire and North Lincolnshire

BEVERLEY

Objects D'Art, St. Crispin Arcade, 11 Butcher Row, Beverley, Humberside HU17 0AA. Prop: Bernard & Norma Johnson. Tel: (01482) 869583. Est: 1988. Shop; open 7 days a week 10–5. NEW stock - medium. Spec: miniatures; brass; copper; dolls houses and furniture; jewellery; photograph frames; pottery. OLD general stock - very small. PR: £1–100. CC: A; V.

The Toy Gallery, 46 Lairgate, Beverley, East Yorkshire HU17 8EU. Prop: J.C. & K.M. Kendrew. Tel: (01482) 864890. Est: 1990. Shop; open Monday to Saturday 9–5.30. NEW stock - large. Spec: dolls/dolls clothes; teddy bears; musical boxes; rocking horses; wooden toys. OLD stock - very small. Spec: dolls/dolls clothes; teddy bears. PR: £5–3,000. CC: V; A; EC; MC. Mem: Chamber of Trade.

BRIDLINGTON

C.J. and A.J. Dixon, 1st Floor, 23 Prospect Street, Bridlington, Humberside. Tel: (01262) 676877. Fax: 606600. Est: 1969. Shop; open 9–5.30. Fairs: O.M.R.S., Brittania and other medal fairs. NEW general stock - medium. Spec: medals and miniature medals. OLD general stock - medium. PR: £5–6,000. CC: V; A; EC; MC; AE. Cata: 3 a year.

CLEETHORPES

T.J.'s, 4 Short Street, Cleethorpes, Humberside DN35 8LZ. Prop: Mr M. & Mrs C. Jackson. Tel: & Fax: (01472) 291643. Est: 1990. Shop; open Monday to Saturday 8.30–6, (Sunday in Summer months). NEW stock - small. Spec: diecast toys; model cars; general toys. OLD stock - very small. Spec: diecast toys. PR: £5–55. Also, cards, stationery, confectionery & tobacco.

DRIFFIELD

Crested China Company, Station House, Driffield, East Riding of Yorkshire YO25 7PY. Prop: David & Elisabeth Taylor. Tel: (01377) 257042 and 255002. Est: 1978. Private premises; appointment advised. Fairs: Alexandra Palace, London and specialist fairs. OLD stock - medium. Spec: Goss and Crested china; souvenir ware. PR: £5–40 (some more valuable) CC: DC; V; A; AE; MC; EC; BC. Cata: 4 a year.

GRIMSBY

Robin Fowler (Period Clocks), Washing Dales, Washing Dales Lane, Aylesby, Grimsby DN37 7LH. Tel: & Fax: (01472) 751335. Est: 1976. Storeroom; appointment necessary. Fairs: Crown, Cooper, Galloway, Bailey. OLD stock. Spec: clocks barometers; scientific instruments. PR: £200–5,000. CC: V. Mem: B.H.I.

Scarthoe Antiques, 38A Louth Road, Scarthoe, Grimsby DN32 0BX. Prop: P.Bridges. Tel: (01472) 877394. Est: 1975. Shop; open Tuesday, Wednesday, Friday and Saturday 10–5. NEW stock - small. OLD stock - very small. PR: £1–100.

HOWDEN

Lewis Hickson FBHI, Sober Hill Farm, Gilberdyke, East Yorkshire HU15 2TB. Tel: (01430) 449113. Est: 1961. Private premises; appointment necessary. Fairs: Newark etc. NEW stock - very small. OLD stock - very small. Spec: clocks; barometers; scientific instruments. PR: £200–5,000. Cata: occasionally. Also, repairs and conservation. Mem: British Horological Institute, Antiquarian Horological Society.

HULL

Grannies Parlour Antiques, 33 Anlaby Road, Hull, Humberside HU1 2PG. Prop: Nita & Alan Pye. Tel: (01482) 228258. Est: 1974. Shop; open Monday to Saturday 11–5. Fairs: locally. OLD general stock - large. Spec: toys; dolls; teddy bears. PR: 25p–£500. Also, supplies items to museums, film companies etc. Mem: Hull Chamber of Trade.

Lesley's Antiques, 329 Hessle Road, Hull, Humberside HU3 4BL. Tel: (01482) 323986 and 646280. Est: 1967. Shop; open Monday to Saturday 10–4 or by appointment. OLD general stock - very large. PR: £1–100 and higher sometimes. Also, valuations, restorations and repairs. Corresp: French, Spanish. Mem: Hessle Road Traders Association.

Marine Art Posters, 71 Harbour Way, Merchants Landing, Victoria Dock, Hull HU9 1PL. Prop: Audrey E. Newsome. Tel: & Fax: (01482) 321173. Est: 1988. Private premises; appointment necessary. NEW stock - very large. Spec: badges; posters; all maritime subjects. PR: £1.25–45. CC: all. Cata: 2 or 3 a year.

Penny Farthing Antiques, Albion House, Westgate, North Cave, Nr. Brough, North Humberside HU15 2NJ. (•) Prop: Caroline E. Dennett. Tel: (01430) 422958. Est: 1986. Shop; open Monday to Saturday 9.30–6. Fairs: Newark. OLD general stock - medium. PR: £10–3,000. Also, brass and iron beds.

SCUNTHORPE

Guns and Tackle, 251A Ashby High Street, Scunthorpe, Humberside. Prop: J.A. Bowden. Tel: & Fax: (01724) 865445. Est: 1965. Shop; open 9–5. NEW stock - medium. Spec: guns. OLD stock - very small. Spec: antique guns and clocks. PR: £40–2,000. CC: all. Also, repairs on guns.

ISLE OF WIGHT

BEMBRIDGE

Windmill Antiques, 1 Foreland Road, Bembridge, Isle of Wight PO35 5XR. Prop: E.J. de Kort. Tel: & Fax: (01983) 873666. Est: 1973. Shop; open 9.30–1 and 2.15–5. OLD stock - very large. Spec: ceramics; jewellery; objets de vertu; wrist and chain watches. CC: V; MC. Corresp: German, Dutch. Mem: L.A.P.A.D.A.

COWES

J.M. Cameron Gallery, 90B High Street, Cowes, Isle of Wight PO31 7AW. Prop: Jean Flynn. Tel: (01983) 290404. Est: 1990. Shop; open 10–5. OLD stock - small. Spec: badges; bookmarkers; brass; buttonhooks; commemorative ware; crochet; fine art; hatpins & holders; lace; maritime/nautical; paperweights; photograph frames; photographic pictures; railways; spoons; teddy bears; thimbles; Victorian; writing - general. PR: £25.

FRESHWATER

Aladdins Cave, 1/2 School Green Road, Freshwater, Isle of Wight PO40 9BB. Prop: Mrs Jane Dunn. Tel: (01983) 752934, home: 753846. Est: 1984. Shop at: 2 Golden Villas, Heathfield Road, Freshwater; open 7 days a week 9.30–4.30. OLD stock - small. Spec: writing - general; Art Deco; badges; binoculars; bookmarkers; boot scrapers; bottles; boxes; brass; candles/candlesticks; ceramics; china; copper; corkscrews & bottle openers; costume jewellery; games; kitchenalia; mirrors; plates; playing cards; scales, weights & measures; Victorian. PR: £1–500.

GODSHILL

Nostalgia Toy Museum, High Street, Godshill, Ventnor, Isle of Wight PO38 3HZ. Prop: Malcolm Lake. Tel: (01983) 730055. Fax: 821296. Est: 1989. Shop; open from Easter to end of October 7 days a week 10–5, mail order service all year. Toy Fairs: Sandown Park, N.E.C., Gloucester, Windsor, Brussels. NEW stock - medium. Spec: diecast toys; model trains, aircraft and cars; teddy bears; general toys. OLD stock - very large. Spec: diecast toys; model trains, aircraft and cars; tinplate toys; general toys. PR: £10–1,000. CC: A; V; D. Cata: monthly. Also, wants lists welcomed.

RYDE

Uriah's Heap, 9 Royal Victoria Arcade, Union Street, Ryde, Isle of Wight PO33 2LQ. Prop: Frank Cross. Tel: (01983) 564661. Est: 1975. Shop; open Wednesday, Friday and Saturday 10–5. OLD stock - small. Spec: brass; ceramics; costume jewellery; drawing instruments; fans; glass; inkstands; ivory; jewellery; lace; objets de vertu; pens; pincushions; portrait miniatures; silhouettes; silver; treen; tribal; wrist watches; fountain pens. PR: £1–500. CC: V; MC.

ISLE OF WIGHT

VENTNOR

Emporium Books, 58 High Street, Ventnor, Isle of Wight PO38 1LT. Prop: Capt. Keith A. Hockney. Tel: (01983) 852514 (24hr answerphone). Est: 1953. Shop; open in business hours. NEW stock - large and OLD stock - medium. Spec: binoculars; bottles; china; corkscrews & bottle openers; Edwardian; kitchenalia; medals; motor car mascots; motoring; pen knives; playing cards; radio & television; railways; scales, weights and measures; sewing machines; spoons; Staffordshire; tinplate toys; tools; Victorian. PR: 50p–£500. *Also at:* Elsie May Antiques, 17 Pier Street, Ventnor (q.v.).

Elsie May Antiques, 17 Pier Street, Ventnor, Isle of Wight PO38 1ST. Prop: Capt. Keith A. Hockney. Tel: (01983) 852514 (24hr answerphone). For shop details and specialities see entry for Emporium Books, Ventnor.

YARMOUTH

Marlborough House Antiques, 21 The Square, Yarmouth, Isle of Wight PO41 0NS. Prop: Peter A. Webb. Tel: (01983) 760498. Est: 1972. Shop; open Monday to Saturday 9.30–5.30, Sunday 9.30–3.30. OLD stock. Spec: Art Deco; Art Nouveau; Victorian; brass; candles/candlesticks; copper; jewellery; Georgian; glass; heraldry; Staffordshire; china; pottery. PR: £20–2,000. CC: BC; A; MC; AE; DC; V.

KENT

B & B Military, 1 Kings Avenue, Ashford, Kent TN23 1LU. Prop: Len Buller. Tel: (01233) 632923. Est: 1977. Private premises; postal business only. NEW stock. Spec: military models; repro Dinky military; 28/30mm figures for Dinky military. PR: £11.50–35.50. Cata: available with frequent updates.

BECKENHAM

J. Designs, 17 Eden Road, Elmers End, Beckenham, Kent BR3 4AS. Prop: Tina Newman and Paula Shilson. Tel: (0181) 650-4031. Private premises; appointment necessary. Fairs: London Dollshouse Festival (May) and Miniatura (March & October). NEW stock - very small. Spec: dolls in 1/12th scale; porcelain heads, fully posable, dressed to order. PR: £60–100. Cata: on request.

BOUGHTON UNDER BLEAN

Jean Collyer Antiques, 194 The Street, Boughton under Blean, Faversham, Kent ME13 9AL. Tel: (01227) 751454. Est: 1977. Shop; open Tuesday & Friday 2–5, Saturday 10–5. OLD stock - small. Spec: porcelain, glass and silver 1780–1830. Also, furniture. Corresp: French, German.

BRASTED

J. Read, The Old Manor House, The Green, Brasted, Kent TN16 1JL. Prop: J.E. & J.R. Read. Tel: (01959) 562536. Est: 1982. Shop; open Monday to Thursday and Saturday 11–5.30, Sunday by appointment. OLD stock - medium. Spec: arts & crafts; barometers; boxes; brass; buckets; chandeliers; clocks; copper; cutlery; jardinières; letter boxes; lighting; metalware; mirrors; musical boxes; spoons; trays; vases; Victorian; chain watches. PR: £1–4,000. Also, small furniture.

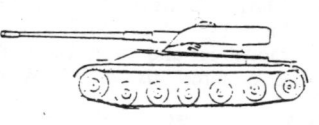

BROADSTAIRS

Broadstairs Antiques & Collectables, 49 Belvedere Road, Broadstairs, Kent CT10 1PF. Tel: (01843) 861965. Est: 1983. Shop; open Monday to Saturday 10–4.30 (Winter), 10–5 (Summer), closed Wednesday. OLD stock - small. Spec: Victorian & Edwardian plates, linen and lace. PR: 50p–£1,000.

Gillycraft, 11 Eastern Esplanade, Broadstairs, Kent CT10 1DR. Prop: M. & G. Faulkner. Tel: (01843) 868591. Est: 1992. Shop at: 11A Albion Street, Broadstairs, Kent; open Tuesday 9–11.30, Thursday and Friday 12–3, Saturday 9–3 or by appointment. NEW stock - very small. Spec: teddy bears. Also, pewter dragons and figures. Mem: F.S.B. and Local Chamber of Commerce.

CANTERBURY

Bridge Antiques, 97 High Street, Wingham, Canterbury, Kent CT3 1DE. Prop: Alan & Clarrie Cripps. Tel: (01227) 720445. Est: 1960. Shop; open Monday to Saturday 9–5, closed Wednesday and by appointment. OLD stock - very large. Spec: brass; chandeliers; china; clocks; copper; dolls/dolls clothes; Georgian. PR: £1–8,000. Also, valuations, inventories and full or part house clearance. Corresp: French, German.

Brocanterbury: Curios, 68 Stour Street, Nr. Heritage Museum, Canterbury, Kent CT1 2NZ. Prop: Mrs Nan Leith. Tel: (01227) 454519. Est: 1982. Shop; open Monday, Wednesday, Friday & Saturday 12–6, other times by appointment. OLD stock - medium. Spec: brass and glass 1900–1960's; Art Deco; ceramics; costume; cutlery; egg cups; kitchenalia; letter boxes. PR: £3–35.

Burgate Antiques, 10c Burgate, Canterbury, Kent CT1 2HG. Prop: Paul & Ann Winterflood. Tel: (01227) 456500. Est: 1989. Shop; open 6 days a week 10–5. NEW stock - small. Spec: toy soldiers. OLD stock - medium. Spec: Art Deco; boxes; brass; ceramics; china; clocks; copper; costume jewellery; diecast toys; Edwardian; fine art; Georgian; glass; jewellery; medals; militaria; silver; toy soldiers; Victorian; writing - general. PR: £2–2,000. CC: V; MC; AE; JCB; D; E. Also, 12 dealers within antique centre. Corresp: French, Spanish.

The English Teddy Bear Co., 4 St. Peters Street, Canterbury, Kent CT1 2AD. Prop: Alise & Jonty Crossick & Dominic Richards. Tel: (01227) 784640. Fax: 788016. Est: 1990. Shop; open during business hours. NEW stock - large. Spec: teddy bears, limited edition bears and related gifts. PR: £5–200 (bears). CC: V; M. Cata: quarterly. *Also shops in:* Bath, Cambridge, Carnaby Street (London), Meadowhall, Newcastle, Oxford, Regent Street (London), Stratford, Windsor, York.

The Hobby Shop, 57 Palace Street, Canterbury, Kent CT21 2DY. Prop: Mark & Margaret Alexander. Tel: (01227) 785699. Est: 1988. Shop; open Monday to Saturday 9–5.30. NEW stock - very large. Spec: model railways; diecast vehicles; model car and aircraft kits. PR: £4–300. CC: A; V; MC; AE. Mem: Chamber of Commerce. *Also at:* 122 West Street, Faversham (q.v.).

The Magpies Nest, 14 Palace Street, Canterbury, Kent CT1 2DZ. Prop: Diane Cleavely. Tel: (01227) 764883. Est: 1990. Shop; open Monday to Saturday 10.30–6. NEW stock - large. Spec: dolls/dolls clothes; dolls houses; miniatures; teddy bears; thimbles; photograph frames; musical boxes. CC: V; MC; A; AE. Also, Limoge boxes; miniature Austrian bronzes.

World Coins, 35-36 Broad Street, Canterbury, Kent CT1 2LR. Prop: David Mason. Tel: (01227) 768887. Est: 1970. Shop; open Monday to Saturday 9.30–5, except Thursday 9.30–1. NEW stock - very small. Spec: GB proof & mint sets; paper money (latest issues). OLD stock - large. Spec: coins; tokens; medallions; militaria; paper money; stamps; postal history. PR: 10p–£300. Cata: 2 a year. Corresp: French.

CRANBROOK

Cranbrook Antiques, 15 High Street, Cranbrook, Kent. Prop: Raj & Sue Bisram. Tel: (01580) 712173. Est: 1983. Shop; open Monday to Saturday 10–5. OLD stock - small with major specialities. PR: £5–1,500. CC: V; A. Also, proprietors of Cranbrook Auctions Rooms.

DARTFORD

Rupert by Post, 3 Canterbury Close, Dartford, Kent DA1 1RR. Prop: Terry & Glenys Theobald. Tel: (01322) 273108. Est: 1990. Private premises; appointment necessary. Fairs: Sandown Park Toy Fair. NEW stock - large. Spec: Rupert Bear memorabilia/merchandise only. OLD stock - very small. PR: £1–1,000. CC: MC; V; A. Cata: 2 a year.

DEAL

Serendipity, 168 High Street, Deal, Kent CT14 6DU. Prop: Marion Short and Jayne Eschalier. Tel: (01304) 369165. Est: 1979. Shop; open Monday to Wednesday and Friday 10–12.30 and 2–4.30, Saturday 9–5, and postal business. Fairs: Chilham Castle. OLD stock. Spec: ceramics; Staffordshire; fine art. PR: £10–500. CC: V. Cata: every 3 months. Corresp: French. Mem: Chamber of Trade.

DOVER

The Warehouse, 29-30 Queens Gardens, Dover, Kent CT17 9AH. Prop: Julian Chambers. Tel: (01304) 242006. Est: 1989. Shop; open Tuesday to Saturday 9.30–4.30. Fairs: Sandown Park, Maidstone, Ashford, Canterbury, Bromley. OLD stock - very large. Spec: Diecast toys; model trains and cars; tinplate toys. PR: £1–1,500. Also, antique furniture and architectural salvage.

FAVERSHAM

Collectors Corner, East Street/Crescent Road, Faversham, Kent ME13 8AD. Prop: George Mileham. Tel: (01795) 539721 (daytime). Est: 1988. Shop; open Monday to Friday 10–3, Thursday 10–2. Fairs: attended every weekend. OLD stock - medium. Spec: aeronautica; arms & armour; arts & crafts; Art Deco; Art Nouveau; automobilia; badges; bamboo; barometers; beadwork; bells; binoculars; bookmarkers; bottles; boxes; brass; bronze; buckets; buckles & clasps; buttons and many others. PR: £1–15,000. Also, free valuation service on antiques & collectables.

The Hobby Shop, 122 West Street, Faversham, Kent ME13 7JB. Prop: Mark & Margaret Alexander. Tel: (01795) 531666. Est: 1988. Shop; open Monday to Saturday 9–5.30. NEW stock - very large. Spec: model railways; diecast vehicles; model car and aircraft kits. PR: £4–300. CC: A; V; MC; AE. Mem: Chamber of Commerce. *Also at:* 57 Palace Street, Canterbury (q.v.).

FOLKESTONE

Chris Easton Cards, 8-8A Old High Street, Folkestone, Kent CT20 1RL. Tel: (01303) 850672. Fax: 245542. Est: 1990. Shop; open Monday to Saturday 9–5. Fairs: Bloomsbury. OLD stock - large. Spec: badges; commemorative ware; diecast toys; jewellery; militaria; paper money; writing - general; stamps. PR: £5–200. CC: V; A; MC. Mem: Postcard Traders Association.

Jonathan Greenwall Antiques, The Sandgate Antiques Centre, 61–63 Sandgate High Street, Sandgate, Nr. Folkestone, Kent CT20 3AH. Tel: (01303) 248987. Est: 1968. Shop; open Monday to Saturday 9.30–5.30, Bank Holidays 11–5. OLD stock - very large. Spec: china; decanters; fine art; glass; jewellery; objets de vertu; pottery; silver; walking sticks; wrist watches; writing - general. PR: £5–10,000. CC: AE; A; V; MC. Corresp: French. Mem: L.A.P.A.D.A., Kent Chamber of Commerce & Industry.

LEIGH

Anthony Woodburn Ltd., Orchard House, High Street, Leigh, Kent TN11 8RH. Tel: (01732) 832258. Fax: 838023. Est: 1976. Shop; open Monday to Saturday 9–5, preferably by appointment. Fairs: B.A.D.A. Fair, Grosvenor House, Olympia (November). OLD stock - very small. Spec: clocks. Cata: every 18 months approximately. Mem: B.A.D.A., L.A.P.A.D.A.

MAIDSTONE

Cornfield Miniatures, Unit 12D, The Corn Exchange, Market Buildings, Maidstone, Kent ME14 1HP. Prop: Jim & Susan Cutler. Tel: (01622) 755116. Est: 1995. Shop; open Tuesday to Friday 10–4, Saturday 9–4. Fairs: Dolls house fairs – Gt. Danes Hotel, Maidstone, Inn on the Lake, Gravesend. NEW stock - large. Spec: dolls houses; miniatures. PR: 20p–£500.

Maxitrak, 4 Larkstore Park, Lodge Road, Staplehurst, Kent TN12 0QY. (•) Prop: A. Probyn & C.W. Bridges. Tel: & Fax: (01580) 893030. Est: 1978. Storeroom; open Monday to Friday 9–4.30, Saturday 9–12. NEW and OLD stock - very small. Spec: railway models; road steam models. CC: V; MC; BC. Cata: annually.

MARGATE

The Collectors Toy & Model Shop, 52 Canterbury Road, Westbrook, Margate, Kent CT9 5BG. Prop: Mr David S. Leach. Tel: (01843) 232301 or Tel: & Fax: 291905. Fax: 860404. Est: 1991. Shop; open Monday to Saturday 12–5.30, Sunday by appointment. Fairs: Kent toy & train fairs. NEW stock - medium. Spec: Dinky; Corgi; Matchbox; Scalextrics; Star Wars; Star Trek; sci-fi; tin; figures; constructional toys; diecast toys; miniatures; teddy bears; toys - general. OLD stock - very large. Spec: Dinky; Corgi; Matchbox; Spot-on; Hornby; Triang; Scalextrics; Star Wars; constructional toys; diecast toys; miniatures; teddy bears; toys - general. PR: £5–500. CC: A; V; EC; MC. Cata: every 3 months. Also, worldwide mail order business. Mem: many associations.

ORPINGTON

C.J. Denton, P.O. Box 25, Orpington, Kent BR6 8PU. Tel: (01689) 873690. Est: 1969. Private premises; postal business only. Fairs: quarterly Cumberland Hotel (Marble Arch). NEW stock -medium. Spec: telephone cards - better/more exclusive BT issues and Irish and Irish-theme. OLD stock - small. Spec: telephone cards; Irish coins and medallions; antiquities. PR: £2–500. Cata: monthly. Mem: B.N.T.A., A.D.A.

RAMSGATE

De Tavener Antiques, 24 Addington Street, Ramsgate, Kent. Prop: Mr & Mrs I.E. Gregg. Tel: (01843) 582213. Est: 1983. Shop; open Monday to Saturday 9.30–5.30. OLD general stock. Spec: antique clocks and barometers. CC: A; V; AE; DC; EC.

Granny's Attic, 2 Addington Street, Ramsgate, Kent CT11 9JL. Prop: Miss Penelope J. Warn. Tel: (01843) 588955 or 596288. Est: 1986. Shop; open Monday to Saturday 10–5, closed Thursday pm. NEW and OLD general stock - medium. PR 20p–£2,000. CC: V; A. Also, shipping goods.

RIVERHEAD

Roundabout, 28a London Road, Riverhead, Kent. Prop: Mrs L. Lopez Fonseca & Mrs C. Ledamun. Tel: (01732) 741873. Est: 1992. Shop; open Monday to Friday 9.30–5, closed Wednesday. OLD stock - small. Spec: crochet; lace; costume jewellery; Victorian. PR: £2–350. Corresp: Spanish.

ROCHESTER

Dolls House Shop, 68 High Street, Rochester, Kent ME1 1JY. Prop: Carol Chambers & Michelle Burford. Tel: & Fax: (01634) 831615. Est: 1989. Shop; open Monday to Saturday 9.30–5. Fairs: specialist dolls house fairs. NEW stock. Spec: dolls houses; teddy bears. PR: £1–500. CC: V; A; MC.

'Lillian Trigg' of Rochester, 58 Tern Crescent, Strood, Rochester, Kent ME2 2RG. Prop: Linda Stewart. Tel: (01634) 713131. Est: 1994. Private premises; appointment necessary. Fairs: very few. NEW stock - very small. Spec: collectors teddy bears only. PR: £36–300.

ROLVENDEN

Falstaff Antiques, 63/67 High Street, Rolvenden, Cranbrook, Kent TN17 4LP. Prop: Mr C.M. Booth. Tel: (01580) 241234. Est: 1964. Shop; open Monday to Saturday 10–6. NEW general stock - medium. OLD general stock - medium. Spec: automobilia; model cars; motor car mascots; motoring. PR: £1–300. CC: V; MC; AE; JCB. Also, a museum specialising in Morgan cars.

SANDHURST

Forge Antiques, Rye Road, Sandhurst, Cranbrook, Kent TN18 5JG. Prop: James Nesfield. Tel: (01580) 850308 or 850665. Est: 1968. Shop and market stand; appointment advised as irregular hours. Fairs: Ardingly, Penshurst. OLD stock - small. Spec: badges; brass; ceramics; china; clocks; commemorative ware; costume; farriers/blacksmiths; glass; iron working; ivory; kitchenalia; mirrors; treen. PR: £1–2,000. Also, restoration of anything wooden. Corresp: French. Mem: N.F.S.B.

SEVENOAKS

Amherst Antiques, 23 London Road, Riverhead, Sevenoaks, Kent TN13 2BU. Prop: Dianne Brick. Tel: (01732) 455047. Est: 1987. Shop; open Monday to Saturday 9.30–5, closed Wednesday. Fairs: NEC, Buxton, Guildford, West London, Chester. OLD stock - medium. Spec: ceramics; glass; silver; treen; Tunbridge ware. PR: £20–3,000. CC: V; A; AE.

Bradbourne Gallery, 4 St. John's Hill, Sevenoaks, Kent TN13 3NP. Prop: Mrs Jane Ross. Shop; open Monday to Friday 9.30–5, Saturday 9–1. Fairs: Petersfield, Penshurst, Sutton Valence. NEW stock - very small. Spec: lamps; glass; ceramics. OLD stock - small. Spec: boxes; brass; candles/candlesticks; china; copper; Edwardian; Georgian; horticultural and farm equipment; jewellery; kitchenalia; mirrors; silver; Victorian. PR: £5–1,000. CC: V; A; MC; EC. Also, interior design, curtain making and upholstery service. Corresp: French.

Peppercorns Antique and Craft Centre, 57/59 High Street, Sevenoaks, Kent TN13 1JF. Prop: Miss M. Hubert. Tel: (01732) 740329. Est: 1994. Shop; open Monday to Saturday 10.15–5.30. NEW general stock - very small. OLD general stock - medium. PR: £1–100. CC: V; A; MC.

SIDCUP

Racing Wheels, 72 Warwick Road, Sidcup, Kent DA14 6LJ. Prop: Roberto & Alison Capella. Tel: & Fax: (0181) 300-3558. Est: 1993. Shop; open Tuesday to Saturday 10–6.30. Fairs: Norwich, Donington, Sandown, Kempton. NEW stock - large. Spec: Formula 7 - Group C - model cars. PR: £10–1,000. Cata: annually. Also, 1/43rd scale model building - dioramas. Corresp: Italian.

TENTERDEN

Bears Galore, 8 The Fairings, Tenterden, Kent TN30 6QX. Prop: Richard & Susan Tatham. Tel: & Fax: (01580) 765233. Est: 1994. Shop; Monday to Saturday 10–5. Fairs: Kensington, Stratford, Birmingham NEC, Nuremberg, Hove, Croydon. NEW stock - small. Spec: teddy bears - Steiff, Merrythought; dolls; badges; bookmarkers; miniatures; wrist watches; toys - general. PR: £1–1,000. CC: A; V; MC. Cata: 2 a year and a newsletter for genuine collectors and customers.

TUNBRIDGE WELLS (ROYAL)

Hadlow Antiques, P.O. Box 134, Tunbridge Wells, Kent TN2 5YA. Prop: Michael & Linda Adler. Tel: & Fax: (01825) 830368. Appointment necessary. Old stock. Spec: barometers; calculating machines; dolls/dolls clothes; dolls houses; globes; gramophones; ivory; medical instruments; musical boxes; objets de vertu; optical toys; radio & television; scientific instruments; snuff boxes; teddy bears; typewriters. Corresp: Spanish, French, Italian.

Tunbridge Wells Antique Centre, Union Square, The Pantiles, Tunbridge Wells, Kent. Prop: A. & N. Harding. Tel: (01892) 533708. Est: 1986. Shop; open Monday to Saturday 9.30–5. OLD general stock - very large. Spec: Victorian Staffordshire figures; arms & armour; Art Deco; Art Nouveau; boxes; buttonhooks; ceramics; chandeliers; china; clocks; commemorative ware; cutlery; decanters; firearms; photograph frames; pottery; Royal memorabilia; scent bottles; serviette rings etc. PR: £1–5,000. CC: V; AE.

Up Country Ltd., The Old Corn Stores, 68 St. Johns Road, Tunbridge Wells, Kent TN4 9PE. Prop: Colin M. Springett. Tel: (01892) 523341. Fax: 530382. Est: 1988. Shop; open Monday to Saturday 9–5.30. OLD stock - medium. Spec: decorative; kitchenalia; treen. PR: £10–2,000. CC: A; EC; MC; V; DC. Also, antique country furniture. Corresp: French.

The Variety Box, 16 Chapel Place, Tunbridge Wells, Kent TN1 1YQ. Tel: (01892) 531868. Est: c1960. Shop; open Monday to Saturday 9.30–5, closed Wednesday. OLD stock - large. Spec: buttonhooks; costume jewellery; cuff links; cutlery; fans; glass; hatpins & holders; match boxes/books; Mother-of-Pearl; pen knives; pens; pincushions; sovereign holders; spectacles, lorgnettes and monacles; spoons; Stanhopes; thimbles; treen; Victorian; writing accessories; Tunbridge ware. PR: £1–150. Corresp: French.

WESTERHAM

Castle Antiques Centre, 1 London Road, Westerham, Nr Sevenoaks, Kent TN16 1BB. Prop: Stewart Ward Properties. Tel: (01959) 562492. Est: 1987. Shop; open Monday to Saturday 10–5. NEW stock - very small. OLD stock - large. Spec: bottles; costume jewellery; crochet; cutlery; eccentrics; glass; hatpins & holders; kitchenalia; lace; metalware; Osborne Plaques; tools; Victorian. PR: £1–100. Also, clock repair.

Regal Antiques, 2 Market Square, Westerham, Kent. Tel: (01959) 561778. Shop; open Wednesday to Saturday 10–5. OLD stock - medium. Spec: vintage wrist and pocket watches; jewellery; portrait miniatures; china. PR: £50–10,000. CC: A; BC.

Tortoise Antiques, c/o Castle Antiques, 1 London Road, Westerham, Nr Sevenoaks, Kent TN16 1BB. Prop: Ian White. Tel: (01959) 562492 (Thursday & Saturday). Est: 1980. Market stand; appointment necessary. Fairs: Tonbridge (Friday), Alexandra Palace, Lea Valley (monthly), Orpington Collectors Evening (monthly). OLD stock - large. Spec: badges; bottles; corkscrews & bottle openers; eccentrics; metalware; tins, signs & advertising; Victorian. PR: £1–100. Also, house clearance, illustrated talks on antiques and a writer on antiques.

WHITSTABLE

Chuffa Trains Railmania Museum, 82 High Street, Whitstable, Kent CT5 1AZ. Prop: Bryan & Catherine Rising. Tel: (01227) 277339. Est: 1991. Shop; open Monday, Tuesday and Thursday to Saturday 10–3. Fairs: Ashford, Ditton, Romford, Gillingham, Canterbury, Littlebourne. NEW stock - medium. Spec: model trains. OLD stock - small. Spec: model trains. PR: £1–150. Also, museum of model trains and railwayana open during shop hours. Mem: Kent Museums Group.

LANCASHIRE

ACCRINGTON

The Coin and Jewellery Shop, 129a Blackburn Road, Accrington, Lancashire BB5 0AA. Prop: James & Sandra Bridgeman. Tel: (01254) 384757. Est: 1977. Shop; open Monday to Saturday 9.30–5, closed Wednesday. Fairs: Bradford Coin Fair, Morley, Leeds; Cumberland Hotel, Marble Arch, London. NEW stock - medium. Spec: jewellery. OLD stock - medium. Spec: jewellery; medals; militaria; tins, signs & advertising; tobacco & associated; coins & banknotes. PR: £1–100. CC: A; V.

BLACKBURN

Little House Miniatures, 81 King William Street, Blackburn, Lancashire BB1 7DT. Prop: Mrs Linda Mattock. Tel: (01254) 580611. Fax: 678300. Est: 1994. Shop; open Monday to Friday 9–5.30, Saturday 9–4, Sunday 2–4. Fairs: Lancashire, Cheshire, West Yorkshire (please ring for details). NEW stock. Spec: dolls/dolls clothes; dolls houses; miniatures; pewter. PR: £50–500 (for houses). Cata: 2 a year, free of charge. Also, local agent for Hantel Victorian Pewter Miniatures.

BLACKPOOL

Old Manse Books, 166 Preston Old Road, Marton, Blackpool, Lancashire FY3 9QY. Prop: Mr L. McLair. Tel: (01253) 763853. Private premises; appointment necessary. OLD stock - small. Spec: bookmarkers; boxes; corkscrews and bottle openers; games; gramophone needle tins; playing cards; tins, signs & advertising; tobacco and associated. PR: 20p–£100. Cata: very infrequently. Mem: English Playing Card Society.

CHORLEY

Park Toys, 17 Market Street, Adlington, Chorley, Lancashire PR7 4HE. Prop: B.A. Ferner. Tel: (01257) 483121. Fax: 482848. Est: 1979. Shop; open Monday to Friday 9.30–5.30 or by appointment. NEW and OLD stock - medium. Spec: constructional toys; diecast toys; model cars; tinplate toys; toys - general; toy soldiers. CC: V; A; MC; AE; DC. Corresp: French, German, Italian.

CLITHEROE

Farmhouse Antiques, Corner Shop, 23 Main Street, Bolton-by-Bowland, Clitheroe, Lancashire BB7 4NW. Prop: Marian Howard. Tel: (01200) 447294 or 441457. Est: 1988. Shop; open Saturday, Sunday and Bank Holidays or by appointment. Fairs: Antique Textile Fair in Manchester. OLD stock - medium. Spec: antique textiles and needlework; beadwork; buckles & clasps; buttons; buttonhooks; crochet; embroideries; embroidered pictures; fans; hatpins & holders; jewellery; kitchenalia; lace; objets de vertu; pinchushions; rugs; smaplers; shawls; tapestries. PR: £1–500. Mem: Ribble Valley Tourist Association, Lancashire Hill Country Tourist Attraction.

DARWEN

Cottage Antiques, 135 Blackburn Road, Darwen, Lancashire BB3 1ET. Tel: (01254) 775891 (24hr answering service). Shop; appointment necessary. OLD stock - very large. Spec: quality antiques.

GREAT HARWOOD

Benny Charlesworth's Snuff Box, 51 Blackburn Road, Great Harwood, Nr. Blackburn, Lancashire. Prop: N. Walsh & J.A. Bartholomew. Tel: (01254) 888550. Est: 1984. Shop; open Monday and Wednesday to Saturday 10–1 and 2–5. Fairs: G. Mex Manchester, Bolton, Bury. NEW stock - very small. Spec: teddy bears; pottery. OLD stock. Spec: writing - general; pottery; fine art; Edwardian; Victorian; jewellery. PR: £1–1,000. CC: A; EC; MC; V.

HASLINGDEN

Fieldings Antiques, 176–180 Blackburn Road, Haslingden, Lancashire. Prop: Andrew Fielding. Tel: (01706) 214254. Est: 1968. Shop; open 11–5. OLD general stock - small. Spec: clocks; musical boxes. PR: £100–3,000. CC: BC. Also, furniture.

LANCASTER

G.B. Antiques Ltd., G.B. Antiques Centre, Lancaster Leisure Park, Wyresdale Road, Lancaster LA1 3LA. Prop: Mr A. & Mrs G. Blackburn. Tel: (01524) 844734. Fax: 844735. Est: 1990. Warehouse; open 7 days a week 10–5. OLD general stock - very large. PR: £5–500. CC: A; MC; V. Also, reproduction furniture (pine, oak and mahogany). *Note:* this is an antique centre with 110 plus dealers.

LYTHAM ST. ANNES

Toy and Teddy Bear Museum Shop, 373 Clifton Drive North, St. Annes, Lytham St. Annes, Lancashire FY8 2PA. Prop: Mrs Irena Thompson. Tel: (01253) 713705. Est: 1989. Shop; open Whitsun to 31 October: Wednesday to Sunday 11–5, Winter months: Sundays 11–5 and school holidays. NEW stock - small. Spec: teddy bears. PR: £4–200. Also, Toy & Teddy Bear Museum.

111

LANCASHIRE

PRESTON

Joys, 83 Berry Lane, Longridge, Preston, Lancashire PR3 3WH. Prop: E.E. Hamlet. Tel: (01772) 782083. Est: 1986. Shop; open Monday, Tuesday and Thursday to Saturday 10.30–4.30. NEW stock - very small. OLD stock - very small. Spec: Art Deco; Art Nouveau; brass; copper; decanters; Edwardian; Georgian; jewellery; mirrors; pottery; shawls; silver; vases; Victorian. PR: £5–500.

Samlesbury Hall, Preston New Road, Samlesbury, Preston, Lancashire PR5 0UP. Prop: Samlesbury Hall Trust. Tel: (01254) 812010. Fax: 812174. Est: 1970. Shop; open Tuesday to Sunday 11–4.30. OLD general stock - small. PR: £1–8,000.

Swag, 24-26 Leyland Road, Penwortham, Preston, Lancashire PR1 9XS. Prop: Marcella Fletcher. Tel: (01772) 744970. Est: 1967. Shop; open 10–6. Fairs: Harrowgate G.N.I. OLD general stock - medium. Spec: dolls; porcelain; pottery. PR: £1–2,000. Also, furniture.

Ray Wade Antiques, 113 New Hall Lane, Preston, Lancashire PR1 5PB. Tel: (01772) 792950. Fax: 651415. Mobile: (0836) 291336. Est: 1977. Shop; open Monday to Friday 10–5.30, Saturday 12.30–5. OLD stock - medium. Spec: Oriental items; Grand Tour objects; ceramics. PR: £10–5,000. Also, furniture, paintings and restoration arranged.

LEICESTERSHIRE

ASHBY-DE-LA-ZOUCH

Yesteryear Homes, Windy Willows, 59 Station Hill, Swannington, Leicestershire LE67 8RJ. (•) Prop: Mike & Mary Marsden. Tel: & Fax: (01530) 838138. Est: 1992. Private premises; appointment necessary. Fairs: Miniatura, Hove, Maidstone. NEW stock - very small. Spec: dolls houses. PR: £450–5,500. Cata: 1 a year.

COALVILLE

Keystone Antiques, 9 Ashby Road, Coalville, Leicestershire. Prop: Iris & Heather McPherson N.A.G. Registered Valuer. Tel: (01530) 835966. Est: 1979. Shop; open Monday to Friday 10–5, Saturday 10–4.30, closed Wednesday and Sunday. Fairs: NEC (April and August). OLD stock - small. Spec: boxes; buttonhooks; costume jewellery; cuff links; cutlery; Edwardian; fashion accessories; glass; jewellery; match boxes/books; scent bottles; serviette rings; silver; snuff boxes; sovereign holders; spoons; Victorian; chain watches; writing. PR: £20–1,000. CC: V; A; MC. Also, Liberon wax polishes, gem testing and jewellery valuations for probate and insurance. Mem: L.A.P.A.D.A., G.A.G.T.L., N.A.G.

HINCKLEY

Parade Figures, 65 Shilton Road, Barwell, Leicestershire LE9 8HB. Prop: Gordon Upton. Tel: & Fax: (01455) 230952. Est: 1992. Private premises; appointment necessary. Fairs: Euro Militaire. Spec: toy soldiers. PR: £5–15. CC: all. Cata: send S.A.E. for current list. Also, a retail model shop. Mem: F.S.B.

LEICESTER

Black Cat Bookshop, 36/39 Silver Arcade, Leicester, Leicestershire LE1 5FB. Prop: Mr & Mrs P. Woolley. Tel: (0116) 251-2756. Est: 1987. Shop; open Monday to Saturday 9.30–5. NEW stock - very small. Spec: Rock & Pop; Seventies; toys - general. OLD stock - small. Spec: badges; bookmarkers; diecast toys; films & entertainment; games; posters; Rock & Pop; The Sixties & Seventies; toys - gerneal; Sherlock Holmes; James Bond. PR: £1–100. CC: V; MC. Cata: occasional.

LEICESTERSHIRE

Letty's Antiques, 6 Rutland Street, Leicester, Leicestershire LE1 1RA. Prop: Ian Dubberley. Tel: (0116) 262-6435. Est: 1952. Shop; open Monday to Saturday 9.30–5, closed Thursday. NEW stock - very small. Spec: bookmarkers; brass; bottles; buckles & clasps; copper; inkstands; jewellery; Mother-of-Pearl; scent bottles; silver. OLD general stock - small. Spec: Art Nouveau; Art Deco; brass; bottles; buckles & clasps; buttonhooks; candle extinguishers; commemorative ware; copper; cuff links; decanters; glass; jewellery; Mother-of-Pearl; pewter; scent bottles; serviette rings; silver; snuff boxes; sovereign holders; teapots; thimbles; Toby Jugs; chain watches. PR: £5–5,000. CC: V; MC.

K.H. Norton, 1-5 Roman Street, Narborough Road, Leicester, Leicestershire LE3 0BD. Prop: D.K., P.G. & P.J. Norton and A.M. Vanheusen. Tel: (0116) 254-9953 Fax: 233-6631. E-Mail: 100523.3154@compuserve.com. Est: 1961. Storeroom; open Monday, Tuesday and Thursday 9–5.30, Wednesday 9–7.45, Friday 9–5, Sunday 10–1. Faris: trade fairs only. NEW stock - very large. Spec: constructional toys; diecast toys; model cars and aircraft; traction/steam engines; transport; toys - general. PR: £1–250. CC: A; V; D; MC. Cata: 1 a year. Mem: Lion Group of Wholesalers.

Pooks Motor Books, Unit 4 Fowke Street, Rothley, Leicestershire LE7 7PJ. (•) Prop: Barry Pook. Tel: (0116) 237-6222. Fax: 237-6491. Est: 1985. Open Monday to Friday 9–5.30, some Saturday mornings. Fairs: major Autojumbles. OLD stock - very large. Spec: automobilia; bicycles; horticultural & farm equipment; model cars; motor car mascots; motoring; posters; tins, signs & advertising; traction/steam engines; transport. PR: £1–2,000. CC: all except AE. Also, car brochures.

LOUGHBOROUGH

Fennel St. Galleries, 21A Fennel Street, Loughborough, Leicestershire. Tel: (01509) 269860. E-Mail: malcolm@gang.demon.co.uk. Est: 1983. Shop; open Thursday and Saturday 9.30–5.30, Friday 9.30–7. Fairs: Bloomsbury book fair. OLD specialist stock - small. Spec: co-operative memorabilia; old wireless sets. PR: £10–250. Corresp: French, German, Spanish.

MARKET HARBOROUGH

Reg Leete, The Old Granary, Lubenham, Market Harborough, Leicestershire. Tel: (01858) 465787. Est: 1954. Showrooms and workshop; appointment necessary. OLD stock - medium. Spec: fishing; dogs; all sporting items; horse brasses; medals; militaria. PR: £5 plus. Also, picture framing and restoration. Mem: R.C.B.P.A.

MARKFIELD

H.G. Images, P.O. Box 6, Markfield, Leicestershire LE67 9ZY. Prop: Hava Getz. Tel: & Fax: (01530) 244354. Est: 1986. Storeroom and private premises; postal business or by appointment. Fairs: Donington, N.E.C. OLD stock - medium. Spec: playing cards; phonecards; tobacco & associated; badges; match boxes/books; writing - general. Cata: 2 a year. Also, specialising in Thematics. Mem: I.P.C.S., T.C.C., C.P.C.C.

UPPINGHAM

Clutter, 14A Orange Street, Uppingham, Rutland LE15 9SQ. Prop: Maureen Campbell Sumner. Tel: (01572) 823745. Est: 1982. Shop; open Monday to Wednesday and Friday 10–5, Saturday 10–6, Thursday 10–5 (Summer) and other times by appointment. NEW stock. Spec: candle extinguishers; candles/candlesticks; Victorian replica bath requisites. OLD general stock - small. Spec: textiles; lace; Victorian. PR: 50p–£600. CC: V; MC etc. Corresp: French, German, Italian. Mem: Rutland Tourist Association.

John Garner Antiques, 51-53 High Street East, Uppingham, Leicestershire LE15 9PY. Tel: (01572) 823607. Fax: 821654. Est: 1966. Shop and storeroom; open Monday to Saturday 9–5.30, Sunday by appointment. Fairs: Newark, East of England Agricultural, Royal Norfolk Show, Royal Show, Miami Beach Antique Show. OLD stock - medium. Spec: barometers; bronze; chandeliers; clocks; decanters; Edwardian; fine art; Georgian; miniatures; posters; sports - general; golf; vases; Victorian; writing - general. PR: £1–500. CC: MC; V; AE. Cata: 1 a year. Also, 18th and 20th century furniture and oil paintings. Corresp: German. Mem: Fine Art Trade Guild.

LINCOLNSHIRE

BOSTON

Grandads Playroom, 275 Church Green Road, Fishtoft, Boston, Lincolnshire PE21 0RP. Prop: David Betts. Tel: & Fax: (01205) 360663. Est: 1993. Private premises; appointment necessary. Fairs: Miniatura - Hove and many others. NEW stock - very small. Spec: candles/candlesticks; ceramics - brickwork; chandeliers; tudor specialist dolls houses; embroideries and tapestries - miniature carpets; miniatures (1/12 and 1/24); oil lamps; room boxes; lighting. PR: £5 plus. CC: all major cards. Cata: ongoing. Mem: British Toy Makers Guild.

Portobello Row Antique Centre, 93-95 High Street, Boston, Lincolnshire. Prop: A. Murphy. Tel: & Fax: (01205) 368692. Shop; open Monday to Saturday 10.30–4. NEW stock - very small. Spec: kitchenalia; clothing; blue & white china; copper; French. OLD stock - small. Spec: kitchenalia; clothing; blue & white china; copper; French. PR: £1–300 plus.

CONINGSBY

Great Britain & the Empire Toy Soldiers, The Cedars, 97 High Street, Coningsby, Lincolnshire LN4 4RF. Prop: A.P.N. Humphries. Tel: (01526) 342012. Est: 1982. Private premises; appointment necessary. NEW stock - small. Spec: high quality traditional toy soldiers painted to order. PR: £5–500. Cata: on request. Also, suppliers to Buckingham Palace, Windsor Castle and Holyrood House, and restoration of old toy soldiers. Corresp: French, German, Italian, Russian.

GRANTHAM

Grantham Clocks, 30 Lodge Way, Grantham, Lincolnshire NG31 8DD. Prop: Mr R. & Mrs M. Conder. Tel: (01476) 61784. Est: 1986. Private premises; appointment necessary. Fairs: Kelham Hall, Grantham. Spec: clocks.

HORNCASTLE

Junktion, The Old Railway Station, New Bolingbroke, Boston, Lincolnshire PE22 7LN. (•) Prop: J. Rundle. Tel: (01205) 480068 and 480087. Fax: 480132. Est: 1983. Shop; open Wednesday, Thursday & Saturday 10–5. Fairs: Newark. OLD stock. Spec: aeronautica; amusement machines; Art Deco; automobilia; bicycles; cameras; dolls houses; early plastics; fairground relics; games; lawn mowers; model trains and aircraft; motor car mascots; motoring; radio & television; rocking horses; tinplate toys; tins, signs & advertising; traction/steam engines. PR: £3–3,000.

Laurence Shaw Antiques, 77 East Street, Horncastle, Lincolnshire LN9 6AA. Prop: L.D. & C.R. Shaw. Tel: (01507) 527638. Est: 1970. Shop; open Monday to Saturday 8.30–5. Fairs: Newark, Ardingly. OLD stock. Spec: brass; ceramics; china; clocks; decanters; glass; metalware. PR: £5–10,000. Mem: N.F.S.E.

LINCOLN

20th Century Frocks, 65 Steep Hill, Lincoln, Lincolnshire LN1 1YN. Prop: Patricia Rowberry. Tel: (01522) 545916. Est: 1986. Shop; open 11–4.30. Fairs: Newark. OLD stock. Spec: vintage clothes; costumes; textiles; jewellery; fashion accessories. PR: £3–150.

B & H Models, 13 Corporation Street, Lincoln, Lincolnshire LN2 1HL. Prop: Ben Krause. Tel: (01522) 538717. Fax: (01427) 615968. Est: 1980. Shop; open 6 days a week 9.30–5.30. NEW and OLD stock - large. Spec: constructional toys; diecast toys; dolls/dolls clothes; dolls houses; early plastics; model trains, cars and aircraft; railways; tinplate toys; tools; toy soldiers; traction/steam engines; transport. PR: £1–1,000. CC: A; V. Cata: 1 a year. Also, certificate and business card printing.

Balmoral Books, 2 Castle View, Walcott, Lincolnshire LN4 3TB. Prop: Len Godfrey. Tel: (01526) 860044. Est: 1956. Private premises; postal business only. Fairs: Tattershall - Lincoln, Spilsby - Lincolnshire. OLD general stock - medium. PR: £1–150. Cata: 2 a year. Corresp: German. Mem: N.A.B.O.B., B.O.A.R.D.

No. 9 Gifts & Games, 9 Steep Hill, Lincoln, Lincolnshire LN2 1LT. Prop: John & Sandra Davis. Tel: & Fax: (01522) 510524. Est: 1986. Shop; open Monday to Saturday 10–5.30, Sunday 11–4. NEW stock - medium. Spec: dolls houses; teddy bears; miniatures. PR: 25p–£750. CC: all major. Cata: 1 a year. Mem: M.I.N.T.A.; F.S.B (Federation of Small Businesses).

Vanhefflins, 12 High Street, Kirton Lindsey, North Lincolnshire DN21 4LY. (•) Prop: Keith Vanhefflin. Tel: & Fax: (01652) 648044. Est: 1820. Shop and private premises; open 10–5. OLD general stock - very large. Spec: fine art; jewellery; pottery. PR: £1–50,000.

SPALDING

Crossway Models, Crossways, 2 Salem Street, Gosberton, Lincolnshire PE11 4NQ. (•) Prop: Roger Tennyson. Tel: & Fax: (01775) 841171. Est: 1992. Private premises; appointment necessary. Fairs: D & J fairs at Donington and N.E.C. NEW stock - very small. Spec: model cars - 1/43 scale hand built white metal model cars. OLD stock - very small. Spec: diecast toys, Dinky, Corgi and Spit On model cars. PR: £10–100. CC: V; A; MC; EC. Cata: quarterly newsletter.

STAMFORD

GRA's Models, 65 Scotgate, Stamford, Lincolnshire PE9 2YB. Prop: J. Gradon Forsyth. Tel: & Fax: (01780) 51826. Est: 1989. Shop; open 10–5.30, except Wednesday and Sunday. NEW stock - medium. OLD general stock - small. Spec: diecast toys. PR: £1–1,000. CC: V.

St. Martins Antique Centre, 23A High Street, St Martins, Stamford, Lincolnshire PE9 2LF. Prop: Peter Light. Tel: (01780) 481158. Fax: 56210. Est: 1993. Shop; open 7 days a week 10–5. Fairs: Newark, Newmarket, Stoneleigh and Peterborough. OLD general stock - small. Spec: arts & crafts; Art Deco; china; clocks; fine art; glass; jewellery; militaria; model aircraft; papier mâché; rugs; scientific instruments; silver; toys - general; wrist watches. PR: £500–1,000. CC: V; MC.

LINCOLNSHIRE

Stamford Antiques Centre, The Exchange Hall, Broad Street, Stamford, Lincolnshire PE9 1PX. Prop: Catherine P.A. Turner. Tel: (01780) 62605. Est: 1990. Shop; open 7 days a week 10–5 or by appointment. Fairs: West London, N.E.C. (April & August). OLD stock - large. Spec: arts & crafts; Art Nouveau; badges; brass; costume jewellery; cutlery; lace; linen; writing - general. PR: 50p–£5,000. CC: A; V; MC. Also, Art Nouveau Originals c1900 is based in the centre. Corresp: French. Mem: L.A.P.A.D.A.

SUTTON-ON-SEA

Knicks Knacks Antiques, 41 High Street, Sutton-on-Sea, Lincolnshire LN12 2EY. Prop: Robin & Jeannie Nicholson. Tel: (01507) 441916. Est: 1984. Shop; open Tuesday to Sunday 10–5. Fairs: Newark. OLD stock - large. Spec: Victorian lighting; Art Deco; Art Nouveau; bottles; brass; cameras; candles/candlesticks; chandeliers; china; clocks; commemorative ware; costume jewellery; cutlery; dolls/dolls clothes. PR: £1–1,000. CC: V; A; EC; MC. Also, brass and iron beds and fireplaces.

LONDON
(EAST POSTAL DISTRICTS)

Boxes & Musical Instruments, 2 Middleton Road, Hackney, London E8 4BL. Prop: Joseph M. O'Kelly. Tel: (0171) 254-7074. Est: 1975. Shop; strictly appointment necessary. NEW stock - very large. Spec: boxes; musical instruments; Anglo-Indian; inkstands; ivory; musical; objets de vertu; Oriental; papier mâché; snuff boxes; tortoiseshell; treen; writing boxes; Tumbridgeware. CC: AE. Also, conservation and restoration. Corresp: Greek, French. Mem: F.O.M.R.H.I.

House of Usher, Unit 9, Antique City, 98 Wood Street, Walthamstow, London E17. Prop: C.R. Usher. Tel: (0181) 478-8553. Est: 1992. Shop; open Monday to Wednesday, Friday and Saturday 10–5.30. OLD stock - medium. Spec: constructional toys; diecast toys; films & entertainment; musical; photographic pictures; rock & pop; The Sixties; toys; toy soldiers; transport. PR: 25p–£50.

Record Detector, 3 & 4 Station Approach, Station Road, Chingford, London E4. Prop: Nick & Jack Salter. Tel: (0181) 529-6361. Fax: 559-3438. Est: 1990. Shop; open Monday to Saturday 10–5, closed Thursday. NEW stock - medium. Spec: CD's. OLD stock - very large. Spec: major Rock music types, soul and jazz, UK & foreign releases. PR: 50p–£250. Cata: to order.

Simmons & Simmons Ltd., P.O. Box 104, Leytonstone, London E11 1ND. Prop: Howard & Frances Simmons. Tel: (0181) 989-8097. Fax: 518-8421. Est: 1982. Private premises; postal business only. Fairs: Coinex, London coin fairs. NEW stock - medium. Spec: fine art; medals; sculpture; bronze; silver. OLD stock - large. Spec: Art Deco; Art Nouveau; bronze; coins; fine art; medals; scales, weights & measures; sculpture; silver. PR: £10–1,000. CC: V; A; AE. Cata: speciality catalogues 2 a year. Corresp: French, Spanish. Mem: B.N.T.A.

LONDON
(EAST CENTRAL POSTAL DISTRICTS)

Angel Dollshouse Workshop, 400 St. John Street, Islington, London EC1V 4NJ. Prop: William Davis. Tel: (0171) 713-5000. Est: 1986. Shop; open Monday to Saturday 10–5. NEW stock - large. Spec: handmade dolls houses; teddy bears; dolls/dolls clothes; diecast toys; tinplate toys; toys - general; miniatures; rocking horses; scooters. OLD general stock - small. PR: £10–1,000. Mem: British Toymakers Guild.

City Clocks, 31 Amwell Street, Islington, London EC1R 1UN. Prop: Jeffrey Rosson FBHI. Tel: (0171) 278-1154. Fax: 278-2932. Est: 1883. Shop; open Tuesday to Friday 8.30–5.30, Saturday 9–3. Fairs: Westpoint, Birmingham clock fairs. NEW and OLD stock - small. Spec: clocks; musical boxes; wrist watches; writing. PR: £50–5,000. CC: AE; V; MC; A; DC. Also, clock and watch repair and restoration. Mem: British Horological Institute.

C.R. Frost & Son Ltd., 60–62 Clerkenwell Road, London EC1 5PX. Prop: Ian Franklin. Tel: (0171) 253-0315. Fax: 253-7454. Shop; open Monday to Friday 9.30–5.30. OLD stock - very small. Spec: barometers; clocks; wrist watches; tools. PR: £60–2,500. CC: A; V; AE. Mem: Watch and Clockmakers Guild.

Halcyon Days, 4 Royal Exchange, London EC3V 3LL. Prop: Mrs S. Benjamin. Tel: (0171) 626-1120. Fax: 283-1876. Est: 1984. Shop; open Monday to Friday 10–5.30. Fairs: Grosvenor House Antiques, Olympia. NEW stock - medium. Spec: enamels; porcelain. OLD stock - medium. Spec: antique enamels; candles/candlesticks; ceramics; clocks; cuff links; decorative; French; Mauchline ware; mother-of-pearl; musical boxes; objets de vertu; papier mâché; Royal memorabilia; scent bottles; snuff boxes; Staffordshire; tea caddies; teddy bears; treen; tortoiseshell; wine antiques. PR: £30 plus. CC: A; V; DC; AE; JCB. Cata: 4 a year. Corresp: French, German, Dutch. Mem: Bond Street Association. *See also:* London W1 (q.v.).

L.A.S.S.C.O., Mark Street (Off Paul Street), London EC2A 4ER. Tel: (0171) 739-0448. Fax: 729-6853. Est: 1985. Shop; open 7 days a week 10–5. OLD stock - large. Spec: architectural antiques; aeronautica; amusement machines; arts & crafts; Art Nouveau; Art Deco; boot scrapers; brass; bronze; chandeliers; doorstops; fairground relics; French; Georgian; heraldry; kitchenalia; London Transport; marbles; maritime/nautical. PR: £100–50,000. CC: all. Cata: quarterly.

Searle and Co. Ltd., 1 Royal Exchange, Cornhill, London EC3 3LL. Directors: N. Bird & S. Carson. Tel: (0171) 626-2456. Fax: 283-6384. Est: 1893. Shop; open Monday to Friday 9–5.30. NEW and OLD stock - medium. Spec: Art Nouveau; Art Deco; card cases; clocks; cuff links; cutlery; decanters; Georgian; globes; inkstands; jewellery; pens; pewter; photograph frames; serviette rings; tea caddies; teapots; toiletries; wrist and chain watches; wine antiques; writing accessories. PR: £50–4,000. CC: V; MC; AE. Also, fine quality pearls and many individual hand-made pieces. Mem: N.A.G.

LONDON
(NORTH POSTAL DISTRICTS)

Ashingtons, Number 9, The Georgian Village, 30-31 Islington Green, London N1. Prop: Tina M. Ashington. Tel: (0171) 226-9907. Fax: 226-8634. Est: 1993. Shop; open Wednesday 7–3, Saturday 8–4. Fairs: major I.A.C.F. and selected Sunday fairs. NEW stock - medium. Spec: silver; photograph frames. OLD stock - medium. Spec: silver; arts & crafts; Art Nouveau; Art Deco; candles/candlesticks; cutlery; decorative; objets de vertu; photograph frames; serviette rings; silver; spoons; vases; walking sticks. PR: £15–15,000. CC: V; MC; JCB. Also, specialist in modern silver and valuations. Mem: Camden Passage Traders Association.

Banbury Fayre, 6 Pierrepont Arcade, Camden Passage, Islington, London N1. Prop: Nadine Steel. Tel: (0181) 852-5675. Est: 1984. Shop; open Wednesday 7–3, Saturday 8–5. OLD stock - small. Spec: aeronautica; badges; bookmarkers; boxes; buttonhooks; card cases; ceramics; china; commemorative ware; corkscrews & bottle openers; egg cups; fans; games; writing - general; transport; scent bottles; Osborne Plaques; pen knives; maritime/nautical; ship memorabilia; Boer War; Baden-Powell. PR: £5–200. Corresp: French. Mem: Camden Passage Traders Association.

Patric Capon, 350 Upper Street, Islington, London N1 0PD. Tel: (0171) 354-0487. Fax: (0181) 295-1475. Est: 1969. Shop; open Wednesday and Saturday only. Fairs: Olympia (June). OLD stock - very small. Spec: fine antique clocks; barometers; scientific instruments; maritime/nautical. PR: £1,000–25,000. Corresp: French. Mem: B.A.D.A.

Cat Box, York Arcade, Camden Passage, 80 Islington High Street, London N1. Prop: Heather Lotinga. Tel: (0181) 744-9277. Est: 1986. Shop in arcade; open Wednesday and Saturday. Fairs: Cat Show - Olympia, NEC Cat Show - Birmingham, Sunday fairs - Tolworth and Croydon. NEW stock - very small. OLD stock - small. Spec: eccentrics; cat objects. PR: £20–100. CC: A; MC. Cata: 4 a year. Corresp: French, Italian.

Copycat Models, 21 Norfolk Close, London N13 6AN. Prop: Mr C.J. & Mrs M.J. Penn. Tel: & Fax: (0181) 888-4485. Est: 1983. Private premises; postal business only. Fairs: most in South East England. NEW stock - very large. Spec: diecast toys; model cars. OLD stock - large. Spec: diecast; model cars, trains and aircraft; toy soldiers. PR: £1–20.

Decodence, Shop 13, The Mall, 359 Upper Street, London N1 0PD. Prop: Gad Sassower. Est: 1989. Shop; open Wednesday and Saturday 10–5 or by appointment. OLD stock - small. Spec: bakelite – radio & television. PR: £20–2,000. CC: MC; V.

Dinosaur Collectors Club, 71 Hoppers Road, Winchmore Hill, London N21 3LP. Prop: Michael E. Howgate M.Sc. Tel: (0181) 882-2606. Est: 1991. Private premises; postal business only. Fairs: Dinosaur Convention (2 a year). NEW and OLD stock - medium. Spec: fossils, geology and prehistory; toys. PR: 50p–£1,000. Cata: quarterly. Also, produce a bi-monhthly club newsletter. Corresp: French, German.

LONDON NORTH POSTAL DISTRICTS

Dolly Land, 864 Green Lanes, Winchmore Hill, London N21 2RS. Prop: G.K. Hollman. Tel: (0181) 360-1053. Fax: 364-1370. Est: 1987. Shop; open Tuesday and Thursday to Saturday 9.30–4.30. Fairs: London doll and teddy fairs. NEW and OLD stock - medium. Spec: collectors dolls and bears. PR: £1–600.

Dolphin Diecasts, London N17 7DB. Prop: S.M. Belanger and M. Goodyear. Tel: (0181) 885-4250. Est: 1990. Private premises; postal business only. Fairs: most toy fairs NEC, Donington etc. NEW stock - small. Spec: model cars; toys; Lledo; Hotwheels from U.S.A.; American items. PR: £1–20. Cata: 2 a year. Also, American contacts, most American items obtainable.

Donay Antiques, 35 Camden Passage, Islington, London N1 8EA. Prop: D.C. Goddard and C.E. Dulling. Tel: (0171) 359-1880. Fax: 704-0488. Est: 1980. Shop; open Wednesday and Saturday 8.30–5. NEW stock - very small. Spec: games; miniatures; tins, signs & advertising. OLD stock - very small. Spec: games; jukeboxes & slot machines; amusement machines; marbles; money boxes. PR: £5–3,000. CC: V; MC; AE. Also, custom made chess sets and boards/games tables.

Vincent Freeman Antiques, 1 Camden Passage, Islington, London N1 2UD. Tel: (0171) 226-6178. Fax: 226-7231. Est: 1966. Shop; open Tuesday, Wednesday, Friday and Saturday 10–5. Fairs: Olympia (June). OLD stock -large. Spec: glass; musical boxes; objets de vertu; oil lamps. PR: £100–10,000. CC: all.

Gazebo, Top Floor Fleamarket, Pierrpoint Row, Camden Passage, Angel Islington, London N1. Prop: Mrs Drene Brennan. Tel: (0171) 226-6627. Est: 1975. Open Wednesday and Saturday 9.30–3.30. OLD stock - medium. Spec: badges; bookmarkers; buttons; chocolate; corkscrews & bottle openers; egg cups; fans; films & entertainment; games; money boxes; paper money; photographic pictures; playing cards; pottery; railways; Rock & Pop; stationery; phonecards; tobacco & associated. PR: 20p–£12. Also, the biggest egg cup shop in London.

Get Stuffed, 105 Essex Road, Islington, London N1 2SL. Prop: Amdrell Limited. Tel: (0171) 226-1364. Fax: 359-8253. Est: 1971. Shop; open Monday 1–5, Tuesday, Wednesday & Friday 12–5, Saturday 12–3. NEW stock - small. Spec: taxidermy only. OLD stock - very small. Spec: taxidermy. PR: £75–10,000. Also, suppliers of glass domes and manufacturers of display cases.

Hart & Rosenberg, 2 & 3 Gateway Arcade, Camden Passsage, Islington, London N1 0PG. Prop: Enid Hart & Harry Rosenberg. Tel: (0171) 359-6839. Fax: (0181) 676-9006. Est: 1968. Shop; open Wednesday & Saturday 9–5, Tuesday & Friday 10.30–5 or by appointment. OLD stock - large. Spec: card cases; Oriental ceramics; china; decorative; fine art; glass; heraldry; jardinières; tankards; tea caddies; teapots; trays; vases. PR: £100–1,000. CC: A; AE; DC; JCB; MC; V; EC; D. Mem: Camden Passage Traders Association.

Intercol London, 43 Templars Crescent, London N3 3QR. Prop: Yasha Beresiner. Tel: (0181) 349-2207. Fax: 346-9539. E-Mail: 100447.3341@compuserve.com. Est: 1979. Shop at: 114 Islington High Street, London N1; open Wednesday to Saturday 9.30–5.30. Fairs: international. NEW and OLD stock - large. Spec: playing cards; paper money; games; globes; medals; oil lamps. PR: £10–2,000. CC: V; MC; AE. Cata: 4 a year. Also, valuations and lectures. Corresp: French, Italian, Spanish, Hebrew. Mem: I.B.N.S., A.N.A., B.N.T.A.

Jubilee Photographica, 10 Pierrepont Row, Camden Passage, Islington, London N1. Prop: Beryl Vosburgh. E-Mail: beryl@winks.demon.co.uk. Est: 1966. Shop; open Wednesday & Saturday 10.30–3.30. Fairs: Bonnington Photographica (2 a year). OLD stock - very large. Spec: early photography; daguerreutypes; ambrotypes; cameras; magic lanterns & slides; stereocards & viewers. PR: 5p–£1,500. Also, cartes de visite, cabinet cards, topographic, ethnic, wedding, children, military & Royalty subjects.

Carol Ketley Antiques, 4–5 Pierrepont Arcade, Camden Passage, Islington, London N1. Tel: (0171) 359-5529 and (0831) 827284. Fax: (0171) 266-4589. Est: 1981. Shop; open Wednesday 8.30–3.30, Saturday 9.30–4.30. Fairs: Olympia, Decorative Antiques & Textile Fair Little Chelsea. OLD stock (pre 1900) - medium. Spec: glass; decanters; bamboo; ceramics; blue & white transferware; decorative; china; mirrors; pottery; Georgian. CC: V; MC; AE. Corresp: French. Mem: L.A.P.A.D.A.

Judith Lassalle, 7 Pierrepont Arcade, Camden Passage, London N1 8EF. Tel: (0171) 607-7121 and 354-9344. Est: 1765. Shop; open Wednesday 7.30–4 and Saturday 9.30–4 or by appointment. Fairs: Ephemera and Atlantic City USA and American Ephemera. OLD stock - medium. Spec: games; marbles; optical toys; playing cards; Royal memorabilia; tinplate toys. PR: £1–5,000. CC: V; MC; D; EC. Cata: occassionally. Also, moving paper and peep shows and toys. Corresp: French. Mem: English and American Ephemera Societies.

John Laurie Antiques Ltd., 352 Upper Street, Islington, London N1 0PD. Prop: John Sewiktz. Tel: (0171) 226-0913 Fax: 226-4599. Shop; open Monday to Saturday 9.30–5. NEW stock - very small. Spec: silver. OLD stock - very large. Spec: silver. PR: £20–10,000. CC: V; AE; DC. Corresp: Italian, French. Mem: L.A.P.A.D.A.

Andrew Lineham Fine Glass, The Mall, Camden Passage, London N1 8ED. Tel: (01243) 576241. Est: 1976. Shop; open Wednesday 7.30–3, Saturday 10–4 or by appointment. Fairs: Olympia. OLD stock - medium. Spec: Art Nouveau; Art Deco; glass; ceramics; decorative; night lights; paperweights; scent bottles; tankards. PR: £100–10,000. CC: V; MC; AE; D. Mem: B.A.D.A.

The London Barometer Co., 5, The Lower Mall, The Mall Antiques Arcade, Camden Passage, Islington, London N1 0PD. Tel: & Fax: (0171) 226-4992. Est: 1991. Shop; open Wednesday 8–4, Friday 10–4, Saturday 9–6. OLD stock - very large. Spec: barometers. barographs; stereoscopes; scientific instruments. PR: £20–40,000 (average £700). CC: MC; A; V. Corresp: French, German, Spanish.

London Militaria Market, 55A High Street, Marlow, Buckinghamshire SL7 1BA. Prop: S. Bosley & M. Warren. Tel: & Fax: (01628) 822503. Est: 1985. Market stand at: Angel Arcade, Camden Passage, London N1; open Saturdays 8–2.

Laurence Mitchell Antiques, 13 Camden Passage, Islington, London N1 8EA. Tel: (0171) 359-7579. Fax: 226-1738. E-Mail: l.mitchell@mail.bogo.uk. Est: 1974. Shop; open Tuesday, Thursday & Friday 10–5, Wednesday 8–5, Saturday 9–5. Fairs: Olympia Fine Art & Antiques. OLD stock - small. Spec: ceramics; bronze; antique Meissen porcelain; Oriental porcelain; ivory. PR: £150–15,000. CC: V; AE; A; JCB; DC. Mem: Camden Passage Traders; Chamber of Commerce.

Monika, No. 16 The Mall, Camden Passage, London N1 0PD. Prop: Mrs M.G. Jàrtelius. Tel: (0171) 354-3125. Est: 1986. Shop; open Wednesday and Saturday 10–5, Friday 12–4 or by appointment. OLD stock of period pieces - medium. Spec: ceramics - Art Deco, Edwardian and 1940's; beadwork; card cases; costume; cuff links; early plastics; embroideries; fans; fashion accessories; jewellery; leather; mirrors; objets de vertu; scent bottles; vases. PR: £45–650. CC: major cards. Also, hire service. Corresp: German, Swedish, French, Italian. Mem: L.A.P.A.D.A.

Terence Plank, 23 The Mall, 359 Upper Street, Islington, London N1 0PD. Tel: (0171) 226-2426. Fax: (01689) 819456. Est: 1976. Shop; open during normal business hours. OLD stock - small. Spec: clocks; wrist & chain watches. PR: £250–6,000. CC: V; AE; JCB. Mem: L.A.P.A.D.A.

Robin Quy Antiques, G11 The Mall Antiques Arcade, 359 Upper Street, Islington, London N1 0PD. Tel: (0171) 359-8671. Est: 1996. Shop; open Tuesday to Saturday 10–6. OLD stock - very small. Spec: bottles; corkscrews & bottle openers; cutlery; Georgian; glass; silver; snuff boxes; spoons; trays; wine antiques. PR: £20–2,000. CC: all.

The Shunting Yard, 121 Lordship Lane, Tottenham, London N17 6XE. Prop: Mr E. & Mrs V. Collins. Tel: (0181) 801-8151. Est: 1980. Shop; open Wednesday to Saturday 10–5.30. Fairs: Dunstable, Enfield, Letchworth and Rochford. NEW and OLD stock - medium. Spec: constructional toys; diecast toys; early plastics; model trains and cars; railways; tinplate toys; toys - general; toy soldiers; transport. PR: £2–250.

Style, 1 Georgian Village, Camden Passage, Islington Green, London N1. Prop: Mr M. Webb & Ms P. Coakley. Tel: (0171) 359-7867 or Tel: & Fax: (0181) 449-2588. Est: 1979. Shop; open Wednesday 9–3, Saturday 9.30–4. OLD stock - medium. Spec: Art Nouveau; Art Deco; bronze; ivory; pewter. PR: £500–10,000. CC: V; MC; AE; DC; JCB. Also, arts & crafts 1880–1930.

Templar Antiques, 12 York Arcade, Camden Passage, 80 Islington High Street, London N1 8EQ. Prop: Mrs Pamela Wilson. Tel: (0171) 833-2640. Est: 1975. Market stand; open Wednesday and Saturday 8–5.30. OLD stock - small. Spec: glass; bottles; candles/candlesticks; chandeliers; china; decanters; mirrors; night lights; Oriental; paperweights; scent bottles; vases. PR: £20–1,000.

Alfred Terry Coins Ltd., Reco House, 928 High Road, North Finchley, London N12 9RW. Tel: (0181) 446-9319. Fax: 446-9719. Est: 1908. Private premises; appointment necessary. NEW stock - very large. Spec: jewellery. OLD stock - very small. Spec: Victorian design jewellery; gold coins. PR: £60 upwards. Mem: N.A.G.

Turn On Lighting, 116–118 Islington High Street Camden Passage, London N1 8EG. Prop: Mrs Janet Holdstock. Tel: & Fax: (0171) 359-7616. Est: 1976. Shop; open Tuesday to Saturday 10.30–5 and by appointment. OLD stock - medium/large. Spec: c.1840–c.1940 lighting; Art Deco, Art Nouveau, Edwardian and Victorian lighting; arts & crafts. PR: £300 upwards. CC: V; A; AE. Also, museum work. Mem: Historic Lighting Club, Decorative Arts Society.

Yesterday Child, Angel Arcade, 118 Islington High Street, London N1 8EG. Prop: David & Gisela Barrington. Tel: & Fax: (01908) 583403. Est: 1971. Shop; open Wednesday and Saturday 9–3. OLD stock - very large. Spec: antique dolls only. PR: £100–10,000. Corresp: German, French, Dutch, Russian. Mem: L.A.P.A.D.A.

LONDON
(NORTH WEST POSTAL DISTRICTS)

Alfies Antique Market, 13–25 Church Street, London NW8 8DT. Tel: (0171) 723-6066. Fax: 724-0999. Est: 1976. Open Tuesday to Saturday 10–6. OLD stock - very large. Spec: arts & crafts; Art Deco; Art Nouveau; ceramics; china; costume jewellery; decorative; dolls/dolls clothes; Edwardian; fashion accessories; games; Georgian; glass; jewellery; kitchenalia; posters; textiles; tins, signs & advertising; toys; Victorian. PR: £5–10,000. Also, restoration, framing and upholstery.

Alvin's Dolls and Toys, Stand G9/10/11, Alfies Antique Market, 13-25 Church Street, Marleybon London NW8 8DT. Prop: Alvin Ross. Tel: (0171) 723-1513. Est: 1988. Market stand; open Tuesday to Saturday 10–5.30. OLD stock - medium. Spec: jigsaws; constructional toys; dolls/dolls clothes; games; model trains and cars; teddy bears; tinplate toys; toys - general; toy soldiers. PR: £1–500. CC: V; MC; AE; JCB. Corresp: French.

Kristin Baybars, 7 Mansfield Road, Gospel Oak Village, London NW3 2JD. Tel: (0171) 267-0934. Est: 1957. Shop; open Tuesday to Saturday 11–6. NEW stock - medium. Spec: dolls houses; teddy bears; miniatures; toys - general; constructional toys; rocking horses. OLD stock - very small. Spec: dolls houses; miniatures; toys - general. PR: 5p–£2,000.

Beverley, 30 Church Street, Marylebone, London NW8 8EP. Prop: Beverley & Beth. Tel: (0171) 262-1576. Shop; open Monday to Thursday 11–6.30, Friday & Saturday 9.30–6.30. Fairs: NEC Birmingham (April & August), Newark, Warwick. OLD stock. Spec: Art Deco.

BR Collectors Corner, Cobourg Street, Euston, London NW1 2HP. Prop: British Rail. Tel: (0171) 922-6436. Fax: 922-6435. Est: 1969. Shop; Monday to Saturday 9–4.30, closed Bank Holidays. NEW stock - small. Spec: railwayana – badges; ceramics; posters; tins, signs & advertising; trains; writing. OLD stock - very large. Spec: buckets; buttons; clocks; cutlery; egg cups; glass; keys; lighting; mirrors; plates; posters; railways; stationery; teapots; telephones; tins, signs & advertising; trains; transport; typewriters; walking sticks; writing. PR: 10p–£1,500. CC: V; MC; AE; DC. Cata: 1 a year, with bi-monthly supplements.

The Collector/Tableware, 9 Church Street, London NW8 8EE. Prop: Tom Power. Tel: (0171) 706-4586. Fax: 706-2948. Shop; open Monday to Saturday 9.30–5.30, Sunday 10–2. Fairs: Stafford, Birmingham. NEW general stock - medium. Spec: ceramics; china; commemorative ware; jardinières; Toby jugs; Royal Doulton; Beswick; Moorcroft; David Winter; Wedgwood; Lilliput Lane; Royal Worcester etc. OLD stock - large. PR: £6–3,000. CC: AE; MC; V. Cata: 2 a year (subscription and non-subscription). Also, specialise in discontinued tableware. Corresp: French.

Laurence Corner, 62-64 Hampstead Road, London NW1 2NU. Tel: (0171) 813-1010. Fax: 813-1413. Est: 1960. Shop; open Monday to Saturday 9.30–6. OLD stock - very large. Spec: militaria; badges; medical instruments. PR: £1–150. CC: all. Cata: 2 a year. Also, theatre and costume hire.

Gallery on Church Street, 12 Church Street, London NW8 8EP. Prop: Eve Phillips. Tel: & Fax: (0171) 723-3389. Est: 1985. Shop; open Tuesday to Friday 10–5 or by appointment. NEW stock - medium. Spec: fine art; posters; costume jewellery; glass. OLD stock. Spec: Art Nouveau; Art Deco; fine art; posters; glass. PR: £25–3,000. CC: V; MC; EC; JCB; AE. Corresp: French, German, Spanish, Italian, Portuguese.

Gillian Gould Antiques, 32 Flask Walk, London NW3 1HE. Tel: (0171) 433-1747. Fax: 431-7716. Private premises; postal business only. *For stock details see:* Gillian Gould Antiques, at Ocean Leisure, Embankment Place, London WC2.

Granny's Goodies, Stand S001, Alfies Antique Market, 13-25 Church Street, London NW8. Prop: Brenda Gerwat-Clark. Tel: (0171) 706-4699. Est: 1976. Shop; open Tuesday to Saturday 12–5. Fairs: London International Doll, Toy, Miniatures and Teddy Bear, Kensington Town Hall. OLD stock. Spec: antique dolls, toys and teddy bears. PR: £1–3,000. CC: V; MC; EC. Corresp: German.

'Legacy', G50 & 51, Alfie's Antique Market, 13–25 Church Street, London NW8 8DT. Prop: W.A. Garraway & J. Rosser. Tel: (0171) 723-0449. Est: 1988. Market stand; open Monday to Saturday 10–5. OLD stock - very large. Spec: aeronautica; automobilia; badges; bells; binoculars; bookmarkers; bottles; boxes; brass; buttonhooks; card cases; commemorative ware; corkscrews & bottle openers; decorative; diecast toys; egg cups; fans; films & entertainment; gramophone needle tins; hatpins & holders. PR: £1–250.

Stevie Pearce, G144 Alfies Antique Market, 13–25 Church Street, London NW8 8DT. Tel: (0171) 723-1513. Est: 1993. Market stand; open 10.30–5.30. OLD stock - medium. Spec: costume jewellery; cuff links; fashion accessories; laundry bygones. PR: £3.50–15.

Romantic Robot, 54 Deanscroft Avenue, London NW9 8EN. Prop: Sacha. Tel: (0181) 200-8870. Fax: 200-4075. E-Mail: chag@private.nethead.co.uk. Est: 1983. Private premises; postal business only. Spec: model cars - Mollo, Lesney, Matchbox. Corresp: French, German, Czech, Russian.

Silver Belle Antiques, 48 Church Street, London NW8 8EP. Prop: Mr & Mrs B. Bowman. Tel: & Fax: (0171) 723-2908. Est: 1991. Shop; open during normal business hours. NEW stock - very small. Spec: photograph frames. OLD stock - very large. Spec: candles/candlesticks; china; card cases; cutlery; decanters; Georgian; inkstands; serviette rings; The Sixties; spoons; tankards; tea caddies; teapots; trays. PR: £10–3,500. CC: all major. Corresp: Spanish, Italian, German, French.

Soviet Carpet & Art Centre, 303-305 Cricklewood Broadway, London NW2 6PG. Tel: (0181) 452-2445. Fax: 450-2642. Est: 1983. Shop; open Sunday 10.30–5.30, Monday to Friday by appointment. NEW stock - very large. Spec: badges; bronze; ceramics; costume; costume jewellery; dolls/dolls clothes; fine art; rugs; sculpture; shawls; textiles. OLD stock - large. Spec: arms & armour; fine art; rugs. PR: 10p–£10,000. CC: all. Cata: 1 a year. Also, fine and applied arts from former U.S.S.R. Corresp: Russian. Mem: Fine Art Trade Guild.

The Talking Machine, 30 Watford Way, London NW4 3AL. Prop: D. Smith. Tel: & Fax: (0181) 202-3473 and (0374) 103139. Est: 1975. Shop; open variable hours. OLD stock - very small. Spec: records; gramophones; phonographs; sewing machines; typewriters; juke boxes. PR: £1 plus.

LONDON
(SOUTH EAST POSTAL DISTRICTS)

Acorn Antiques, 111 Rosendale Road, West Dulwich, London SE21 8EZ. Prop: Mrs Gaynor Kingham. Tel: (0181) 761-3349. Est: 1977. Shop; open Monday to Friday 10–6, Saturday 10–5.30. NEW stock - small. Spec: jewellery. OLD stock - small. Spec: silver; jewellery; ceramics. PR: £1–200. CC: all except DC. Also, greeting cards and fire tools/fenders.

Nigel A. Clark, 28 Ulundi Road, Blackheath, London SE3 7UG. Tel: (0171) 858-4020. Est: 1975. Private premises; postal business only. OLD stock - medium. Spec: ceramics; fine art; medals; silver; British copper coins; tradesmen's tokens of 17th Century. PR: £1-1,000 plus. Cata: irregular.

T.A. Hillyer, 301 Sydenham Road, London SE26 5EW. Tel: Shop (0181) 778-6361, Home 777-2506. Est: 1953. Shop; open Monday to Friday 9.30–4, closed Wednesday, Saturday 9.30–2. OLD general stock - medium. Spec: pre 1930 china and glass. Also, bric–a–brac and furniture.

Peter Laurie, 28 Greenwich Church Street, Greenwich, London SE10 9BJ. Prop: Peter Wollen. Tel: (0181) 853-5777. Open 7 days a week 10.30–5, except Friday morning. OLD stock - medium. Spec: maritime/nautical; aeronautica; arms & armour; binoculars; cameras; scientific instruments; telescopes. PR: £1–1,000. CC: EC; MC; A; V.

Spread Eagle Antiques, 1 Stockwell Street, Greenwich, London SE10 9JL. Prop: Richard Moy. Tel: & Fax: (0181) 305-1666. Est: 1956. Shop; open 7 days a week 10–5.30. OLD general stock - large. Spec: Art Deco; bookmarkers; cameras; ceramics; commemorative ware; costume; decorative; films & entertainment; fine art; games; kitchenalia; maritime/nautical; pen knives; photographic pictures; railways; textiles; tins, signs & advertising; toys - general; Victorian. PR: £1–100. CC: all. Corresp: French.

Nigel Thursting Die-Cast Models, 3 Prendegast Road, Blackheath, London SE3 9LR. Tel: (0181) 333-9039 or 852-1570. Est: 1993. Private premises; postal business only. Fairs: NEC, Picketts Lock, Donington Park, Brentwood. NEW stock - very small. Spec: diecast models - Lledo. OLD stock - large. Spec: diecast Lledo. PR: £4–250. Cata: every 2 months.

Unique Collections, 52 Greenwich Church Street, London SE10 9BL. Prop: Glen Chapman. Tel: (0181) 305-0867. Fax: 853-1066. Est: 1987. Shop; open 7 days a week 11–5. Fairs: Norman Joplins Toy Soldier Show. NEW stock - very small. OLD stock - medium. Spec: badges; diecast toys; fire fighting equipment; model cars; police memorabilia; toy soldiers. CC: V; A; AE. Cata: 2 a year, on diecast toys.

LONDON SOUTH EAST POSTAL DISTRICTS

'Vale', 21 Tranquil Vale, Blackheath, London SE3 0BU. Prop: Richard Varnham. Tel: (0181) 852-9817. Est: 1952. Shop; open Monday to Saturday, closed Thursday. NEW stock - very small. OLD general stock - very small. Spec: jewellery; coins; medals; stamps. PR: £20–350. CC: all. Mem: P.T.S., A.D.A., B.N.T.A.

Vintage Cameras Ltd., 256 Kirkdale, Sydenham SE26 4NL. Prop: John Jenkins. Tel: (0181) 778-5416. Fax: 778-5841. Est: 1959. Shop; open Monday to Saturday 9–5. Fairs: photographica. OLD stock - medium. Spec: cameras; photographica. PR: £10–5,000. CC: A; V; JCB; AE; DC. Cata: monthly. Also, mail order photographica.

LONDON
(SOUTH WEST POSTAL DISTRICTS)

Charles Allix & Associates, 32 Bury Street, London, SW1Y 6AU. Prop: Charles Allix, David Penney & Philip Whyte. Tel: (0171) 321-0353. Fax: 321-0350. Est: 1934. Shop; appointment necessary. OLD stock - medium. Spec: horology - clocks, wrist and chain watches; walking sticks. PR: £1–20,000. CC: V; A; MC. Cata: 1 or 2 a year. Also, appraisals and commission buying.

Maria Andipa & Son Icon Gallery, 162 Walton Street, London SW3 2JL. Prop: Maria & Mr Acoris Andipa. Tel: (0171) 589-2371. Fax: 225-0305. E-Mail: andipa@icons.demon.co.uk. Est: 1969. Shop; open Monday to Saturday 11–6 or by appointment. NEW stock - very small. OLD stock - very small. Spec: icons; fine art; objets de vertu; oil lamps; cast brass; Italian/Venetian art. PR: £250–50,000 plus. CC: AE; MC; V; EC. Cata: on request. Corresp: Greek, Spanish, Portuguese, French, Arabic. Mem: L.A.P.A.D.A., G.M.C.

Robert Barley Antiques, 48 Fulham High Street, London SW6 3LQ. Tel: & Fax: (0171) 736-4429. Est: 1968. Shop; open Monday to Friday 9.30–5.30, Saturday 10.30–1. Fairs: Olympia (Spring, Summer & November), Decorative Antiques & Textiles Fair (March & September). NEW stock - medium. Spec: bronze; candles/candlesticks; fine art; fossils, geology & prehistory; ivory; objets de vertu; sculpture; weather vanes; scientific instruments. PR: £25–25,000. CC: V; MC; A; AE.

R.A. Barnes (Antiques), 26 Lower Richmond Road, London SW15 1JP. Prop: J.M. Langin. Tel: (0181) 789-3371. Fax: 780-3195. Est: 1970. Shop; open Monday to Friday 10–5.30. Fairs: Portobello Road, Roger's Gallery (every Saturday). OLD stock - very large. Spec: Staffordshire; Art Nouveau; boxes; candles/candle sticks; ceramics; brass; bronze; decanters; embroideries; glass; objets de vertu; Oriental; photograph frames; pottery; scent bottles; snuff boxes. PR: £5–5,000. CC: V; A. Also, antique furniture. Corresp: French, Spanish. Mem: L.A.P.A.D.A.

Beaver Coin Room, Beaver Hotel, 57 Philbeach Gardens, London SW5 9ED. Prop: Mr Jan Lis. Tel: (0171) 373-4553. Fax: 373-4555. Est: 1971. Private premises; appointment necessary. Fairs: London Coin Fair, Coinex. OLD stock - small. Spec: Art Nouveau; Art Deco; commemorative medals; paper money; coins. PR: £5–1,000. CC: V; AE; DC. Corresp: French, German, Polish. Mem: British Numismatic Trade Association.

Big Ben, 5 Broxholme House, New King's Road, London SW6 4AA. Prop: Roger Lascelles. Tel: (0171) 731-0072. Fax: 384-1957. Est: 1975. Shop; open by appointment. NEW stock. Spec: reproduction clocks. OLD stock - medium. Spec: antique clocks. CC: AE; V. Corresp: German; French.

J.H. Bourdon–Smith Ltd., 24 Mason's Yard, Duke Street, St James's, London SW1Y 6BA. Tel: (0171) 839-4714. Fax: 839-3951. Shop; open 9.30–6. Fairs: B.A.D.A., Grosvenor House, N.E.C. and others abroad inc. New York. OLD stock. Spec: boxes; card cases; inkstands; snuff boxes; spoons; tea caddies; trays. Cata: annually. Also valuations & repairs. Mem: B.A.D.A.

Christine Bridge Antiques, 78 Castelnau, London SW13 9EX. Prop: Christine Bridge and Darryl Bowles. Tel: & Fax: (0181) 741-5501. Est: 1972. Private premises; appointment necessary. Fairs: Olympia, L.A.P.A.D. Show, West London. OLD stock- large. Spec: glass; decanters; Georgian; beadwork; bronze; ceramics; chandeliers; clocks; ivory; oil lamps; vases; wine antiques; Victorian. PR: £100–8,000. CC: A; V; JCB. Also, sole UK agent for ABACUS, the Antique Dealers computer system. Mem: L.A.P.A.D.A.

Jasmin Cameron, Antiquarius, Stand J6, 131-141 King's Road, London SW3 5ST. Tel: (0171) 351-4154. Fax: (01494) 774276. Est: 1980. Shop; open Monday to Saturday 10–5.45. OLD stock - very small. Spec: fountain pens; gold/silver pencils; inkstands; drinking glasses; decanters; wine antiques. PR: £15–800. CC: V; A; AE.

Chelsea Antiques Market, 253 King's Road, London SW3 5EL. Prop: Peter & Adrian Harrington. Tel: (0171) 668-5945. Fax: 823-3449. Est: 1967. Shop; open Monday to Saturday 10–6. OLD stock - very large. Spec: china; costume jewellery; decorative; glass; globes; jewellery; maritime/nautical; scientific instruments; silver; telescopes; Victorian; wrist watches. Corresp: French, German, Italian. Mem: A.B.A.

The Clock Clinic, 85 Lower Richmond Road, Putney, London SW15 1EU. Prop: Robert S. Pedler. Tel: (0181) 788-1407. Fax: 780-2838. Est: 1971. Shop; open Tuesday to Friday 9–6, Saturday 9–1. Fairs: Olympia (June & November), L.A.P.A.D.A. NEC (January). OLD stock - small. Spec: barometers; clocks. PR: £200–15,000. CC: V; MC; AE. Mem: L.A.P.A.D.A.

Clocks & General Collectables, Stand H 3-4, Antiquarius, 135 King's Road, London SW3 4PW. Prop: Peter Dixon. Tel: (0171) 376-4585. Fax: 376-4591. Est: 1978. Market stand; open Monday to Saturday 10–5.30. Fairs: Decorative, Kings College, London. OLD stock - medium. Spec: barometers; brass; clocks; copper; corkscrews & bottle openers; decanters; doorstops; globes; inkstands; letter boxes; money boxes; oil lamps; stationery; Victorian; writing accessories. PR: £10–5,000. CC: V; MC.

Clunes Antiques, 9 West Place, Wimbledon Common, London SW19. Prop: Daphne Clunes. Tel: (0181) 946-1643. Est: 1973. Shop; open Tuesday to Saturday 10–4.30. Fairs: Dorking Halls, Dog & Fox, Ardingly, Brocante. OLD general stock. Spec: binoculars; birdcages; boxes; brass; buckets; buttons; china; commemmorative ware; decorative; Edwardian; egg cups; films & entertainment; kitchenalia; marbles; metalware; night lights; pottery; Royal Memorabilia; scales, weights & measures; Staffordshire; tools; toys - general; treen; Victorian; writing - general. PR: £3–100.

Galerie Moderne Ltd., 10 Halkin Arcade, Motcomb Street, London SW1. Prop: Mark Waller. Tel: (0171) 245-6907. Fax: 245-6341. Est: 1982. Shop; open Monday to Friday 10–6 and Saturday by appointment. Fairs: Art Asia, Hong Kong. OLD stock - small. Spec: antique ceramics, glass, posters and motoring collectables. CC: AE. Corresp: French.

Elizabeth Gibbons, Stand N15/16, Antiquarius, 131/141 King's Road, London SW3 4PW. Tel: Mobile (0956) 427172, Home (01989) 750243. Est: 1989. Shop; open Monday to Friday 10–5.30. Fairs: major antique fairs. OLD stock - very large. Spec: beadwork; buttons; costume; dolls clothes; embroideries; embroidered pictures; lace; laundry bygones; samplers; shawls; textiles; tribal; Victorian. PR: £1–500. CC: all major. Corresp: French. Mem: Textile Society, Costume Society, Lace Guild.

Joss Graham Oriental Textiles, 10 Eccleston Street, London SW1W 9LT. Tel: & Fax: (0171) 730-4370. Est: 1980. Shop; open Monday to Saturday 10–6. NEW stock - medium. Spec: ceramics; costume; glass; jewellery; lighting; looms & weaving; mirrors; Oriental; silk industry; silver; teapots; textiles. OLD stock - medium. Spec: Anglo-Indian; beadwork; boxes; ceramics; costume; embroideries; glass; icons; jewellery; lighting; looms & weaving; metalware; Oriental; rugs; shawls; silk industry; silver; teapots; textiles; tiles; trays; tribal. PR: £10–1,000. CC: A; V; MC. Also, restoration and conservation of textiles. Corresp: French.

Gregory, Bottley & Lloyd, 13 Seagrave Road, London SW6 1RP. Tel: (0171) 381-5522. Fax: 381-5512. Est: 1850. Shop; open weekdays 9.30–5, Saturday 9.30–2, closed Bank Holiday weekends. NEW and OLD stock - very large. Spec: fossils, geology & prehistory. PR: £1–5,000. CC: A; V; DC; MC. Cata: 2 a year.

Gutlin Clocks, 616 King's Road, London SW6 2DU. Prop: Mr J.M. & Mrs U.F. Coxhead. Tel: & Fax: (0171) 384-2439. Est: 1994. Shop; open Monday to Saturday 9.30–7. NEW stock - very small. Spec: clocks. OLD stock - very large. Spec: clocks; mirrors; barometers; boxes; candlesticks. PR: £200–7,000. CC: A; V; MC; EC. Also, restoration of clocks and barometers. Corresp: German, French.

Hayman & Hayman, Antiquarius, Stand K3, 135 King's Road, London SW3 4PW. Prop: M.C. Hayman & G. Hayman. Tel: (0171) 351-6568. Fax: (0181) 994-8010. Est: 1975. Market stand; open 10.30–5.30. NEW stock - medium. Spec: photograph frames; scent bottles; a few decanters, silhouettes, inkstands. OLD stock - very small. Spec: Imoges boxes; silver boxes. PR: £20–800. CC: V; A; AE. Corresp: French, Spanish.

Kensington Bear, 15 Exhibition Road, South Kensington, London SW7 2HE. Prop: Glen Jones. Tel: (0171) 823-9295. Est: 1993. Shop; open Monday to Saturday 10–6. NEW stock - small. Spec: teddy bears – Steiff, Deans, Merrythought and limited edition artist bears. PR: £1–450. CC: all major. Also, mail order service available.

Stanley Leslie, 15 Beauchamp Place, London SW3 1NQ. Prop: Mr G. Hyams. Tel: (0171) 589-2333. Fax: 589-3530. Est: 1955. Shop; open Monday to Saturday 9–5. NEW and OLD stock - variable stock size. Spec: antique and modern silver. CC: V; A; AE; DC; JCB.

M.P. Levene Ltd., 5 Thurloe Place, London SW7 2RR. Tel: (0171) 589-3755. Fax: 589-9908. Est: 1926. Shop; open Monday to Friday 9.30–5.30, Saturday 9.30–1. NEW and OLD stock - medium. Spec: jewellery; silver. PR: £30–25,000. CC: all. Corresp: French, Spanish, German, Italian. Mem: B.A.D.A.

Sylvanna Llewelyn, Stand E2, Antiquarius, 131/141 King's Road, Chelsea, London SW3. Tel: (0171) 351-4981. Est: 1993. Market stand; open Monday to Saturday 10–6. OLD stock - large. Spec: buttons; costume jewellery. PR: £1–100.

Longmire, 12 Bury Street, St. James's, London SW1Y 6AB. Tel: (0171) 930-8720. Est: 1962. Shop; open Monday to Friday 10–5. NEW stock - medium. Spec: cuff links; jewellery. OLD stock - small. Spec: cuff links; jewellery. PR: £250–5,000. CC: V; MC. Also, custom enamelling. Corresp: French, Spanish, Italian. Mem: Royal Warrant Holder.

Fay Lucas, B4 Antiquarius, 135 Kings Road, Chelsea, London SW3 4PW. Tel: & Fax: (0171) 351-6004. Est: 1979. Gallery; open 10.30–6. Fairs: Olympia fine arts and antiques. NEW stock. Spec: silver, continental and English rare novelties. CC: A; V; AE; DC. Also, art. Corresp: French, Italian, Spanish. Mem: L.A.P.A.D.A.

Magpies, 152 Wandsworth Bridge Road, Fulham, London SW6 2UH. Prop: Mrs C. Whitrow & Mrs P. Kavanaugh. Tel: (0171) 736-3531. Est: 1985. Shop; open Monday to Saturday 10–5. OLD general stock - large. PR: £1–300.

David Martin–Taylor Antiques, 558 Kings Road, London SW6 2DZ. Prop: C. Cavet & A. Bigozzi. Tel: (0171) 731-4135. Fax: 371-0029. Est: 1968. Shop; open Monday to Saturday 10–6. Fairs: London Decorative (March & September), Olympia (June & November). OLD stock - very large. Spec: bamboo; boxes; candles/candlesticks; decorative; doorstops; French; jardinières; leather; mirrors; objets de vertu; Oriental; Papier Maché; tobacco & associated; trays. PR: £300–20,000. CC: AE; V; A; MC. Also, furniture. Corresp: French, Italian, Greek, Spanish. Mem: L.A.P.A.D.A.

McKenna & Co., 28 Beauchamp Place, Knightsbridge, London SW3 1NJ. Tel: (0171) 584-1966. Fax: 225-2893. Est: 1982. Shop; open Monday to Saturday 10.15–5.45. Fairs: Olympia, Claridges, Miami. NEW stock - small. Spec: jewellery. OLD stock - medium. Spec: jewellery. PR: £20–50,000. CC: all major. Cata: 1 a year. Also, valuations, repair and buying-in from the public. Mem: L.A.P.A.D.A., N.A.G.

MKL Models, The Guards Museum, Wellington Barracks, Birdcage Walk, London SW1 6HQ. Prop: Lynn and Tricia Kenwood. Tel: (01734) 733690. Fax: 733947. Est: 1981. Shop; open Saturday to Thursday 10–4. Fairs: Donington, Windsor, Farnham, N.E.C., Kempton, Sandown. NEW stock - very large. Spec: toy soldiers; badges; bookmarkers; cuff links; horsebrasses & harnesses; thimbles. OLD stock - medium. Spec: toy soldiers. PR: £3–2,000. CC: V; A; MC; EC.

R.S. & S. Necus, H-1, Antiquarius, 135 King's Road, Chelsea, London SW3 4PW. Tel: & Fax: (0171) 352-2405. Est: 1971. Market stand; open 10–5.30. NEW stock - very small. OLD stock - medium. Spec: silver. PR: £200–5,000. CC: V; A; AE; MC.

Sue Norman, L4 Antiquarius, 135 King's Road, Chelsea, London SW3 4PW. Prop: Sue & Nick Alloway. Tel: (0171) 352-7217. Fax: (0181) 870-4677. Est: 1972. Market stand; open Monday to Saturday 10–5.30. Fairs: Olympia (June), West London (August & January). OLD stock - very large. Spec: blue & white china; pottery. PR: £50–500. CC: V; MC; AE.

Numismatic Arts of London, 233 Wandsworth Bridge Road, London SW6 2TU. Prop: Art Rubino. Tel: & Fax: (0171) 731-2919. E-Mail: art rubino@msn.com. Est: 1977. Private premises; appointment necessary. NEW stock - medium. Spec: trays. OLD stock - large. Spec: trays; badges; bottles; paper money; photographic pictures; militaria. PR: £10–1,000. CC: MC; V. Cata: by Email, monthly. Corresp: French, Italian. Mem: R.N.A., R.P.A., A.N.A., A.N.S.

Paul Orssich, 117 Munster Road, London SW6 6DH. Tel: (0171) 736-3869. Fax: 371-9886. E-Mail: orssich@citscape.co.uk. Est: 1980. Shop; open Monday to Friday 10–6 and other times by appointment. Fairs: Kensington Town Hall Art Deco Fairs, P.B.F.A. Royal Academy Fair (June). OLD stock - medium. Spec: Art Deco illustrations. PR: £2 upwards. CC: V; A; MC. Also, Hispanic studies. Corresp: Spanish, French, German. Mem: P.B.F.A.

The Singing Tree, 69 New Kings Road, London SW6 4SQ. Prop: T. Sanders, M. Daccombe, H. Wilkins & C. O'Reilly. Tel: (0171) 736-4527. Est: 1977. Shop; open Monday to Saturday 10–5.30. NEW stock - very large. Spec: handmade dolls houses; miniature furniture, silver, glass and porcelain. CC: V; AE; A. Cata: every 2 years. Corresp: French.

Peta Smyth Antique Textiles, 42 Moreton Street, Pimlico, London SW1V 2PB. Tel: (0171) 630-9898. Fax: 630-5398. Est: 1976. Shop; open Monday to Friday 9.30–5.30. Fairs: Olympia (June and November). OLD stock - medium. Spec: antique embroideries and embroidered pictures, tapestries, textiles. PR: £20–14,500. CC: A; V; MC. Corresp: French. Mem: L.A.P.A.D., Guild of Master Craftsmen.

Spink & Son Ltd., 5-7 King Street, St James's, London SW1. Tel: (0171) 930-7888. Fax: 839-4853. Est: 1666. Shop; open 9–5.30. NEW and OLD stock - large. Spec: numismatics - coins, medals, paper money. PR: £1–5,000. CC: AE; V; MC; A. Cata: 10 a year. Also, fine art. Corresp: most European.

Steinberg & Tolkien, 193 King's Road, London SW3. Prop: Mark Steinberg. Tel: (0171) 376-3660. Est: 1991. Shop; open during business hours. OLD stock - very large. Spec: American costume jewellery 1900–1950's; vintage Haute Couture and American Couture 1900–1970's. PR: £20–3,000. CC: all. Corresp: French, Italian, Spanish, German.

Theodore's Bear Emporium, The Old Waiting Room, Mortlake Station, Sheen Lane, London SW14 8LN. Prop: Karl & Sheila Gibbons. Tel: (0181) 876-2996. Fax: 876-9916. Shop; open Tuesday to Saturday 10–5 and postal business. Fairs: major national and international. NEW stock - medium. Spec: teddy bears – from artists and manufacturers around the globe. PR: £3–2,500. CC: A; MC; D; JCB. Cata: 3 a year. Mem: Richmond upon Thames Chamber of Commerce.

Wilton Cycle & Wireless Co., 28 Upper Tachbrook Street, London SW1V 1SW. Prop: Mr R.D. Head. Tel: (0171) 834-1367. Est: 1895. Shop; open Monday to Friday 9.30–6 (½ day Thursday), Saturday 9.30–5. NEW stock - very large. Spec: bicycles; constructional toys; Diecast toys; model trains, cars and aircraft; railways; toy soldiers. PR: £1–200. CC: A; V.

Harriet Wynter Ltd, 50 Redcliffe Road, London SW10 9NJ. Tel: (0171) 352-6494. Fax: 352-9312. Est: 1956. Private premises; postal business only. Fairs: Scientific Instrument fair (May & October). OLD stock. Spec: early antique scientific instruments and works of art; calculating machines; sculpture; sundials; drawing instruments; fine art; maritime/nautical. PR: £500 plus. Corresp: French, German. Mem: B.A.D.A.

Robert Young Antiques, 68 Battersea Bridge Road, London SW11 3AG. Prop: Robert & Josyane Young. Tel: (0171) 228-7847. Fax: 585-0489. Est: 1978. Shop; open Tuesday to Saturday 10–6. Fairs: Chelsea, Olympia. OLD stock - medium. Spec: candle extinguishers; candles/candle sticks; fairground relics; fire fighting equipment; fishing; laundry bygones; pen knives; samplers; snuff boxes; tankards; treen. PR: £100–5,000. CC: AE; MC; V. Also, reproduction ironwork and lighting. Corresp: French.

LONDON
(WEST POSTAL DISTRICTS)

Abacus Antiques, Grays Antique Market, 58 Davies Street, London W1Y 2LP. Prop: Paul Lesbirel. Tel: (0171) 629-9681. Est: 1968. Market stand; open Monday to Friday 10–6. OLD stock - medium. Spec: glass; ivory; jewellery; silver; wrist watches. PR: up to £500. CC: AE; A; MC; V; D.

Aberdeen House Antiques, 75 St. Mary's Road, London W5 5RH. Prop: Nicholas Schwartz. Tel: & Fax: (0181) 567-5194. Est: 1972. Shop; open Monday to Saturday 10–5.30. Fairs: Olympia (June). OLD stock - medium. Spec: decorative; lighting; mirrors. PR: £50–3,000. CC: V; MC; A; AE; JCB; DC. Corresp: Portuguese. Mem: L.A.P.A.D.A.

The Antique Clothing Shop, 282 Portobello Road, London W10. Prop: Sandy Stagg. Tel: (0181) 993-4162. Est: 1993. Shop; open Friday and Saturday 9–6 or by appointment. Fairs: many. OLD stock - very large. Spec: costumes; crochet; dolls/dolls clothes; fashion accessories; handbags and purses; lace; shawls; shoes; smocks; textiles. PR: £2–200. CC: V; MC. Mem: P.A.D.A.

Argyll Etkin Ltd., 48 Conduit Street, New Bond Street, London W1R 9FB. Prop: Eric Etkin. Tel: (0171) 432-7800. Fax: 434-1060. Est: 1976. Gallery; 'Stampex' London (Spring & Autumn) and overseas fairs. OLD stock - very large. Spec: stamps; postal history; stamp boxes. PR: £35–100,000. CC: MC; V; AE. Corresp: German, French. Mem: P.T.S.(London), A.S.D.A.(USA), A.S.D.A.(Austr.), S.A.P.D.A.(S. Africa).

Clayre Armytage and Anne Music, Unit 32, Bond Street Antique Centre, 124 New Bond Street, London W1. Tel: (0171) 493-5830. Est: 1970. Market stand; open 10.30–5.30. OLD stock - medium. Spec: antique jewellery. PR: £100-500. CC: V; A. Also, some objet d'art.

Sean Arnold, Gray's Antique Market, 58 Davies Street, London W1Y 2LP. Tel: (0171) 409-7358. Fax: 499-5890. Est: 1986. Shop; open Monday to Friday 10–6. NEW stock - small. Spec: silver jewellery; hand painted gift items. OLD stock - large. Spec: golf; sports; luggage. PR: £10–25,000. CC: V; A; MC. Also, clubhouse decoration and tournament prizes. Corresp: German. Mem: Portobello Traders Association.

Sean Arnold Antiques, Portwine Gallery, 173-175 Portobello Road, London W11. Tel: (0171) 409-7358. Fax: 499-5890. Est: 1988. Shop, storeroom and private premises; open Monday to Friday 1–6, Saturday 8–5 or by appointment. NEW stock - small and OLD stock - medium. Spec: golf; luggage; bronze; leather; spoons. PR: £10–10,000. CC: V; MC; A. Also, tournament prizes and club house decor. Corresp: German. Mem: Portobello Traders Association. *Also market stand at:* Grays Antique Market, 58 Davies Street, London W1.

Art Direct, 22 Upper Grosvenor Street, London W1Y 3WD. Prop: Iain M. Brunt and Nathanial Gee. Tel: (0171) 499-7012. Fax: 499-7015. Est: 1995. Private premises; appointment necessary. NEW and OLD general stock - very large. PR: £500–100,000. CC: V; MC. Cata: on the Internet.

Astarte Gallery, Shop 14, The Bond Street Antiques Centre, 124 New Bond Street, London W1Y 9AE. Prop: A.G. Davies. Tel: & Fax: (0171) 409-1875. URL: http://www.desiderata.com. Est: 1956. Shop; open Monday to Friday 10.30–5. OLD stock - medium. Spec: antiquities; works of art; medallions; coins. PR: £15–20,000. CC: V; A; AE. Cata: infrequently. Mem: A.D.A.

B. & T. Antiques, 79–81 Ledbury Road, London W11 2AG. Prop: Mrs Bernadette Lewis. Tel: (0171) 229-7001. Fax: 224-8508. Est: 1971. Shop; open 10–6. Fairs: 2 a year. OLD general stock - very large. Spec: objects, mirrors and lights from 18th Century to 1920. CC: V. Corresp: French. Mem: L.A.P.A.D.A.

Gregg Baker Oriental Art, 132 Kensington Church Street, London W8 4BH. Tel: (0171) 221-3533. Fax: 221-4410. Est: 1986. Shop; open Monday to Friday 10–6 or by appointment. Fairs: Olympia (June), Arts of Pacific Asia - Santa Monica (March) and New York (October). OLD stock - small. Spec: Oriental; bronze; ivory; metalware. PR: £500–50,000. CC: V. Mem: B.A.D.A., L.A.P.A.D.A.

Linda Bee, Grays Mews Antiques Market, 1–7 Davies Mews, London W1 2LP. Tel: (0171) 629-5921. Fax: 493-9344. Market stand; open 11–6. NEW stock - medium. Spec: costume jewellery. OLD stock - large. Spec: arts & crafts; Art Deco; Art Nouveau; buckles & clasps; costume; costume jewellery; cuff links; early plastics; eccentrics; Edwardian; fans; fashion accessories; golf; photograph frames; pincushions; scent bottles; shoes/shoe making; teddy bears; wrist watches; handbags and compacts 1910–1950. PR: £15–500. CC: V; AE; MC. Corresp: Italian, French.

Brian Beet, 111 New Bond Street, London W1Y 0BQ. Tel: (0171) 437-4975. Fax: 495-8635. Est: 1979. Private premises; open Monday, Tuesday and Friday 2–5.30. Fairs: Olympia (June). OLD stock - very small. Spec: Anglo-Indian; brass; card cases; corkscrews & bottle openers; objets de vertu; Oriental; scales, weights & measures; silver; snuff boxes; wine antiques; writing accessories. PR: £250–2,500. CC: V; MC; AE; JCB. Also, stamp boxes and dampers. Corresp: French.

N. Bloom & Son (1912) Ltd., Bond Street Antique Centre, 124 New Bond Street, London W1Y 9AE. Prop: Ian Harris. Tel: (0171) 629-5060. Fax: 493-2528. Est: 1912. Market stand; open Monday to Friday 10.30–5.30. Fairs: Olympia (June & November), Claridges. NEW stock - very small. OLD stock - medium. Spec: jewellery; wrist watches; some arts & crafts, Art Nouveau, binoculars, bronze, costume jewellery and silver. PR: £200–15,000. CC: all. Cata: 1 or 2 a year. Corresp: French, German. Mem: L.A.P.A.D.A.

LONDON WEST POSTAL DISTRICTS

Boodle and Dunthorne Ltd., 128 Regent Street, London W1R 5FE. Directors: Nicholas & Michael Wainwright. Tel: (0171) 437-5050. Est: 1798. Shop; open Monday to Saturday 9.30–6. NEW and OLD stock. Spec: jewellery; silversmiths. PR: £500–10,000. CC: all. Cata: 1 a year (October). Mem: N.A.G.

The Box Department at Hayloft Woodwork, 3 Bond Street, Chiswick, London W4 1QZ. Prop: Janet & Cole Manson. Tel: (0181) 747-3510. Fax: 742-1860. Est: 1984. Shop; open Monday to Friday and most Saturdays 10–3. OLD general stock - very small. Spec: all kinds of small boxes. PR: £2–90. Also, custom-built furniture. Mem: Guild of Master Craftsmen.

Brandt Oriental Art, 1st Floor, 29 New Bond Street, London W1Y 9HD. Prop: Robert Brandt. Tel: & Fax: (0171) 499-8835. Est: 1980. Private premises; appointment necessary. Fairs: Olympia (June & November), Arts of Pacific Asia - New York and Santa Monica. OLD stock - very small. Spec: fans; metalware; Oriental; textiles. PR: £500–10,000. Mem: B.A.D.A.

David Brower Antiques, 113 Kensington Church Street, London W8 7LN. Tel: (0171) 221-4155. Fax: 221-6211. Est: 1966. Shop; open Monday to Friday 10–6. OLD stock - large. Spec: fine quality antiques incl. bronze, ceramics, decorative, Oriental, sculpture. PR: £250–20,000. CC: AE; V; MC.

Bruford & Heming Ltd., 28 Conduit Street, London W1R 9TA. Prop: Alan Kinsey. Tel: (0171) 499-7644. Fax: 493-5879. Est: 1858. Shop; open Monday to Friday 9–5.30. NEW and OLD stock - very large. Spec: jewellery; domestic silverware; cutlery. PR: £30–5,000. CC: MC; V; AE. Cata: end of October. Also, valuations & repairs. Mem: L.A.P.A.D.A., N.A.G.

The Button Queen, 19 Marylebone Lane, London W1M 5FE. Prop: Martyn & Isabel Frith. Tel: & Fax: (0171) 935-1505. Est: 1953. Shop; open Monday to Wednesday 10–5, Thursday and Friday 10–6, Saturday 10–4. NEW and OLD stock - medium. Spec: buttons; some buckles & clasps. CC: V; A; MC. Also, earings and cuff links made from old buttons and wheelchair access. Mem: British Button Society.

Pamela M. Caunt, 292 Westbourne Grove, London W11 2PS. Tel: & Fax: (0171) 226-5221. Est: 1973. Market stand; open Saturday 7–4. Fairs: Newark. OLD stock - medium. Spec: medals; jewellery; militaria; chain watches; Victorian. PR: £20–35. CC: V; MC. Also, books on military jewellery.

Charleville Gallery, 7 Charleville Road, London W14 9JL. Prop: F. King. Est: 1986. Shop; open Wednesday to Friday 10–6 or by appointment. Fairs: Bagatelle. OLD stock - medium. Spec: textiles. PR: £1–3,000. CC: V; MC. Corresp: French.

Garrick D. Coleman, 75 Portobello Road, London W11 2QB. Tel: (0171) 937-5524. Fax: 937-5530. Est: 1970. Shop; open Tuesday to Friday 10–4, Saturday 8–4. OLD stock - small. Spec: games; ivory; paperweights; chess sets and boards; backgammon; conjuring items. PR: £100–10,000. CC: all. Corresp: French.

Continuum, Stand 124, Grays Antique Market, 58 Davies Street, London W1Y 2LP. Prop: F. & E. Joy. Tel: (0171) 493-4909. Est: 1969. Market stand; open Monday to Friday 11–6. OLD stock - very small. Spec: Oriental; tribal. CC: MC; V; AE; DC; JVC. Corresp: French, German.

John Dale Antiques, 87 Portobello Road, London W11 2QB. Prop: Jo Cairns. Tel: (0171) 727-1304. Est: 1960. Shop; open Monday to Friday 10–4, Saturday 7–5. NEW stock - very small. Spec: trays. OLD stock - small. Spec: cameras; Edwardian; Georgian; medals; Victorian. PR: £20–1,000. CC: V; MC; AE; DC. Mem: P.A.D.A.

A.B. Davis Ltd., 18 Brook Street, (corner New Bond Street), London W1Y 1AA. Managing Director: Mr A. Douglas Chaplin. Tel: (0171) 629-1053. Fax: 499-6454. Est: 1970. Shop; open Monday to Friday 10–4. NEW and OLD stock - very large. Spec: jewellery; silver; wrist and chain watches. PR: up to £2-3,000 R.S.P. CC: all major. Mem: N.A.G.

Jehanne de Biolley Oriental Art, 29 Conduit Street, London W1R 9JA. Tel: (0171) 495-4257. Fax: 493-2604. Est: 1990. Private premises; appointment necessary. OLD stock. Spec: Oriental; Chinese and Korean ceramics; jewellery; Indian miniatures on ivory. Corresp: French.

Peter Delehar, 146 Portobello Road, London W11 2DZ. Tel: (0181) 866-8659. Est: 1919. Shop; open Saturday 9–4. Fairs: Antique Scientific and Medical Instrument Fair (2 a year). OLD stock - very small. Spec: antique scientific and medical instruments. PR: £50–5,000. CC: AE; V; A; MC; JCB; DC. Also, organizer of the Antique Scientific and Medical Instrument Fair. Mem: founder member of the Scientific Instrument Society.

Didier Antiques, Unit 2, Kensington Church Street Antique Centre, 58-60 Kensington Church Street London W8 4DB. Tel: & Fax: (0171) 938-2537. Est: 1980. Shop; open Monday to Saturday 11–6. Fairs: NEC Birmingham (Easter and August), Olympia (June and November). OLD stock. Spec: arts & crafts; Art Nouveau; Art Deco; cuff links; jewellery; silver. PR: £50–5,000. CC: V; AE; DC; MC; JCB. Corresp: French, Dutch, German. Mem: P.A.D.A.

The English Teddy Bear Co., 24 Carnaby Street, London W1 1PH. Prop: Alise & Jonty Crossick & Dominic Richards. Tel: (0171) 439-2406. Fax: 734-2783. Est: 1990. Shop; open during business hours. NEW stock - large. Spec: teddy bears, limited edition bears and related gifts. PR: £5–200 (bears). CC: V; M. Cata: quarterly. *Also shops in:* Bath, Canterbury, Cambridge, Meadowhall, Newcastle, Oxford, Regent Street (London), Stratford, Windsor, York.

The English Teddy Bear Co., 153 Regent Street, London W1 7FD. Prop: Alise & Jonty Crossick & Dominic Richards. Tel: (0171) 287-3273. Fax: 434-3815. Est: 1990. Shop; open during business hours. NEW stock - large. Spec: teddy bears, limited edition bears and related gifts. PR: £5–200 (bears). CC: V; M. Cata: quarterly. *Also shops in:* Bath, Canterbury, Cambridge, Carnaby Street (London), Meadowhall, Newcastle, Oxford, Stratford, Windsor, York.

Ermitage Fine Arts Ltd., 14 Hay Hill, London W1X 7LJ. Tel: & Fax: (0171) 499-5459. Est: 1984. Shop; open Monday to Friday 10.30–5. Fairs: European Fine Arts Fair, Maastricht. OLD stock - very large. Spec: Fabergé, Russian and continental silver. PR: £1,000–100,000. Corresp: German, French, Russian. Mem: B.A.D.A.

Eureka Antiques, 105 Portobello Road, London W11. Prop: Noel Gibson & Alex O'Donnell. Tel: (0161) 941-5453. Est: 1966. Market stand; open Saturday 7–3 by appointment. Fairs: Olympia (3), Kensington (2), Little Chelsea (3). OLD stock. Spec: papier mâché; tartanware. PR: £50–10,000. CC: BC.

Frydman, Bond Street Silver Galleries, 111-112 New Bond Street, London W1Y 0BQ. Prop: G. Barnett. Tel: & Fax: (0171) 493-4895. Est: 1930. Gallery shop; open Monday to Friday 9–5.30. OLD stock - medium. Spec: Art Nouveau; Art Deco; bells; candle extinguishers; candles/candlesticks; card cases; cutlery; mirrors; Mother-of-Pearl; silver; spoons; tea caddies; teapots; wine antiques. PR: £5–5,000. Corresp: German, French.

G.P. Mobilia, 309 Uxbridge Road, Acton, London W3 9QU. Prop: G.P. Mobilia. Tel: & Fax: (0181) 992-1182. Est: 1989. Shop; open Tuesday to Friday 10–6, Saturday 10–4. Fairs: NEC and Donington toy fairs. NEW stock - medium. Spec: toys; diecast toys; motoring related; model cars. OLD stock - small. Spec: toys; TV & film related items; sci-fiction; motoring; diecast toys; model cars. PR: £1–2,000. CC: AE; A; BC; V.

Michael German (Antiques), 38B Kensington Church Street, London W8 4BX. Tel: (0171) 937-2771. Fax: 937-8566. Est: 1971. Shop; open Monday to Friday 10–5, Saturday 10–2. OLD stock - medium. Spec: walking sticks; arms & armour. PR: £50–15,000. CC: all. Mem: B.A.D.A., L.A.P.A.D.A.

Golfiana, P.O. Box 178, Cambridge, CB4 3UF. Prop: Sarah Fabian-Baddiel. Tel: (0171) 408-1239. Fax: 493-9344. Est: 1970. Stand at: Grays-in-the-Mews, B24, Davis Mews, London W1; open Monday to Friday 10–6. NEW stock - small. Spec: golf; Diecast toys; tinplate toys; toy soldiers; trains; transport. OLD stock - small. PR: £10–1,000. CC: V; A. Cata: occasionally, to known clients. Mem: P.B.F.A.

Patrick & Susan Gould, Stand L17, Grays Mews Antique Market, 1–7 Davies Mews, London W1Y 2LP. Tel: (0171) 408-0129. Est: 1973. Market stand; open 10–5.30. OLD stock - very small. Spec: Art Deco and Art Nouveau (glass only). PR: £100–10,000. CC: V; MC. Corresp: French.

Graham and Oxley (Antiques) Ltd., 73 Gloucester Terrace, London W2 3DH. Prop: Michael Graham. Tel: (0171) 402-0982. Fax: 706-7517. Est: 1965. Private premises; appointment necessary. Fairs: Olympia. OLD stock. Spec: antique ceramics and decorative accessories. PR: £100–20,000.

Anthony Green Antiques, Unit 39, The Bond Street Antique Centre 124 New Bond Street, London W1Y 9AE. Tel: (0171) 409-2854. Fax: 408-0010. E-Mail: vintagewatches@easyme.co.uk. Est: 1978. Shop; open Monday to Friday 10–5. OLD stock - medium. Spec: vintage wrist watches; antique pocket watches. PR: £200–20,000. CC: all major. Cata: available on request.

Green's Antique Galleries, 117 Kensington Church Street, London W8 7LN. Prop: Mr Sidney Green. Tel: (0171) 229-9618. Est: 1958. Shop; open Monday to Saturday 9.30–5, closed for lunch Monday to Friday 1.30–2.30. OLD stock - large. Spec: antique jewellery and silver. PR: £10–2,000. CC: V; MC; A; AE. Corresp: French, Italian. Mem: Kensington Chamber of Commerce.

Halcyon Days, 14 Brook Street, London W1Y 1AA. Prop: Mrs Susan Benjamin. Tel: (0171) 629-8811. Fax: 409-7901. Est: 1950. Shop; open Monday to Friday 9.15–5.30, Saturday 9.30–5.30. Fairs: Grosvenor House, Olympia, B.A.D.A. NEW stock - medium. Spec: enamels; porcelain. OLD stock - medium. Spec: candles/candlesticks; ceramics; clocks; cuff links; decorative; French; Mauchline ware; mother-of-pearl; musical boxes; objets de vertu; papier mâché; Royal memorabilia; scent bottles; snuff boxes; Staffordshire; tea caddies; teddy bears; treen; tortoiseshell; wine antiques. PR: £30 plus. CC: A; V; DC; AE; JCB. Cata: 4 a year. Corresp: French, German, Dutch, Italian. Mem: Bond Street Associaiton. *See also:* London EC (q.v.).

Hampson & Lewis, Unit 139, Grays Antique Centre, 58 Davies Street, London W1. Prop: Susan Lewis. Tel: (0171) 409-1350. Est: 1981. Market stand; open Monday to Friday 10–5.30. OLD stock - small. Spec: arts & crafts; jewellery; silver. PR: £50–5,000. CC: V; MC. Corresp: French.

Patricia Harbottle, Geoffrey Van Arcade, 105 Portobello Road, London W11 2QB. Tel: (0171) 731-1972. Fax: 731-3663. Est: 1988. Market stand inside arcade; open Saturday 8–3. Fairs: West London, Kensington, Wilton House, Snape, NEC. OLD stock - small. Spec: corkscrews and bottle openers; decanters; glass; wine antiques. PR: £5–2,000. CC: V; MC. Cata: occasionally. Also, trading at the Boston Antiques Centre, Mass., U.S.A. Mem: P.A.D.A.

Harlequin House, 3 Kensington Mall, London W8 4EB. Prop: Jennifer Raison. Tel: (0171) 221-8629. Est: 1984. Shop; open Tuesday, Friday and Saturday 11–5.30 or by appointment. NEW stock - medium. Spec: masks; puppets. OLD stock - small. Spec: antique puppets - Pelhams range. PR: 50p–£500.

Brian Haughton Antiques, 3$_B$ Burlington Gardens, London W1X 1LE. Tel: (0171) 734-5491. Fax: 494-4604. Est: 1962. Shop; open 10–5. Fairs: International Ceramics Fair & Seminar - London (June), International Antique Dealers Show - New York (October). OLD stock - very large. Spec: antique porcelain, pottery, glass and works of art. PR: £200–50,000. CC: AE; V. Also, antique fair organiser. Corresp: French, German.

Heraldry of Mayfair, 1 White Horse Street, Mayfair, London W1V 7LA. Prop: M.J. & J.M. Geoghegan. Tel: & Fax: (0171) 499-8335. Est: 1994. Shop and market stand; open Monday to Saturday 10–7, Sunday 10–4. Fairs: Green Park and English Heritage re-enactments. NEW stock - very small. Spec: heraldic badges, buttons, china, cuff links, embroideries, jewellery, stationery. PR: £55–1,500. CC: BC; V; MC; D; AE. Cata: available on request. Also, genealogy.

Erna Hiscock, 47 High Street, New Romney, Kent. Tel: (01797) 367774. Est: 1970. Shop at: Chelsea Galleries, Portobello Road, London; open Saturdays 7–4. Fairs: N.E.C. Birmingham, Ardingly and Newark. OLD stock - very large. Spec: antique samplers. PR: £250–2,500. CC: A; V.

Hope & Glory, 131a Kensington Church Street, (entrance in Peel Street), London W8 7LP. Prop: Robert R. Lower. Tel: (0171) 727-8424. Est: 1982. Shop; open Monday to Saturday 10–5. OLD stock. Spec: commemorative ware; Royal memorabilia; political commemoratives. PR: £10–1,000. CC: V; MC; EC. Note: 800–1,000 different items stocked.

Jonathan Horne Antiques Ltd., 66C Kensington Church Street, London W8 4BY. Tel: (0171) 221-5658. Fax: 792-3090. Est: 1968. Shop; open Monday to Friday 9.30–5.30. Fairs: The International Fine Art and Antique Dealers Show (New York), The Fine Art and Antiques Fair (Olympia, London), The International Ceramics Fair (London) and B.A.D.A. Antiques Fair (London). OLD stock - small. Spec: early English pottery. Cata: 1 exhibition catalogue a year. Mem: B.A.D.A.

Valerie Howard, 2 Campden Street, off Kensington Church Street, London W8 7EP. Tel: (0171) 792-9702. Fax: (0181) 948-2096. Est: 1988. Shop; open Monday to Friday 10–5.30, Saturday 10–4. Fairs: Olympia (June). OLD stock - large. Spec: china; pottery. PR: £80–15,000. CC: V; MC; AE. Corresp: French. Mem: L.A.P.A.D.A.

David Ireland, 99 Elgin Crescent, London W11 2JF. Tel: & Fax: (0171) 221-4188. Est: 1985. Market stand at: Westbourne Antiques Arcade, 283 Westbourne Grove, London; open Saturday 8–4. Fairs: Textile Society's Antique Textile Fair. OLD stock - small. Spec: antique costume, embroideries, embroidered pictures, Oriental, shawls, shoes and textiles. PR: £20–2,000. CC: A; V; MC.

Jag Decorative Arts, 58–60 Kensington Church Stree London W8 4DB. Prop: G. Morgan, G. Strickland and C. Warner. Tel: (0171) 938-4404. Fax: 937-3400. Est: 1988. Shop; open Monday to Saturday 10.30–5.30. OLD stock - very large. Spec: arts & crafts; Art Nouveau; bronze; ceramics; glass; metalware; pewter. PR: £100–5,000. CC: A; V; MC; EC; DC; AE. Corresp: French.

Jones Antique Lighting, 194 Westbourne Grove, London W11 2RH. Prop: Judy Jones. Tel: & Fax: (0171) 229-6866. Est: 1982. Shop; open Monday to Saturday 9.30–6. OLD stock - medium. Spec: lighting; arts & crafts; Art Nouveau; Art Deco; brass; bronze; chandeliers; copper; French; glass; globes; iron working; night lights; oil lamps. CC: V; AE. Mem: L.A.P.A.D.A.

Kleanthous Antiques Ltd., Stouts Antiques Market, 144 Portobello Road, London W11 2DZ. Prop: Chris & Costas Kleanthous. Tel: (0171) 727-3649. Fax: (0181) 980-1199 and (01923) 897618. Est: 1969. Shop; open Saturday 6.30–4. Fairs: Olympia. OLD stock - medium. Spec: jewellery - Georgian, Victorian, Art Nouveau and Art Deco; watches - vintage wrist and pocket by Rolex, Cartier, Patek Pillipe, Vacheron and Constantin, Jeager le Coultre Reverso and others; objets de vertu; silver - 18th and 19th Century; clocks; tortoiseshell; ivory. PR: £200–10,000. CC: V; MC; A; AE; DC. Corresp: French, German, Greek, Italian. Mem: L.A.P.A.D.A.

Enid Lawson Gallery, 36A Kensington Church Street, London W8 4BX. Tel: (0171) 937-8444. Fax: 938-4786. Est: 1995. Shop; open Tuesday to Saturday 10.30–6 and other times by appointment. NEW stock - very small. Spec: studio ceramics & pottery. PR: £20–500. CC: MC; V. Also, contemporary fine art. Mem: Kensington & Chelsea Chamber of Commerce.

London Curiosity Shop, 66E Kensington Church Street, London W8 4BY. Prop: Mr & Mrs C.D. Wertheim. Tel: & Fax: (0171) 229-2934. Est: 1994. Shop; open Monday to Saturday 10–6. OLD stock - very small. Spec: chandeliers; china; dolls/dolls clothes; jewellery; phonecards; paperweights. PR: £5–500. CC: V; AE; JCB. Also, restoration of china and dolls. Corresp: Japanese, French.

William Mansell, 24 Connaught Street, London W2 2AT. Prop: Bill Salisbury. Tel: (0171) 723-4154. Est: 1864. Shop; open during business hours. NEW and OLD general stock - small. Spec: barometers; buckles & clasps; buttonhooks; card cases; clocks; costume jewellery; cuff links; cutlery; decanters; inkstands; jewellery; miniatures; pewter; photograph frames; scent bottles; serviette rings; silver; tankards; wrist & chain watches. PR: £50–2,500. CC: all major. Also, repair and restoration. Corresp: French, German. Mem: B.W. & C.M.G., B.H.I.

Allison Massey, 376, Grays Antique Market, 58 Davies Street, London W1Y 1LB. Tel: (0171) 493-1634. Fax: 493-9344. Est: 1977. Market stand; open Monday to Friday 10–6. OLD stock - medium. Spec: jet - Art Nouveau, buckles & clasps, buttons, early plastics, fashion accessories, hatpins & holders, jewellery etc. PR: £5–500. CC: V; MC; AE; JCB. Corresp: French.

Mayflower Antiques, 117 Portobello Road, London W11. Prop: John, Sue & Kevin Odgers. Tel: & Fax: (01255) 504079. Est: 1970. Shop; open Saturday 7–5. Fairs: Scientific fairs - London. OLD stock - very small. Spec: barometers; calculating machines; cameras; dolls/dolls clothes; drawing instruments; gramophones; ivory; maritime/nautical; medical instruments; model trains; musical boxes; scientific instruments; sewing machines; stereoscopes; sundials; telescopes; tinplate toys; traction/steam engines; typewriters. PR: £5–5,000. CC: V; MC; EC; JCB. Mem: Portobello Antique Dealers Association.

Pete McAskie Toys, Stand A12/13, Basement, Gray's Mews Antiques, 1-7 Davies Mews, London W1Y 1AR. Tel: (0171) 629-2813. Fax: 493-9344. Est: 1976. Market stand; open Monday to Friday 10–6. Fairs: Sandown Park Toy Fair, Toy Show - Paris, Toy Swapmeet Woluwe - Bruxelles, Jaarbeurs - Utrecht. OLD stock - medium. Spec: diecast toys; model trains, cars and aircraft; tinplate toys; general toys; toy soldiers. PR: 25p–£3,000. CC: MC; V; A. Corresp: French.

Michael Coins, 6 Hillgate Street, off Notting Hill Gate, London W8 7SR. Prop: Michael Goby. Tel: & Fax: (0171) 727-1518. Est: 1967. Shop; open Monday to Friday 10–5. NEW stock - very small. Spec: coins. OLD stock - medium Spec: coins. PR: £1–500.

Stephen Naegel, Stand B23, Grays Antique Market, 1-7 Davies Mews, London W1 1AR. Tel: (0171) 491-3066. Fax: 493-9344. Est: 1976. Market stand; open Monday to Friday 10–4. OLD stock - large. Spec: toy soldiers; militaria; dolls/dolls clothes; medals; tins, signs & advertising. PR: £3–5,000 plus. CC: MC; V; AE.

Noonstar, Abstract, 58–60 Kensington Church Stree London W8 4DB. Prop: Galya Aytac. Tel: (0171) 376-2652. Fax: 229-5492. Est: 1979. Shop; open 11–5.30. NEW and OLD stock - large. Spec: Art Nouveau; Art Deco; bottles; bronze; ceramics; clocks; costume jewellery; decanters; decorative; early plastics; eccentrics; glass; iron working; ivory; marbles; pewter; scent bottles; sculpture; The Seventies; The Sixties; vases. PR: £50–10,000. CC: AE; A; V; DC; JCB. Also, Cameo, Lalique. Corresp: French, Russian, Turkish, Italian, German. Mem: L.A.P.A.D.A.

The Old Cinema, 160 Chiswick High Road, London W4 1PR. Prop: Martin Hanness. Tel: (0181) 995-4166. Fax: (0181) 995-4167. E-Mail: 100572.2146@ compuserve.com. Est: 1979. Open Monday to Saturday 9.30–6, Sunday 12–5. NEW stock - very large. Spec: architectural; props. OLD stock - very large. Spec: architectural antiques. CC: V; A. Cata: quarterly. Also, shopfittings and furniture. Corresp: Spanish, Italian. Mem: L.A.P.A.D.A.

You want it - You got it !

The Old Father Time Clock Centre
1st Floor, 101 Portobello Road, London, W11 2QB
Tel/Fax: 0181 546-6299 (24 hrs)
Mobile: 0836 712088
Open Friday 9-1 & Saturday 6-4
or by appointment

Old Father Time Clock Centre, 1st Floor Portobello Studios, 101 Portobello Road, London W11 2QB. Prop: John Denvir. Tel: & Fax: (0181) 546-6299. Mobile: (0836) 712088. Est: 1986. Shop; open Friday 9–2, Saturday 6.30–4, other times by appointment. Fairs: specialist clock fairs. NEW stock - very small. Spec: clocks; barometers. OLD stock - large. Spec: clocks; barometers. PR: £10–10,000. CC: A; V. Also, glass domes, spares and repairs.

Pairs Limited, 22 Upper Grosvenor Street, London W1Y 3WD. Prop: Iain Michael Brunt. Tel: (0171) 499-7012. Fax: 499-7015. E-Mail: natg@portman. demon.co.uk. Est: 1995. Shop; open 9.30–5.30. Fairs: Olympia. NEW general stock - large and OLD general stock - very large. Spec: arts & crafts; Art Nouveau; Art Deco; boxes; ceramics; chandeliers; china; decanters; decorative; doorstops; Edwardian; french; Georgian; glass; jardinières; lighting; mirrors; objets de vertu; sculpture; tapestries; Victorian. PR: £500–10,000. CC: V; MC. Cata: 3 a year. Corresp: French. *At same premises:* Antique Search with catalogue on Internet: http://www.demon.co.uk/antiques.

Pars Antiques, Stand A14/15, Grays in the Mews, 1-7 Davies Mews, London W1Y 1AR. Prop: Katy Williams. Tel: (0171) 491-9889. Fax: (0181) 255-0779. Est: 1986. Market stand; open Monday to Friday 10.30–6. OLD stock - very large. Spec: ancient art (Egyptian, Greek, Roman, Persian) including ancient metalware, ancient pottery, ancient jewellery and ancient glass. PR: £5–5,000. CC: V; A; MC; AE; DC. Cata: infrequently. Mem: A.D.A.

Peter Petrou, 195 Westbourne Grove, London W11 2SB. Est: 1974. Shop; open Monday to Saturday 10–6. Fairs: Olympia Fine Art and Antiques Fairs. OLD stock - very large. Spec: Anglo–Indian; boxes; brass; bronze; candles/candlesticks; ceramics; eccentrics; embroideries; embroidered pictures; fine art; fossils, geology & prehistory; globes; ivory; jardinières; letter boxes; lighting; marbles; maritime/ nautical; metalware; miniatures. PR: £1,000–150,000. Corresp: French, Greek. Mem: L.A.P.A.D.A.

Pieces of Time, 1/7 Davies Mews, Units 17–19, London W1Y 2LP. Prop: Jonathan A. Wachsmann. Tel: (0171) 629-2422. Fax: 409-1625. E-Mail: sales@p-o-time.demon.co.uk. Open Monday to Friday 10–6. OLD stock - small. Spec: walking sticks; clocks; snuff boxes; maritime/nautical; musical boxes. PR: £100–40,000. CC: all. Cata: 4 a year, on the Internet http://www.antique-watch.com/welcome.html. Mem: L.A.P.A.D.A.

Madeleine C. Popper FGA, DGA, L12/L13 Grays-in-the-Mews, 1–7 Davies Mews, London W1Y 2LP. Tel: (0171) 493-2996. Fax: 493-9344. E-Mail: 100034.2225@compuserve.com. Est: 1966. Market stand; open Monday to Friday 11–5.30. Fairs: Olympia (June & November). OLD stock. Spec: Art Nouveau; antique costume jewellery (ie cut steel, Berlin iron, pinchbell, paste etc.); Georgian; jewellery; objets de vertu; Victorian; gold & gem set jewellery. PR: £40–5,000. CC: all (inc. JCB). Corresp: French, German. Mem: L.A.P.A.D.A., Fellow of the Pemmological Association of Great Britain, G.A.G.T.L., Society of Jewellery Historians.

Raffety, 34 Kensington Church Street, London W8. Prop: N. Raffety & H. Walwyn. Tel: & Fax: (0171) 938-1100. Est: 1982. Shop; open Monday to Friday 10.30–5.30, Saturday 10.30–2 or by appointment. Fairs: Olympia, B.A.D.A. OLD stock - very large. Spec: barometers; clocks; musical boxes. PR: £250–35,000. CC: V; AE; DC. Also, restore longcase and bracket clock movements. Corresp: French, German, Spanish, Portuguese, Danish, Italian. Mem: B.A.D.A., L.A.P.A.D.A.

Raffety, 39 Ledbury Road, Notting Hill Gate, London W11 2AA. Prop: Nigel Raffety. Tel: & Fax: (0171) 229-4947. Est: 1979. Shop; open Monday to Friday 10–5, Saturday 11–3, or by appointment. Fairs: Olympia, B.A.D.A. OLD stock - medium. Spec: antique clocks and barometers from 1650–1880. PR: £500–15,000. CC: AE; V; MC; DC. Corresp: French, German, Spanish. Mem: B.A.D.A., L.A.P.A.D.A.

S. & G. Antiques, Stouts Antiques Market, 144 Portobello Road, London W11 2DZ. Prop: Gary Sirett. Tel: (0181) 907-7140. Fax: 909-3277. Mobile: (0468) 366677. Est: 1970. Shop; open Saturday 6.30–4.30. Fairs: Newark, Ardingly, N.E.C. OLD stock - very large. Spec: ceramics; glass; china; miniature porcelain. PR: £20–5,000. CC: V; MC; JCB. Mem: P.A.D.A.

Seaby Coins & Antiquities, 14 Old Bond Street, London W1X 3DB. Tel: (0171) 495-1888. Fax: 499-5916. Shop; open Monday to Friday 10–5. Fairs: Coinex, London Coin Fairs. OLD stock. Spec: coins. Cata: 4 auction catalogues and 2 price lists per year. Mem: British Numismatic Trade Association.

Nicholas Shaw Antiques, 111/112 New Bond Street, London W1Y 9AB. Tel: & Fax: (0171) 629-1853. Est: 1993. Shop; open Monday to Friday 9.30–5.30. Fairs: Dorchester, Claridges, Olympia, N.E.C., Kensington, Harrogate. NEW and OLD stock - medium. Spec: antique silver; provincial Scottish and Irish silver. PR: £1–1,000. CC: V; AE. Mem: L.A.P.A.D.A.

M. & L. Silver Partnership, 111-112 New Bond Street, London W1Y 0BQ. Prop: Mr & Mrs C. Lasher. Tel: & Fax: (0171) 499-5170. Est: 1952. Shop in gallery; open Tuesday to Friday 9.30–4. NEW stock - very small. Spec: silver; silver plate. OLD stock - medium. Spec: silver; silver plate; Sheffield; picture frames. PR: £50–10,000. CC: A; V; DC.

Sladmore Gallery, 32 Bruton Place, Berkeley Square, London W1X 7AA. Tel: (0171) 499-0365. Fax: 409-1381. Est: 1971. Shop; open Monday to Friday 10–6, Saturday by appointment. Fairs: B.A.D.A. Antiques Fair. NEW stock - very small. Spec: bronzes by 3 contemporary sculptors: Geoffrey Dashwood, Mark Coreth and David Williams-Ellis. OLD stock - very small. Spec: 19th and early 20th Century animalier and figurative bronze sculpture. PR: £750 upwards. CC: AE. Cata: 3 a year. Corresp: French, Spanish. Mem: B.A.D.A., S.L.A.D.

Colin Smith and Gerald Robinson Antiques, 105 Portobello Road, London W11. Tel: (0171) 225-1163. Est: 1981. Shop; open Saturday 8–3 or by appointment. Fairs: Olympia (June & November). OLD stock - medium. Spec: card cases; ivory; mother-of-pearl; snuff boxes; tea caddies; tortoiseshell. PR: £100–3,000. CC: all major.

Boris Sosna T/A C. & B. Gems & Antique Jewellery, K-34/35 Grays Mews Antique Mar Davies Mews, London W1P 2RX. Tel: (0171) 629-2371. Fax: (0181) 348-1646. Market stand; open Monday to Friday 10–6. NEW stock - small. Spec: jewellery; silver; wrist & chain watches; boxes; Art Deco; Art Nouveau; scent bottles; serviette rings; candles/candlesticks; snuff boxes; teapots; Victorian. OLD stock - very large. Spec: jewellery; silver; cuff links; boxes; wrist & chain watches; Art Deco; Art Nouveau; card cases; Georgian; militaria. PR: £50–5,000. CC: V; A; MC; AE. Corresp: Russian. Mem: F.G.A., D.G.A.

Stockspring Antiques, 114 Kensington Church Street, London W8 4BH. Prop: Mrs A. Agnew & Mrs F. Marno. Tel: & Fax: (0171) 727-7995. Est: 1980. Shop; open Monday to Friday 10–5.30, Saturday 10–1. Fairs: Olympia, Northern Antique Dealers fair. OLD stock - very large. Spec: English porcelain. PR: £5–5,000. CC: MC; AE. Mem: L.A.P.A.D.A.

June & Tony Stone Fine Antique Boxes, 75 Portobello Road, London W11 2QB. Tel: (01273) 500212. Fax: 500024. E-Mail: fineboxes@acid.co.uk. Est: 1991. Shop; open Tuesday to Friday 10–4, Saturday 7–5. Fairs: Olympia (June, November, February). OLD stock - medium. Spec: boxes; decanters; decorative; games; Georgian; letter boxes; money boxes; mother-of-pearl; objets de vertu; tea caddies; tortoiseshell; Victorian. PR: £300 plus. CC: all major. Cata: 2 a year. Also, on the Internet: http://www.acid.co.uk/fab. Mem: L.A.P.A.D.A., P.A.D.A.

Terrace Antiques, 10 South Ealing Road, London W5 4QA. Prop: Nicholas Schwartz. Tel: (0181) 567-5194. Est: 1972. Shop; open Monday to Saturday 10–5.30. Fairs: Olympia (June). NEW stock - small. Spec: paperweights; photograph frames. OLD general stock - large. PR: £10–1,000. CC: V; A; MC; AE; DC; JCB. Corresp: Portuguese. Mem: L.A.P.A.D.A.

Themes & Variations, 231 Westbourne Grove, London W11 2SE. Prop: Mrs Liliane Fawcett. Tel: (0171) 727 5531. Fax: 221-6378. Est: 1984. Shop; Monday to Friday 10–1 and 2–6, Saturday 10–6. NEW and OLD stock - very large. Spec: Art Deco; eccentrics; fashion accessories; glass. CC: AE; V; A; MC. Corresp: French, Italian, Spanish.

Tradition of London Ltd., 33 Curzon Street, Mayfair, London W1Y 7AE. Prop: Alan Lewis, Steve Hare & David Scheinmann. Tel: (0171) 493-7452. Fax: 355-1224. Est: 1960. Shop; open Monday to Friday 9–5.30, Saturday 9.30–3. Fairs: Euro-Militaire, London Toy Soldier Shows, Napoleonic Fair. NEW stock - large. Spec: toy style soldiers; military miniatures; hobby kits. PR: £4–400. CC: V; MC; AE; DC. Cata: 1 a year with supplements.

Under Two Flags, 4 St. Christopher's Place, London W1M 5HB. Prop: A. & R. Coutts. Tel: & Fax: (0171) 935-6934. Est: 1972. Shop; open Tuesday to Saturday 10–5. NEW stock - medium. Spec: toy and model soldiers. OLD stock - very small. PR: £8–700. CC: V; A; MC. Also, paints, brushes, military uniform books.

W.H. Collectables, 500 Chesham House, 150 Regent Street, London W1R 5FA. Prop: Mr Michael A. Wheeler. Tel: (01394) 385021. Est: 1981. Storeroom; appointment necessary or postal business. OLD stock - very large. Spec: aeronautica; Anglo-Indian; automobilia; canal memorabilia; games; Georgian; gramophones; London transport; maritime/nautical; match boxes/books; militaria; paper money; playing cards; railways; Royal memorabilia; sewing machines; sports; tobacco & associated; transport. PR: £10–500. CC: V; MC; AE. Cata: 3 a year. Mem: Ephemera Society; International Bond & Share Society.

Captain O.M. Watts, 7 Dover Street, London W1X 3PJ. Prop: Mariner - Watts plc. Tel: (0171) 493-4633. Fax: 495-0755. Est: 1926. Shop; open Monday to Saturday 9–6. OLD stock - very small. Spec: maritime/nautical. CC: AE; A; V. Also, chandlery. Corresp: Spanish, French. Mem: B.M.I.F.

Zeitgeist, 58 Kensington Church Street, London W8 4DB. Prop: A. Self & P. Robinson. Tel: & Fax: (0171) 938-4817. Est: 1991. Shop; open Monday to Saturday 11–6. Fairs: N.E.C. Birmingham (August). OLD stock - very small. Spec: arts & crafts; Art Nouveau; glass; lighting; mirrors; pewter; silver. PR: £100–5,000. CC: V; AE; DC; JCB.

LONDON
(WEST CENTRAL POSTAL DISTRICTS)

A.H. Baldwin & Sons Ltd., 11 Adelphi Terrace, London WC2N 6BJ. Tel: (0171) 930-6879. Fax: 930-9450. Est: 1872. Shop; open Monday to Friday 9–5. Fairs: Olympia Fine Arts & Antiques Fairs (June & Nov), Coinex (October). OLD stock - Spec: commemorative medals and coins. CC: all major. Cata: occasionally. Corresp: French, German. Mem: B.A.D.A.; B.N.T.A.; B.N.S.

Ballantyne & Date, 38 Museum Street, Bloomsbury, London WC1A 1LP. Prop: Roger Ballantyne–Way & Robert Date. Tel: (0171) 242-4249. Fax: 430-0684. Shop; open Monday to Saturday 10.30–6, Sunday 12–6. Fairs: monthly P.B.F.A. London (Hotel Russell, Russell Square WC1), other P.B.F.A., Ephemera Society. NEW stock - very small. OLD stock - large. Spec: arts & crafts; Art Nouveau; Art Deco; automobilia; canal memorabilia; ceramics; fine art; London Transport; maritime/nautical; motoring; posters; railways; tins, signs & advertising; transport. PR: £1–1,000. CC: all except DC. Mem: P.B.F.A.; E.S.

Classic Collection, 2 Pied Bull Yard, Bury Place, London WC1A 2JR. Tel: (0171) 831-6000. Fax: 831-5424. Email: classic collection@leica.demon.co.uk. Est: 1991. Shop; open Monday to Saturday 9–5.30. NEW stock - medium. Spec: cameras - Leica and Minox; optical toys. PR: £20–2,000. CC: AE; V; A; JCB. Cata: 4 a year. Corresp: Japanese.

Philip Cohen Coins, 20 Cecil Court, Leicester Square, London WC2N 4HE. Tel: (0171) 379-0615. Fax: 240-4300. Est: 1975. Shop; open Monday to Friday 11–5.30, Saturday 12–5. Fairs: Coinex - London. OLD stock - very large. Spec: coins; sovereigns and Krugerrands (bullion). PR: £1–1,000. CC: V; MC. Mem: B.N.T.A., A.N.A.

Lewis Davenport Ltd., 7 Charing Cross Underground, Concourse, The Strand, London WC2N 4HZ. Prop: Mrs Betty Davenport. Tel: (0171) 836-0408. Fax: 379-8828. Est: 1898. Shop; open Monday to Friday 9.30–5.30. NEW stock - medium. Spec: magic and conjuring. OLD stock - small. Spec: magic and conjuring. PR: £2–1,000. Cata: every 2 years.

Deco Inspired, 67 Monmouth Street, Covent Garden, London WC2H 9DG. Prop: Mr & Mrs Chaman. Tel: & Fax: (0171) 240-5719. Est: 1993. Shop; open Monday to Saturday 11–7. OLD general stock - small. Spec: American lifestyle 1920-1959 including: tins, signs & advertising; trays; Art Deco; bamboo; birdcages; candles/candlesticks; ceramics; clocks; costume jewellery; decorative; early plastics; eccentrics; fans; glass; globes; jukeboxes & slot machines; lighting; metalware; mirrors; radio & television; scales, weights & measures; telephone. PR: £1–5,000. CC: V; MC; AE. Also, custom finished frames - gilt speciality. Corresp; French, Spanish.

Frasers Autographs, 1st Floor, Stanley Gibbons, 399 Strand, London WC2R 0LX. Prop: Paul Fraser. Tel: (0171) 836-8444. Fax: 836-9325. Est: 1976. Shop; open 9.30–5.30. NEW and OLD stock - very large. Spec: autographed rock & pop, films & entertainment, fine art, paperweights, posters, The Sixties and sports items. PR: £20–20,000. CC: V; AE; MC. Cata: bi-monthly.

145

Gillian Gould Antiques, at Ocean Leisure, Embankment Place, 11-14 Northumberland Avenue, London WC2. Tel: (0171) 930-5050. Fax: 903-3032. Est: 1989. Shop; open Monday to Wednesday & Friday 9.30–6, Thusday 9.30–7, Saturday 9.30–5.30. OLD stock - medium. Spec: globes; Mauchline ware; spectacles, lorgnettes & monacles; maritime/nautical; scientific instruments; barometers; binoculars; brass; drawing instruments; medical instruments; optical toys; science; sundials; telescopes; tools. PR: £50–350. CC: all. Cata: 1 a year. Also, hire and restoration. Corresp: French. *Also at:* Gillian Gould Antiques, 32 Flash Walk, London NW3 1HE (q.v.).

Grosvenor Prints, 28–32 Shelton Street, Covent Garden, London WC2H 9HP. Prop: Nigel Talbot. Tel: (0171) 836-1979. Fax: 379-6695. Est: 1976. Shop; open during normal business hours. OLD stock - very large. Spec: aeronautica; arms & armour; canal memorabilia; costume; eccentrics; fairground relics; fishing; fossils, geology & prehistory; maritime/nautical; militaria; musical instruments; optical toys; Royal memorabilia; silhouettes; sports; tobacco & associated; transport; Victoriana. PR: £5–1,000. CC: AE; V; A.

The Jessop Group Ltd., 98 Scudamore Road, Leicester, Leicestershire LE3 1TZ. Manager: Mr Martin Frost. Tel: (0171) 831-3640. Fax: 831-3956. Est: 1988. Shop at: Jessop Classic, 67 Great Russell Street, London WC1; open Monday to Saturday 9–5.30. Fairs: major UK camera fairs. NEW and OLD stock - very large. Spec: binoculars; cameras; optical toys; photographic pictures; stereoscopes. PR: £10–10,000. CC: MC; A; V; AE; Jessop Card. Cata: 4 a year. Mem: Photographic Marketing Association.

Langfords, Vault 8/10, The London Silver Vaults, Chancery Lane, London WC2A 1QS. Prop: Joel & Adam Langford. Tel: (0171) 242-5506. Fax: 405-6401. Est: 1950. Shop; open Monday to Friday 9–5.30, Saturday 9–1. NEW stock - very small. Spec: silver. OLD stock - large. Spec: silver. PR £10–50,000. CC: A; V; AE; DC; MC; D. Mem: L.A.P.A.D.A.

The London Dolls House Company, 29 The Market, Covent Garden, London WC2E 8RE. Tel: (0171) 240-8681. Est: 1995. Shop; open Monday to Saturday 10–7, Sundays and Bank Holidays 12–5. NEW stock - very large. Spec: miniatures; dolls houses. OLD stock - very small. PR: £1–1,000. CC: MC; V; AE. Cata: annually.

Arthur Middleton, 12 New Road, Covent Garden, London WC2N 4LF. Tel: (0171) 836-7042. Fax: 497-2486. Shop; open 10–6. Fairs: Scientific Instrument Fair (April and October). OLD stock - small. Spec: antique globes and scientific instruments. PR: £100–100,000. CC: AE; DC. Also, props hire and large stock of films, TV and photography. Corresp: French, German.

LONDON
(OUTER)

BROMLEY

Peter Morris, 1 Station Concourse, Bromley North BR Station, Bromley, Kent BR1 4EQ. (•) Tel: (0181) 313-3410. Fax: 466-8502. Est: 1983. Shop; open Monday to Friday 10–6, closed Wednesday, Saturday 9–2. Faris: Coinex, London, Cumberland, many European Shows. NEW stock - very small. Spec: coins; medals; militaria. OLD stock - very large. Spec: coins; medals; bank notes; antiquities. PR: 50p–£500. CC: all except AE. Cata: quarterly on coins, bi-annual on medals. Corresp: German, French. Mem: B.N.T.A., A.N.A., O.M.R.S., F.R.N.S., A.D.A.

CROYDON

Oscar Dahling Antiques, 87 Cherry Orchard Road, Croydon, Surrey CR0 6BE. Tel: (0181) 681-8090. Est: 1991. Shop; open Monday to Saturday 10.30–6.30 and by appointment. Fairs: Dorking Halls. OLD general stock - very small. Spec: Art Deco; textiles; Victorian; wrist watches. PR: £1–300. CC: DC. Corresp: French.

The Hobby House, 92 Church Street, Croydon, Surrey CR0 1RD. Prop: Mrs Salmon and Mrs Talbot. Tel: (0181) 667-0441. Est: 1995. Shop; open Tuesday to Saturday. NEW general stock - medium. Spec: Tudor houses. CC: all.

Sock It To Me Trading Co., 25 Howard Road, Woodside, London SE25 5BU. (•) Prop: Jane Goldsmith. Tel: & Fax: (0181) 656-3207. Est: 1985. Private premises; appointment necessary. Fairs: Croydon Fairfield, Wallington Pub. Halls, Surrey. OLD stock - medium. Spec: Poole dinnerware; 1950's ceramics; Moorcroft Powder Blue; the Fifties, Sixties and Seventies. PR: £5–40 (Ceramics). Also, furniture and fabrics.

ENFIELD

Terence J. McGee, 20 Slades Close, Enfield, Middlesex EN2 7EB. (•) Tel: (0181) 366-5727. Est: 1972. Private premises; appointment necessary. Fairs: London and main venues in the South of England. OLD stock - medium. Spec: gramophones; gramophone needle tins; records; musical; calculating machines; cameras; commemorative ware; films & entertainment; photographic pictures; posters; radio & television; rock & pop; science; scientific instruments; the Sixties and Seventies; stereoscopes; Edwardian; Victorian. PR: £1–1,000. Cata: 1 a year. Corresp: Italian, French, German. Mem: E.S., British Vintage Wireless Society.

GREENFORD

Jack Ben–Nathan, 22 Teignmouth Gardens, Perivale, Greenford, Middlesex UB6 8BX. (•) Tel: (0181) 997-6574. Est: 1980. Private premises; appointment necessary. NEW and OLD stock - very small. Spec: games; billiards and snooker. PR: £1–1,100. Cata: 1 a year.

LONDON (OUTER)

HARROW

Harrow Coin & Stamp Centre, Victoria House, 93 Manor Farm Road, Wembley, Middlesex HA0 1XB. Tel: (0181) 997-5055. Fax: 997-8410. Est: 1965. Private premises; appointment necessary or postal business. NEW general stock - very large. OLD stock - very large. Spec: stamps; coins; medals; tokens; banknotes. Cata: on request. Corresp: French. Mem: P.T.S., B.N.T.A.

Mrs Peggotty's Miniatures Ltd., 92 Hampden Road, Harrow Weald, Middlesex HA3 5PR. Prop: Mr & Mrs M.J. Clifford. Tel: (01374) 918029. Est: 1993. Shop; open Wednesday to Friday 12.30–5, Saturday 10.30–4. NEW stock - small. Spec: dolls/dolls clothes; dolls houses; miniatures. PR: 50p–£250. Cata: annually.

HOUNSLOW

Joan & Bob Anderson, 132 Springwell Road, Heston, Hounslow, Middlesex TW5 9BP. Tel: (0181) 572-4328. Private premises; appointment necessary. OLD stock - small. Spec: ceramics; china - especially Midwinter; the Sixties. PR: £1–150.

ICKENHAM

Peter Lane, 17 Milton Road, Ickenham, Uxbridge, Middlesex UB10 8NH. (•) Tel: (01895) 674124. Est: 1984. Private premises; postal business only. OLD stock - very small. Spec: conjuring, magic. PR: £1–300.

NORTHWOOD

Hobday Toys, 44 High Street, Northwood, Middlesex HA4. Prop: Ken Hobday. Tel: (01895) 636737 or (01923) 84000. Fax: (01895) 621042. Est: 1985. Shop; open Monday to Friday 9–5, weekends by appointment. Fairs: Sandown, Reading, Stoneleigh, Gloucester, Shepton Mallett. OLD stock - very large. Spec: model trains and cars; tinplate toys; transport; gauge '0' trains pre 1939. PR: up to £10,000. Corresp: French, German. Mem: H.R.C.A., Bassett-Lowke Society, Gauge '0' Guild.

RICHMOND-UPON-THAMES

The Gooday Gallery, 20 Richmond Hill, Richmond, Surrey TW10 6QX. Prop: Mrs Debbie Gooday. Tel: (0181) 940-8652. Est: 1971. Shop; open Tuesday, Thursday to Saturday 11-5.30, Sunday 2–5.30 or by appointment. OLD stock - very small. Spec: arts & crafts; Art Nouveau; Art Deco; ceramics; decorative; early plastics; glass; Liberty jewellery and pewter; lighting; metalware; mirrors; The Sixties; African tribal. PR: £20–5,000. Mem: Decorative Arts Society.

Quelque Chose, 9 King Street, Richmond, Surrey TW9 1ND. Prop: Ian & Belinda McCarbaher. Tel: (0181) 948-3036. Est: before 1976. Shops at: 9 King Street and 5 Paved Court, Richmond; open Monday to Saturday 10.30–5.30, Sunday 12.30–5.30. NEW stock - very large. Spec: dolls; teddy bears; traditional toys; limited edition artist dolls and teddy bears; dolls houses; fine miniatures and accessories; arts & crafts; constructional toys; diecast toys; marbles; model cars; musical boxes; pewter; stationery; tinplate toys. PR: 50p–£1,000 plus. CC: V; MC. Also, greetings cards, soft toys and children's clothing. Corresp: French.

SHEPPERTON

Smalltalk, 96A High Street, Shepperton, Middlesex TW17 9BB. (•) Prop: Mrs Michelle Cambridge and Mrs J. Burgess. Tel: (01932) 247686. Est: 1987. Shop; open Monday to Saturday 9–5.30. Fairs: miniature fairs throughout London & Southern England. NEW stock - medium. Spec: dolls/dolls clothes; dolls houses; pewter; photographic pictures; toys - general. PR: £2–500. CC: A; V.

SUTTON

West Promotions, P.O. Box 257, Sutton, Surrey SM3 9WW. (•) Prop: Mrs Pamela West. Tel: & Fax: (0181) 641-3224. Est: 1993. Private premises; postal business only. Fairs: London Paper Money Fair. NEW and OLD stock - large. Spec: paper money; postal orders. PR: £1–5,000. Cata: 4 to 6 a year. Corresp: French.

TEDDINGTON

Pinocchio, 79 High Street, Teddington, Middlesex TW11 8HG. Prop: Mr & Mrs F.A. Langella. Tel: (0181) 977-8995. Fax: 977-8890. Est: 1988. Shop; open Monday to Saturday 9.30–5.30, Wednesday 11–4, Sunday by appointment only. NEW stock - large. Spec: teddy bears; jewellery; cuff links; games; fountain pens; teapots; toys - general. OLD stock - very small. Spec: teddy bears. PR: £1–2,500. CC: all major. Also, teddy/dolls hospital.

TWICKENHAM

The Dolls House Estate Agents, 18 Crown Road, St Margaret's, Twickenham, Middlesex TW1 3EE. Prop: Mrs Joy Plummer. Tel: (0181) 891-3035. Est: 1977. Shop; postal business only (shop re-opening Summer 1996). NEW stock - very small. Spec: handmade character teddy bears. OLD stock - very small. Spec: dolls houses; miniatures; teddy bears; needlepoint carpets and oil paintings in miniature to order. PR: £1–500. Cata: 2 a year.

Golden Oldies, 113 London Road, Twickenham, Middlesex TW1 1EE. Prop: J.S. Wooster. Tel: (0181) 891-3067. Fax: 744-3133. Est: 1964. Shop; open Tuesday to Friday 10–6, Saturday 10–4. NEW stock - large and OLD stock - small. Spec: film memorabilia. PR: 50p–£2,000. CC: A; V; EC. Cata: 2 a year.

Marion Pitman, 29 Hampton Road, Twickenham, Middlesex TW2 5QE. Tel: (0181) 898-7165. Est: 1978. Shop; open variable hours - please phone first. Fairs: Ephemera Society. OLD stock - medium. Spec: tins, signs & advertising; bottles; commemorative ware; tankards. Cata: erratically.

MERSEYSIDE

*Including the Unitary Authorities of Knowsley, Liverpool,
St. Helens, Sefton and Wirral*

LIVERPOOL

Stefani Antiques, 497 Smithdown Road, Liverpool, Merseyside LI5 5AE. Prop: Mrs T. Stefani. Tel: (0151) 734-1933. Est: 1980. Shop; open Monday to Saturday 10–5. OLD general stock. Spec: Edwardian, Georgian and Victorian antiques. PR: £50–5,000. CC: A; EC; MC; V. Corresp: Greek.

SOUTHPORT

ABS International Ltd, The Shakespeare Centre, 45 Shakespeare Street, Southport, Merseyside PR8 5AB. Prop: M.I. Weighill and M. Youssefi. Tel: (01704) 549920. Fax: 549921. Est: 1991. Office; postal business only. NEW stock - medium. Spec: diecast toys; model cars and aircraft (Russian only). PR: £7.50–50. CC: A; D; EC; MC; V. Cata: 1 or 2 a year, £1 including P & P. Corresp: French.

Gingers, 657 Lord Street, Southport, Merseyside PR9 0AW. Prop: Jean & Roy Griffiths. Tel: (01704) 533054. Fax: 880251. Est: 1989. Shop; open Monday to Saturday 10–5.30, Sunday 11–6. Fairs: N.E.C., Donington, Doncaster. NEW stock - small. Spec: diecast toys; model cars; tinplate toys; toy soldiers. OLD stock. Spec: diecast toys; model cars; tinplate toys. PR: £3.75–200. CC: V; A. Also, promotional products for individual businesses.

Osiris Antiques, 104 Shakespeare Street, Southport, Merseyside. Prop: C.A. & P.A. Wood. Tel: (01704) 560418. Est: 1980. Shop; open Monday & Wednesday to Saturday 11–5. OLD stock - medium. Spec: Art Deco; Art Nouveau; costume. PR: £1–800.

Sue's N Dave's, 13 Stanley Street, Southport, Merseyside PR9 OBY. Prop: Susan Shore & Dave Walton. Tel: (01704) 546296. Est: 1992. Shop; open Tuesday to Friday 10–5, Saturday 9–5. Fairs: many. NEW stock - very large. Spec: dolls houses; miniatures. CC: V; A; MC.

NORFOLK

AYLSHAM

Chris Rudd, P.O. Box 222, Aylsham, Norfolk NR11 6TY. Tel: (01263) 735007. Fax: 731777. Est: 1991. Private premises; postal business only. OLD stock - very small. Spec: Celtic coins. Cata: 6 a year. Mem: British Numismatic Trade Association.

BURNHAM MARKET

Anne Hamilton Antiques, 21 North Street, Burnham Market, Norfolk PE31 8HG. Tel: (01328) 738187. Est: 1989. Shop; open Monday to Saturday 10–1 and 2–5. OLD stock - medium. Spec: porcelain; small decorative items. PR: £5–2,000. CC: BC; V; MC. Also, English furniture.

COLTISHALL

Coltishall Antiques Centre, High Street, Coltishall, Norfolk. Prop: Mrs Isobel Ford. Tel: (01603) 767898 and 612582, Mobile (0836) 330233. Est: 1980. Shop; open Tuesday to Saturday 10–5. Fairs: Lomay Antiques Fairs (London and Norwich), North Walsham Fair. OLD stock - medium. Spec: Art Deco; Art Nouveau; ceramics; china; costume jewellery; cutlery; decanters; firearms; glass; heraldry; medals; militaria; objets de vertu; oil lamps; Oriental; pottery; scent bottles; serviette rings; silver; spoons; Staffordshire; swords; teapots; teddy bears. PR: £10–3,000.

FAKENHAM

Market Place Antiques, 28 Upper Market, Fakenham, Norfolk NR21 9BX. Prop: Jean Hannent. Tel: (01328) 862962. Est: 1987. Shop; open 10–4.30. OLD stock. Spec: silver; Victorian jewellery; writing - general. PR: £5–500. CC: A.

GREAT YARMOUTH

Barry's Antiques, 35 King Street, Great Yarmouth, Norfolk. Prop: B. Nichols. Tel: (01493) 842713. Est: 1985. Shop; open 9.30–5. NEW and OLD general stock - medium. PR: £10–10,000. CC: all.

Curiosity Corner, 166 Northgate Street, Great Yarmouth, Norfolk NR30 1BY. Prop: Mr G.M. & Mrs L. Curtis. Tel: & Fax: (01493) 859690. Shop; open Monday to Wednesday, Friday and Saturday 10–4.30. OLD stock - medium. Spec: Art Deco; brass; ceramics; china; commemorative ware; copper; costume jewellery; Edwardian; Georgian; glass; jewellery; Oriental; paperweights; plates; pottery; Staffordshire; teapots; vases; Victorian; writing - general. PR: 50p plus.

HOLT

Curios, 4 Albert Street, Holt, Norfolk NR25 6HX. Prop: Stephanie Harrison. Tel: (01263) 711084. Est: 1991. Shop; open 9.30–5. NEW general stock - large. Spec: dolls house furniture and fittings. OLD general stock - medium. PR: £1–500. CC: A; MC; V; EC. Corresp: French. Mem: Chamber of Trade.

NORFOLK

Sue Miller Antiques & Collectables, The Courtyard, Langham Glass, Langham, Holt, Norfolk NR25 7DQ. Prop: Sue Miller. Tel: (01328) 830511. Fax: 830787. Est: 1993. Shop; open 7 days a week 10–5. NEW stock - small. OLD stock - very large. Spec: Art Deco; Art Nouveau; candles/candlesticks; ceramics; china; fishing; Georgian; glass; horsebrasses & harnesses; mirrors; paperweights; scent bottles; Victorian. PR: £1–100. CC: A; MC; EC; V. Also, high level glassware.

HUNSTANTON

Delawood Antiques, 10 Westgate, Hunstanton, Norfolk PE36 5AL. Prop: Mr R.C. Woodhouse. Tel: (01485) 532903. Est: 1981. Shop; open Monday, Wednesday, Friday and Saturday 10–5 other times by appointment. OLD stock - small. Spec: barometers; clocks; writing - general. PR: £1–1,000 plus. Also, repairs, restoration and valuations. Mem: B.W. & C.M.G.

KING'S LYNN

Old Curiosity Shop, 25 St. James Street, King's Lynn, Norfolk. Prop: Mrs R.S. Wright. Tel: (01553) 766591. Est: 1979. Shop; open Monday and Thursday to Saturday 11–5. Fairs: Alexandra Palace, Lee Valley, Newark. NEW stock - very small. OLD stock - medium. Spec: jewellery; lighting; original fittings; teddy bears; watches; writing - general. PR: £1–1,000. Also, teddy repairs.

NORTH WALSHAM

Kensington Pottery, Cat Pottery, 1 Grammar School Road, North Walsham, Norfolk NR28 9JH. Prop: Ken & Nick Allen. Tel: (01692) 402962. Est: 1953. Workshop; open Monday to Friday 9–5, Saturday 11–1. NEW stock - medium. Spec: pottery cats and dogs; some cat dolls. OLD stock. Spec: pottery cats and dogs. PR: £3–50. Corresp: French.

NORWICH

The Bear Shop, 18 Elm Hill, Norwich, Norfolk NR3 1HN. Prop: Robert J. Stone. Tel: (01603) 766866. Est: 1991. Shop; open Monday to Saturday 10–5. NEW stock - large. Spec: teddy bears, collectors bears and associated merchandise. PR: £2–500. CC: V; MC; A. Cata: 1 a year.

Cloisters Antiques Fair, St. Andrew's & Blackfriars Hall St. Andrew's Plain, Norwich, Norfolk. Tel: (01603) 425158. Est: 1975. Market stand; open Wednesday 8–3.30. NEW stock - very small. Spec: ceramics; china. OLD stock - medium. Spec: cameras; ceramics; china; costume jewellery; decorative; jewellery; photographic pictures; silver; spoons; stereoscopes; textiles; watches – wrist and chain. PR: £1–200.

Collectors Toyshop, St. Mary's Antique Centre, Duke Street, Norwich, Norfolk NR3 3AF. Prop: Steve Marshall. Tel: (01603) 457761. Est: 1985. Shop; open Monday to Saturday 10–4.30. Fairs: East Anglian. NEW stock - very small. Spec: diecast toys. OLD stock - medium. Spec: diecast toys; dolls/dolls clothes; teddy bears; tinplate toys; toys - general; toy soldiers; trains. PR: £1–300. CC: all major.

Mrs I.M. Eade, The Old Post Office Stores, The Green, Aldborough, Norfolk NR11 7AA. (•) Prop: K.R. & Mrs I.M. Eade. Tel: (01263) 768456. Est: 1990. Private premises; appointment necessary. Fairs: Anglian Fairs, Reepham, Norfolk; St. Andrews Hall, Norwich, Norfolk; Orpington Collectors (Summer only). OLD stock - medium. Spec: badges; metal buttons; medals; militaria. PR: £1–50.

Elm Hill Craft Shop, 12 Elm Hill, Norwich, Norfolk NR3 1HN. Prop: Christina Morris. Tel: (01603) 621076. Est: 1936. Shop; open Monday to Saturday 10–5. NEW stock - medium. Spec: dolls houses; miniatures; toys; dolls/dolls clothes. PR: 50p–£200. CC: AE; V; MC; A; D; EC. Mem: B.T.G. (associate member).

Elm Hill Stamps & Coins, 27 Elm Hill, Norwich, Norfolk NR3 1HN. Prop: J. Gotte. Tel: (01603) 627413. Est: 1950. Shop; open Monday to Saturday 9–5, except Thursday 9–1. NEW stock - very large. Spec: stamps; coins; medals. OLD stock - very large. Spec: stamps; coins; medals; antiquities. PR: £1–5,000. Corresp: German, Dutch. Mem: P.T.S., P.T.A.

Leona Levine, Silver Specialist, 35 St. Giles Street, Norwich, Norfolk NR2 1JN. Prop: Leona Levine & Bruce Thompson. Tel: & Fax: (01603) 628709. Est: 1865. Shop; open Monday to Saturday 9–5, closed Thursday. NEW stock - small and OLD stock - medium. Spec: silver; wine antiques; spoons; serviette rings; teapots. PR: £10–3,000. CC: V; MC; AE. Also, repairs and valuations. Corresp: French. Mem: B.A.D.A.

Pottergate Stamps & Cards, 5-7 Bagleys Court, Pottergate, Norwich, Norfolk NR2 1TW. Prop: A. Boulter, R. Ransom & D. Wild. Tel: (01603) 762916. Est: 1994. Shop; open Monday to Friday 9–5.30, Saturday 9–4.30. Fairs: major postcard & stamp fairs countrywide. NEW stock - medium. Spec: stamps; collectors albums. OLD stock - large. Spec: stamps; coins; medals. Cata: auction catalogues every 8 weeks. Mem: Philatelic Traders' Society; Postcard Traders Association.

St. Mary's Antique Centre, St. Mary's Plain, Duke Street, Norwich, Norfolk. Prop: Mrs Isobel Ford. Tel: (01603) 612582. Est: 1992. Shop; open Monday to Saturday 10–4.30. OLD general stock - medium. Spec: teddy bears; tinplate toys; bottles; china; clocks; costume jewellery; cutlery; diecast toys; dolls/dolls clothes; firearms; gramophone needle tins; jewellery; medals; militaria; model trains and cars; plates; toys - general; vases; Victorian; writing - general. PR: £1–1,000. CC: V; A.

St. Michael at Plea Antique & Collectors Centre, St. Michael at Plea Church, Bank Plain, Norwich, Norfolk NR2 4SN. Prop: David Clarke. Manager: Keith Burton. Tel: (01603) 618989. Est: 1986. Market stand; open Monday to Saturday 9.30–5. OLD stock - very large. Spec: Art Deco; badges; boxes; brass; ceramics; china; commemorative ware; cutlery; embroideries; glass; medals; militaria; plates; silver. PR: £1–1,000. Mem: P.B.F.A.

Trains & Olde Tyme Toys, 3 Aylsham Crescent, Aylsham Road, Norwich, Norfolk NR3 2RZ. Prop: Brian & Glenda Secker. Tel: (01603) 413585. Est: 1986. Shop; open Monday to Saturday 10–5. NEW and OLD stock - very large. Spec: diecast toys including Dinky, Corgi, Matchbox; model railways 'N' and 'OO' and 'O' tinplate; tinplate toys; toy soldiers. PR: £10–150. CC: A; D; V.

Tudor Rose D.H. Miniatures, 5 Taverham Craft Centre, Fir Covert Road, Taverham, Norwich NR8 6HT. Prop: D. Ames and J.E. Tudor. Tel: (01603) 260462. Est: 1993. Shop; Tuesday to Sunday 10.30–4.30. NEW stock - large. Spec: dolls houses; miniatures. PR: 50p–£400. CC: V; A; MC. Also, electrical service for dolls houses and gift vouchers available. Mem: M.I.N.T.A.

WELLS-NEXT-THE-SEA

Church Street Antiques, 2 Church Street, Wells-next-the-Sea, Norfolk. Prop: Lesley Ann Irons & Paula Ford. Tel: (01328) 711698. Est: 1988. Shop; open Tuesday to Sunday 10–4. OLD stock - medium. Spec: beadwork; buckles & clasps; buttons; costume; costume jewellery; crochet; embroideries; fashion accessories; hatpins & holders; kitchenalia; lace; pincushions; textiles. PR: 50p–£200.

Holkham Antiques, Main Road, Holkham, Nr. Wells-next-the-Sea, Norfolk. Prop: W. Jellings. Tel: (01692) 402424. Est: 1993. Shop; open most weekends Easter to mid-October 11–5. Fairs: I.A.C.F. Newark (Stand F025) and Ardingly. OLD stock - small. Spec: maritime/nautical. PR: £1–150. Also, decorative items for interior and garden designers.

NORTH YORKSHIRE

Including the Unitary Authority of York

FILEY

Cairncross and Sons, 31 Bellevue Street, Filey, North Yorkshire YO14 9HU. Prop: Mr
G.T.R. Cairncross. Tel: (01723) 513287. Est: 1971. Shop; open Monday to
Saturday 9.30–12.30 and 2.30–4.30, closed Wednesday November to March.
NEW stock - medium. Spec: badges; medals; militaria. OLD stock - very large.
Spec: badges; medals; militaria. PR: £1–100. CC: V; MC. Cata: monthly £1.50
each.

HARROGATE

Anglo–Scandinavian Antiques, The Ginnel Antique Centre, The Ginnel, Harrogate,
North Yorkshire HG1 2RB. Prop: Karin M.K. Lilleengen. Tel: (01423) 567182 or
Tel: & Fax: 508857. Est: 1974. Antique centre; open Monday to Saturday 9.30–
5.30. Fairs: Heritage Antiques Fairs in London. OLD stock - large. Spec:
inkstands; cutlery; egg cups. PR: £5–500. CC: MC; V. Corresp: German, Swedish,
Norwegian.

Michael Green Traditional Interiors, Library House, Regent Parade, Harrogate, North
Yorkshire HG1 5AN. Tel: (01423) 560452. Est: 1977. Shop; open Monday to
Friday 9–5.30, Saturday 9–4. OLD stock - medium. Spec: brass; china; copper;
decorative; horticultural & farm equipment; kitchenalia; laundry bygones; plates;
pottery; spoons; treen; writing - general. PR: £1–1,500. CC: all. Corresp: French.

Grove Collectors Centre, 55 Grove Road, Harrogate, North Yorkshire H61 5EP. Prop:
C. & S.J. Robinson, Harrogate Rustproofing Cntr Ltd. Tel: (01423) 561680. Est:
1980. Shop; open Monday to Saturday 10–4, closed Friday and Sunday. OLD
general stock - large. PR: £1–1,000.

Paraphernalia, 38A Cold Bath Road, Harrogate, North Yorkshire HG1 2JG. Prop:
Peter F. Hacker. Tel: (01423) 567968. Est: 1990. Shop; open Monday to Saturday
10–5. Fairs: Newark Showground. OLD stock - medium. Spec: bamboo; candles/
candlesticks; ceramics; china; commemorative ware; costume jewellery; cutlery;
decanters; Edwardian; egg cups; glass; Mauchline ware; Osborne plaques;
paperweights; plates; pottery; Royal memorabilia; Toby jugs; vases; Victorian;
Goss & Crested china. Also, small furniture.

Windmill Antiques, 4 Montpellier Mews, Harrogate, North Yorkshire HG1 2TJ. Prop:
Brian & Jean Tildesley. Tel: (01423) 530502, home (01845) 501330. Est: 1980.
Shop; open Monday to Saturday 10–5.30. NEW stock - medium. Spec: copies of
Victorian rocking horses. OLD stock - medium. Spec: genuine Victorian and
Edwardian rocking horses and childrens chairs; boxes; copper; brass. PR: £30–
5,000. CC: A; V; JCB. Cata: on rocking horses, by request. Also, 18th and 19th
Century furniture.

KNARESBOROUGH

Pennymead Books, 1 Brewerton Street, Knaresborough, North Yorkshire HG5 8AZ. Prop: David Druett. Tel: & Fax: (01423) 865962. Est: 1984. Private premises; appointment necessary. OLD stock - small. Spec: stamps. Cata: 2 a year. Also, philatelic auctioneer. Mem: P.B.F.A.

Gordon Reece Gallery, Finkle Street, Knaresborough, North Yorkshire HG5 8AA. Tel: (01423) 866219. Fax: 868165. Est: 1980. Shop; open 10.30–5, Sunday 2–5, closed Thursday. OLD stock - very large. Spec: beadwork; bronze; costume jewellery; embroideries; jewellery; miniatures; Oriental; pottery; rugs; sculpture; tribal; antique kilns. PR: £15–6,000. CC: A; V; EC; MC. Cata: permanent carpet catalogue only. Also, AA listed. Corresp: French.

PATELEY BRIDGE

Cat in the Window Antiques, 22 High Street, Pateley Bridge, Nr. Harrogate, North Yorkshire HG3 5JU. Prop: Mrs Sheila Morgan. Tel: (01423) 711343. Est: 1976. Shop; open Tuesday and Thursday to Saturday 2–5. OLD general stock - small. PR: £1–500.

Brian Loomes, Calf Haugh Farmhouse, Pateley Bridge, Harrogate, North Yorkshire HG3 5HW. Tel: & Fax: (01423) 711163. Est: 1966. Showroom; open Monday to Saturday 9–5. OLD stock - very large. Spec: antique clocks only. PR: £500–15,000.

PICKERING

'Country Collector', 11–12 Birdgate, (top of the Market Place), Pickering, North Yorkshire YO18 7AL. Prop: Mr & Mrs G. Berney. Tel: (01751) 477481. Est: 1990. Shop; open Tuesday and Thursday to Saturday 10–5. OLD stock - medium. Spec: Art Deco ceramics; blue & white china; decorative ceramics 1800–1940; Victoriana. PR: £5–1,000. CC: V; A.

RIPON

Dollshouse Gallery, 2 Bedern Bank, Ripon, North Yorkshire HG4 1ED. Prop: Christine O'Malley. Tel: (01765) 608851. Est: 1995. Shop; open Monday to Saturday 9–6.30, Sunday 11–4 in Summer/Spring, Monday to Saturday 9–4.45 in Winter. NEW stock - medium. Spec: dolls houses; dolls; miniatures; teddy bears; embroideries. PR: £1–400. CC: A; BC (Soon available). Also, cross stitch and needlecraft.

Sigma Antiques, Sigma, Water Skellgate, Ripon, North Yorkshire. HG4 1BQ. Prop: David Thomson. Tel: (01765) 603163. Fax: 690933. Est: 1966. Shop; open Monday to Saturday 10.30–5 or by appointment. OLD stock - large. Spec: writing. PR: £5–50,000. CC: V; MC; AE.

SELBY

Cawood Antiques, Sherburn Street, Cawood, Nr. Selby, North Yorkshire YO8 0SS. Prop: J.E. Gilham. Tel: (01757) 268533. Est: 1986. Shop and storeroom; open 7 days a week 8–4.30. Fairs: Newark International Antique Fair. OLD stock - very small. Spec: ceramics; china; clocks; firearms; Georgain; militaria; swords; Victorian. PR: £1–4,000. CC: A; V. Also, antique furniture restoration.

SHERBURN IN ELMET

Drey Antiques, 56 Low Street, Sherburn in Elmet, Leeds LS25 6BA. Prop: Valerie L. Keates. Tel: (01977) 681404. Est: 1984. Shop; open Monday, Tuesday & Thursday to Sunday 10–5. Fairs: various in North of England and Newark. NEW stock - very small. Spec: ceramics; commemorative ware; Toby jugs; Royal Doulton; Beswick figures. OLD general stock - medium. PR: £5–1,000. Also, a search service.

SKIPTON

Adamson Armoury, 70 Otley Street, Skipton, North Yorkshire BD20 1ET. Prop: J.K. Adamson. Tel: (01756) 791355. Est: 1977. Shop at: Otley Road, Skipton; open Monday 10–12, Tuesday to Saturday 10–4.15. OLD stock - medium. Spec: antique arms only. PR: £15–1,500.

Craven Model Centre, 1 Back O' the Beck, Water Street, Skipton, North Yorkshire BD23 1PH. Prop: Micheal Humphris. Est: 1992. Shop; open Wednesday to Saturday 10.30–4.30. Fairs: Heywood, Garstang, Skipton, Colne. OLD stock - very large. Spec: diecast toys; model trains, cars and aircraft; motoring; railways; tinplate toys; tins, signs & advertising; toys; transport; writing. OLD general stock - small. Spec: automobilia; diecast toys; dolls houses; horticultural & farm equipment; lawn mowers; maritime/nautical; toys; writing; traction/steam engines. PR: £10–100. Also, garden features, exhibition studies and automobilia.

Ings House Antiques, Thorpe Lane, Linton, Nr Skipton, North Yorkshire. Prop: Sonia & Patricia Barnes. Tel: (01756) 730301. Est: 1988. Barn/storeroom; open 7 days a week (advised to phone first). NEW and OLD general stock. PR: £10–500. Also, Victoriana and country furniture.

THIRSK

Victoria Miniatures, 1 Castlegate, Thirsk, North Yorkshire YO7 1HL. Prop: B.M., S.E. & A.R. Vie. Tel: (01845) 524600. Est: 1995. Shop; open Monday to Friday 9.30–5.30, Saturday 9–5, Wednesday half day, also a postal business. NEW stock - small. Spec: arts & crafts; dolls houses; model cars; clocks; fine art; teddy bears; diecast toys; dolls/dolls clothes; miniatures; model trains; toy soldiers. OLD stock - very small. Spec: diecast toys; model cars and trains; tinplate toys. PR: £1–300. CC: A; BC; V; E; D. Also, repair service for model trains, woodcarving, woodturning and miniature furniture making courses.

WHITBY

Allan Clewlow, 6 Skinner Street, Whitby, North Yorkshire YO21 3AJ. Tel: (01947) 821655. Shop; open Monday to Saturday 10–5, Sundays during the Summer. OLD general stock - medium. PR: £1–500.

John R. Hoggarth, Thorneywaite House, Glaisdale, Whitby, North Yorkshire YO21 2QU. Tel: & Fax: (01947) 897338. Est: 1976. Private premises; appointment necessary. OLD stock. Spec: Lord & Lady Baden–Powell memorabilia; scouting & guiding; football. PR: £1–200. Cata: 1 every 6 weeks.

YORK

The English Teddy Bear Co., 36 Stonegate, York YO1 2AS. Prop: Alise & Jonty Crossick & Dominic Richards. Tel: (01904) 622822. Fax: 620200. Est: 1990. Shop; open during business hours. NEW stock - large. Spec: teddy bears, limited edition bears and related gifts. PR: £5–200 (bears). CC: V; M. Cata: quarterly. *Also shops in:* Bath, Canterbury, Cambridge, Carnaby Street (London), Meadowhall, Newcastle, Oxford, Regent Street (London), Stratford, Windsor.

Harry Kipling, Back Lane, Holme on Spaldingmoor, York, North Yorkshire YO4 4AU. Tel: (01430) 860300. Est: 1970. Storeroom and private premises; open any time. Fairs: Newark. NEW stock - very small. OLD stock - medium. Spec: automobilia; badges; bicycles; diecast toys; dolls houses; fairground relics; gramophones; model trains, cars and aircraft; motor car mascots; motoring; musical instruments; scooters; tinplate toys; tins, signs and advertising; traction/ steam engines; transport. PR: £1–500. Also, motoring books.

National Railway Museum, Leeman Road, York, North Yorkshire YO2 4XJ. Prop: National Museum of Science and Industry. Tel: (01904) 621261. Fax: 611112. Est: 1975. Open Monday to Saturday 10–6, Sunday 11–6. NEW stock - large. Spec: railways; model trains; commemorative ware; traction/steam engines.

Pond Cottage Antiques, Pond Cottage, Brandsby Road, Stillington, York YO6 1NY. Prop: Christopher & Dianne Thurstans. Tel: & Fax: (01347) 810796. Est: 1973. Shop and private premises; open 7 days a week 9–dusk. OLD stock - medium. Spec: automobilia; decorative; kitchenalia; laundry bygones; metalware; motor car mascots; pottery; scales, weights & measures; spinning/spinning wheels; tools; treen; writing - general; quilts. PR: £1–300. Also, pine furniture.

Mary Shortle, 9 Lord Mayor's Walk, York, North Yorkshire. Tel: & Fax: (01904) 425168. Est: 1980. Shop; open 10–5. Fairs: Kensington, Victoria, Derby, Leicester. NEW and OLD stock - medium. Spec: dolls/dolls clothes; dolls houses; miniatures; rocking horses; teddy bears; toys - general; PR: £1–3,000. CC: V; MC; AE. Cata: 1 a year. Corresp: German. Also, artist dolls German, Swiss, American.

Stonegate Teddy Bears, 54 Stonegate, York, North Yorkshire YO1 2AS. Prop: K.J. Scott. Tel: (01904) 641074. Est: 1990. Shop; Monday to Friday 9.30–5, Saturday 9.30–5.30, Sunday 11–4. NEW stock - medium. Spec: teddy bears (traditional). PR: £1–500. CC: V; MC; D; AE; JCB. Also, teddy bear related items. Corresp: German.

NORTHAMPTONSHIRE

DAVENTRY

Kenna Models, 49 London End, Nr Daventry, Northamptonshire NN11 6DP. Prop: P.J. Kenna. Tel: & Fax: (01327) 260835. Est: 1986. Private premises; postal business only. OLD stock. Spec: model cars. PR: £70.

FINEDON

Aspidistra Antiques, 51 High Street, Finedon, Northamptonshire. Prop: Patricia & Geoffrey Moss. Tel: (01933) 680196. Est: 1991. Shop; open Monday to Saturday 9–5.30, Sunday 11–5. Fairs: Newark, Ardingly, Alexandra Palace, N.E.C. OLD stock - medium. Spec: arts & crafts; Art Deco; Art Nouveau; Victorian. PR: £1–1,000. CC: V; A. Also, restoration of furniture.

CB Antiques, 13 High Street, Finedon, Northamptonshire NN9 5JN. Prop: Mr R. Cheney. Tel: (01933) 681048. Est: 1992. Shop; open Monday to Saturday 9–5.30, Sundays 11–5. NEW stock - very small. OLD stock - medium. Spec: china; films & entertainment; fine art; glass; kitchenalia; oil lamps; Oriental; pottery; Victorian. PR: £1–1,000. Also, oak and country furniture and mahogany.

E.K. Antiques, 37 High Street, Finedon, Northamptonshire NN9 5JN. Prop: Edward Kubacki. Tel: (01933) 681882. Est: 1993. Shop; open Monday to Saturday 9–5, Sunday 11–5. OLD stock - medium. Spec: arts & crafts; Art Deco; Art Nouveau; barometers; boxes; brass; bronze; buttons; buttonhooks; candles/candlesticks; ceramics; clocks; costume jewellery; decanters; decorative; Edwardian; embroidered pictures; fine art; Georgian; glass and many others. PR: £1–5,000. Also, French polishing, furniture restoration and house clearances. Corresp: Danish, Polish.

FLORE

Christopher Jones Antiques, Flore House, The Avenue, Flore, Northamptonshire NN7 4LZ. Tel: (01327) 342165. Fax: 349230. Est: 1990. Shop; open Monday to Friday 10–5, Saturday 11–4.30, Sunday by appointment. Fairs: Olympia. OLD stock - large. Spec: antiques for interior decoration incl. Anglo-Indian, bamboo, birdcages, boxes, brass, bronze, ceramics, chandeliers, china, decanters, embroidered pictures, French, glass, inkstands, jardinières, lighting, marbles, metalware, mirrors, Mother-of-Pearl and many others.

NORTHAMPTON

Penny's Antiques, 83 Kettering Road, Northampton, Northamptonshire NN1 4AW. Prop: Mrs Penny Mawby. Tel: (01604) 32429. Est: 1975. Shop; open Monday to Wednesday and Friday 11–4, Saturday 10–5. OLD general stock - medium. PR: £1–200. CC: V; MC.

NORTHAMPTONSHIRE

Swapmeet Models, 'Threeways', Church Street, Brixworth, Northampton NN6 9BZ. Prop: Mr J.P. Smith & Mrs D.L. Rumble–Smith. Tel: & Fax: (01604) 882594. Est: 1988. Shop; open by appointment 7 days a week. Fairs: NEC Birmingham, Duxford, Donington. NEW stock - large Spec: diecast toys; dolls houses; model trains, cars and aircraft; railways; toys - general; toy soldiers; traction/steam engines; transport. OLD stock - large. Spec: diecast toys; dolls houses; model trains, cars and aircraft; railways; toys - general; toy soldiers; traction/steam engines; transport. PR: £4–50. CC: A; MC; V. Cata: 1 a week. Also, swaps cars for trains, vice-versa, etc. Mem: I.Mech.Eng.

TOWCESTER

Shelron, 9½ Brackley Road, Towcester, Northamptonshire NN12 6DH. Prop: Ron Grosvenor. Tel: & Fax: (01327) 350242. Est: 1986. Shop; open Tuesday to Friday 10–4, Saturday 10–1. OLD stock - very large. Spec: coins; badges; bookmarkers; bottles; canal memorabilia; diecast toys; films & entertainment; motoring; Royal memorabilia; sports; tins, signs & advertising; tobacco & associated. PR: 10p–£350. CC: A; V. Cata: mail bid sales, 9 a year. Mem: P.T.A., Forum of Small Businesses.

NORTHUMBERLAND

ALNWICK

Tamblyn, 12 Bondgate Without, Alnwick, Northumberland NE66 1PP. Prop: S.M. Hirst. Tel: (01665) 603024. Est: 1981. Shop; open 10–4.30. OLD stock - large. Spec: glass; arts & crafts; fine art; boxes; snuff boxes; treen. PR: £1–350. Also, Stone Age implements and Chinese artefacts.

BERWICK-UPON-TWEED

Treasure Chest, 43 Bridge Street, Berwick-on-Tweed, Northumberland. Prop: Yvonne Scott. Tel: (01289) 307736. Est: 1989. Shop; open Friday to Wednesday 10.30–4. OLD general stock - small. Spec: Art Deco; boxes; brass; buttons; buttonhooks; china; commemorative ware; costume jewellery; cutlery; decanters; egg cups; fashion accessories; glass; hatpins & holders; jewellery; kitchenalia; lace; luggage; Mauchline ware; plates; pottery; spectacles, lorgnettes & monacles; Victoriana. PR: £1–800. Also, restoration of china. Corresp: French.

CRAMLINGTON

British Toy Soldiers, 29 Greenlaw Road, Southfield Green, Cramlington, Northumberland NE23 6NP. Prop: Norman Joplin. Tel: (01670) 714522. Fax: 590683. Est: 1983. Private premises; postal business only. Fairs: British Toy Soldier & Figure Show - Royal National Hotel, London (last Saturday in June & first Saturday in December) OLD stock - large. Spec: toy soldiers; lead figures. PR: £5–3,000. Cata: bi-monthly. Also, organiser of British Toy Soldier & Figure Show and consultant to Christie's, South Kensington. Mem: British Model Soldier Society.

FELTON

Felton Park Antiques, Felton Park, Felton, Nr. Morpeth, Northumberland NE6 5 9HN. Prop: Dennis and Anne Burton. Tel: & Fax: (01670) 787319. Est: 1973. Storeroom; appointment necessary. Fairs: Newark, Ardingly, Harrogate, Shepton. OLD stock - very small. Spec: ceramics; pottery. PR: £1–100. Also, restoration of furniture only. Corresp: Italian, French.

HEXHAM

Fewsters Model Shop, 44 Priestopple, Hexham, Northumberland NE46 1PP. Shop manager: Scott Wilson. Tel: (01434) 603516. Fax: 600442. Est: 1991. Shop; open 9–5. NEW stock - large. Spec: radio controlled models; model cars; constructional toys; diecast toys; dolls houses. PR: £2–500. CC: MC; V; D; JCB.

WARKWORTH

Bank of Nostalgia, 19 Castle Street, Warkworth, Northumberland NE65 0UW. Prop: Mr T.G. Mohon. Tel: (01665) 711799. Est: 1993. Shop; open daily 11–5. OLD stock - medium. Spec: diecast toys; commemorative ware; model trains; toys - general; curios. PR: £1–150. CC: all major.

NOTTINGHAMSHIRE

NEWARK-ON-TRENT

The Keyhole, Dragonwyck, Far Back Lane, Farnsfield, Newark, Nottinghamshire NG22 8 Prop: George & Valerie Olifent. Tel: & Fax: (01623) 882590. Est: 1983. Private premises; appointment necessary. OLD stock - very small. Spec: keys and locks. PR: £2.50–500. Also, repair and refurbishment. Mem: Master Locksmiths Association.

Newark Antiques Centre, Regent House, Lombard Street, Newark-on-Trent, Nottinghamshire NG24 1XP. Prop: Mr Tinsley. Tel: (01636) 605504. Est: 1988. Antique centre; open Monday to Saturday 9.30–5, Sundays and Bank Holidays 11–4. NEW stock - very small. OLD stock - very large. Spec: Art Nouveau; Art Deco; badges; boxes; brass; cameras; ceramics; china; clocks; commemorative ware; costume jewellery; Georgian; glass; medals; mirrors; pottery; silver; Staffordshire; textiles; toys - general. PR: £1–2,500. Also, furniture upholstery, caning, fabrics, free valuations, metal polishing and clock mending. Corresp: French, German.

Scallywags, Market Place, Ollerton, Newark, Nottinghamshire NG22 9BL. Prop: Tony & Barbara Hesford. Tel: (01623) 825600. Est: 1994. Shop; open Tuesday to Saturday 10–5.30, Sunday 2–4. NEW general stock - medium. Spec: dolls houses; miniatures. PR: £1–100. CC: A; EC; MC; V; D. Also, specialist items made to order and advisory service. Corresp: French. Mem: M.I.N.T.A.

Tudor Rose Antiques Centre, 12–13 Market Place, Newark, Nottinghamshire NG24 1DY. Prop: Mr D.H. & Mrs C. Rose. Tel: (01636) 610311. Est: 1995. Shop; open Monday to Saturday 10–5. Fairs: Stafford (3 day), Bowman, Newark, I.A.C.F. OLD general stock- large. Spec: quality antiques (datelined 1940); writing - general. PR: £1–5,000. CC: MC; A; V; D. Also, furniture restoration.

Simon Wilson, Unit 52, Newark Antique Centre, Lombard Street, Newark, Nottinghamshire.

NOTTINGHAM

The Chassis Shop, Leonard House, 99 Annesley Road, Hucknall, Nottinghamshire NG15 7DR. Prop: J. Reeve. Tel: & Fax: (0115) 963-3667. Est: 1957. Shop; open Monday to Saturday 9–5, half day Wednesday. NEW stock - medium. Spec: model cars; diecast toys; tinplate toys. PR: £1–200. CC: A; V. Corresp: French.

Richard Davie Autographs, 11A Lenton Avenue, The Park, Nottingham NG7 1DX. Tel: (0115) 950-8828. Fax: 950-8269. E-Mail: 100737.2131@compuserve. Est: 1994. Private premises; appointment necessary. Fairs: UACC show - London and New York, Koschal Fair - Florida. OLD stock - large. Spec: signed photographs; autograph letters. PR: £50–5,000. CC: V; A; MC. Cata: every 2 months. Mem: U.A.C.C., C.A.C.C., Manuscript Society.

Melville Kemp Limited, 79–81 Derby Road, Nottingham, Nottinghamshire NG5 1BA. Tel: & Fax: (0115) 941-7055. Shop; Monday to Wednesday, Friday and Saturday 9–5.30. Fairs: N.E.C., Grosvenor House, Olympia. NEW and OLD stock - very large. Spec: jewellery; silver. PR: £20–5,000. CC: most. Corresp: French. Mem: N.A.G., L.A.P.A.D.A., National Registered Valuers.

David & Carole Potter, 76 Derby Road, Nottingham, Nottinghamshire NG1 5FD. Tel: (0115) 941-7911. Est: 1966. Shop; open Tuesday to Saturday 10–4. OLD general stock - medium. CC: V; AE; DC. Mem: L.A.P.A.D.A.

The Rather Nice Bear Shop, The Sherwood Bear Clinic, 3rd Floor, 5 The Poultry, Nottingham NG1 2HW. Prop: Russell Sherwood. Tel: (0115) 924-3276. Fax: 950-8045. Est: 1993. Shop; open Monday to Friday 9.30–4.30, Saturday 9.30–3.30 please ring first. Fairs: Kensington Bear Fair, Ruddington Bear Fest. NEW stock - very small. Spec: teddy bears; dolls/dolls clothes; dolls houses; rocking horses. OLD stock - very small. Spec: teddy bears; dolls/dolls clothes; dolls houses; rocking horses. PR: £25–500. Also, restorers of bears, dolls, puppets and rocking horses. Corresp: French, German. Mem: B.C.U.K.

Small World, Old Melton Road, Plumtree, Nottingham NG12 5NH. Prop: R.E. Rampley. Tel: (0115) 937-6771. Est: 1988. Workshop; appointment necessary. NEW stock - very small. Spec: dolls houses. PR: £100–1,000. CC: V; MC; A.

Val Smith Coins, 170 Derby Road, Nottingham, Nottinghamshire NG7 1LR. Tel: (0115) 978-1194. Est: 1966. Shop; open Monday to Saturday 10–5. OLD stock - medium. Spec: badges; buttons; diecast toys; medals; militaria; money boxes; paper money; police memorabilia; silver; toy soldiers; coins. PR: £1–500.

Top Hat Antiques Centre, 70-72 Derby Road, Nottingham, Nottinghamshire NG1 5FD. Prop: John & Sylvia Weedon. Tel: (0115) 941-9143. Est: 1978. Shop; open Monday to Saturday 9.30–5. OLD general stock - very small. PR: £1–10,000. CC: A; V; AE; DC. Mem: Nottingham Antique Dealers Association.

Trident Arms, 74 Derby Road, Nottingham, Nottinghamshire NG1 5FD. Prop: Mr Michael Long. Tel: (0115) 947-4137. Fax: 941-4199. Est: 1981. Shop; open Monday to Friday 9.30–5.15, Saturday 10–4. Fairs: London, Nottingham, N.E.C. Birmingham, Leeds etc. NEW and OLD stock - very large. Spec: arms & armour; buttons; firearms; militaria; Police memorabilia; tribal; medals; maritime/nautical. PR: £1–5,000. CC: MC; V; A; AE. Mem: Gun Trade Association.

SOUTHWELL

Facet Books, 15 Marrison Way, Southwell, Nottinghamshire NG25 OED. Prop: J.B.F. Allinson. Tel: (01636) 814735, mobile (0589) 818622. Est: 1983. Private premises; strictly by appointment only. Fairs: 2 or 3 a year. OLD stock - very small. Spec: Guiness items; comic give-aways; film/TV toys. PR: £1–100. Cata: 1 a year. Corresp: German.

SUTTON-IN-ASHFIELD

Harringtons, 51 Outram Street, Sutton-in-Ashfield, Nottinghamshire NG17 4BG. Prop: Mr G.E. Bramwell. Tel: (01623) 440594. Est: 1990. Shop; open Monday to Saturday 9–5. NEW stock - large. Spec: diecast toys; model trains and cars. OLD stock - very small. Spec: diecast toys; model trains and cars; tinplate toys. PR: £5–200. Mem: F.S.B.

OXFORDSHIRE

ABINGDON

Robert Longstaff Workshops, Appleton Road, Longworth, Oxfordshire OX13 5EF. (•) Tel: (01865) 820206. Fax: 821089. Est: 1976. Shop and workshops; open Monday to Thursday 9–5, Friday 9–3, weekends by appointment. Fairs: many. NEW stock - small. Spec: arts & crafts; Art Deco; Art Nouveau; clocks; constructional toys; dolls houses; musical instruments; toys - general. PR: 50p–£1,500. CC: V; A. Cata: 1 a year, with updates £2.50. Corresp: French, German. Mem: B.T.H.A.

BICESTER

Collector Merchants Ltd., Unit 10, Murdock Road, Bicester, Oxfordshire OX6 7PP. Tel: (01869) 369400. Fax: 369500. Est: 1994. Wholesale storeroom; open 6 days a week 8.30–5.30, Thursday 8.30–9. NEW general stock - very large. PR: minimum order £100 plus. CC: A; V; DC. Cata: monthly.

BLEWBURY

Blewbury Antiques, London Road, Blewbury, Oxfordshire OX11 9NX. Prop: Sheila & Eric Richardson. Tel: (01235) 850366. Est: 1971. Shop; open Wednesday to Monday 10–6. NEW general stock - very small. Spec: oil lamp parts (chimneys etc.). OLD stock - medium. Spec: Edwardian; Victorian; 20th Century collectables.

BURFORD

Jonathan Fyson Antiques, 50/52 High Street, Burford, Oxfordshire OX18 4QF. Tel: & Fax: (01993) 823204. Est: 1970. Shop; open Monday to Saturday 9.30–5.30. OLD stock - medium. Spec: brass; candles/candlesticks; chandeliers; glass; jewellery; lighting; metalware; mirrors; objets de vertu; treen. PR: £10–5,000. CC: A; V. Also, valuations for probate and insurance. Corresp: French. Mem: Cotswold Antique Dealers Association.

Gateway Antiques, Cheltenham Road, Burford Roundabout, Burford, Oxfordshire OX18 4JA. Prop: Michael Ford & Paul Brown. Tel: & Fax: (01993) 823678. Est: 1985. Shop; open Monday to Saturday 10–5.30, Sunday 2–5. OLD stock - very large. Spec: Anglo-Indian; arts & crafts; Art Nouveau; brass; candles/candlesticks; clocks; Edwardian; embroidered pictures; French; Georgian; glass; metalware; mirrors; Oriental; pottery; samplers; Staffordshire; tea caddies; treen; Victorian. PR: £5–6,000. CC: A; V. Cata: annually. Also, a courier service and shipping. Corresp: French, German. Mem: Cotswold Antique Dealers Association (C.A.D.A.).

Tony Radman, Denver House, 17 Witney Street, Burford, Oxfordshire OX18 4RU. Tel: (01993) 822040. Fax: 822769. Est: 1983. Shop; appointment necessary. OLD stock. Spec: medals; orders; decorations; badges; militaria; stamps; covers; banknotes & coins; tokens. CC: all. Cata: many on different subjects. Corresp: Italian, French, Russian. Mem: O.M.R.S., O.M.S.A.

Manfred Schotten Antiques, 109 High Street, Burford, Oxfordshire OX18 4RH. Tel: (01993) 822302. Fax: 822055. Shop; open Monday to Saturday 9–5.30. Fairs: Fine Art and Antiques Fair, Olympia (June). OLD stock - large. Spec: sporting antiques - golf, tennis, football, rugby, cricket, rowing etc. PR: £20–60,000. CC: V; MC; A; AE. Corresp: German. Mem: C.A.D.A.

DEDDINGTON

Castle Antiques Ltd., Manor Farm, Clifton, Deddington, Oxfordshire. Prop: John & Judy Vaughan. Tel: (01869) 338688. Est: 1974. Shop; open Monday to Saturday 10–6, Sunday 10–4. OLD stock. Spec: brass; ceramics; copper; decorative; glass; kitchenalia; metalware; Victorian. PR: £1–1,000. CC: V; A; AE. Also, garden furniture and furniture 1750–1930. Mem: L.A.P.A.D.A.

HENLEY-ON-THAMES

Russell Jones Books, The Coach House, High Street, Hurley, Berkshire SL6 5NB. (•) Tel: (01628) 824237. Est: 1940. Private premises; appointment necessary. NEW stock - medium and OLD stock - large. Spec: automobilia; constructional toys; diecast toys; horticultural and farm equipment; motoring; photographic pictures; traction/steam engines; transport. PR: £20–400. Cata: monthly. Corresp: French.

OXFORD

Auto Models, The Collectors Corner, Evans Yard, Bicester OX6 7TJ. (•) Tel: (01869) 323252. Fax: 324242. Est: 1983. Shop; open 6 days a week 8.30–5.30. NEW stock - very large. Spec: diecast toys. OLD stock - small. Spec: diecast toys. PR: £2–300 (£25 average). CC: A; V. Cata: monthly.

Reginald Davis Ltd., 34 High Street, Oxford, Oxfordshire OX1 4AN. Tel: (01865) 248347. Fax: 200915. Est: 1939. Shop; open Monday to Wednesday, Friday and Saturday 9–4.30. NEW stock - medium. Spec: jewellery; silver. OLD stock - medium. Spec: arts & crafts; jewellery; silver. PR: £10–5,000. CC: V; AE; A. Also, repairs and valuations. Mem: N.A.G., B.A.D.A.

The English Teddy Bear Co., 135 High Street, Oxford OX1 4DN. Prop: Alise & Jonty Crossick & Dominic Richards. Tel: & Fax: (01865) 721165. Est: 1990. Shop; open during business hours. NEW stock - large. Spec: teddy bears, limited edition bears and related gifts. PR: £5–200 (bears). CC: V; M. Cata: quarterly. *Also shops in:* Bath, Canterbury, Cambridge, Carnaby Street (London), Meadowhall, Newcastle, Regent Street (London), Stratford, Windsor, York.

TETSWORTH

Joanna C. Glyn, Fourways, Station Road, Chinnor, Oxfordshire OX9 4QB. (•) Prop: Swan Holdings. Tel: (01844) 281777. Fax: 281770. Est: 1995. Market stand at: The Swan at Tetsworth Antiques Centre, High Street, Tetsworth, Oxfordshire; open 7 days a week 10–6. OLD stock - very small. Spec: fine British porcelain c.1740–1820. PR: £100–2,000. CC: A; V etc.

OXFORDSHIRE

THAME

Key Miniatures, 7 Swan Walk, Upper High Street, Thame, Oxfordshire OX9 3HN. Prop: Veronica Keating. Tel: (01844) 216680. Fax: (01296) 748232. Est: 1994. Shop; open Monday to Saturday 10–5, closed Wednesday. NEW stock - medium. Spec: dolls houses; miniatures; teddy bears. PR: £1–500. CC: MC; V; A; D. Mem: M.I.N.T.A.

WALLINGFORD

Lamb Arcade Antiques Centre, High Street, Wallingford, Oxon OX10 OBX. Tel: (01491) 835766. Est: 1979. 30 shops and showcases; open Monday to Friday 10–5, Saturday 10–5.30, Sundays and Bank Holidays 11–5. OLD stock. Spec: antique porcelain, glass, rugs, boxes, crafts, jewellery and linen. Also, furniture and brass bedsteads, furniture restorer and a coffee shop and winebar.

O'Donnell Antiques, 26 High Street, Wallingford, Oxfordshire OX10 8EJ. Prop: Lin & Chris O'Donnell. Tel: (01491) 839332. Est: 1973. Shop; open Monday to Friday 9.30–1 and 2–5, Sunday 11–5. Fairs: Fawley Court, Henley-on-Thames, Kempton Park. OLD general stock - medium. Spec: boxes; candles/candlesticks; copper; kitchenalia; lighting; metalware; oil lamps; Oriental; rugs; Staffordshire; Victorian. PR: £1–1,000. CC: V; MC; EC; A. Corresp: French.

Tags Antiques, The Lamb Arcade, High Street, Wallingford, Oxfordshire OX10 0BS. Prop: Tom & Ann Green. Tel: (01491) 835048. Est: 1979. Shop; open 7 days a week 10–5. OLD stock - small. Spec: arms & armour; china; costume jewellery; dolls houses; jewellery; militaria; tools. PR: £1–1,000. Mem: Thames Vallery Dealers Association.

WITNEY

'Teddy Bears' of Witney, 99 High Street, Witney, Oxfordshire OX8 6LY. Prop: Ian Pout. Tel: (01993) 702616. Fax: 702344. Est: 1985. Shop; open Monday to Friday 9.30–5.30, Saturday 9.30–5, Sunday 10.30–4.30. Fairs: August Bearfest. NEW and OLD stock - very large. Spec: teddy bears. PR: £20–2,000. CC: V; MC. Cata: 1 a year.

WOODSTOCK

Asylum House Antiques, 7 Market Street, Woodstock, Oxfordshire OX20 1SU. Prop: Peter Jacobs. Tel: (01993) 813704. Fax: 813705. Est: 1988. Private premises; appointment necessary. OLD stock - small. Spec: Georgian glasses and decanters. PR: £50–3,000.

Bees Antiques, 30 High Street, Woodstock, Oxfordshire OX20 1TG. Prop: Jo & Jim Bateman. Tel: (01993) 811062. Open Monday to Saturday 10–1 and 1.30–5, Sunday 11–5, closed Tuesday. Fairs: T.V.A.D.A. at Eton and Oxford, Marlborough. OLD stock - small. Spec: ceramics; glass; brass; copper; jewellery; china; decanters; egg cups; inkstands; jardinières; paperweights; plates; pottery; scent bottles; teapots; Toby Jugs; vases. PR: £10–2,000. CC: V; MC; EC; JCB. Corresp: French, Dutch. Mem: T.V.A.D.A.

Hall–Bakker Decorative Arts, Span Antiques, 6 Market Place, Woodstock, Oxfordshire. Prop: Elisabeth Hall–Bakker & Les Hall. Tel: & Fax: (01993) 705275. Shop; open Monday to Saturday 10–1 and 2–5, Sunday 1–5. Fairs: Giant Alexandra Palace (Stand R29), Birmingham N.E.C. (April & August), Kensington Town Hall - London Decorative Arts Fairs. OLD stock - small. Spec: arts & crafts - brass and copper; Art Deco; Art Nouveau - incl. pewter; art pottery; glass. PR: £5–600. Corresp: Dutch, French, German. Mem: T.V.A.D.A.

Le Print Antique Centre, 16 High Street, Woodstock, Oxfordshire OX20 1TF. Manager: G.G. Beament. Tel: (01993) 813900. Est: 1970's. Shop with 20 plus dealers; open Monday to Saturday 10–5, Sunday 11–5. NEW general stock - small. OLD stock - medium. Spec: Art Deco; Art Nouveau; brass; ceramics; china; commemorative ware; cutlery; glass; metalware; paperweights; pottery; silver; Victorian. PR: £1–1,000. CC: V; A; MC. Also, a travel agency on the premises.

SHROPSHIRE

BRIDGNORTH

Bridgnorth Miniatures, Museum Shop, 1 Postern Gate, High Street, Bridgnorth, Shropshire WV16 4AA. Prop: Linda Keeling. Tel: (01746) 768085. Est: 1994. Shop; open Tuesday to Saturday 10–5. NEW stock - medium. Spec: dolls houses; miniatures. PR: 10p–£500 (approx.).

CHURCH STRETTON

Antiques on the Square, 2 Sandford Court, Sandford Avenue, Church Stretton, Shropshire SY6 6BH. Prop: Mr C.J. Radford. Tel: (01694) 724111. Fax: 724138. Est: 1988. Shop; open 7 days a week 9.30–1 and 2–5. Fairs: Loughborough Deco Fair, Warwick Deco Fair. OLD stock - large. Spec: Art Nouveau; Art Deco; Art Deco china; ceramics; arts & crafts; Clarice Cliff china; Thirties memorabilia. PR: £30–500 plus. CC: AE; V; MC; D; E. Cata: monthly. Also, Central Antique Couriers (export). Corresp: French, German.

IRONBRIDGE

Bears on the Square, 2 The Square, Ironbridge, Shropshire TF8 7AQ. Prop: Bernard Beech and Margaret Phillips. Tel: (01952) 433924. Fax: 433926. Est: 1993. Shop; open 7 days a week 10.30–4.30. NEW stock - small. Spec: teddy bears. OLD stock - very small. Spec: teddy bears. PR: £5–500. CC: all. Cata: 1 a year. Corresp: French, German.

Ironbridge Antique Centre, Dale End, Ironbridge, Telford TF8 7DS. Prop: F.G. Cooke. Tel: (01952) 433784. Est: 1981. Warehouse; open Monday to Saturday 10–5, Sunday 2–5. NEW stock - medium. Spec: writing. OLD stock - large. Spec: general antiques. PR: 50p–£1,000.

Ironbridge Toy Museum, 1 The Square, Ironbridge, Shropshire TF8 7AQ. Prop: Bernard Beech & Margaret Phillips. Tel: & Fax: (01952) 433926. Est: 1991. Shop; open 7 days a week 10–5. NEW stock - small. Spec: diecast toys; games; model cars; tinplate toys; toys - general. OLD stock - very small. Spec: constructional toys; diecast toys; dolls/dolls clothes; dolls houses; games; model trains and cars; tinplate toys; toys - general. PR: £2–250. CC: all. Corresp: French, German.

LUDLOW

Curiosity Shop, 127 Old Street, Ludlow, Shropshire SY8 1NU. Prop: Mr J.D. Luffman. Tel: & Fax: (01584) 875927. Est: 1966. Shop; open 6 days a week 9–5 or by appointment. OLD general stock - very small. Spec: barometers; clocks; fine art; horsebrasses & harnesses; metalware; militaria; musical boxes; objets de vertu; oil lamps; Oriental; samplers; scientific instruments; swords; taxidermy. PR: £25–10,000.

Little Paws, 4 Castle Street, Ludlow, Shropshire SY8 1AT. Prop: Martyn Rees–Evans. Tel: (01584) 875286. Est: 1995. Shop; open Monday to Saturday 10–5.30. NEW stock - very small. Spec: teddy bears. PR: £5–300. CC: V; AE.

Teme Valley Antiques, 1 The Bull Ring, Ludlow, Shropshire SY8 1AD. Prop: C.S. Harvey. Tel: (01584) 874686. Est: 1979. Shop; open Monday to Saturday 10–5. NEW stock - small. Spec: cuff links; jewellery; silver. OLD stock - small. Spec: spoons; vases; ceramics; Victorian; china; wine antiques; cuff links; cutlery; Edwardian; Georgian; jewellery; miniatures; objets de vertu; plates; portrait miniatures; serviette rings; silver; teapots. PR: £5–2,500. CC: V; A; AE; DC. Also, valuations. Mem: National Association of Goldsmiths.

OSWESTRY

Newgate Antiques, 20 and 35 Church Street, Oswestry, Shropshire SY11 2SP. Prop: John & Beryl Read. Tel: (01691) 679786. Fax: 679995. Est: 1961. Shop open Monday to Saturday 9.30–5. NEW and OLD general stock - very small. PR: £5– 500. CC: V; A.

SHREWSBURY

F.C. Manser & Son Ltd., 53/4 Wyle Cop, Shrewsbury, Shropshire SY1 1XJ. Tel: (01743) 351120. Fax: 271047. Est: 1944. Shop; open 9–5.30 except Thursday 9–1, Saturday 9–5, closed Sunday. Fairs: L.A.P.A.D.A. (January). NEW general stock - medium. OLD general stock - very large. PR: £5–15,000. CC: V; A. Also, full restoration services and valuations. Mem: L.A.P.A.D.A.

Tiffany Antiques, Unit 1, Welsh Bridge Ant. Cent 135 Frankwell, Shrewsbury, Shropshire SY3 8JX. Prop: A. Wilcox. Tel: (01270) 257425. Mobile: (0370) 380261. Est: 1989. Shop; open 10–5.30. OLD general stock - small. Spec: bottles; boxes; brass; buttonhooks; cameras; china; copper; corkscrews & bottle openers; fishing; glass; golf; horsebrasses & harnesses; inkstands; jewellery; kitchenalia; Mauchline ware; metalware; Mother-of-Pearl; musical instruments; Osborne Plaques.

Welsh Bridge Antique Centre, 135 Frankwell, Shrewsbury, Shropshire SY3 8JX. Prop: Peter Commor. Tel: & Fax: (01743) 248822. Est: 1994. Shop; open Monday to Saturday 9.30–5.30, Sunday 1–5. OLD general stock - medium. PR: £1–500.

WHITCHURCH

The Rocking Horse Workshop, The Cottage Farm, Tilstock Road, Whitchurch, Shropshire SY13 3JQ. Prop: Mr D. & Mrs N. Kiss. Tel: (01948) 666777. Est: 1988. Private premises; open Monday to Saturday 9–5. Fairs: 8 a year, varied. NEW and OLD stock - very small. Spec: rocking horses. PR: £50–5,000. CC: A; V; DC. Cata: available on request. Also, rocking horse gifts (£1–50).

Something Else, 60 High Street, Whitchurch, Shropshire SY13 1BB. Prop: Janet & Rod Forster. Tel: (01948) 664780. Est: 1989. Shop; open Monday to Saturday 9.30–5. OLD stock - medium. Spec: automobilia; badges; ceramics; constructional toys; Diecast toys; games; gramophones; militaria; model trains and cars; motoring; oil lamps; timplate toys; tins, signs & advertising; toys - general; traction/steam engines; transport. PR: £1–250.

SOMERSET

AXBRIDGE

John Hawley MBHI Antique Clocks, Court Barn, Church Lane, Badgworth, Axbridge, Somerset BS26 2QP. Tel: (01934) 733444. Est: 1970. Private premises; appointment necessary. Fairs: Brunel and Midlands watch and clock fairs. OLD stock - very small. Spec: clocks longcases, bracket, wall and carriage; tools horological; barometers. PR: £100–3,000. Also, restoration of antique clocks. Mem: British Horological Institute; British Guild of Watch & Clockmakers.

BRIDGWATER

Bridgwater Antiques Market, Marycourt Antiques Mart, St. Marys Street, Bridgwater, Somerset. Contact: Colin Munro. Tel: (01823) 451433. Market stand; open Friday and Saturday 9.30–5. OLD stock - medium. Spec: costume jewellery; glass; jewellery; lace; toys - general; Victorian. PR: £1–700. Also, small furniture.

Bridgwater Collectors Shop, Unit 6, Marycourt Shopping Mall, 39 St. Marys Street, Bridgwater, Somerset. Prop: W.I. Loudon. Tel: (01278) 431112. Est: 1993. Shop; open Monday to Saturday 9.30–5. NEW stock - very small. OLD stock - large. Spec: coins; medals; militaria; diecast toys; phonecards; police memorabilia; paper money. PR: £1 plus.

BURNHAM-ON-SEA

Castle Antiques, Victoria Court, Victoria Street, Burnham-on-Sea, Somerset. Prop: T.C. German. Tel: & Fax: (01278) 785031. Est: 1953. Shop; open 10–5, closed Wednesday. OLD general stock. PR: £30–3,000. CC: A; V; JCB; D; MC. Corresp: German, Scandinavian, French.

The Command Post, 23 Ashcott Close, Burnham-on-Sea, Somerset TA8 1HW. Prop: Tony Moore. Tel: (01278) 786858. Est: 1989. Private premises; appointment necessary. Fairs: Gloucester, Bristol, Malvern, Shepton Mallet, Plymouth, Exeter. NEW stock - very small. Spec: toy soldiers. OLD stock - small. Spec: toy soldiers. PR: £3–250. Cata: 4 a year to mail order customers. Also, dog related items (cards, mugs, memos etc.).

CHEDDAR

One Twelfth Homes, Unit 9 Wessex Business Centre, Wedmore Road, Cheddar, Somerset BS27 3EB. Prop: Bess & Terry Childs. Tel: (01934) 744766. Private premises; open 5 days a week 9–6 and postal business. Fairs: 42 attended a year. NEW general stock - very small. Spec: dolls houses. PR: £70–500. CC: V; MC; D; A; CN. Cata: annually.

CREWKERNE

Oscars Antiques, 13-15 Market Square, Crewkerne, Somerset TA18 7LE. Prop: Mr Bryan & Mrs Helen Hall. Tel: (01460) 72718. Est: 1966. Shop; open Monday to Saturday 10–1 and 2.15–5. NEW general stock - large. OLD general stock - large. PR: £1–1,500.

SOMERSET

Margaret Spencer & Co., Goulds Nap, Chard Road, Crewkerne, Somerset TA18 8BA. Prop: Margaret & Marion Spencer. Tel: (01460) 72362. Est: late 1960's. Storeroom; open Monday to Friday 9–5. NEW stock - small. Spec: rocking horse accessories. PR: £1–100. CC: MC; V. Cata: 1 a year.

FROME

Margaret's Miniatures, 13 Catherine Hill, Frome, Somerset BA11 1BZ. Prop: Margaret & Brian Burgin. Tel: (01373) 453727. Fax: 452989. Est: 1993. Shop; open Tuesday to Saturday 10–5. Fairs: Bath, Bristol, Salisbury, Winchester, Sherborne. NEW stock - very large. Spec: dolls/dolls clothes; dolls houses; miniatures. Cata: 1 a year. Also, mail order service, Dolls House Clubs discount.

ILMINSTER

M. Wood Ceramics, Church Cottage, Donyatt, Nr. Ilminster, Somerset. Tel: (01460) 54283. Est: 1979. Private premises; appointment necessary. Fairs: Exeter, Westpoint. OLD general stock - small. Spec: antique pottery, porcelain and glass. PR: £1–300.

TAUNTON

Taunton Antiques Market, 27 Silver Street, Taunton, Somerset TA1 3DH. Prop: Bath Antiques Market Ltd. Tel: & Fax: (01823) 289327. Est: 1978. Market with over 100 dealers; open Mondays (inc. Bank Holidys) 9–4. OLD general stock.

WILLITON

Blackmores, 6 High Street, Williton, Somerset TA4 4NW. Prop: Mrs Mary Lintott. Tel: (01984) 632227. Fax: 641147. Shop; open Monday to Friday 9.30–5, Saturday 9.30–1. NEW general stock - medium. OLD stock - small. PR: £1–100. CC: MC; V. Also, a tearoom. Mem: B.A.

WIVELISCOMBE

Heads N' Tails, Bournes House, 41 Church Street, Wiveliscombe, Somerset TA4 2LT. Prop: D.N. McKinley. Tel: (01984) 623097. Fax: 624556. Est: 1981. Private premises; appointment necessary. NEW and OLD stock - medium. Spec: taxidermy; fishing. PR: £5–5,000. CC: V; MC; AE. Cata: available on request. Also, prop hire for film and TV photoshoot etc., commissions and restoration work. Mem: Guild of Taxidermists.

YEOVIL

John Hamblin, Unit 6, 15 Oxford Road, Pen Mill Trading Estate, Yeovil, Somerset BA21 5HR. Tel: & Fax: (01935) 71154. Est: 1994. Shop; open Monday to Saturday 9–5. NEW stock - small. Spec: model cars and aircraft. PR: £5–200. CC: V; A; EC; MC. Cata: 2 every 3 months.

Teddy's Corner, Farquharsons, Middle Street, Yeovil, Somerset BA20 1JZ. Prop: John & Fran Farquharson. Tel: (01935) 75803. Est: 1990. Shop; open Monday to Saturday 9–5. NEW stock - medium. Spec: teddy bears. PR: £1–500. CC: BC; MC; V. Also, sewing machines and haberdashery.

Yeovil Collectors Centre, 16 Hendford, Yeovil, Somerset BA20 1TE. Prop: Barry Scott. Tel: (01935) 33739. Est: 1993. Shop; open Monday to Saturday 9.30–6, closed some Tuesdays and Wednesdays. Fairs: major fairs in Wessex. NEW stock. Spec: china; commemorative ware; diecast toys; model trains, cars and aircraft; paperweights; thimbles. OLD stock. Spec: badges; buttons; china; commemorative ware; diecast toys; films & entertainment; medals; militaria; paper money; plates; playing cards; police memorabilia; pottery; radio & television; rock & pop; Royal memorabilia; spoons; stereoscopes; teapots; teddy bears; phonecards; Toby Jugs; toys - general; records (78 rpm); stamps. PR: £5–200.

SOUTH YORKSHIRE

Including the Unitary Authorities of Barnsely, Doncaster, Rotherham and Sheffield

BARNSLEY

British Bottle Review, 5 Ironworks Row, (Elsecar Heritage Centre), Wath Road, Elsecar, Barnsley, South Yorkshire S74 Prop: A.R. Blakeman. Tel: & Fax: (01226) 745156. Shop; open Monday to Friday 9–4. OLD stock - small. Spec: bottles, pot lids and advertising. PR: £1–1,000. CC: A; V. Cata: 8 a year (fully illustrated).

Hazelhatch Miniatures, 1 Brick Cottages, Low Laithes, Barnsley, South Yorkshire S71 5HD. Prop: Rosalene Walters. Tel: & Fax: (01226) 755243. Est: 1995. Private premises; postal business only. NEW stock - very small. Spec: miniatures including crochet, embroideries, embroidered pictures, rugs and samplers. PR: 35p–£125. Cata: 1 a year (4 x 1st class stamps) with 2 or 3 free updates.

MEADOWHALL

The English Teddy Bear Co., 21b The Lanes, Meadowhall Centre, Sheffield S9 1EP. Prop: Alise & Jonty Crossick & Dominic Richards. Tel: (0114) 256-9632. Fax: 256-9210. Est: 1990. Shop; open during business hours. NEW stock - large. Spec: teddy bears, limited edition bears and related gifts. PR: £5–200 (bears). CC: V; M. Cata: quarterly. *Also shops in:* Bath, Canterbury, Cambridge, Carnaby Street (London), Newcastle, Oxford, Regent Street (London), Stratford, Windsor, York.

SHEFFIELD

Basically Bears, 390 Sharrowvale Road, Hunters Bar, Sheffield, South Yorkshire S11 8ZP. Prop: Miss Kathleen Fells. Tel: (0114) 268-7183. Est: 1990. Shop; open Tuesday to Saturday 10–5.30. NEW stock - small. Spec: teddy bears. OLD stock - very small. Spec: teddy bears. PR: 50p–£500. CC: A; V; AE.

Causeway House Crafts, Castleton, Sheffield, South Yorkshire S30 2WE. Prop: Roger Vincent. Tel: (01433) 620343. Est: 1979. Shop; open 7 days a week 10–5 Easter to Christmas, January to March limited opening. NEW stock - large. Spec: china; costume jewellery; fine art; lace; miniatures; teddy bears. PR: £1–100. CC: A; V; AE. Also, picture framing and a coffee shop. Mem: Local Chamber of Trade; Forum for Private Businesses.

Fun Antiques, 72 Abbeydale Road, Sheffield, South Yorkshire S7 1FD. Prop: Bill Harrap. Tel: (0114) 255-3424. Fax: 258-8599. Est: 1984. Shop; appointment necessary. Fairs: Newark, Ardingly, Birmingham, Donington, Wembley. OLD stock. Spec: amusement machines; decorative; dolls/dolls clothes; eccentrics; fairground relics; games; jukeboxes & slot machines; model trains and cars; money boxes; optical toys; Rock & Pop; The Seventies; sports; teddy bears; tinplate toys; tins, signs & advertising; toys - general. PR: £50–500. Also, supply and fit all themed bric-a-brac to restaurants, bars pubs and shopping malls, research and find eye catchers and decorate, frame & case special items.

A.E. Jameson & Co., 257 Glossop Road, Sheffield, S10 2GZ. Prop: Philip, Mark & Andrea Jameson. Tel: (0114) 272-3846. Est: 1883. Shop; open 8.30–5.30. NEW stock - large. Spec: Georgian; glass; curios. OLD stock - very small. PR: £5–10,000. Also, restorations and valuations. Mem: L.A.P.A.D.A.

Rails, 29 Chesterfield Road, Sheffield, South Yorkshire S8 0RL. Prop: John, Hedley & Margaret Barber. Tel: (0114) 255-1436. Fax: 255-5982. Est: 1987. Shop; open Monday to Saturday 10.15–4.15. Fairs: northern Swapmeets. NEW and OLD stock - very large. Spec: model cars. PR: £1–600. CC: V; MC; AE; JAL. Cata: bimonthly.

WOMBWELL

Bijou Books, 'Nimrod', 55 Aldham House Lane Wombwell, South Yorkshire S73 8RG. Prop: Maureen Firth. Tel: & Fax: (01226) 755012. Est: 1984. Private premises; postal business only. OLD stock - medium. Spec: arts & crafts; fine art; writing - general. PR: £1–500. Cata: occasionally.

STAFFORDSHIRE

BREWOOD

The Mad Hatter, 24 Sandy Lane, Brewood, Staffordshire ST19 9ET. Prop: Sheila & Barry Collins. Tel: (01902) 850011. Fax: 851542. Est: 1993. Private premises; appointment necessary. Fairs: Miniatura, Lyndhurst, Dorking, Altrincham. NEW stock - medium. Spec: miniatures (12th scale), hats & accessories; hat boxes; hat stands; luggage. PR: £2.50–35. Cata: regularly updated (min. 2 a year). Mem: M.I.N.T.A.

BURNTWOOD

Massey's Miniatures, 153 Cannock Road, Chase Terrace, Burntwood, Staffordshire WS7 8JT. Prop: Paul & Irene Massey. Tel: (01543) 270134. Est: 1990. Shop and market stand; open Tuesday to Saturday 10–4. Fairs: Gollys Friends, East Midlands. NEW general stock - medium. Spec: dolls houses; miniatures. PR: £1–1,000 and upwards. CC: V; A; MC. Cata: available on request. Also, commission work undertaken. Mem: M.I.N.T.A.

HANLEY

Five Towns Antiques, 17 Broad Street, Hanley, Stoke-on-Trent, Staffordshire ST1 4HS. Prop: B. & B. Arkinstall. Tel: (01782) 272930. Est: 1986. Shop; open during normal business hours. OLD general stock - medium. Spec: arts & crafts; Art Nouveau; Art Deco; ceramics; china; early plastics; lighting; mirrors; pottery; writing - general. PR: £1–400. Corresp: French, German.

KINGSLEY

Country Cottage Interiors, Newhall Farmhouse, Hazles Cross Road, Kingsley, Nr. Leek, Staffordshire. Prop: Linda Salmon. Tel: (01538) 754762. Est: 1982. Storeroom; appointment necessary. NEW stock - small. Spec: kitchenalia; horticultural and farm equipment; bamboo; tins, signs & advertising; laundry bygones. PR: £1–500. Also, a self catering cottage available.

KINVER

Kinver Antiques Centre, 128 High Street, Kinver, Stourbridge, Staffordshire. Prop: Ray Williams. Tel: (01384) 277918. Shop; open 10–6. NEW stock - very small. OLD stock - large. Spec: Art Nouveau; Art Deco; automobilia; bells; brass; china; clocks; copper; dolls/dolls clothes; fairground relics; Georgian; gramophones; gramophone needle tins; metalware; musical; musical boxes; posters; street furniture; swords; tinplate toys; traction/steam engines; Victorian; walking sticks; writing - general. PR: £1–1,000.

LEEK

Sylvia Chapman Antiques, 56 St. Edward Street, Leek, Staffordshire ST13 5DL. Tel: (01538) 399116. Est: 1983. Shop; open Monday to Saturday 10–5.30, but closed Thursday. Fairs: Newark. OLD stock - very large. Spec: Art Nouveau; china; glass; kitchenalia; pewter; pottery; treen; Victorian; Art Deco; Edwardian. PR: £10–400. Also, antique furniture.

LICHFIELD

The Antique Shop, 31 Tamworth Street, Lichfield, Staffordshire WS13 6JP. Prop: Mrs P.M. Rackham. Tel: (01543) 268324. Est: 1982. Shop; open Monday to Saturday 9.30–1.30 and 2.30–5.30. OLD general stock - medium. Spec: boxes; brass; ceramics; copper; decanters; hatpins & holders; jewellery; mirrors; objets de vertu; photograph frames; scent bottles; serviette rings; silver; spoons; Staffordshire; thimbles; wine antiques; fountain pens. PR: £5–1,000. CC: MC.

The Dolls House Shop, 47 Tamworth Street, Lichfield, Staffordshire WS13 6JW. Prop: Keith W. Jones. Tel: (01543) 256865. Est: 1977. Shop; open Monday to Saturday 9–5.30. NEW stock - very large. OLD stock - small. Spec: barometers; ceramics; clocks; porcelain dolls; dolls houses; glass; jewellery; miniatures; mirrors. PR: 25p–£500. CC: A; V; AE; DC; JCB. Also, pictures. Mem: M.I.N.T.A.

Images, 4 & 6 Dam Street, Lichfield, Staffordshire WS13 6AA. Prop: Peter Stockham. Tel: (01543) 264093. Est: 1975. Shop; open during normal business hours. NEW general stock. OLD stock. Spec: bookmarkers; dolls/dolls clothes; dolls houses; fine art; games; heraldry; marbles; medals; miniatures; optical toys; playing cards; samplers; stationery; teddy bears; tins, signs & advertising; toys - general; tribal; Victorian. PR: £1–1,000. Mem: B.A.

Ken Palmer, The Courtyard, Lichfield Road, Pipe Hill, Lichfield, Staffordshire WS13 8JR. Tel: (01543) 415186. Est: 1952. Private premises; appointment necessary. Fairs: major dolls house fairs inc. Minitura and Kensington. NEW stock - small. Spec: miniatures; silver; dolls house artifacts; automata. PR: £10–1,000. Cata: 1 a year in January. Mem: M.I.N.T.A.

Tudor of Lichfield Antique Centre, Lichfield House, Bore Street, Lichfield, Staffordshire WS13 6LL. Prop: Sophie M. Burns–Mace. Tel: (01543) 263951. Est: 1992. Shop; open Monday to Saturday 10–5. OLD stock - medium. Spec: glass; china; brassware; silver; plate; copper; jewellery etc. PR: £1–3,000. CC: MC; V. Also, family restaurant below in 16th Century half timbered building.

RUGELEY

Rugeley Antique Centre, 161 Main Road, Brereton, Rugeley, Staffordshire WS15 1DX. Prop: Mr & Mrs D.F. Edwards. Tel: & Fax: (01889) 577166. Est: 1980. Shop; open Monday to Saturday 9–5, Sundays and Bank Holidays 12–4.30. NEW stock - very small. OLD general stock - large. PR: £1–500. CC: A; MC; BC. Also, 30 dealers within this antique centre. Corresp: French.

STAFFORD

Promod Ltd., P.O. Box 366, Stafford, Staffordshire ST16 3UR. Tel: (01785) 224212. Fax: 227994. Est: 1982. Storeroom; postal business only. NEW stock - very large. Spec: diecast toys; model cars. OLD stock - large. Spec: diecast toys; model cars. PR: £5–150. CC: V; A; MC. Cata: monthly to Collectors club members. Mem: Guild of Master Craftsmen.

STOKE-ON-TRENT

Cartographics, 49 Grange Road, Biddulph, Stoke-on-Trent, Staffordshire ST8 7RY. Prop: R.J. & S.W. Dean. Tel: (01782) 513449. Est: 1969. Private premises; appointment necessary or postal business. OLD stock - medium. Spec: canal memorabilia. PR: £2–500. Cata: occasionally.

Dinky Toy Town, 49 Chapel street, Forsbrook, Stoke-on-Trent, Staffordshire ST11 9DA. Prop: Graham Warren. Tel: (01782) 394075. Est: 1979. Market stand at weekends. Fairs: NEC, Buxton, Donington, Brentwood, Walsall, Stoke. NEW stock - very small. Spec: diecast toys. OLD stock - medium. Spec: badges; diecast toys; model cars and aircraft; tinplate toys; toys - general; toy soldiers; trains. PR: £5–500 (Dinky toys). Cata: 2 a year, in Summer and Winter. Also, football items. Corresp: Spanish.

North Staffs Railmania, 8 Hassall Road, Alsager, Stoke-on-Trent, Staffordshire ST7 2HQ. Prop: P. Hallam and N.R.B. King. Tel: (01270) 878519. Est: 1982. Private premises; appointment necessary. Fairs: 10 a year. OLD stock - very small. Spec: model trains - expensive and old collectable 'O' gauge. PR: £50–500. Also, fair organiser.

The Potteries Antique Centre, 271 Waterloo Road, Cobridge, Stoke-on-Trent, Staffordshire. Prop: William Buckley. Tel: (01782) 201455. Fax: 201518. Est: 1991. Shop; open Monday to Saturday 9.30–6, Sunday 10–4.30. Fairs: Newark, Ardingly. OLD stock - very large. Spec: Art Deco; Art Nouveau; bamboo; brass; ceramics; china; clocks; commemorative ware; Edwardian; Georgian; glass; jardinières; jewellery; mirrors; plates; pottery; tins, signs & advertising; Toby jugs; tiles; wrist watches. PR: £1–5,000. CC: A; V. Cata: 3 a year. Also, specialist container shipping, and antique & reproduction furniture.

Toys 'N' Heroes, 49 Chapel Street, Forsbrook, Stoke-on-Trent, Staffs ST11 9DA. Prop: Mrs Aileen Warren. Tel: (01782) 394075. Est: 1990. Market stand; appointment necessary. Fairs: NEC and Donington toy fairs. OLD stock - medium. Spec: Star Wars; T.V. toys. PR: £1–200. Cata: 4 a year, monthly lists in Collectors Gazette. Corresp: Spanish.

SUFFOLK

ALDEBURGH

Aldeburgh Galleries, 132 High Street, Aldeburgh, Suffolk IP15 5AQ. Prop: W.T. & K. Dandy & Mr S. Haslam. Tel: (01728) 453963. Est: 1988. Shop; open Monday to Saturday 10–5, Sunday 2–4.30. OLD general stock - medium. Spec: arts & crafts; Art Nouveau; Art Deco; bottles; boxes; brass; buckles & clasps; buttons; buttonhooks; ceramics; china; costume jewellery; cuff links; early plastics; Edwardian; glass; jewellery; teddy bears; thimbles; Victorian; writing; silver. PR: £1–1,000. CC: V; A; MC.

BECCLES

Saltgate Antiques, 11 Saltgate, Beccles, Suffolk NR34 9AN. Prop: Ann Ratcliffe. Tel: (01502) 712776. Est: 1971. Shop; open Monday to Saturday 10–5, Wednesday 10–1. OLD general stock - large. Spec: writing - general.

Wren House Antiques, 1 High Street, Wrentham, Nr. Beccles, Suffolk. Prop: Tony & Velerie Kemp. Tel: (01502) 675276. Est: 1986. Shop; open Friday & Saturday 10.30–5, Sunday 11–4 or by appointment. OLD general stock - medium. PR: £1–1,000.

Wrentham Antiques Centre, 7 High Street, Wrentham, Beccles, Suffolk NR34 7HD. Prop: Anthony Rush & Katie Walker. Tel: (01502) 675376. Fax: (01206) 263681. Est: 1968. Shop; open Monday to Saturday 10–5, closed Wednesday, Sunday 11–4. OLD general stock - very large. Spec: antiques and collectables. PR: £1–5,000. CC: MC; A; EC. Also, restoration and valuations. Corresp: French, Portuguese, Italian. Mem: M.A.D.A.

BUNGAY

Blackdog Antiques, 51 Earsham Street, Bungay, Suffolk NR35. Prop: Mr Button. Tel: (01986) 895554. Est: 1986. Shop; open 10–5, Sunday 11–4.30. Fairs: Newark and many others. OLD general stock. Spec: antiques from Roman to 1950's in all subjects. PR: £1–100. Also, antique furniture.

BURY ST. EDMUNDS

Risby Barn, The Barn, Risby, Bury St Edmunds, Suffolk. Prop: Richard & Susan Martin. Tel: (01284) 811126. Est: 1986. Shop; open 7 days a week 10–5. NEW stock - very small. OLD stock - medium. PR: 50p–£2,000. CC: V; A. Also, garden centre and a coffee shop.

Corner Shop Antiques, 1 Guildhall Street, Bury St. Edmunds, Suffolk IP33 1PR. Prop: Mrs Gillian Howard. Tel: (01284) 701007. Est: 1981. Shop; open daily except Thursday and Sunday 10–5. OLD stock - medium. Spec: Art Nouveau; Art Deco; brass; ceramics; china; copper; costume jewellery; glass; Victorian. PR: £1–150. Corresp: French.

The Enchanted Aviary, 'Lapwings', Rushbrooke Lane, Bury St. Edmunds, Suffolk IP33 2RS. Prop: Christopher C. Frost. Tel: (01284) 725430. Est: 1971. Private premises; appointment necessary. NEW and OLD stock - very small. Spec: taxidermy. PR: £10–800. Cata: 2 a year. Also, natural history items, paintings and curios.

CLARE

Clare Antique Warehouse, The Mill, Malting Lane, Clare, Nr Sudbury, Suffolk. Prop: David A. Edwards. Tel: (01787) 278449. Est: 1989. Antiques centre; open Monday to Saturday 9.30–5.30. NEW and OLD general stock - medium. PR: £1–500.

Clare Bears, 15 Station Road, Clare, Suffolk, CO10 8NJ. Prop: Steve Bryant. Tel: (01787) 277429. Est: 1996. Private premises; appointment necessary. Fairs: The Event of 1996 (Bear Show) - Alexandra Palace, November 1996. NEW stock - very small. Spec: teddy bears (specialist mohair collectors bears). PR: £50–200. Cata: available on request. Also, exclusive designs and one off bears and layaway service. Corresp: French, German, Japanese.

IPSWICH

Tony Adams Wireless & Bygones, 175 Spring Road, Ipswich, Suffolk IP4 5NQ. Tel: (01473) 714362. Est: 1967. Shop; open Monday, Tuesday, Friday & Saturday 10–12.30 and 2.30–4.30. OLD stock - small. Spec: cameras; model trains and cars; radios. PR: £1–300. Also, repair of period radios. Corresp: German.

Roy Arnold, 77 High Street, Needham Market, Ipswich IP6 8AN. Tel: (01449) 720110. Fax: 722498. E-Mail: 100733.1513@compuserve.com. Est: 1974. Shop; open 10–5. OLD stock - medium. Spec: tools; corkscrews & bottle openers; drawing instruments; pen knives; scientific instruments; spinning/spinning wheels. PR: £5–2,000. Also, new books on the above specialities. Mem: T.A.T.H.S., L.A.P.B.D.S., E.A.I.A., M.W.T.E.A.

Kathleen Ann Holian, 306 Spring Road, Ipswich, Suffolk IP4 5NL. Prop: Kathleen Holian & Craig Hammond. Tel: (01473) 274051. Est: 1993. Private premises; appointment necessary. Fairs: London. NEW stock - very small. Spec: teddy bears. PR: £50–200. Cata: 1 a year.

LAVENHAM

One Bell, 46 High Street, Lavenham, Suffolk CO10 9PY. Prop: J.F. & M.A. Tinworth. Tel: (01787) 248206. Est: 1986. Shop; open Monday, Tuesday and Friday 11–4.30, Saturday and Sunday 11–5. OLD general stock - medium. Spec: militaria. PR: 50p–£200.

LONG MELFORD

Country Antiques, 10 Westgate Street, Long Melford, Suffolk CO10 9DS. Prop: Elaine Pink. Tel: (01787) 310617. E-Mail: fn44@dial.pipex.com. Est: 1994. Shop; open Tuesday, Wednesday, Friday and Saturday 11–5. OLD general stock - small. PR: £50–500. CC: V; MC.

LOWESTOFT

Kessingland Antiques, 36A High Street, Kessingland, Lowestoft NR33 7QQ. Prop: Thomas A. Hammond. Tel: (01502) 740562. Est: 1976. Shop; open Monday to Sunday 10–5.30, closed Thursday. Fairs: Newark. OLD general stock - large. Spec: clocks; walking sticks; wrist and chain watches. PR: £1–1,000.

NEWMARKET

Neate Militaria & Antiques, P.O. Box 26, Newmarket, Suffolk CB8 9JE. Prop: Mr G.C. Neate. Tel: (01638) 660288. Fax: 560207. Est: 1984. Private premises; postal business. Fairs: major medal & militaria fair. OLD stock - large. Spec: decorations & medals. PR: £2–2,000. CC: V; MC; A; D. Cata: 5 a year. Mem: O.M.R.S., O.M.S.A., M.M.S.S.A., M.C.C. of C.

STOWMARKET

Trench Puzzles, Three Cow Green, Bacton, Stowmarket, Suffolk IP14 4HJ. Prop: Mr K.G. Holmes. Est: 1981. Private premises; appointment necessary. Fairs: twice weekly market stall for new stock (London WC2). NEW and OLD stock - very small. Spec: games. PR: £1–500. Cata: annually for new puzzles, occasionally for old puzzles. Also, puzzle design, searching, making, evaluation and restoration. Corresp: French, Spanish.

SUDBURY

Perfect Miniatures, 86/88 Friars Street, Sudbury, Suffolk CO10 6AJ. Prop: Peter Jonathan Hunt. Tel: (01787) 375884. Est: 1979. Shop; open Monday to Saturday 10–6 (ring first) and by appointment. NEW stock - small. Spec: kits; dolls houses; miniatures. PR: £2–4,000. Cata: colour pictures £5, price list only send S.A.E. Corresp: French, German.

WOODBRIDGE

David Gibbins Antiques, 21 Market Hill, Woodbridge, Suffolk IP12 4LX. Tel: & Fax: (01394) 383531. Est: 1966. Shop; open 9.30–5, Wednesday 9.30–1. Fairs: B.A.D.A. - North Harrogate. OLD stock. Spec: Lowestoft porcelain; decanters; embroidered pictures; Georgian; metalware; mirrors; objets de vertu; samplers; silhouettes. PR: £250–20,000. CC: V. Cata: occasionally. Also, 18th Century English furniture. Mem: B.A.D.A.

Melton Antiques, The Street, Melton, Woodbridge, Suffolk. Prop: Mrs Anna Harvey Jones. Tel: (01394) 386232. Est: 1980. Shop; open Monday to Saturday 9.30–5. Fairs: Sandown Park, Long Melford (monthly). OLD stock - medium. Spec: decorative; embroidered pictures; beadwork; buckets; buttonhooks; lighting; Mauchline ware; Mother-of-Pearl; papier mâché; photograph frames; pincushions; samplers; scent bottles; silver; snuff boxes; tapestries; thimbles; tortoiseshell; trays. PR: £1–600.

SURREY

ASHTEAD

Temptations (Antique Jewellery), 88 The Street, Ashtead, Surrey KT21 1AW. Prop: Pauline Watson F.G.A. Tel: (01372) 277713. Est: 1965. Shop; open Monday to Saturday 9.30–5. NEW stock - small. Spec: jewellery; buckles & clasps; cuff links; Edwardian; silver; photograph frames; sovereign holders; spectacles, lorgnettes & monacles; thimbles; chain watches. OLD stock - medium. Spec: Georgian, Victorian and Edwardian jewellery and silver. PR: £30–1,500. CC: V; MC. Also, annual evening invitation only events, talks on jewellery, valuations and photography. Corresp: French. Mem: N.A.G., Fellow of Gemmological Association. *See also:* Temptations, 5 Old kings Head Court, Dorking (q.v.).

BADSHOT LEA

The Antiques Warehouse, Badshot Farm, St. George's Road, Badshot Lea, Nr. Farnham, Surrey GU19 9HY. Prop: Hilary & Peter Burroughs. Tel: (01252) 317590. Fax: 879751. Est: 1995. Antique centre; open Tuesday to Sunday 10–5.30. OLD general stock - very large. Spec: arts & crafts; Art Deco; Art Nouveau; bottles; boxes; brass; ceramics; china; clocks; costume jewellery; cutlery; decanters; diecast toys; embroidered pictures; games; glass; gramophones; jewellery; kitchenalia; mirrors. PR: £1–400. CC: A; EC; MC; V. Also, open most Bank Holidays. Corresp: French.

BOOKHAM

Conan Doyle Books, 6 Sharon Close, Bookham, Leatherhead, Surrey KT23 3LB. Prop: Mr J.M. Gibson. Tel: (01372) 453147. Est: 1981. Private premises; postal business. OLD stock - very small. Spec: Sherlock Holmes/Conan Doyle collectables. Cata: 1 a year. Mem: P.B.F.A.

BRAMLEY

Memories Antiques Centre, High Street, Bramley, Nr. Guildford, Surrey GU5 0HG. Prop: Mrs Pauline Kelsey. Tel: (01483) 892205. Est: 1985. Shop; open Monday to Saturday 10–5. Fairs: Ardingly, Sandown. OLD general stock - large. PR: £1–2,000. Also, finding service for furniture, collectors etc.

COULSDON

Decodream, 233 Chipstead Valley Road, Coulsdon, Surrey CR5 3BY. Prop: David Mobbs. Tel: (0181) 668-5534. Est: 1968. Shop with free parking; appointment necessary. OLD stock - medium. Spec: ceramics; china; pottery; Clarice Cliff; Shelley; F. & C. Rhead; S. Cooper. PR: £100–300. Corresp: French.

DORKING

Camelot Collection, Fairfield House, Beare Green, Surrey RM5 4QQ. (•) Prop: Susie Banks. Tel: (01306) 711330. Fax: 713106. Est: 1992. Private premises; postal business only. Fairs: Dorking. NEW stock - small. Spec: miniature garden and Christmas items. PR: £1–50. Cata: 1 a year.

Optical Antiques, 6 Clifton Terrace, Cliftonville, Dorking, Surrey RH4 2JG. Prop: E. Tombs. Tel: (01306) 889645. Est: 1992. Shop; open Monday to Saturday 9.30–5.30. Fairs: Ardingly. OLD stock - medium. Spec: binoculars; cameras; optical toys; photograph frames; photographic pictures; stereoscopes; telescopes. PR: £50–1,500. CC: V; A. Corresp: French.

Temptations Jewellers, 5 Old Kings Head Court, 11 High Street, Dorking, Surrey RH4 1AR. Tel: (01306) 885452. *For stock details see:* Temptations, 88 The Street, Ashtead.

Victoria & Edward Antique Centre, 61 West Street, Dorking, Surrey RH4 1BS. Prop: Mr A.J. Crowe & Mr N. Packington. Tel: (01306) 889645. Shop; open 9.30–5.30. OLD general stock - very large. Spec: arts & crafts; Art Nouveau; Art Deco; bamboo; barometers; binoculars; boot scrapers; bottles; boxes; brass; bronze; candles/candlesticks; ceramics; commemorative ware; copper; corkscrews & bottle openers; costume jewellery; cutlery; decanters; decorative; Edwardian; fishing; Georgian; glass; gramophones; kitchenalia; metalware; mirrors; objets de vertu. PR: £1–4,000. CC: A; V.

West St. Antiques, 63 West Street, Dorking, Surrey RH4 1BS. Prop: J.G. & P.J. Spooner and R.A. Rasner. Tel: & Fax: (01306) 883487. Est: 1984. Open Monday to Saturday 9.30–5.30 or by appointment. Fairs: London Arms Fair, Regents Park Fair, Winchester, Dorking and Farnham Arms Fairs. OLD stock - very large. Spec: arms & armour; swords; porcelain; silver; glass. PR: £50–15,000. CC: V; AE. Cata: 4 a year (cost £5 a year) Also, furniture and paintings. Mem: Dorking Chamber of Commerce.

EAST MOLESEY

Hampton Court Emporium, 52-54 Bridge Road, Hampton Court, East Molesey, Surrey KT8 9HA. Tel: (0181) 941-8876. Shop; open 7 days a week 9.30–5.30. OLD stock - small. Spec: cameras; stereoscopes; scientific instruments; optical toys; playing cards; binoculars; photographs. PR: £1–500. CC: V. Corresp: French.

EPSOM

Discount Diecasts, 19 Welbeck Close, West Ewell, Surrey KT17 2BJ. (•) Prop: Mr D. Wright. Tel: (0181) 393-4259. Mobile: (0956) 422891. Est: 1991. Private premises; postal business only. Fairs: Sandown, Farnham Maltings, Dorking, Leatherhead, Dulwich. NEW stock - small. Spec: diecast toys. OLD stock - very small. Spec: diecast toys. PR: £5–500.

EWHURST

Jes Models, Parliement Farm, Ewhurst Green, Ewhurst, Surrey GU6 7RR. Prop: Mr A.M. Bennett. Tel: (01802) 421656. Est: 1993. Private premises; postal business only. NEW stock - small. Spec: model cars; toys - general; writing. OLD stock - very small. Spec: model cars; toys - general; writing. PR: £5–180. Cata: monthly.

FARNHAM

Casque and Gauntlet Militaria, 55–59 Badshot Lea Road, Badshot Lea, Farnham, Surrey GU9 9LP. Prop: R.L. & A. Colt. Tel: (01252) 20745. Shop; open Monday to Saturday 10–5.30. OLD stock - very large. Spec: aeronautica; arms & armour; badges; militaria; swords. PR: 50p–£3,000. CC: V; MC; A. Also, repairs to all metal work, cleaning and polishing of copper and brass and re-silvering and re-gilding.

Childhood Memories, 27 South Street, Farnham, Surrey GU9 7QU. Prop: Miss M.A. Stanford. Tel: (01252) 724475. Est: 1975. Shop; open 9.30–5. OLD stock - large. Spec: constructional toys; diecast toys; dolls/dolls clothes; film & entertainment; games; marbles; miniatures; model trains, cars and aircraft; optical toys; playing cards; railways; Rock & Pop; rocking horses; teddy bears; tinplate toys; toys - general; toy soldiers. PR: 50p–£3,000. CC: V; MC; AE.

The Craft & Dollshouse Emporium, 11 Upper Church Lane, Farnham, Surrey GU9 7PW. Prop: Mrs D. Holden. Tel: (01252) 711191. Est: 1994. Shop; open Monday to Saturday 9.30–5, Wednesday 9.30–3. NEW stock - small. Spec: dolls houses; dolls house furniture, miniature accessories (glassware, woodturning, porcelain) and DIY items (windows, doors, wallpapers and lighting). PR: 50p–£1,000. CC: V; A; EC; MC. Cata: £3 available from end of March. Also, local crafts.

GODALMING

Church Street Miniatures, 26 Church Street, Godalming, Surrey GU7 1EW. Prop: Mrs B.H. Walton. Tel: (01483) 427023. Fax: 427024. Est: 1995. Shop; open 10–4, closed Wednesday. NEW stock - very large. Spec: dolls houses; miniatures. PR: £1–500. CC: V; A; MC; EC.

Galerie du Pape, 120 High Street, Godalming, Surrey. Prop: A.J. Pope. Tel: (01483) 421815. Fax: 452374. Est: 1995. Shop; open Tuesday to Saturday 9.30–4.30. NEW and OLD general stock - very small. Spec: toy soldiers. PR: 10p–£35. CC: V; MC; EC; A.

The Olde Curiosity Shoppe, 99 High Street, Godalming, Surrey GU7 1AQ. Prop: Mr & Mrs R.A. Trendle. Tel: (01483) 415889. Est: 1975. Shop; open Monday to Saturday 10–5, Wednesday 10–3. NEW stock - medium. Spec: ceramics; china; brass; cuff links; cutlery; decanters; dolls/dolls clothes; jewellery; photograph frames. OLD stock - medium. Spec: ceramics; china; glass; jewellery; objets de vertu; Victorian. PR: £1–200. CC: MC; V; D.

GUILDFORD

Antique's Centre, 22 Haydon Place, Guildford, Surrey GU1 1SP. Prop: Mrs J.M. Carter. Tel: (01483) 567817. Est: 1968. Shop; open Tuesday, Thursday and Friday 10–4, Saturday 10–4.30. OLD general stock - very large. Spec: Art Nouveau; Art Deco; ceramics; jewellery; Victorian. PR: £1–500.

The Bear Garden and Dolls Attic, 10 Jeffries Passage, Guildford, Surrey GU1 4AP. Prop: Andrew Colborne–Baber. Tel: (01483) 302581. Fax: 301514. E-Mail: emmlac@surrey.ac.uk. Est: 1992. Shop; open Monday to Saturday 9.30–5.30. Fairs: selected fairs. NEW stock - medium. Spec: teddy bears; dolls/dolls clothes; dolls houses. OLD stock - very small. Spec: teddy bears; dolls/dolls clothes; dolls houses. PR: £1–1,500. CC: V; MC; JCB; DC; AE; D; EC; E. Cata: 2 a year. Also, mail order service. Corresp: French, German, Welsh.

Denning Antiques, 1 Chapel Street, Guildford, Surrey. Prop: Mrs Denning. Tel: (01483) 39595. Est: 1986. Shop; open Monday to Saturday 10–5. NEW stock - very small. Spec: silver. OLD stock - medium. Spec: silver; lace. PR: £1–1,000.

Drummond's of Bramley, Birtley Farm Buildings, Bramley, Guildford, Surrey GU5 OLA. (•) Prop: D.J.H. Shaw. Tel: (01483) 898766. Fax: 894393. Est: 1988. Open 7 days a week 9–5.30. Fairs: Chelsea Flower Show, Antiques & Textiles, Chelsea and others. OLD stock - very large. Spec: Art Nouveau; Art Deco; boot scrapers; chandeliers; doorstops; Edwardian; Georgian; jardinières; letter boxes; lighting; mirrors; sundials; telephone boxes; tiles; toiletries; treen; Victorian; weather vanes; writing - general. PR: £50–100,000. Also, period antique bathrooms. Corresp: French, German, Japanese.

Guildford Antique Centre, 22 Haydon Place, Guildford, Surrey GU1 4LL. Est: 1969. Shop; open Tuesday, Thurdsay & Friday 10–4, Saturday 10–4.30. OLD stock - large. Spec: jewellery; silver; buckles & clasps; buttonhooks; card cases; cuff links; Georgian; objets de vertu. PR: £4–500. Also, Devon ware.

Horological Workshops, 204 Worplesdon Road, Guildford, Surrey GU2 6UY. Prop: Mr & Mrs M.D. Tooke. Tel: (01483) 576496. Est: 1968. Shop; open Monday to Friday 8.30–5.30, Saturday 9–12.30. Fairs: Olympia (June). NEW stock - very small. Spec: wrist watches; clocks. OLD stock. Spec: barometers; clocks; musical boxes; watches. Cata: 2 or 3 a year. Also, restoration of clocks, watches, barometers and turret clocks. Mem: B.A.D.A., C.I.N.O.A., B.H.I.

Sheric Mini Auto's, 217 Worplesdon Road, Guildford, Surrey GU2 6XJ. Prop: Eric & Sheila Bonner. Tel: (01483) 235127. Est: 1991. Private premises; appointment necessary or postal business (worldwide). Fairs: Farnham Maltings, Kempton Park, Picketts Lock, Havant. NEW stock - small. Spec: emergency service models; diecast toys; model cars. OLD stock - very small. PR: £1–50. CC: A; MC; V. Cata: in March, updated through the year. Corresp: French, German (translater if necessary).

HASLEMERE

Wood's Wharf Antiques, 56 High Street, Haslemere, Surrey. Prop: Mrs C.M. Lunnon. Tel: (01428) 642125. Fax: 725045. Est: 1975. Shop; open Monday to Saturday 9.30–5. NEW stock ·· very small. Spec: silver photograph frames; Staffordshire. OLD stock - large. Spec: porcelain; brass. PR: £1–600. CC: V; MC; EC. Also, 18th & 19th Century furniture, antique pine, rustic french and picture.

LINGFIELD

I.O.U. (Interesting, Old and Unusual), Paris House, 52/56 High Street, Lingfield, Surrey RH7 6AA. Prop: Keith Wheeler. Tel: & Fax: (01342) 836565. Est: 1994. Shop; open Monday 9.30–4.30, Tuesday to Saturday 9.30–5, closed Sundays and public holidays. NEW general stock - medium. OLD general stock - large. PR: £1–3,000. Also, house clearance.

OXTED

Antiques Centre, 80–84 Station Road, East Oxted, Surrey RH8 0PG. Prop: D. Quigley & J. Wagstaff. Tel: (01883) 712806. Est: 1992. Shop; open Monday to Friday 9.30–5.30. OLD stock. Spec: boxes; brass; ceramics; chandeliers; copper; Georgian; jewellery; mirrors; paperweights; photograph frames; portrait miniatures; samplers; serviette rings; silver; Staffordshire; tea caddies; Toby Jugs; vases; Victorian; chain watches. PR: £1–5,000. CC: A; V; MC; AE. Also, antique furniture.

SURREY

Postings, P.O. Box 1, Oxted, Surrey RH8 0FD. Prop: R.N. Haffner. Tel: & Fax: (01883) 722646. Est: 1992. Private premises; postal business only. Fairs: Philatelic Federations (Kent, Surrey, Sussex and Hampshire). OLD stock - very small. Spec: postal memorabilia; stamp boxes and cases; model letter boxes - tin and crested china; model post vans; post office signs and badges. PR: £10–750. CC: V; MC; JCB. Cata: 2 a year. Mem: P.T.S., P.T.A., E.S.

Treasures, 151 Station Road East, Oxted, Surrey. Prop: Mrs B. Ward–Lee. Tel: (01883) 713301. Shop; open 10–5. OLD general stock - very large. PR: £1–500. CC: A; V.

RUNFOLD

Runfold Collectables, Abbot's Shingle, Botany Hill, The Sands, Farnham, Surrey GU10 1LZ. Prop: Bernard & Peggy Green. Tel: & Fax: (01252) 781124. Est: 1994. Shop; open 7 days a week 12–5. Fairs: Newark, Ardingly. NEW stock - very small. Spec: boxes; mirrors. OLD stock - medium. Spec: aeronautica; Art Deco; ceramics; china; commemorative ware; decorative; glass; gramophones; radio & television. Corresp: French.

SUNBURY-ON-THAMES

Fantazia/Angelique Miniatures, 12 Camilla Close, Sunbury, Middlesex TW16 7PZ. (•) Prop: L.M. Goldsborough. Tel: (01932) 780934. Est: 1988. Private premises; appointment necessary. NEW stock - very small. Spec: dolls/dolls clothes. PR: £1–150. Cata: on request, £1 and S.A.E.

THAMES DITTON

Ladybirds Collectables, 33 High Street, Thames Ditton, Esher, Surrey KT7 0SD. Prop: Ms Bernice Saxony. Tel: (0181) 398-8877. Fax: 399-7474. Est: 1987. Shop; open 9.30–5.30. NEW stock - small. OLD stock - medium. Spec: Art Nouveau; Art Deco; brass; ceramics; china; decorative; dolls houses; doorstops; horticultural and farm equipment; miniatures incl. furniture; objets de vertu; Oriental; plates; rugs; samplers; teapots; thimbles; tins, signs & advertising; Toby Jugs. PR: £4–300. CC: all.

WHYTELEAFE

Modellers Loft, 4 Wellesley Parade, Godstone Road, Whyteleafe, Surrey CR3 0BL. Prop: Patricia Jones. Tel: (01883) 625417. Est: 1983. Shop; open Tuesday to Saturday 9–5.15. Fairs: Toyman, L. Johnsons. OLD stock - very large. Spec: model boats, trains, cars, aircraft and steam/traction engines; diecast toys; toys - general; constructional toys; dolls/dolls clothes; dolls houses; early plastic toys; marbles; money boxes; optical toys; rocking horses; scooters; tinplate toys; toy soldiers. PR: 50p–£3,000. CC: V; MC; JCB; V; D. Mem: F.S.B., Chamber of Trade, Caterham.

TYNE AND WEAR

Including the Unitary Authorities of Gateshead, Newcastle upon Tyne, North Tyneside, South Tyneside and Sunderland

NEWCASTLE UPON TYNE

Antiques at H. & S. Collectables, 149 Salters Road, Gosforth, Newcastle upon Tyne, Tyne and Wear NE3 1DU. Prop: Mr Harry & Mrs Sheila Shorrick. Tel: (0191) 284-6626. Est: 1986. Shop; open Monday to Saturday 10–5. OLD stock - small. Spec: Art Deco; Art Nouveau; boxes; candles/candlesticks; ceramics; china; clocks; decanters; glass; inkstands; jardinières; objets de vertu; plates; scent bottles; serviette rings; silver; spoons; tea caddies; teapots; Toby Jugs; treen; Victorian. PR: £5–1,000.

D.H.N. Phonecards, 5 Beanley Avenue, Lemington, Newcastle-upon-Tyne NE15 8SP. Prop: David Norris. Tel: (0191) 267-9699. Fax: 265-9183. Est: 1992. Private premises; appointment necessary. Fairs: all major phonecard fairs. NEW stock - medium. Spec: phonecards. OLD stock - large. Spec: phonecards. PR: £1–300. Cata: every six weeks.

The English Teddy Bear Co., Unit A3, 23 The Boulevard, Antiques Village, Metro Centre, Gateshead NE11 9YN. (•) Prop: Alise & Jonty Crossick & Dominic Richards. Tel: & Fax: (0191) 460-4949. Est: 1990. Shop; open during business hours. NEW stock - large. Spec: teddy bears, limited edition bears and related gifts. PR: £5–200 (bears). CC: V; M. Cata: quarterly. *Also shops in:* Bath, Canterbury, Cambridge, Carnaby Street (London), Meadowhall, Oxford, Regent Street (London), Stratford, Windsor, York.

Glasscraft, Unit 3 Willington Marina, Willington Quay, Wallsend, Tyne & Wear NE28 6QS. (•) Prop: Philip Grenyer. Tel: & Fax: (0191) 234-2254. Est: 1989. Open Monday to Thursday 8.45–5.15, Friday 8.45–3.15. Fairs: all major shows. NEW stock - small. Spec: glass; miniatures (hand made specialising in Cranberry). CC: V; MC. Mem: M.I.N.T.A.

Geoffrey Hugall Antiques, 19 Clayton Road, Jesmond, Nr. Newcastle-upon-Tyne, Tyne and Wear. Tel: (0191) 281-8408. Est: 1970. Shop; open Monday to Friday 10–5, Saturday 10–4.30 and other times by appointment. OLD stock - medium. Spec: antique ceramics, silver, glass; Georgian. PR: £10–10,000. CC: V; MC. Corresp: French.

NORTH SHIELDS

Maggie May's, 49 Kirton Park Terrace, North Shields, Tyne and Wear. Est: 1989. Shop; Thursday, Friday and Saturday 11–5.30. OLD stock - medium. Spec: Art Deco; fine art; glass; gramophones; mirrors; model trains and cars; musical instruments; objets de vertu; oil lamps; teddy bears; tinplate toys; toys - general. PR: £1–1,000. Also, furniture.

TYNE AND WEAR

SOUTH SHIELDS

Dolly Domain, The Dolls Hospital, 45 Henderson Road, Simonside, South Shields, Tyne & Wear NE34 9QW. Prop: Liz Bonner. Tel: (0191) 427-6214. Fax: 424-0400. Est: 1988. Shop; open Tuesday to Thursday 10–5, Saturday 10–5 (when not at fairs), Monday and Friday by appointment. Fairs: doll, doll & teddy, and dolls house miniature fairs. NEW stock - large. Spec: dolls/dolls clothes; dolls houses; teddy bears. OLD stock - medium. Spec: dolls/dolls clothes; teddy bears. PR: £80–3,000. CC: V; MC. Also, organizer of regional doll & teddy and dolls house fairs.

SUNDERLAND

Peter Smith Antiques, 12–14 Borough Road, Sunderland, Tyne and Wear SR1 1EP. Prop: Peter & Jean Smith. Tel: (0191) 567-3537. Fax: 514-2286. Est: 1968. Storeroom; open Monday to Friday 9.30–4.30, Saturday 10–1. NEW stock - very small. OLD stock - very large. Spec: arts & crafts; Art Deco; Art Nouveau; barometers; china; decanters; Georgian; musical boxes; oil lamps; pottery; Victorian. PR: £5–8,000. CC: V; A; DC; AE. Also, vast stocks of furniture. Corresp: German. Mem: L.A.P.A.D.A.

TYNEMOUTH

Ian Sharp Antiques, 23 Front Street, Tynemouth Village, Northumberland NE30 4DX. Tel: & Fax: (0191) 296-0656. Est: 1988. Shop; open Monday to Saturday 10–1 and 1.30–5.30. Fairs: Newark. OLD stock. Spec: all ceramics pre 1900; clocks; pottery; writing - general. PR: £30–3,000. CC: V; A; MC; EC; AE. Also, furniture c.1700–1900.

WARWICKSHIRE

ALCESTER

Malthouse Antiques Centre, 4 Market Place, Alcester, Warwickshire B49 5AE. Prop: J.W. & P.M. Allcock. Tel: (01789) 764032. Est: 1984. Shop; open Monday to Saturday 10–5, Sunday 2–5. NEW general stock - very small. OLD general stock - medium. PR: £1–500. CC: MC.

LEAMINGTON SPA

Dolls Domain, 1 Satchwell Court, Royal Priors Shopping Centre, Leamington Spa, Warwickshire CV32 4QE. Prop: Mr Gordon W. Fortnum. Tel: & Fax: (01926) 314341. Est: 1993. Shop; open Monday to Saturday 9–5.30. NEW stock - large. Spec: dolls/dolls clothes; dolls house kits, DIY & decorating materials; miniatures. PR: 20p–£500. CC: V; MC; EC; A. Mem: M.I.N.T.A., Guild of Master Craftsmen.

STRATFORD-UPON-AVON

Art Deco Ceramics, Shop Units 3 & 4, Stratford-upon-Avon Antique Cn Ely Street, Stratford-upon-Avon CV37 6LN. Prop: Howard & Pat Watson. Tel: (01789) 204351. Est: 1980. Market stand; open Monday to Wednesday, Friday and Saturday 10–5. Fairs: Alexandra Palace, Midlands Art Deco Fair, Warwick. OLD stock - medium. Spec: Art Deco ceramics; some post-war pottery. PR: £10–500. Also, authors on Clarice Cliff and Art Deco.

Chaucer Head Bookshop, 21 Chapel Street, Stratford-upon-Avon, Warwickshire CV37 6EP. Prop: Mr L.W. Bailey & Mr R. Pierce. Est: 1970. Shop; open Monday to Saturday 10–5.30, Sunday 12–5 or by appointment. NEW stock - medium. OLD stock - very large. Spec: theatre; Shakespeare. PR: 25p–£2,000. CC: AE. Corresp: French, Italian. Mem: B.A.

The English Teddy Bear Co., 15 High Street, Stratford-upon-Avon, Warwickshire CV37 6AU. Prop: Alise & Jonty Crossick & Dominic Richards. Tel: & Fax: (01789) 414724. Est: 1990. Shop; open during business hours. NEW stock - large. Spec: teddy bears, limited edition bears and related gifts. PR: £5–200 (bears). CC: V; M. Cata: quarterly. *Also shops in:* Bath, Canterbury, Cambridge, Carnaby Street (London), Meadowhall, Newcastle, Oxford, Regent Street (London), Windsor, York.

Meer Street Antique Arcade, 10a/11 Meer Street, Stratford-upon-Avon, Warwickshire CV37 6QB. Prop: Roy Griffith. Manager: Edith Prosser. Tel: (01789) 297249. Est: 1993. Shop; open Monday to Friday 10–5, Saturday 10–5.30. OLD stock - medium. Spec: Art Deco; candles/candlesticks; ceramics; costume; costume jewellery; decorative; Edwardian; embroideries; fans; fine art; Georgian; hatpins & holders; inkstands; jewellery; lace; lighting; mirrors; musical instruments; plates; pottery and many others. PR: £1–3,000. CC: V; MC. Corresp: German, French, Spanish.

Stratford Antiques Centre, Ely Street, Stratford-upon-Avon, Warwickshire CV37 6LN. Prop: London & Birmingham Properties. Tel: (01789) 204180. Est: 1982. Shop; open 7 days a week 10–5.30. OLD general stock - very large. Spec: Art Nouveau; Art Deco; ceramics; commemorative ware; diecast toys; dolls/dolls clothes; jewellery; model trains; police memorabilia; railways; tinplate toys; toy soldiers. PR: £1–2,000. CC: up to each stallholder. Also, craft shops in courtyard and cafe.

The Trading Post, 1 High Street, Stratford-upon-Avon, Warwickshire CV37 6AU. Prop: Leitch and Baker Ltd. Tel: (01789) 267228. Fax: 262112. Est: 1975. Shop; open 7 days a week 9–6. NEW stock - large. Spec: dolls/dolls clothes; dolls houses; miniatures; teddy bears. PR: £1–500. CC: V; A; MC; AE; D. Cata: bi-annually. Also, British gifts. Mem: M.I.N.T.A.

James Wigington Arms and Armour, P.O. Box 82, Stratford-upon-Avon, Warwickshire CV37 6ZT. Tel: (01789) 261418.

WARWICK

Antiques & Collectables, 68 Smith Street, Warwick, Warwickshire CV34 4HU. Prop: David & Lorraine Wilkes. Tel: (01926) 401828. Est: 1968. Shop; open Sunday to Saturday 10–6. OLD stock - very large. Spec: crested china; crochet; diecast toys; dolls/dolls clothes; early plastics; films & entertainment; lace; miniatures; model trains & cars; motoring; teddy bears; textiles; tinplate toys; toys - general; toy soldiers. PR: £3–1,000. CC: V; MC; EC; JCB.

John Goodwin & Sons, 38 West Street, Westgate, Warwick, Warwickshire. Prop: N. Goodwin. Tel: & Fax: (01926) 491191. Est: 1982. Shop and storeroom; open Monday to Friday 8.30–5.30, Saturday 9.30–5.30. NEW general stock - medium. Old stock - very small. PR: £5–500. Also, furniture and pictures. Corresp: French.

Midlands Goss & Commemoratives, The Old Cornmarket Antique Cen 70 Market Place, Warwick, Warwickshire CV34 4SO. Prop: Betty & Nevil Malin. Tel: (01926) 419119. Est: 1980. Market stand; open Monday to Saturday 9–5. OLD stock - medium. Spec: commemorative ware; Goss and crested ware. PR: £5–500. Cata: quarterly. Corresp: French.

Pentoy Ltd., The Old Garage, Priors Marston, Warwickshire CV23 8RT. (•) Prop: Mr D. Adams. Tel: (01327) 261631. Fax: 261040. E-Mail: 101374.547@ compuserve.com. Est: 1985. Warehouse; open to trade Monday to Friday 9–5.30 and by appointment for private dealers. Fairs: International Toy Fair, Olympia (trade only). NEW stock - large. Spec: bicycles; diecast toys; miniatures; model trains, cars and aircraft; tinplate toys. PR: £5–150. CC: V; AE; MC; A; CB. Cata: available with regular updates. Corresp: French.

Warwick Antique Centre, 20-22 High Street, Warwick, Warwickshire CV34 4AP. Tel: (01926) 491382 and 495704. Est: 1978. Shop; open Monday to Saturday 10–5. NEW stock - very small. OLD stock - very large. Spec: Art Deco; badges; cameras; china; costume jewellery; diecast toys; Edwardian; fishing; jewellery; Mauchline ware; medals; militaria; paper money; police memorabilia; silver; thimbles; tools; toys - general; Victorian; fountain pens; coins; stamps. PR: £1–250. Also, fountain pen repairs, teddy bear restoration and insurance valuations.

Warwick Antiques, 16–18 High Street, Warwick, Warwickshire CV34 4AP. Prop: Michael Morrison. Tel: (01926) 492482. Fax: 493867. Est: 1969. Shop; Monday to Saturday 9–5. OLD stock - large. Spec: brass; clocks; copper; golf; handbells; horsebrasses & harnesses; inkstands; ivory; metalware; mirrors; musical boxes; oil lamps; pewter; scales, weights & measures; scientific instruments; Staffordshire; tankards; telescopes; Toby Jugs. PR: £1–2,000. CC: V; AE. Corresp: Spanish, French, German, Danish.

WEST MIDLANDS

Including the Unitary Authorities of Birmingham, Coventry, Dudley, Sandwell, Solihull, Walsall and Wolverhampton

BIRMINGHAM

Birmingham Railway Auctions & Publications, 7 Ascot Road, Moseley, Birmingham, West Midlands B13 9EN. Prop: John Mander. Tel: & Fax: (0121) 449-9707. Est: 1985. Private premises; appointment necessary. OLD stock - small. Spec: railways; badges; bookmarkers; buttons; china; clocks; cutlery; glass; match boxes/books; metalware; playing cards; posters; silver; spoons; teapots; trains; transport. PR: £1–5,000. Cata: 10 a year. Also, monthly collectors journal and collectors guides no. 1 to 4, and auctions at Sheffield, Kidlington (nr Oxford), Quorn and Matlock.

Format of Birmingham Ltd., Room 5, 1st Floor, 18–19 Bennetts Hill, Birmingham B2 5QJ. Prop: Garry Charman & David Vice. Tel: (0121) 643-2058. Fax: 643-2210. Est: 1971. Private premises; open Monday to Friday 9.30–5. Fairs: Coinex - London. OLD stock. Spec: British and foreign coins; banknotes; medallions. Cata: 2 a year. Mem: B.N.T.A., International Association of Professional Numismatics.

COVENTRY

Maxine Aston, 19 Styvechale Avenue, Earlsdon, Coventry, West Midlands CV5 6DW. Prop: Maxine Carole. Tel: & Fax: (01203) 711711. Est: 1988. Private premises; appointment necessary. Fairs: cat shows. OLD stock - small. Spec: felines, anything cat related. PR: £1–1,500. Cata: 3 or 4 a year.

David Fletcher - Mint Coins, P.O. Box 64, Coventry CV5 6SN. Tel: (01203) 715425. Fax: 677985. Est: 1973. Private premises; postal business only. Fairs: National Motor Cycle Museum, Coinex - London and overseas. NEW and OLD stock - very large. Spec: modern coins of the world. PR: 25p–£250. CC: A; V. Cata: quarterly. Corresp: French, German, Mandarin. Mem: B.N.T.A.

Memories Antiques & Collectables, 400A Stoney Stanton Road, Coventry, West Midlands CV6 5DH. Tel: (01203) 687994. Est: 1968. Shop; open 10.30–2.30. OLD stock - very small. Spec: bronze; china; clocks; commemorative ware; Edwardian; Georgian; Mauchline ware; medals; militaria; miniatures; oil lamps; Oriental; Royal memorabilia; rugs; silver; snuff boxes; swords; teapots; Toby jugs; vases; Victorian; writing - general. PR: £1–1,000.

Peeping Tom's, 172 The Chesils, Cheylesmore, Coventry, West Midlands CV3 5BH. Prop: Mrs Janet & Mr Michael John Sharp. Tel: & Fax: (01203) 502975. Est: 1990. Shop; open Tuesday to Saturday 10.30–5.30. Fairs: Farnham, NEC, Donington, Kempton Park, Sandown. NEW stock - small. Spec: ceramics; dolls/ dolls clothes; dolls houses; teddy bears; tinplate toys; toy soldiers. OLD stock - very small. Spec: ceramics; dolls/dolls clothes; dolls houses; teddy bears; tinplate toys; toy soldiers. PR: £20–600. CC: V; MC. Mem: Federation of Small Businesses.

The Time Machine, 242 Abbey Road, Whitley, Coventry CV3 4BE. Prop: Paul Michael Kennelly. Tel: (01203) 307700. Est: 1983. Shop; open Wednesday to Saturday 9.30–6. Fairs: Coventry Diecast Model Club - The Sports Connexion. NEW and OLD stock - very large. Spec: diecast toys; model cars and aircraft; toys - general; toy soldiers; trains. PR: 50p–£500. Also, valuation.

FOUR OAKS

Robert Taylor, Windy Ridge, Worcester Lane, Four Oaks, Nr. Sutton Coldfield, West Midlands. Tel: (0121) 308-4209. Fax: 323-3473. Est: 1986. Open 7 days a week 9–7. Fairs: N.E.C., Donington. OLD stock - very large. Spec: constructional toys; diecast toys; model cars and aircraft; tinplate toys; toys - general; toy soldiers; Dinky; Corgi; Schackelton. PR: £1–1,000. CC: V; MC. Cata: available on request. Corresp: French.

STOURBRIDGE

Des Morgan, F11 Swincross Road, Old Swinford, Stourbridge, West Midlands DY8 1NL. Tel: (01384) 397033. Fax: 394416. Est: 1990. Private premises; appointment necessary. Fairs: Big Brum, Newark, Stafford. OLD stock - very small. Spec: artists materials. PR: £10–1,000.

Jenny Morgan, F11 Swincross Road, Stourbridge, West Midlands DY8 1NL. Tel: (01384) 397033. Fax: 394416. Est: 1988. Private premises; postal business only. Fairs: Hugglets Teddy Bear Fairs, Town Hall, Kensington, London (February and August). NEW stock - medium. Spec: teddy bears. OLD stock - very large. Spec: teddy bears. PR: £20–12,000. Cata: 1 a year.

Nostalgia Bears, 22 Drew Road, Pedmore, Stourbridge, West Midlands DY9 0UY. Est: 1965. Private premises; appointment necessary. Fairs: Hagley Hall (Spring & Autumn). NEW stock - very small. Spec: teddy bears.

Stourbridge Models, Birmingham Street, Stourbridge, West Midlands DY8 1JE. Prop: Mr N.D. Douglas. Tel: (01384) 441002. Fax: 371499. Est: 1990. Shop; open Monday to Saturday 10–5 (closed Wednesday and Sunday). NEW stock - very small. Spec: dolls houses. PR: £1–400. CC: V; MC; D; JCB; EC; Also, general model kits and accessories.

SUTTON COLDFIELD

Arlette's Miniatures, 15 Augustine Grove, Four Oaks, Sutton Coldfield, West Midlands B74 4XX. Prop: Arlette Shelton. Tel: (0121) 308-5903 (answerphone). Est: 1993. Private premises; postal business only. Fairs: Miniatura. NEW stock - very small. Spec: miniatures; hand made upholstered furniture in 1/12th scale mainly in mahogany. PR: £10–50. Cata: 1 a year. Mem: M.I.N.T.A., B.T.G.

Collectable Toys, Windyridge, Worcester Lane, Sutton Coldfield, West Midlands B75 5QS. Prop: Robert Taylor. Tel: (0121) 308-4209. Fax: 323-3473. Est: 1982. Private premises and storeroom; postal business only. Fairs: NEC, Donington. OLD stock - very large. Spec: badges; constructional toys; diecast toys; Dinky; Corgi; dolls/dolls clothes; model cars and aircraft; tinplate toys; toys - general; toy soldiers; military models. PR: £1–500. CC: A; V; MC. Cata: monthly. Corresp: French.

WEST MIDLANDS

WALSALL

The Doghouse, 309 Bloxwich Road, Walsall, West Midlands WS1 2DQ. Prop: Jon Rutter. Tel: (01922) 30829. Fax: 31236. Est: 1972. Shop; open 9.30–5.30. NEW general stock - small. Spec: dolls/dolls clothes. OLD general stock - large. Spec: toys - general. Stock changes daily. PR: 50p–£5,000. CC: D; V; A; AE. Also, fireplaces, lamposts, telephone and post boxes, architectural.

Jennifers of Walsall, 51 George Street, Walsall, West Midlands WS1 1RS. Prop: A.J. & J.M. Roberts. Tel: (01922) 23382. Est: 1947. Shop; open Monday to Saturday 9.30–5 (half day Thursday). Fairs: attended. NEW stock - large. Spec: dolls houses; miniatures; model trains, cars and aircraft; teddy bears; railways. OLD stock - medium. Spec: model cars and trains. CC: V; A; AE. Cata: updated yearly. Mem: M.I.N.T.A.

Past and Present, 66 George Street, Walsall, West Midlands WS1 1RS. Prop: Geoff Ellis. Tel: (01922) 611151. Est: 1988. Shop; open 10–5. NEW stock - very large. Spec: lighting; mirrors; glass; ornaments; silver. OLD stock - large. Spec: silver; jewellery; glass; china; ornaments. PR: £1–1,000. CC: V.

WEDNESBURY

Transtar Promotions, 37 Comberford Drive, Tiffany Green, Wednesbury, West Midlands WS10 OUA. Prop: Geoff & Linda Price. Tel: (0121) 502-3713. Private premises; appointment necessary. Fairs: toy fairs in the Midlands area. NEW general stock - medium. Spec: diecast toys; model cars. PR: £2–10. Cata: 2 a year. Also, promoters of toy collectors fairs.

WEST SUSSEX

ARUNDEL

Pat Golding, 6 Castle Mews, Tarrant Street, Arundel, West Sussex BN18 9DG. Tel: (01903) 883980. Est: 1984. Shop; open Monday to Saturday 10–1 and 2–5. Fairs: Ardingly. OLD stock - small. Spec: ceramics; china; commemorative ware; glass; paperweights; pottery; Royal memorabilia; Goss & Crested china. PR: £1–500.

Spencer Swaffer, 30 High Street, Arundel, West Sussex. Tel: (01903) 882132. Fax: 884564. Est: 1972. Shop; open Monday to Saturday 9–6, Sunday by appointment. OLD stock - very large. Spec: bamboo; birdcages; boot scrapers; brass; candles/candlesticks; ceramics; chandeliers; decanters; decorative; doorstops; eccentrics; French; Georgian; inkstands; luggage; metalware; mirrors; plates; pottery; Staffordshire. PR: £20–15,000. CC: AE; A; V. Corresp: French. Mem: L.A.P.A.D.A.

BILLINGSHURST

Great Grooms Antique Centre, Great Grooms, Parbrook, Billingshurst, West Sussex RH14 9EU. Prop: Mr T.J. & Mrs S.B.M. Podger. Tel: (01403) 786202. Fax: 786224. Est: 1993. Shop; open Monday to Saturday 9.30–5.30, Thursday 9.30–8, Sunday 10.30–4.30. OLD stock - very large. Spec: boxes; brass; bronze; ceramics; chandeliers; china; clocks; cutlery; Edwardian; fine art; firearms; Georgian; jewellery; lighting; mirrors; paperweights; photograph frames; rugs; silver; spoons; writing - general. PR: £4–30,000. CC: V; MC; AE; A; EC. Cata: quarterly. Also, valuations and interest free credit and involved in an anti-fraud network. Corresp: French, German, Swedish, Spanish, Italian.

BOGNOR REGIS

Trains, 67 London Road, Bognor Regis, West Sussex PO21 1DF. Prop: Alan & Judy Wickham. Est: 1976. Shop; open 6 days a week 9.15–5.15. NEW stock - very large, OLD stock - large. Spec: diecast toys; dolls houses; model trains, cars and aircraft; optical toys; railways; tinplate toys; toys - general; traction/steam engines. CC: V; D; BC; MC. Corresp: French.

BURGESS HILL

R.J. Hunt, 42 Janes Lane, Burgess Hill, West Sussex RH15 0QR. Prop: Richard James Hunt. Tel: (01444) 233516. Est: 1963. Private premises; appointment necessary. Fairs: R. Sparks - various venues, Mark Carter - Aldershot. OLD stock - medium. Spec: aeronautica; arms & armour; automobilia; badges; costume; firearms; maritime/nautical; medals; militaria; police memorabilia; swords; writing. Also, 1940's decor and military vehicle hire.

CHICHESTER

Cottage Collectibles. Prop: Chris Wotton. Tel: (01243) 375627. Est: 1993. Private premises; appointment necessary. Fairs: Newark, Ardingly, Shepton, Malvern, Fontwell. OLD stock - very large. Spec: Lilliput Lane Cottages; David Winter Cottages; Pendelfin; myth & magic; enchantica; Colour Box; Cherished Teddies. PR: £1–2,500. CC: A; V. Cata: every 2 months. Corresp: French.

The Delightful Muddle, 82 Fishbourne Road West, Chichester, West Sussex PO19 3JL. Prop: J. & M.F. Storey. Tel: (01243) 773679. Est: 1978. Shop; open Thursday to Saturday 10–5, Wednesday 1–5, 3rd Sunday in month. Fairs: Midhurst monthly market. OLD stock - small. Spec: brass; candlesticks; ceramics; china; decanters; eccentrics; egg cups; embroideries; embroidered pictures; glass; lace; lighting; pewter; scent bottles; silver; Toby jugs; tribal; Victorian; fountain pens. PR: £1–100.

Gems Antiques, 39 West Street, Chichester, West Sussex PO19 1RP. Prop: M. Hancock. Tel: (01243) 786173. Est: 1985. Shop; open 10–1 and 2.30–5.30. OLD general stock - medium. Spec: china; glass; Staffordshire; Victorian. PR: £50–2,000. CC: V; MC; EC.

Peter Hancock, 40-41 West Street, Chichester, West Sussex PO19 1RP. Tel: (01243) 786173. Fax: 778865. Est: 1970 (approx.). Shop; open Monday to Saturday 10–1 and 2–5.30. OLD stock - large. Spec: badges; barometers; brass; cameras; ceramics; clocks; commemorative ware; gramophones; maritime/nautical; medals; militaria; pens; pewter; scientific instruments; serviette rings; silhouettes; silver; stereoscopes; telescopes; Victorian. PR: £1–2,000. CC: all. Also, valuations, repair and restoration lectures.

Saint Pancras Antiques, 150 St. Pancras, Chichester, West Sussex PO19 1SH. Prop: R.F. Willatt. Tel: (01243) 787645. Est: 1980. Shop; open Monday to Saturday 9.30–5, half-day Thursdays. OLD stock - medium. Spec: arms & armour; ceramics; firearms; Georgian; maritime/nautical; medals; militaria; musical instruments; swords; tea caddies. PR: £2–3,000. Also, early furniture. Corresp: French. Mem: National Federation of Small Businesses.

Squirrel Antiques, No. 44, The Hornet, Chichester, West Sussex PO19 4GL. Prop: Mrs Lesley Hampshire. Tel: (01243) 771744. Est: 1986. Shop; open Monday to Saturday 10–4. Fairs: Goodwood Racecourse, Sandown Park. OLD stock - medium. Spec: ceramics; dolls/dolls clothes; Edwardian; embroideries; textiles; Victorian. PR: £1–200.

The Wedgwood Specialist. Prop: Carol Walker. Tel: (01243) 375627. Mobile: (0836) 253394. Est: 1992. Market stand and private premises; appointment necessary. Fairs: St. Crispins, Wokingham, Hartley Wintney, Ardingly, Newark, Shepton Mallet, Westpoint. OLD stock - large. Spec: Wedgwood – bells, boxes, candles/candlesticks, china, cuff links, egg cups, jardinières, miniatures, paperweights, plates, serviette rings, teapots, dinnerware. PR: £3–800. CC: A; V; MC; EC.

CRAWLEY

Foxford Dolls, 12 Hermits Road, Crawley, West Sussex RH10 1QY. Prop: Mr M. Fox. Tel: (01293) 560552. Est: 1993. Private premises; postal business only. Fairs: various. NEW stock - very small. Spec: dolls; miniatures. PR: £1–100. Cata: 2 a year, please send 4 first class stamps.

CUCKFIELD

B. & C. Seago, High Street, Cuckfield, West Sussex RH1 5JX. Tel: (01444) 441775. Est: 1974. Shop; open Tuesday to Saturday 10–5. OLD general stock - medium. PR: £1–1,000. Cata: approx 3.

HORSHAM

Lucy Williamson, 13 Milton Mansions, Queens Club Gardens, London W14 9RP. Tel: (0171) 386-0243. Est: 1994. Market stand at: Horsham Collectors Market; every Saturday and postal business. NEW stock - medium. Spec: dolls houses; miniatures. PR: 15p–£200. Cata: 1 a year.

LITTLEHAMPTON

Small Time, 64 Arundel Road, Angmering, West Sussex BN16 4LL. (•) Prop: Mr Keith Bougourd. Tel: (01903) 850043. Est: 1993. Private premises; appointment necessary. Fairs: Hove, Miniatura, Lords Cricket Ground, LDHF, Lynhurst. NEW stock - very small. Spec: miniatures - working miniature clocks, non-working pocket watches and barometers. PR: £15–800. CC: V; A; MC. Cata: 2 a year. Mem: British Toy Makers Guild, M.I.N.T.A.

PETWORTH

Bacchus Gallery, Lombard Street, Petworth, West Sussex GU28 0AG. Prop: Roger Gillett. Tel: (01798) 342844. Fax: 342634. Est: 1988. Shop; open 10–1 and 2.30–5. Fairs: Olympia. NEW and OLD stock - very large. Spec: bottles; corkscrews and bottle openers; glass; wine antiques. PR: £5–8,000. CC: MC; V; AE. Also, anniversary wines and fine wines.

Petworth Antique Centre & Market, East Street, Petworth, West Sussex GU28 0AB. Prop: Peter & Doris Rayment. Tel: (01798) 342073. Shop; open Monday to Saturday 10–5.30. OLD general stock. PR: £10–5,000. CC: all major. Corresp: French. Mem: P.A.D.A. (Petworth Antique Dealers Association).

SAYERS COMMON

Recollect-Dolls Hospital, The Old School, London Road, Sayers Common, West Sussex BN6 9HX. Prop: Mr Paul Jago. Tel: (01273) 833314. Est: 1968. Shop and Workshop; open Tuesday to Friday 10–5, Saturday 10–1. Fairs: Marion Fancey, Miniatura, Exhibition Team. NEW stock - medium. Spec: porcelain doll reproductions; miniatures; teddy bears. OLD stock - very small. Spec: dolls; dolls parts - eyes, limbs etc. PR: £1–550. CC: A; V. Cata: 1 a year (£2 postage stamps). Also, moulds for dolls and miniatures and a dolls hospital. Mem: U.K.I.C.

WORTHING

D.A. Jull, 7 Clissbury Drive, Findon Valley, Worthing, West Sussex BN14 0DT. Tel: (01903) 872241. Est: 1970. Private premises; appointment necessary. Fairs: Horsham (twice a week), Dorking (monthly), Shere (twice monthly). OLD stock - medium. Spec: cameras; optical toys; photographic pictures; scientific instruments; Stanhopes; stereoscopes; telescopes. PR: £15–1,000.

Steyne Antique Galleries, 29 Brighton Road, Worthing, West Sussex BN11 3EF. Prop: H.W. & V.I. Melling. Tel: (01903) 200079. Est: 1985. Shop; open 9.30–5.30, closed Monday and Wednesday afternoon. OLD general stock - medium. Spec: Doulton collectibles; antique clocks. PR: £1–3,500. CC: V; AE; MC; A etc. Also, high class furniture.

WEST YORKSHIRE

Including the Unitary Authorities of Bradford, Calderdale, Kirklees, Leeds and Wakefield

BRADFORD

A.K. Models, 45 Beacon Road, Wibsey, Bradford, West Yorkshire BD6 3ET. Prop: Janet & Paul Illingworth. Tel: (01274) 690829. Fax: 685757. Est: 1991. Shop; open Monday, Tuesday, Thursday & Friday 12–5.30, Saturday 9.30–5.30. NEW stock - large. Spec: diecast toys; model trains, cars and aircraft. OLD stock - very small. Spec: diecast toys; model trains and cars. PR: £2–100. CC: V; MC. Also, model train repairs.

Plane Crazy, 8 Petergate, Bradford, West Yorkshire BD1 1DW. Prop: Gail & Tony Foster. Tel: (01274) 394994. Fax: 394995. Est: 1993. Shop; open Monday to Friday 9.30–5, Saturday 9–5. NEW stock - very large. Spec: arts & crafts; dolls houses; embroideries; miniatures; model trains, cars and aircraft; railways; samplers; scalextric. PR: 50p–£600. CC: V; AE; MC; D.

Small Wonders, 20 Fourlands Drive, Bradford, West Yorkshire BD10 9SJ. Prop: Doreen Jeffries. Tel: (01274) 616539. Est: 1980. Private premises; appointment necessary. Fairs: Pudsey, Miniatura and most Northern fairs for dolls and dolls houses. NEW stock - very large. Spec: dolls/dolls clothes; dolls houses. PR: 30p–£100. Corresp: French. Mem: M.I.N.T.A.

HALIFAX

Collectors Old Toy Shop, 89 Northgate, Northbridge, Halifax, West Yorkshire HX1 1XF. Prop: Simon Haley. Tel: (01422) 360434. Fax: 824932. Est: 1983. Shop; open Monday to Saturday 10.30–4.45, closed Thursday from 1pm. Fairs: Beverley, Halifax and Donington Toy Fairs. NEW stock - very small. Spec: toys - general. OLD stock - very large. Spec: tinplate toys; trains; diecast toys; toys - general; money boxes; toy soldiers; writing - general; clocks; antiques. CC: V; MC; EC. Corresp: French.

Muir Hewitt Art Deco Originals, Halifax Antiques Centre, Queens Road Mills, Queens Road/Gibbet Street, Halifax, West Yorkshire HX1 4L Tel: & Fax: (01422) 347377. Est: 1982. Shop within antiques centre; open Tuesday to Saturday 10–5. NEW stock - very small. Spec: Clarice Cliff posters with full colour photographs. OLD stock - medium. Spec: Art Deco ceramics by Clarice Cliff, Susie Cooper and Charlotte Rhead; Art Deco mirrors and lighting. PR: £7.50–2,500. CC: A; AE; MC; V. Also, Art Deco furniture.

HEBDEN BRIDGE

'Cornucopia', 9 West End, Hebden Bridge, West Yorkshire HX7 8JP. Prop: C. Nassor. Tel: (01422) 844497. Est: 1976. Shop; open Wednesday to Friday and Sunday 1–5, Saturday 11–5. NEW general stock - very small. OLD stock - medium. Spec: Art Deco; lighting. Also, 1020–40's furniture. Corresp: Swahili.

HUDDERSFIELD

Geoff Neary – Estate Jewellery, 2 Market Walk, Huddersfield, West Yorkshire. Tel: (01484) 531609. Fax: 432688. Est: 1852. Shop; open Monday to Saturday 9–5. NEW stock. Spec: silver; silver plated items. OLD stock. Spec: silver; old Sheffield plate; fine jewellery. CC: all. Corresp: French, Spanish. Mem: National Association of Goldsmiths.

KEIGHLEY

The Camera House, 65 Oakworth Hall, Colne Road, Oakworth, Keighley, West Yorkshire. Prop: Mr C. Cox. Tel: & Fax: (01535) 642333. Est: 1986. Shop; open Wednesday to Friday 10–4.30, Saturday 10–1. OLD stock - large. Spec: cameras; photgraphica. PR: £5–2,000. Also, repairs and video transfers.

LEEDS

Leeds Antique Centre, Waterloo House, Crown Street, (Back of Corn Exchange), Leeds, West Yorkshire. OLD general stock - large.

Leeds Model Centre, 56 North Street, Leeds, West Yorkshire LS2 7PN. Prop: Mr Jonathan C. Haigh. Tel: (0113) 243-0870. Fax: 245-0691. Est: 1990. Shop; open Monday to Saturday 10–5.30. Fairs: all major John Webb Fairs. NEW stock - large. Spec: diecast toys; model trains and cars; plates; phonecards; traction/steam engines; Corgi goldstar. OLD stock - very large. Spec: diecast toys; model trains and cars; plates; phonecards; traction/steam engines. PR: average £5 or £25. CC: most except AE; DC. Also, mail order service available.

Modelauto, P.O. Box SM2, Leeds, West Yorkshire LS25 5XA. Prop: Rod & Val Ward. Managers: J. Hanson & M. Seaward. Tel: (0113) 268-6685. Fax: (01977) 681991. Est: 1977. Shop at: 120 Gledhow Valley Road, Leeds; open Tuesday to Saturday 10–4.30. NEW stock - very large. Spec: model cars and aircraft; automobilia; diecast toys; motoring; transport. OLD stock - small. Spec: model cars and aircraft; automobilia; diecast toys; motoring; transport. PR: £5–200. CC: V; MC; AE; DC. Also, publish a magazine 'Model Auto Review', and produce own range of models. Corresp: French, German.

Tyke Teds, 41 Victoria Road, Headingley, Leeds, West Yorkshire LS6 1AS. Prop: Ms Sarah–Jane Pattison. Tel: & Fax: (0113) 230-6550. Est: 1995. Private premises; appointment necessary. Fairs: details available. NEW stock - small. Spec: cast teddy bears - all hand painted and gift boxed. PR: £5–50. Cata: 1 a year minimum. Also, design and production of limited edition bears for trade. Corresp: French. Mem: Charity Fairs Stallholders Association.

MIRFIELD

'Lawn and Lace', 5 Know Road, Mirfield, West Yorkshire WF14 8DQ. Prop: Norma Gunson & Graham Hurst. Tel: (01924) 491083. Est: 1989. Shop; open Wednesday to Saturday 9.30–5.30. Fairs: Newark. NEW stock - very small. Spec: writing - general. OLD stock - medium. Spec: dolls/dolls clothes; dolls houses; embroideries; embroidered pictures; lace; lace; teddy bears; textiles; Victorian; writing - general. PR: £1–600. Corresp: French.

WEST YORKSHIRE

NEW MILL

Dogs in Print, 7 Kempsway, Hepworth, New Mill, West Yorkshire HD7 7HZ. Prop: Steve Ribbons. Tel: & Fax: (01484) 684043. Est: 1980. Private premises; appointment necessary. Fairs: Crufts, NEC Antiques Fairs (Spring & Summer). OLD stock - large. Spec: dogs. PR: £5–500. CC: MC; V; DC. Corresp: most European.

PONTEFRACT

Cottage Antiques, 5 Ropergate End, Pontefract, West Yorkshire. Prop: S. Whittaker. Tel: (01977) 611146. Est: 1988. Shop; open 12–4, except Thursday. Fairs: Newark International Antiques & Collectors Fair. OLD general stock - medium. Spec: candles/candlesticks; ceramics; china; kitchenalia; pottery; Staffordshire; Victorian.

D.Turner Antiques, The Old Coach House, Bondgate, Pontefract WF8 2JJ. Prop: Dennise Turner. Tel: (01977) 798818. Est: 1990. Shop; open Monday to Wednesday, Friday and Saturday 11–5. Fairs: Newark, Doncaster. NEW stock - very small. OLD general stock - large. PR: £50–100. Mem: F.S.B.

SHIPLEY

John Ayrey Diecasts, 202 Market Street, Shipley, Bradford BD18 2BY. Tel: (01274) 594119. Fax: 531505. Est: 1981. Appointment necessary. NEW stock - very large. Spec: diecast toys. PR: £1–100. Cata: 1 a year.

SOWERBY BRIDGE

Memory Lane, 69 Wakefield Road, Sowerby Bridge, West Yorkshire. Prop: Keith and Lynda Robinson. Tel: (01422) 833223. Est: 1978. Shop; open Monday to Friday 10.30–5, Sunday 12–4. NEW stock - medium. Spec: dolls; teddy bears; pottery; costume jewellery; rugs; tinplate toys; copper. OLD stock - small. Spec: teddy bears; dolls; costume; pottery; bottles; costume jewellery; kitchenalia; lace. PR: £2–1,000's. CC: A; V. Also, pine and oak furniture.

TODMORDEN

Echoes, 650A Halifax Road, Eastwood, Todmorden, West Yorkshire OL14 6DW. Prop: Pat Oldman. Tel: (01706) 817505. Est: 1980. Shop; open Wednesday to Monday 11–6. OLD stock - large. Spec: beadwork; buckles & clasps; buttons; buttonhooks; card cases; costume; costume jewellery; crochet; cuff links; dolls/dolls clothes; embroideries; fans; fashion accessories; hatpins & holders; jewellery; lace; luggage; pincushions; samplers; scent bottles; shawls; shoes/shoe making; taxidermy; textiles; thimbles. PR: £1–500. CC: A; V; JCB.

WILTSHIRE

BRADFORD ON AVON

Moxhams Antiques, 17, 23 & 24 Silver Street, Bradford on Avon, Wiltshire BA15 1JZ. Prop: Roger & Jill Bichard. Tel: (01225) 862789. Fax: 862844. Est: 1967. Shop; open Monday to Saturday 9–5.30. Fairs: Olympia (June and November). OLD stock. CC: V; MC. Also, furniture. Corresp: French. Mem: L.A.P.A.D.A., B.A.B.A.D.A.

CHERHILL

P.A. Oxley Antique Clocks, The Old Rectory, Cherhill, Wiltshire SN11 8UX. Prop: Michael & Patricia Oxley. Tel: (01249) 816227. Fax: 821285. Est: 1971. Shop; open 9.30–5, closed Wednesday and Sunday OLD stock - large. Spec: antique clocks (including longcase) and barometers. PR: £300–30,000. CC: A; V; MC; AE. Cata: brochure and photographs always available. Mem: L.A.P.A.D.A.

MARLBOROUGH

A.B. Loncraine & Mrs P. Loncraine, Stuart Gallery, 4 London Road, Marlborough, Wiltshire SN8 1PH. Tel: (01874) 730569 and (01672) 513593. Est: 1968. Shop; open Thursday, Friday & Saturday 9–6.30. OLD stock - large. Spec: glass; pictures; frames. PR: £1–500. Also, bespoke pine furniture. Corresp: French.

The Marlborough Parade Antique Centre, The Parade, Marlborough, Wiltshire SN8 1NE. Prop: T.M. Page & N.J. Cannon. Tel: (01672) 515331. Est: 1985. Open 7 days a week 10–5. OLD general stock - medium. CC: A; V; AE.

The Old Boathouse, Hilliers Yard, Marlborough, Wiltshire SN8 1BE. Prop: Mr S.E. and Mrs C.R. Butterfield. Tel: (01672) 511755. Est: 1992. Shop; open Monday to Saturday 9.30–5, Sunday 12–5. NEW stock - large. Spec: dolls houses; miniatures. CC: A; V; AE.

Annmarie Turner Antiques, 22 Salisbury Road, Marlborough, Wiltshire SN8 4AD. Tel: (01672) 515396. Est: 1985. Shop; open Monday to Saturday 9–6, other times by appointment. OLD stock - medium. Spec: kitchenalia; treen; writing - general. PR: £3–500.

MELKSHAM

Jaffray Antiques, 16 The Market Place, Melksham, Wiltshire SN12 6EX. Tel: (01225) 702269. Fax: 790413. Est: 1955. Shop and storeroom; open 9–5 and Saturday by appointment. OLD general stock. Spec: bamboo; barometers; boxes; brass; ceramics; copper; glass; horsebrasses and harnesses; inkstands; jardinières; scales, weights and measures; tea caddies; Victorian; writing - general. PR: £10–600. Also, antique furniture.

WILTSHIRE

SALISBURY

Castle Galleries, 81 Castle Street, Salisbury, Wiltshire SP1 3SP. Prop: John C. Lodge. Tel: & Fax: (01722) 333734. Est: 1971. Shop; open Tuesday, Thursday and Friday 9–5, Saturday 9–1. NEW and OLD stock - large. Spec: badges; buckles & clasps; card cases; clocks; jewellery; medals; militaria; paper money; Royal memorabilia; scales, weights & measures; scent bottles; silver; sovereign holders; swords; thimbles; Victoriana; chain watches; writing - accessories and general; coins. PR: £1–1,000 plus. CC: V; A.

Micawber's, 53 Fisherton Street, Salisbury, Wiltshire SP2 7SU. Prop: Mrs Janice Johnson. Tel: (01722) 337822. Est: 1980. Shop; open Monday, Tuesday and Thursday to Saturday 9.30–5. OLD general stock - medium. Spec: jewellery; ceramics; silver; vintage clothes. PR: 50p–£700. CC: A; MC; V. Also, a framing service. Mem: Fisherton Street Traders Association.

Small Sorts, 40 Winchester Street, Salisbury, Wiltshire SP1 1HG. Prop: N.J. Turk. Tel: (01722) 337235. Est: 1989. Shop; open Tuesday to Saturday 10–5. NEW general stock - very large. Spec: dolls houses; miniatures. PR: 15p–£400. CC: A; AE; MC; V. Mem: British Toy Makers Guild (B.T.G.); Miniaturists Trade Association (M.I.N.T.A.).

SWINDON

Allan Smith Antique Clocks, Amity Cottage, 162 Beechcroft Road, Upper Stratton, Swindon, Wiltshire SN2 6QE. Tel: & Fax: (01793) 822977. Est: 1988. Private premises; appointment necessary. OLD stock. Spec: candle extinguishers; long case clocks; English Fusee bracket clocks; barometers. PR: £1,350–8,950. Cata: constantly updated.

WALES

Including the Unitary Authorities of Anglesey, Aberconwy & Colwyn, Blaenau Gwent, Bridgend, Caerphilly, Caernarfonshire & Merionethshire, Cardiff, Cardiganshire, Carmarthenshire, Denbighshire, Flintshire, Merthyr Tydfil, Monmouthshire, Neath & Port Talbot, Newport, Pembrokeshire, Powys, Rhondda Cynon Taff, Swansea, Torfaen, Vale of Glamorgan and Wrexham

CLWYD

COLWYN BAY

Doli Bach Miniatures, Owens Corner, 80 Abergele Road, Colwyn Bay, Clwyd LL29 7PP. Prop: Eifion and Elizabeth Owen. Tel: (01492) 530169. Est: 1986. Shop; open Monday to Saturday 9–5, closed some Wednesdays. Fairs: Pudsey, Brentwood, Decor, Golly's Friends. NEW stock - large. Spec: dolls houses; some dolls and teddy bears. PR: 2p–£400. CC: V; MC. Cata: available (£1). Also, woodturning. Corresp: Welsh.

Yesterday's News, 43 Dundonald Road, Colwyn Bay, Clwyd LL29 7RE. Prop: Mr Elfed Jones. Tel: (01492) 531195 or 531303. Est: 1967. Private premises; open 7 days a week 9–9. Fairs: irregularly. OLD stock - very large. Spec: automobilia; golf; militaria; motoring; paper money; radio & television; The Seventies; tins, signs & advertising; tobacco & associated; writing. PR: £5–100. CC: V; A; AE. Cata: 2 or 3 a year. Also, classic cars. Corresp: French, German, Welsh.

DENBIGH

A.P.E.S. Rocking Horses, Ty Gwyn, Llannefydd, Denbigh, Clwydd LL16 5BH. Prop: Stuart & Pam MacPherson. Tel: (01745) 540365. Est: 1978. Private premises; appointment necessary. Fairs: British Toymakers Guild (annual), Country Living Magazine, The Royal Show. NEW and OLD stock - very small. Spec: rocking horses. PR: £850–3,500. Cata: every 2 or 3 years. Also, restorers and makers. Mem: British Toymakers Guild; Wales Craft Council; U.K.I.C.

North Wales Models, The Square, Trefnant, Nr. Denbigh, Clwyd LL16 5TY. Prop: K.V. Smith. Tel: (01745) 730240. Est: 1993. Shop; open 7 days a week 9–6, half day Thursday and Sunday. NEW and OLD stock - small. Spec: diecast toys; models trains and cars; railways. PR: £1–100. Cata: 3 a year.

C. Rumney (Coins Regd.), 26 Caer Felin, Llanrheadr, Nr. Denbigh, Clwyd LL16 4PR. Tel: (01745) 890621. Est: 1969. Private premises; appointment necessary. Fairs: London Cumberland Hotel, Paddington Great Western (monthly), all continental shows. NEW stock - small. Spec: coins. OLD stock - large. Spec: foreign coins. PR: £1–5,000. Corresp: Flemish, German, Dutch. Mem: B.N.T.A.

LLANGOLLEN

Deco on the Dee, Castle Courtyard, Castle Street, Llangollen, Denbighshire LL20 8NY. Prop: James & Claire Davies. Tel: & Fax: (01978) 860372 or Tel: 810159. Est: 1994. Shop; open Sunday, Monday, Wednesday, Thursday and Saturday 11–5. Fairs: Chester, Loughborough. OLD stock - very small. Spec: Art Deco ceramics; ceramics - Clarice Cliff, Cooper, Rhead, Shelley, Burleigh, Carlton etc; mirrors; chrome; bakelite. PR: £5–500. CC: A; EC; MC; V. Cata: quarterley. Mem: Chamber of Trade & Tourism.

Passers Buy, Oak Street/Chapel Street, Llangollen, Clwyd. Prop: Marie Evans. Tel: (01978) 860861 and 757385. Est: 1973. Shop; open MOnday to Saturday 11.30 onwards. Fairs: Port Meiron Autumn Fair. OLD stock - medium. Spec: gaudy Welsh fairings; ceramics; commemorative ware; copper; dolls/dolls clothes; Georgian; Staffordshire. PR: £5–1,000. CC: MC; V. Also, 18th & 19th Century furniture. Mem: Llangollen Chamber of Trade.

DYFED

ABERYSTWYTH

Howards of Aberystwyth, 10 Alexandra Road, Aberystwyth, Dyfed SY23 1LE. Prop: John Howard. Tel: & Fax: (01970) 624973. Est: 1976. Shop; appointment necessary. Fairs: Olympia (February, June & November). OLD stock - very large. Spec: 18th & 19th century British ceramics. PR: £200–10,000. CC: V; MC. Mem: B.A.D.A., L.A.P.A.D.A.

HAVERFORDWEST

Prendergast Antiques, 162–164 Prendergast, Haverfordwest, Dyfed SA61 2PQ. Prop: Alan Emmins. Tel: (01437) 765695. Shop; open Monday to Saturday 10–5, closed Thursday and Sunday. Fairs: Newark. OLD stock - medium. Spec: Art Deco; bottles; brass; chandeliers; china; clocks; commemorative ware; decorative; Edwardian; gramophones; Georgian; horticulture & farm equipment; kitchenalia; street furniture; tins, signs & advertising; Victorian.

LLANELLI

Somethings Bruin, Neuadd Wen, Drefach, Llanelli, Dyfed SA14 7AW. Prop: Jill Hussey. Tel: & Fax: (01269) 844466. Est: 1993. Private premises; appointment necessary. Fairs: all major bear fairs. NEW stock - very small. Spec: teddy bear artist. PR: £60–400. Cata: 2 a year.

PEMBROKE

Pembroke Antiques Centre, Wesley Chapel, Main Street, Pembroke, Dyfed SA71 4DE. Prop: Michael Blake. Tel: (01646) 687017. Est: 1978. Disused chapel; Monday to Saturday 10–5. OLD general stock - large. Spec: ceramics; china; decorative; fine art; kitchenalia; rugs.

SYNOD INN

Forge Antiques, The Old Forge, Synod Inn, Llandysul, Dyfed SA44 6JX. Prop: Paul & Norman Williams. Tel: (01545) 580707. Est: 1981. Shop and storeroom; open Tuesday and Thursday to Saturday, 7 days a week in the Summer. OLD general stock - small. PR: £1–3,000.

TREGARON

Nigel Bird Books, Brynhir, Llwynygroes, Tregaron, Dyfed SY25 6PY. Prop: Nigel & Sue Bird. Tel: & Fax: (01974) 821281. Est: 1985. Private premises; appointment necessary. Fairs: railway modelling events and fairs. NEW stock - very small. OLD stock - large. Spec: railway relics - signs, china, brassware etc. CC: V; MC; JCB. Cata: 4 or 5 a year.

GWENT

CHEPSTOW

Glance Back Books, 17 Upper Church Street, Chepstow, Gwent NP6 5EX. Prop: Greg & Lee Lance–Watkins. Tel: (01291) 626562. Est: 1980. Shop; open Monday to Saturday 10ish–5.30, Sunday (Easter to October) 2–5.30, Summer Bank Holidays 11ish–5.30. OLD stock - very large. Spec: coins; medals; tokens; cap badges. PR: 20p–£2,000. CC: V; etc. Cata: infrequent.

Tinkers Den, 16A St. Mary Street, Chepstow, Gwent. Prop: Denise Raine. Tel: & Fax: (01291) 620491. Est: 1995. Shop; open Monday to Saturday in Winter, 7 days a week in Summer 9.30–5.30. OLD stock - large. Spec: brass; china; Edwardian; glass; Victorian. PR: £1–100.

GWYNEDD

BEAUMARIS

Museum of Childhood, 1 Castle Street, Beaumaris, Anglesey LL58 8AP. Prop: Robert & Joan Brown. Tel: (01248) 712498. Est: 1973. Shop; open during normal business hours. NEW and OLD stock - very small. Spec: amusement machines; china; games; glass; gramophones; jukeboxes & slot machines; money boxes; optical toys; plates; pottery; Royal memorabilia; samplers; stereoscopes; teddy bears; tinplate toys; toys - general; Victoriana. PR: £1–200. Mem: North Wales Tourist Board, British Heritage.

HOLYHEAD

Anglesey Dolls Houses, 5A Penrhos Industrial Estate, Holyhead, Anglesey LL65 2UQ. Prop: W.G. & J.A. Harley. Tel: & Fax: (01407) 763511. Est: 1989. Factory; open Monday to Friday 9–5, Saturday 9–4.30. Fairs: Miniature fairs - 30 a year. NEW stock - very small. Spec: dolls houses. PR: £30–3,000. CC: V. Cata: annually. Also, manufacture of 1/12th scale components. Mem: M.I.N.T.A.

LLANDUDNO

The Antique Shop, 24 Vaughan Street, Llandudno, Gwynedd LL30 1AH. Prop: M.J. Lee. Tel: (01492) 875575. Est: 1938. Shop; open Monday to Saturday 9.30–5.30. NEW stock - small. Spec: jewellery; silver; china; glass. OLD stock - medium. Spec: Victorian and diamond jewellery; silver; china; glass.

POWYS

HAY-ON-WYE (Y GELLI)

Blinking Images, Photographic Bookshop, Oxford Road, Hay-on-Wye, via Hereford, HR3 5DG. Prop: Haydn Pugh. Tel: (01497) 820171. Est: 1994. Shop; open 7 days a week 10–5. NEW stock - very small. Spec: photographic related. OLD stock - medium. Spec: photographic related. PR: £1–500. CC: MC; V. Cata: starting Spring 1996.

KNIGHTON

Offa's Dyke Antiques Centre, 4 High Street, Knighton, Powys, Wales. Prop: Mrs S. Gwilym, Mrs H. Hood & Mr I. Watkins. Tel: (01547) 528635. Est: 1987. Shop; open Monday to Saturday 10–1 and 2–5. OLD stock - medium. Spec: ceramics; clocks; glass; jewellery; kitchenalia; pottery; Staffordshire; tins, signs & advertising; wrist watches. PR: £5–800. CC: V; MC; EC.

Islwyn Watkins Antiques, 1 High Street, Knighton, Powys LD7 1AT. Tel: (01547) 520145 or 528940 (evenings). Est: 1978. Shop; open Tuesday and Thursday to Saturday 10–1 and 2–5. OLD stock - medium. Spec: ceramics; commemorative ware; kitchenalia; pottery; tools; treen. PR: £5–1,000.

SOUTH GLAMORGAN

CARDIFF

Big Boys Toys, The Pumping Station, Penarth Road, Cardiff, South Glamorgan CF1 7TT. Prop: A.B. Taverner. Tel: (01222) 667225. Fax: 495642. Est: 1993. Shop; open Monday to Saturday 10–5. NEW and OLD stock - medium. Spec: diecast toys; model cars. PR: £10–250. CC: V; A.

San Domenico Stringed Instruments, 175 Kings Road, Cardiff, South Glamorgan CF1 9DF. Prop: H. Morgan. Tel: (01222) 235881. Fax: 344510. Open 10–4.30. OLD stock - very small. Spec: violin; violas; cellos. PR: £300–1M. CC: all. Also, restorer. Corresp: French.

PENARTH

Trophy Miniatures Wales Ltd., Unit 4 Vale Enterprise Centre, Hayes Road, Sully, Penarth, South Glamorgan CF64 5SY. Prop: L.J & S.J. Taylor. Tel: (01446) 721011. Fax: 732483. Est: 1973. Shop; open by appointment Monday to Friday 8.30–5. Fairs: London Toy Soldier Show, Chicago Hackenjack, N.J. West Coaster California. NEW stock - very small. Spec: militaria; miniatures; model soldiers and boats. PR: £9–1,200. CC: V; MC. Cata: updated each year. Corresp: Welsh.

WEST GLAMORGAN

SWANSEA

Maybery Antiques, 1 Brandy Cove Road, Bishopston, Swansea, West Glamorgan. Prop: W. Maybery. Tel: (01792) 232550. Est: 1969. Shop; open Wednesday to Saturday 11–5. OLD stock - medium. Spec: ceramics; china; clocks; fine art; pottery; Victorian; writing - general. PR: £1–3,000. Also, furniture. Corresp: Welsh.

Number "10", The Antique Centre, 21 Oxford Street, Swansea, West Glamorgan. Prop: Peter Rees. Tel: (01792) 475599. Est: 1989. Shop; open Monday to Saturday 9.30–4. OLD stock - small. Spec: badges; diecast toys; medals; model trains; railways; toys - general. PR: £1–200.

Past Times Antiques, 24 Cwmdonkin Terrace, Uplands, Swansea, West Glamorgan. Prop: Grenville & Gladys Richards. Tel: (01792) 465286. Est: 1981. Shop; open Monday to Friday 10–2, Saturday 10–5.30. OLD stock - large. Spec: arms & armour; badges; binoculars; brass; cameras; candles/candlesticks; china; commemorative ware; medals; militaria; model cars; paperweights; pens; stationery; swords; toys - general. PR: £1–500.

Retro World Miniature Scooters, Publicity House, 19-21 Uplands Crescent, Swansea SA2 0NX. Prop: Peter Bailey. Tel:(01792) 405907. Fax: 472303. Mobile: (0860) 319738. E-Mail: pd.bailey@ukonline. Est: 1991. Postal business only. Fairs: toy & craft fairs, scooter & motorcycle shows. NEW stock - small. Spec: model Lambretta & Vespa white metal 1/32 and 1/16. OLD stock - very small. Spec: white metal kits and fully finished models; scooter memorabilia. PR: £9.99–55. CC: V; MC. Cata: always available.

Kim Scurlock Antiques, 25 Russell Street, Swansea, West Glamorgan SA1 4HR. Prop: Brian & Elizabeth Leigh. Tel: (01792) 643085. Est: 1982. Shop; open Monday to Friday 9.30–5, Saturday 9.30–1. NEW and OLD general stock - very small. Spec: china; Edwardian; Victorian. PR: £5–1,200. CC: V; MC.

West Wales Antiques, 18 Manselfield Road, Murton, Swansea, West Glamorgan SA3 3AR. Tel: (01792) 234318. Est: 1956. Shop; open 10–1 and 2–5. OLD stock. Spec: ceramics; Oriental; barometers; Swansea and Nantgarw porcelain. PR: £50–4,000. Corresp: French. Mem: L.A.P.A.D.A.

SCOTLAND

Including the Unitary Authorities of Aberdeenshire, Angus, Argyll & Bute, Borders, Clackmannan, Dumfries & Galloway, Dumbarton & Clydebank, Dundee, East Ayrshire, East Dunbartonshire, East Lothian, East Renfrewshire, Edinburgh, Falkirk, Fife, Glasgow, Highland, Inverclyde, Mid Lothian, Moray, North Ayrshire, North Lanarkshire, Orkney Islands, Perthshire & Kinross, Renfrewshire, Shetland Islands, South Ayrshire, South Lanarkshire, Stirling, Western Isles and West Lothian

BORDERS

COLDSTREAM

Fraser Antiques, 65 High Street, Coldstream, Berwickshire TD12 4DL. Tel: & Fax: (01890) 882450. Est: 1969. Shop; open Wednesday to Friday 10–5.30 or by appointment. OLD general stock - small. PR: £20–3,000. CC: V; A; MC. Also, restorations and valuations.

INNERLEITHEN

Antiques, 16 High Street, Innerleithen, Peebleshire EH44 6HF. Prop: Paul Wheeler & G. Robb. Tel: (0131) 225-6343. Est: 1986. Shop; open Monday and Thursday to Saturday 11–4.30. OLD stock - medium. Spec: china; glass. PR: £1–100.

DUMFRIES & GALLOWAY

BEATTOCK

T.W. Beaty, Lochhouse Farm, Beattock, Dumfriesshire DG10 9SG. Tel: (01683) 300451. Storeroom; open 6 days a week. Faris: Newark. OLD stock - medium. PR: £5–3,000. Also, antique furniture. Mem: L.A.P.A.D.A.

DUMFRIES

The Antiquarian, 71 Queensberry Street, Dumfries DG1 1BH. Prop: Hugh Mulholland. Tel: (01387) 259970. Est: 1990. Shop; open Monday to Saturday 10–5. OLD stock - medium. Spec: bronze; candles/candlesticks; ceramics; chandeliers; china; clocks; costume jewellery; decanters; decorative; Edwardian; fine art; Georgian; jewellery; mirrors; objets de vertu; oil lamps; plates; silver; Staffordshire; Toby Jugs; Victorian; walking sticks. PR: £5–5,000.

KIRKCUDBRIGHT

The Antique Shop, 69 St. Mary Street, Kirkcudbright, Dumfries & Galloway DG6 4JT. Prop: Marisa Mairs & Patricia Willacy. Tel: (01557) 330239. Est: 1993. Shop; open Monday to Saturday 10–5. OLD stock - medium. Spec: arts & crafts; Art Deco; Art Nouveau; Edwardian; Victorian. PR: £1–2,000. Corresp: Italian.

FIFE

ST. ANDREWS

Old St. Andrews Gallery, 9 Albany Place, St. Andrews, Fife KY16 9HH. Prop: David & Shirley Brown. Tel: (01334) 477840. Est: 1968. Shop; open Monday to Saturday 10–5. NEW stock - medium. Spec: Art Deco; Art Nouveau; golf; jewellery; silver. OLD stock - large. Spec: golf memorabilia; Art Deco; Art Nouveau; jewellery; silver; bronze; ceramics; china; cuff links; fine art; Georgian; ivory; Oriental; scent bottles; serviette rings; snuff boxes; sovereign holders; tea caddies; Victorian; chain watches. PR: £1–20,000. CC: AE; V; MC; DC; JCB.

GRAMPIAN

ABERDEEN

Annie Mo's, 103–105 Holburn Street, Aberdeen, Grampian AB1 6BQ. Prop: Judith McDonald. Tel:: (01224) 212646. Fax: 591716. Est: 1994. Shop; open Monday 12–5.30, Tuesday, Wednesday and Friday 10–5.30, Thursday 10–7.30, Saturday 9–5.30. NEW stock - very small. Spec: mohair, cashmere and tweed teddy bears, limited editions. PR: £40–200. CC: A; V; MC. Also, restored antique pine furniture and custom built reproduction furniture.

HIGHLAND

BEAULY

Iain Marr Antiques, 3 Mid Street, Beauly, Inverness-shire IV4 7DP. Prop: Iain and Avril Marr. Tel: (01463) 782372. Est: 1975. Shop; open 10.30–1 and 2–5.30, closed Thursday and Sunday. OLD stock - medium. Spec: arms & armour; brass; ceramics; clocks; firearms; Georgian; jewellery; militaria; objets de vertu; pewter; silver; snuff boxes; Staffordshire. PR: £5–5,000. CC: V; A; D; EC; MC. Mem: H.A.D.A. (Highland Antique Dealers Association).

DINGWALL

Mercat Antiques & Books, 6 Church Street, Dingwall, Ross & Cromarty IV15 9SB. Prop: Hazel MacMillan. Est: 1994. Shop; open 6 days a week 10–5. OLD general stock - medium. PR: £1–200. Mem: Ross & Cromarty Tourist Board.

HELMSDALE

Kildonan Books & Antiques, 11 Dunrobin Street, Helmsdale, Sutherland KW8 6JA. Prop: Hazel MacMillan. Tel: (01431) 821412. Est: 1995. Shop; open 6 days a week 10–5 Easter to October. OLD general stock - small. PR: £1–150.

INVERNESS

Chris Barge Antiques, 5 Southside Place, Inverness IV2 3JF. Prop: Chris & Heather Barge. Tel: (01463) 230128. Fax: 716268. Est: 1986. Private premises; postal business only. OLD stock - small. Spec: antique corkscrews. PR: £1–1,000. CC: V; MC. Cata: on request, updated every 2-4 weeks (£2 UK, £5 overseas).

Hantel Ltd., Bruiach House, Kiltarlity, Inverness IV4 7HG. Prop: Mrs F. Wilson. Tel: (01463) 741297. Fax: 741483. Est: 1973. Private premises; postal business only. Fairs: International Spring Fair - NEC. NEW stock - very small. Spec: hand painted pewter miniatures made to order. Cata: 1 a year. Mem: Giftware Association, Association of British Pewter Cratfsmen.

The Model Shop, 17 Newmarket Hall, Academy Street, Inverness IV1 1PJ. Prop: Jackie Wilson. Tel: & Fax: (01463) 238213. Est: 1971. Shop; open 9–1 and 2–5.30, Wednesday early closing at 1. NEW stock - medium. Spec: model kits; model trains; radio controlled boats and aircraft. OLD stock - very small. CC: V; A; AE.

KINGUSSIE

Another World, St. Helens, Ardbroilach Road, Kingussie, Inverness-shire PH21 1JX. Prop: F.J. & E.C. Jarratt. Tel: (01540) 661430. Est: 1995. Private premises; appointment necessary. Fairs: Miniatura - Birmingham NEC, Miniatura - Glasgow, Scottish Trade Fair. NEW stock - very small. Spec: dolls houses. PR: £1,000 plus.

LOTHIAN

EDINBURGH

Laurance Black Ltd., 60 Thistle Street, Edinburgh EH2 1EN. Prop: Laurance Black & Sarah Jane Campbell. Tel: (0131) 220-3387. Est: 1989. Shop; open Monday to Friday 10.15–5, Saturday 10.15–4. OLD stock - very small. Spec: arts & crafts; Art Nouveau; barometers; boxes; brass; candles/candlesticks; ceramics; clocks; decanters; decorative; embroidered pictures; fine art; Georgian; glass; metalware; mirrors; money boxes; pottery; samplers; tea caddies; treen; walking sticks. PR: £10–4,000. CC: V; MC; A. Mem: B.A.D.A.

Bow Well Antiques, 103–105 West Bow, Edinburgh EH1 2JP. Prop: George Haggarty & Murdo McLeod. Tel: (0131) 225-3335. Fax: 226-1259. Shop; open 10–5. OLD stock - medium. Spec: ceramics; china; commemorative ware; glass; golf; jewellery; Mauchline ware; pottery; scientific instruments; serviette rings; silver; snuff boxes; Staffordshire; telescopes; Toby jugs; Victorian. PR: £20–1,000. CC: V; A; MC; AE; DC; JCB; D; EC. Also, Scottish agate jewellery and Scottish regalia.

D.L. Cavanagh, 49 Cockburn Street, Edinburgh EH1 1BS. Tel: (0131) 226-3391. Est: 1972. Shop; open Monday to Saturday 11–5. OLD stock - medium. Spec: arms & armour; badges; cutlery; jewellery; medals; militaria; paper money; silver; swords; writing; coins; silver plate. PR: £1–1,000. CC: A; MC; V; D; EC. Corresp: little Italian.

Duncan & Reid, 5 Tanfield, Inverleith, Edinburgh EH3 5JS. Prop: Margaret Duncan, Susan Reid & Pippa Scott. Tel: (0131) 556-4591. Fax: 552-7551. Est: 1993. Shop; open Monday to Saturday 12–5.30, closed Wednesday. OLD stock - medium. Spec: boxes; china; glass. PR: £1–500. Corresp: French, German.

Geraldine's of Edinburgh, 35A Dundas Street, Edinburgh, Lothian EH3 6QQ. Prop: Mrs G.S. Elliott. Tel: & Fax: (0131) 556-4295. Est: 1983. Shop; open Monday to Friday 9–5, Saturday 9–1. NEW and OLD stock - very small. Spec: dolls; teddy bears. PR: £30–500. CC: V; MC; A. Cata: 1 a year. Also, manufacturers of porcelain dolls and mohair teddy bears, and Edinburgh Dolls Hospital. Mem: British Toy Guild.

Harburn Hobbies Ltd., 67 Elm Row, (on Leithwalk), Edinburgh EH7 4AQ. Tel: & Fax: (0131) 556-3233. Est: 1930's. Shop; open Monday to Saturday 9.30–6. NEW stock - medium. Spec: model railways; arts & crafts; constructional toys; diecast toys; miniatures; model cars and aircraft; traction/steam engines. PR: £3–250. CC: V; A; MC; AE. Also, own range of building & model railway accessories and specially commissioned model railway items. Corresp: French. Mem: Forum of Private Business.

Ibsen's, 11 Waterloo Place, Edinburgh, Lothian EH1 3BG. Prop: A.S. Winstanley. Tel: & Fax: (0131) 556-7188. Est: 1995. Shop; open Monday to Saturday 9.30–5. NEW stock - medium. Spec: dolls/dolls clothes; dolls houses; miniatures; Georgian; glass; pewter. PR: 50p–£500. CC: V; MC; A; EC. Corresp: French, German, Spanish, Swedish. Mem: M.I.N.T.A.

Now and Then Telephones, 9 West–Crosscauseway, Edinburgh, Lothian EH8 9JW. Prop: Mr David Andrew Gordon. Tel: & Fax: (0131) 668-2927 (Request fax only). Est: 1975. Shop; open Tuesday to Saturday 10.30–5.30. Fairs: NEC Birmingham Communication Fair. OLD stock - medium. Spec: amusement machines; automobilia; badges; bicycles; calculating machines; cameras; constructional toys; diecast toys; dolls/dolls clothes; early plastics; gramophones; gramophone needle tins; jukeboxes & slot machines; model trains, cars and aircraft; money boxes; motor car mascots; optical toys; radio & television; railways; sewing machines; teddy bears; telephones; toys - general; toy soldiers; traction/steam engines. PR: £50–500. CC: A; V; MC; EC. Corresp: French.

Out of The Nomads Tent, 21 St. Leonards Lane, Edinburgh, Lothian EH8 9SH. Prop: Rufus Reade. Tel: (0131) 662-1612. Fax: 667-6107. Est: 1983. Shop; open Tuesday to Saturday 10–5. NEW stock - medium. Spec: costume jewellery; mirrors; Oriental; rugs; silver; textiles; tribal. OLD stock - small. Spec: Anglo-Indian; costume; embroideries; firearms; Oriental; rugs; textiles; tribal. PR: £1–4,000. CC: V; A; MC; AE. Also, tours to India, Turkey, Pakistan and North Cyprus. Corresp: French.

The Owl & The Pussycat, 22 Deanhaugh Street, Stockbridge, Edinburgh EH4 1LY. Prop: Alison M. Jeffrey. Tel: (0131) 343-6893 and 557-4420. Est: 1987. Shop; open Tuesday to Saturday 10–5. NEW stock - very small. Spec: teddy bears; miniatures. PR: 99p–£500. CC: A; V; AE. Also, exclusive teddy bear illustrations by Alison Jeffrey. Mem: British Teddy Bear Association.

Stockbridge Antiques, 8 Deanhaugh Street, Edinburgh, Lothian EH4 1LY. Prop: J. & D. Ross. Tel: (0131) 332-1366. Est: 1989. Shop; open Tuesday to Saturday 2–5.30. OLD stock. Spec: antique toys, dolls, teddy bears and juvenilia. PR: £10–1,000's. Cata: photographs and information available on request. Also, restoration and re-costuming of dolls and teddies.

Timeless Tackle, 1 Blackwood Crescent, Edinburgh, Lothian EH9 1QZ. Prop: Rob Maxtone Graham. Tel: (0131) 667-1407. Fax: 662-4215. E-Mail: tackle@timetack.demon.co.uk. Est: 1979. Shop; open Tuesday to Saturday 10–5.30 or by appointment. Fairs: Game & Fishing/Toy & Train/General Antique fairs. NEW stock - very small. Spec: fishing; musical instruments. OLD stock - medium. Spec: fishing; automobilia; binoculars; constructional toys; diecast toys; dolls houses; golf; model trains and cars; motor car mascots; motoring; musical; musical instruments; railways; rock & pop; tinplate toys; toys - general, soldiers; traction and steam engines. PR: £1–5,000. CC: A; V; MC; EC. Cata: 4 to 6 a year. Corresp: French.

Unicorn Antiques, 65 Dundas Street, Edinburgh, Lothian EH4 1HL. Prop: Nancy Duncan. Tel: (0131) 556-7176. Est: 1967. Shop; open Monday to Saturday 10.30–6. OLD stock - medium. Spec: writing - general; brass. PR: 50p–£500. Corresp: Spanish, French, German.

GULLANE

Gullane Antiques, 5 Rosebery Place, Gullane, East Lothian. Prop: E.A. Lindsey. Tel: (01620) 842326. Est: 1980. Shop; open Monday, Tuesday, Friday & Saturday 10.30–1 and 2.30–5, Thursday 2.30–5 (in Winter open Tuesday, Friday & Saturday only). NEW stock - very small. Spec: photograph frames. OLD general stock - large. Spec: arts & crafts; Art Deco; Art Nouveau; Victorian. PR: £1–200.

LEITH

Collects, Prop: Jean E. Grainge. Tel: & Fax: (0131) 553-3999 or (01344) 777461. Est: 1986. Private premises; appointment necessary. Fairs: in Scotland and Southern England. OLD stock - small. Spec: Jewellery; Mauchline ware; Victorian; Victorian name brooches. PR: £1–500.

LIVINGSTON

Audrey's Bears, 3 Anderson Green, Livingston, West Lothian EH54 8PW. Prop: Audrey Tainsh. Tel: & Fax: (01506) 930266. Est: 1993. Private premises; postal business only. Fairs: British Teddy Bear Festival, Kensington Town Hall, London and Made in Scotland Trade Show, S.E.C.C., Glasgow. NEW stock - very small. Spec: teddy bears. PR: £40–150. Cata: 1 a year. Also, one-off commissions, limited editions and exclusives. Mem: B.T.B.A.

NORTH BERWICK

Lindsey Antiques, Kirkports, North Berwick, East Lothian. Prop: Stephen Lindsey. Est: 1996. Shop; open Monday, Tuesday, Friday & Saturday 10.30–5. OLD stock - large. Spec: arts & crafts; Art Deco; Art Nouveau; Victorian. PR: £5–200.

ORKNEY

HARRAY

Orcadian Company of Bears, Rosebank Cottage, Harray, Orkney. Prop: Effy Everiss. Tel: (01856) 761352. Est: 1985. Private premises; appointment necessary. NEW stock - very small. Spec: teddy bears; toys - general. PR: £25–200. Cata: yearly. Corresp: French, German, Dutch, Slavonic. Mem: Highland Craft Point, Orkney Traders Industrial Association.

STRATHCLYDE

GLASGOW

D & F Models, 56 Bell Street, Glasgow G1 1LQ. Prop: Mrs I. Davies & Mrs E. Ferguson. Tel: & Fax: (0141) 552-8044. Est: 1988. Shop; open Tuesday to Sunday. NEW general stock - medium. Spec: diecast toys; dolls houses; model trains, cars and aircraft; railways; toy soldiers. PR: £1–150. CC: V; A; AE; DC.

Growlies, 15 Thorn Brae, Johnstone, Strathclyde. (•) Prop: Christine Gribbin & Margaret McLean. Tel: (01505) 336551. Fax: 337373. Est: 1990. Shop; open Monday to Saturday 10–5.30. Fairs: Hugglets, Teddy Total Germany & ours in Scotland. NEW stock - very small. Spec: teddy bears; miniatures. OLD stock - very small. Spec: teddy bears. PR: £1–800. CC: A; V. Cata: 1 a year. Also, delivery service and repairs to old bears.

Ibrox Collectables, 20–22 Ibrox Street, Ibrox, Glasgow G51. Prop: Chris Burton. Tel: mobile (0802) 266862. Est: 1994. Shop; open Monday to Saturday 10–6.30, closed most Sundays - ring for details. Fairs: Gateshead, Pudsey, Donington, Aberdeen and others. NEW and OLD stock - medium. Spec: Dinky, Corgi, Matchbox and other diecast models. PR: £1–1,500.

'Nadagay', 34 Moorburn Avenue, Orchard Park, Giffnock, Glasgow G46 7AL. Prop: Frank A. Mooney. Tel: (0141) 638-2368. Est: 1957. Private premises; appointment necessary. NEW stock - small. Spec: Scots militaria including badges, buckles & clasps, buttons, medals, Clan interests. PR: £1–500 plus. Cata: prepared to specialist's requirements. Mem: many UK societies.

Pastimes, 126 Maryhill Road, St. George's Cross, Glasgow, Strathclyde G20 7QS. Prop: Anne & Gordon Brown. Tel: (0141) 331-1008. Fax: 569-1501. Est: 1980. Shop; open Monday to Saturday 9.30–5. Fairs: Dolls house fairs in Edinburgh, Falkirk, Glasgow. NEW stock - large. Spec: dolls houses; model trains and cars. OLD stock - large. Spec: badges; medals; militaria; model trains, cars and aircraft; tinplate toys; toy soldiers. PR: 50p–£500 plus. CC: V; A; AE. Also, organisers of Glasgow Vintage Toy Auctions.

Relics, 14 Kingsborough Gardens, Glasgow, Strathclyde G12 9QB. Prop: Steven Currie. Tel: (0141) 341-0007. Est: 1989. Shop at: 2 Cresswell Lane, Hillhead, Glasgow; open 7 days a week 10–5.30. OLD general stock - large. Spec: films & entertainment; radio & television; Rock & Pop; The Seventies; The Sixties; telephones; tins, signs and advertising.

SCOTLAND

Scotsmann Models, 55 Parnie Street, Glasgow, Strathclyde G1 5LU. Prop: George Mann. Tel: (0141) 552-6759. Est: 1994. Shop; open Tuesday to Sunday 10–5. Fairs: Glasgow, Dundee, Edinburgh. NEW general stock - medium. Spec: diecast toys; tinplate toys; toy soldiers; trains; models trains and cars. OLD stock - medium. Spec: diecast; model trains and cars; tinplate toys; Star Wars. PR: £1–300.

Jeremy Sniders Antiques, 158 Bath Street, Glasgow, Strathclyde G2 4TB. Tel: (0141) 332-4033. Fax: 332-5505. Open 9–5. NEW stock - very small. OLD stock - very large. Spec: all types of antiques from 1700– modern day including objets d'art; silverware; Scandinavian silverware; jewellery and porcelain. PR: £50–500. Also, restoration and repair of silverware and jewellery and antique furniture. Corresp: Danish, Swedish, Norwegian, French, German. Mem: F.S.B.

The Victorian Village, 53 & 57 West Regent Street, Glasgow, Strathclyde. Tel: (0141) 332-0808. Est: 1976. Market stand; open Monday to Saturday 10–5. OLD stock - very large. Spec: Mauchline ware; Art Deco; Art Nouveau; card cases; costume jewellery; Edwardian; silhouettes; lace; pen knives; hatpins & holders; jewellery; minitaures; thimbles; walking sticks; scent bottles; pincushions; snuff boxes; wrist and chain watches. PR: £3 plus. CC: AE; MC; D; V; EC.

Tim Wright Antiques, 147 Bath Street, Glasgow G2 4SQ. Tel: (0141) 221-0364. Est: 1972. Shop; open Monday to Friday 10–5, Saturday 10.30–2. OLD stock - very large. Spec: Art Nouveau; barometers; beadwork; brass; ceramics; Edwardian; embroidered pictures; fans; Georgian; glass; Mauchline ware; mirrors; pewter; samplers; scent bottles; silhouettes; snuff boxes; Staffordshire; tea caddies; textiles. PR: £30–5,000. CC: A; V; MC. Corresp: French. Mem: L.A.P.A.D.A.

LANARK

Midget Gems, 4 Market Court, Lanark ML11 9EX. Prop: David McNeill. Tel: & Fax: (01555) 666050. Est: 1995. Shop at: 1 Nursery Buildings, New Lanark; open 7 days a week 11–5. Fairs: dolls house & toy fairs in Scotland and Northern England. NEW stock - small. Spec: dolls houses; dolls/dolls clothes; fossils, geology and prehistory. PR: £1–500. CC: V; A; D; MC; EC. Also, calligraphy (on request), miniature pictures (not portraits). Corresp: French.

TROON

Old Troon Sporting Antiques, 49 Ayr Street, Troon, Ayrshire KA10 6EB. Prop: Bob Pringle. Tel: (01242) 311822. Fax: 313111. Est: 1985. Shop; open Monday, Tuesday, Thursday & Friday 9–5, Wednesday & Saturday 9–1. Fairs: British Open Golf Championship. NEW stock - very small. Spec: fishing; golf; sports - general. OLD stock - large. Spec: golf antiques. PR: £1–30,000. CC: V; MC. Cata: infrequently. Mem: Golf Collectors Society.

TAYSIDE

DUNDEE

Angus Antiques, 4 St. Andrews Street, Dundee, Tayside DD1 2EX. Prop: Stanley Paget & John Czerek. Tel: (01382) 322128. Est: 1971. Shop; open Monday to Friday 10–4. OLD general stock. Spec: aeronautica; amusement machines; Anglo-Indian; arms & armour; arts & crafts; Art Deco; Art Nouveau; automobilia; badges; barometers; beadwork; bells; binoculars; birdcages; bookmarkers; boot scrapers; bottles; boxes; brass; bronze and many others. PR: £1–1,500. Cata: 4 or 5 a year.

Cornucopia Collectors, 15 King Street, Dundee, Tayside DD1 2JD. Prop: Frank & Carol Tonelli. Tel: (01382) 224946. Open Monday to Saturday 10–5, closed Wednesday, closed in July & August. Fairs: Scotfairs - Dyce, Meadowbank, Edinburgh and Dundee, York Card Expo, Picture Postcard Show (BIPEX) London. OLD stock - very large. Spec: stamps; coins. PR: 5p plus. CC: A; V. Corresp: Italian. Mem: P.T.S., S.P.T.A., P.T.A.

PERTH

Gallery One, Forsyth Antiques, 2 St. Pauls Square, Perth, Tayside. Prop: Alexander McDonald Forsyth. Tel: (01738) 624877. Est: 1975. Shop; open Monday to Friday 10–5, Saturday 10–1. OLD stock - medium. Spec: glass; jewellery; paperweights; rugs; samplers; silver; spoons; thimbles.

Guiscards, Rait, Nr Perth, Perthshire PH2 7RT. Prop: Mr & Mrs J. Wishart. Tel: & Fax: (0181) 670392. Shop; open Monday to Wednesday and Friday to Saturday 10.30–5. NEW stock - medium. Spec: dolls; dolls houses; dolls house miniatures; teddy bears; general toys. OLD stock - small. Spec: dolls; dolls houses; miniatures; teddy bears; general toys; juvenilia. PR: 20p–£3,000. CC: V; A. Mem: M.I.N.T.A.

PITLOCHRY

Blair Antiques, 14 Bonnethill Road, Pitlochry, Perthshire. Prop: A.D. Huie. Tel: (01796) 472624. Fax: 474202. Est: 1976. Shop; open 9–5. NEW general stock - very small. OLD general stock - very large. Spec: Art Nouveau; Art Deco; brass; bronze; ceramics; clocks; copper; glass; ivory; mirrors; objets de vertu; pottery; scent bottles; silver; snuff boxes; Staffordshire; treen. PR: £10–1,000. CC: V; A; MC.

ISLE OF MAN

Manx Models, 3 Michael Street, Peel, Isle of Man IM5 1HA. Prop: John & Annett Eio. Tel: (01624) 843960. Fax: 844411. E-Mail: manxmods@advsys.co.uk. Est 1991. Shop; open Tuesday, Friday and Saturday 10–5 or by appointment. NEW stock - medium and OLD stock - very small. Spec: model cars; Corgi Gold Star planes and selections of varying kits. PR: £1–200. CC: V; A; MC. Also reproduction model boxes and model restoration.

NORTHERN IRELAND

Including the Unitary Authorities of Antrim, Ards, Armagh, Ballymena, Ballymoney, Banridge, Belfast City, Carrickfergus, Castlereagh, Coleraine, Cookstown, Craigavon, Derry City, Down, Dungannon, Fermanagh, Larne, Limavady, Lisburn, Magherafelt, Moyle, Newry & Mourne, Newtonabbey, North Down, Omagh and Strabane

---

CO. ANTRIM

BELFAST

Herbert Gould & Co., 21–25a Church Road, Holywood, Co. Down BT18 9BU. (•) Prop: Stephen Gould. Tel: (01232) 427916. Fax: 428396. Shop; open Monday to Saturday 9.30–5.30, Sundays in October to December. NEW stock - very large. Spec: teddy bears; pottery; kitchenalia; jewellery; candles/candlesticks. OLD stock - small. Spec: kitchenalia. PR: £1–500. CC: V; A. Cata: 1 a year. Also, general gifts, traditional interior accessories and USA stocks. Corresp: German.

BUSHMILLS

Dunluce Antiques, 33 Ballytober Road, Bushmills, Co. Antrim BT57 8UU. Prop: Mrs J.C. Ross. Tel: (01265) 731140. Est: 1978. Shop; open Monday to Thursday 10–6, Saturday 2–6. NEW stock - very small. OLD general stock - very small. Spec: arts & crafts; Art Deco; Art Nouveau; bronze; candles/candlesticks; ceramics; decanters; Edwardian; Georgian; glass; golf; objets de vertu; oil lamps; Oriental; sculpture; treen; Victorian; walking sticks. PR: £5–5,000. CC: V; A. Also, ceramic restoration service, antiques & Irish paintings.

PORTBALLINTRAE

Brian R. Bolt Antiques, 88 Ballaghmore Road, Portballintrae, Bushmills, Co. Antrim BT57 8RL. Prop: Brian & Helen Bolt. Tel: (01265) 731129. Est: 1978. Shop; open Tuesday, Thursday and Saturday 2–5.30 and other times by appointment, also a postal business. OLD stock - very small. Spec: arts & crafts; Art Deco; Art Nouveau; buckles & clasps; buttons; card cases; decanters; glass; medical instruments; metalware; objets de vertu; pottery; spoons; tortoiseshell; treen; fountain pens. PR: £10–2,500. CC: V; MC; A. Cata: 4 to 6 a year on silver & objets de vertu, 2 a year on glass. Also, valuations for insurance & probate. Mem: Irish Antiques Dealers Association.

CO. ARMAGH

PORTADOWN

Moyallon Antiques, 54 Moyallon Road, Portadown, Co. Armagh. Prop: G. Jebb. Tel: (01762) 831615. Est: 1976. Open during business hours. NEW stock - very small. OLD general stock - small. PR: £5–1,000. Also, pine.

CO. DOWN

ASHFIELD

Clifford Auld (Old Cross Antiques), 54 Killysorrell Road, Ashfield, Nr. Dromore, Co. Down BT25 1LB. Tel: c/o(01846) 682129. Mobile: (0850) 183947. Est: 1966. Shop; appointment preferred. OLD stock. Spec: Georgian and Victorian silver. PR: £25–2,000. CC: A; V. Also, antique furniture. Mem: L.A.P.A.D.A., I.A.D.A.

BANGOR

McCullough's of Bangor, 19 Bridge Street, Bangor, Co. Down BT20 5AW. Prop: J. McCullough. Tel: (01247) 270443. Fax: 271502. Est: 1961. Shop; open 9–5.30. Fairs: in Northern Ireland. NEW general stock - very large. Spec: arms & armour; arts & crafts; Art Deco; automobilia; badges; bells; bicycles; ceramics; china; clocks; commemorative ware; constructional toys; cutlery; decanters; decorative; diecast toys; dolls/dolls clothes; dolls houses; egg cups; fine art and many others. OLD stock - very small. PR: £1–700. CC: V; MC; A; AE; DC. Also, china & top quality glass. Mem: Local Trade Association.

CO. TYRONE

COOKSTOWN

Cookstown Antiques, 16 Oldtown Street, Cookstown, Co. Tyrone, Northern Ireland. Prop: G. Jebb. Tel: (01648) 765279. Fax: 762946. Est: 1980. Shop; open Thursday 2–5.30, Friday 2–5.30, Saturday 10.30–5.30. NEW stock - very small. OLD stock - medium. Spec: jewellery; china; militaria; coins. PR: £5–1,000. Cata: coin list. Mem: R.I.C.S.

REPUBLIC OF IRELAND

CO. DUBLIN

DUBLIN

Coins and Medals (Regd.), 10 Cathedral Street, Dublin 1, Ireland. Prop: Emil Szauer. Tel: (01) 8744033. Est: 1972. Shop; open Monday 2–5, Tuesday to Saturday 9.30–5. Spec: Greek, Roman, Byzantine, Medieval, Tokens etc. modern coins. PR: £2.50–500. Also, numismatic publications. Corresp: German, Hungarian. Mem: I.A.P.N., B.N.T.A.

Murphy Models, 2 Wexford Street, Dublin 2, Ireland. Prop: Padraig Murphy. Tel: (01) 475-1365. Fax: 475-3244. Est: 1979. Open during normal business hours. NEW stock - very large. Spec: model trains, cars and aircraft. PR: £1–300. Cata: 1 a year, with updates.

Michael Walton Furniture, 49 St. Agnes Park, Crumlin, Dublin 12, Co. Dublin. Tel: (3531) 4555394. Est: 1993. Private premises; appointment necessary. Fairs: Miniatura - Birmingham & Glasgow, London Dollshouse Festival - Kensington. NEW stock - very small. Spec: dolls houses; miniatures; fine arts. PR: £50–4,000. Cata: £6 UK & Irl, £7.50 Europe, £15 R.O.W. Also, Georgian furniture and restoration.

CO. LIMERICK

ADARE

Michelina & George Stacpoole, Main Street, Adare, Co. Limerick. Tel: (061) 396409. Fax: 396733. E-Mail: stacpool@iol.ie. Est: 1964. Shop; open Monday to Saturday 10–5.30. Fairs: Irish antique dealers fairs. OLD stock - medium. Spec: arts & crafts; boxes; china; decorative; fine art; Georgian; ivory; metalware; miniatures; mirrors; objets de vertu; Oriental; papier mâché; portrait miniatures; sculpture; silhouettes; silver; textiles; Victorian; writing - general. PR: £5–5,000. CC: V; A; AE. Corresp: Italian. Mem: Irish Antique Dealers Association.

THE CHANNEL ISLANDS

GUERNSEY

FOREST

Beam Me Up Scotty, Petit Bot Hill, Forest, Guernsey, Channel Islands GY4 4HP. Prop: Mr A. Philip. Tel: (01481) 37075. Fax: 39527. Est: 1990. Shop; open Monday to Saturday 1–6.30. NEW stock - large. Spec: Star Trek memorabilia. PR: £10. CC: all except DC; AE.

ST. SAMPSON

The Old Curiosity Shop, Commercial Road, St. Sampson, Guernsey, The Channel Islands. Prop: Mrs A. Stevens–Cox. Tel: (01481) 45091 and 45324. Est: 1978. Shop; open Tuesday, Wednesday, Friday and Saturday. Fairs: St. Pierre Park Hotel Antiques Fair. OLD general stock - medium. Spec: silver; ceramics. PR: £1–1,000. Corresp: German, French.

JERSEY

ST. HELIER

Collectables, 62 Stopford Road, St. Helier, Jersey, Channel Islands. Prop: Peter Le Vesconte. Tel: (01534) 32481 also a Fax after 3pm. Est: 1984. Shop; open 10–3. NEW stock - very small. Spec: modern collectors toys Corgi etc. OLD stock - small. Spec: arms & armour; commemorative ware; toy soldiers; tins, signs & advertising; tinplate toys; phonecards; swords; diecast toys; firearms; model trains and cars; medals; militaria. PR: £5–100. CC: V; MC; EC.

ALPHABETICAL INDEX BY NAME OF BUSINESS

ALPHABETICAL INDEX BY NAME OF PROPRIETOR

SPECIALITY INDEX

NEW & REPRODUCTION

DOORSTOPS

EARLY PLASTICS

SPECIALITY INDEX

OLD & ANTIQUE

AERONAUTICA

Angus Antiques, Scotland 215
Banbury Fayre, London (N) 121
Bric–a–Brac, Cornwall 49
Casque and Gauntlet Militaria,
  Surrey 184
Cobwebs (Ocean Liner Memorabilia),
  Hants 90
Collectors Corner, Kent 105
Courts Miscellany, H. & Worcs 93
Cox (Geoff), Devon 60
G M Services, Hants 87
Grosvenor Prints, London (WC) 146
Heydens, Glos 78
Hunt (R.J.), W. Sussex 195
Junktion, Lincs 116
L.A.S.S.C.O., London (EC) 120
Laurie (Peter), London (SE) 127
'Legacy', London (NW) 126
Militaria, Avon 33
Nicholas Nickleby, Devon 56
Queen's Shilling (The), Dorset 63
Runfold Collectables, Surrey 186
W.H. Collectables, London (W) 144

AMERICANA

Western Antique Arms, Hants 91

AMUSEMENT MACHINES

Angus Antiques, Scotland 215
Donay Antiques, London (N) 122
Fun Antiques, S. Yorks 174
Haybarn Antiques, Essex 71
Junktion, Lincs 116
L.A.S.S.C.O., London (EC) 120
Museum of Childhood, Wales 205
Now and Then Telephones, Scotland .. 211

ANCIENT ART

Pars Antiques, London (W) 142

ANGLO-INDIAN

Angus Antiques, Scotland 215
Beet (Brian), London (W) 135
Cox (Geoff), Devon 60
Gateway Antiques, Oxon 164
Graham Oriental Textiles (Joss),
  London (SW) 131

Hyndford Antiques, E. Sussex 67
Jones Antiques (Christopher),
  Northants 159
Out of The Nomads Tent, Scotland 211
Petrou (Peter), London (W) 142
W.H. Collectables, London (W) 144

ARCHITECTURAL

Cox (Geoff), Devon 60
L.A.S.S.C.O., London (EC) 120
Old Cinema (The), London (W) 141
Recollections, E. Sussex 67

ARMS & ARMOUR

Adamson Armoury, N. Yorks 157
Angus Antiques, Scotland 215
Boscombe Militaria, Dorset 61
Boulden Antiques (Paul), Devon 58
Bric–a–Brac, Cornwall 49
Casque and Gauntlet Militaria, Surrey. 184
Cavanagh (D.L.), Scotland 210
Collectables, C.I. 220
Collectors Corner, Kent 105
Crispin's Day Antiquarian and
  Out-of-Print Military Books, Essex 77
Durham House Antiques Centre, Glos .. 81
Gainsborough House Antiques, Devon . 59
German (Antiques) (Michael),
  London (W) 138
Grosvenor Prints, London (WC) 146
Heydens, Glos 78
HQ84, The Curiosity Shop, Glos 79
Hunt (R.J.), W. Sussex 195
Lanes Armoury (The), E. Sussex 67
Laurie (Peter), London (SE) 127
Marr Antiques (Iain), Scotland 209
Norden Antiques (Peter), Glos 81
Past Times Antiques, Wales 207
Saint Pancras Antiques, W. Sussex 196
"Second Front", Cambs 42
Soviet Carpet & Art Centre,
  London (NW) 126
Tags Antiques, Oxon 166
Trident Arms, Notts 163
Tunbridge Wells Antique Centre, Kent 108
Watergate Antiques, Cheshire 44
West St. Antiques, Surrey 183
Western Antique Arms, Hants 91

ART NOUVEAU

ARTISTS MATERIALS

ARTS & CRAFTS

AUTOGRAPHS

AUTOMATA

AUTOMOBILIA

LORD BADEN-POWELL

BADGES

BAKELITE

BOXES

Tiffany Antiques, Shropshire 169
Tinkers Den, Wales 205
Treasure Chest, Northumberland 161
Tudor of Lichfield Antique Centre,
  Staffs...................................... 177
Unicorn Antiques, Scotland.............. 212
Uriah's Heap, I. o. W..................... 101
Victoria & Edward Antique Centre,
  Surrey..................................... 183
Walcot Reclamation Ltd., Avon 32
Warwick Antiques, Warwickshire....... 191
Well Cottage Antique Centre, Bucks.... 40
Windmill Antiques, N. Yorks 155
Wood's Wharf Antiques, Surrey 185
Wright Antiques (Tim), Scotland 214

BREWING & RELATED
Facet Books, Notts....................... 163

BRONZE
Angus Antiques, Scotland................ 215
Antiquarian (The), Scotland 208
Antique Galleries (AS), Gr. Manchester 83
Arnold Antiques (Sean), London (W).. 134
Baker Oriental Art (Gregg),
  London (W) 135
Barnes (Antiques) (R.A.),
  London (SW)............................. 129
Blair Antiques, Scotland.................. 215
Bloom & Son (1912) Ltd. (N.),
  London (W) 135
Bridge Antiques (Christine),
  London (SW)............................. 130
Brower Antiques (David), London (W) 136
Collectors Corner, Kent 105
Dunluce Antiques, N. Ireland 217
Durham House Antiques Centre, Glos.. 81
E.K. Antiques, Northants 159
Fenwick and Fenwick Antiques,
  H. & Worcs............................... 92
Garner Antiques (John), Leics........... 115
Great Grooms Antique Centre,
  W. Sussex 195
H.L.B. Antiques, Dorset................... 61
Harriman (David), Herts 96
Highland Antiques Export,
  Gr. Manchester 85
Hyndford Antiques, E. Sussex........... 67
Imperial Antiques, Gr. Manchester..... 84
Jag Decorative Arts, London (W) 140
Jones Antique Lighting, London (W) .. 140
Jones Antiques (Christopher),
  Northants 159
Knight and Sons (B.R.), Cambs.......... 42
L.A.S.S.C.O., London (EC).............. 120

Lanes Armoury (The), E. Sussex......... 67
Memories Antiques & Collectables,
  W. Mids.................................. 192
Mitchell Antiques (Laurence),
  London (N)............................... 123
Moorhead (Patrick), E. Sussex 67
Noonstar, London (W) 141
Norden Antiques (Peter), Glos 81
Oasis Antiques, E. Sussex 67
Old St. Andrews Gallery, Scotland 209
Petrou (Peter), London (W).............. 142
Reece Gallery (Gordon), N. Yorks 156
Shortmead Antiques, Beds 35
Simmons & Simmons Ltd.,
  London (E) 119
Sladmore Gallery, London (W) 143
Style, London (N) 124
Victoria & Edward Antique Centre,
  Surrey..................................... 183
Walcot Reclamation Ltd., Avon 32

BUCKETS
BR Collectors Corner, London (NW).. 125
Clunes Antiques, London (SW) 130
Collectors Corner, Kent 105
Durham House Antiques Centre, Glos.. 81
Melton Antiques, Suffolk................. 181
Read (J.), Kent............................. 103
Walcot Reclamation Ltd., Avon 32

BUCKLES & CLASPS
Aldeburgh Galleries, Suffolk............. 179
Barn Collectors Market & Studio
  Bookshop, E. Sussex 70
Bee (Linda), London (W) 135
Bolt Antiques (Brian R.) N. Ireland.... 217
Button Queen (The), London (W) 136
Castle Galleries, Wilts.................... 202
Church Street Antiques, Norfolk 154
Collectable Costume, Avon 31
Collectors Corner, Kent 105
Echoes, W. Yorks 200
Farmhouse Antiques, Lancs 110
Guildford Antique Centre, Surrey 185
Letty's Antiques, Leics.................... 114
Magpie (The), Devon 60
Mansell (William), London (W)......... 140
"Second Front", Cambs 42

BUSES & TRAMWAYS
Roads and Rails, Gr. Manchester 86

BUTTONHOOKS
Aldeburgh Galleries, Suffolk............. 179
Banbury Fayre, London (N)............. 121

SPECIALITY INDEX - OLD & ANTIQUE

BUTTONS

CALCULATING MACHINES

CAMERAS

CANAL MEMORABILIA

CANDLE EXTINGUISHERS

CANDLES & CANDLESTICKS

CARD CASES

SPECIALITY INDEX - OLD & ANTIQUE

– BESWICK

– DOULTON

– BLUE & WHITE

– CLARICE CLIFF

– GOSS & CRESTED

CHOCOLATE

CLOCKS

COMICS

COMMEMORATIVE WARE

COMPACTS

COSTUMES

COUTURE

CROCHET

CUFF LINKS

CUTLERY

DECANTERS

DECORATIVE

DOGS

DOLLS HOUSES

DOLLS & DOLLS CLOTHES

DOORSTOPS

DRAWING INSTRUMENTS

EGG CUPS

EMBROIDERED PICTURES

EMBROIDERIES

FABERGÉ

FAIRGROUND RELICS

FIRE-FIGHTING EQUIPMENT

FIREARMS

FORTIES (THE)

FOSSILS, GEOLOGY & PREHISTORY

FRANCE

GAMES

GEORGIAN

GLASS

GLOBES

GNOMES

GOLD

GRAMOPHONE NEEDLE TINS

GRAMOPHONES

GRAND TOUR

HANDBAGS & PURSES

HANDBELLS

HATPINS & HOLDERS

HERALDRY

HORSE BRASSES & HARNESS

HORTICULTURAL & FARM EQUIPMENT

ICONS

INKSTANDS

LONDON TRANSPORT

LOOMS & WEAVING

LUGGAGE

MAGIC & CONJURING

MARBLES

MARITIME & NAUTICAL

MATCHBOXES & BOOKS

MAUCHLINE WARE

MEDALS

MEDICAL INSTRUMENTS

METALWARE

MILITARIA

MINIATURES

MIRRORS

MODELS
– AIRCRAFT

– BOATS & SHIPS

– CARS

SPECIALITY INDEX - OLD & ANTIQUE

MONEY BOXES

MOTHER-OF-PEARL

MOTORCAR MASCOTS

OIL LAMPS

ORIENTAL

PRINTING

PUPPETS

RADIO & TELEVISION

RAILWAYANA

RECORDS

ROCK & POP

SILVER-PLATE

SIXTIES (THE)

SMOCKS

SNUFF BOXES

SOVEREIGN HOLDERS

SPECTACLES, LORGNETTES & MONACLES

SPINNING & SPINNING WHEELS

SPOONS

SPORTS
– GENERAL

– BILLIARDS & SNOOKER

– CRICKET

– CROQUET

– FISHING

SPECIALITY INDEX - OLD & ANTIQUE

TEAPOTS

TEDDY BEARS

TORTOISESHELL

TOYS

– GENERAL

WALKING STICKS

WAR

WATCHES
– CHAIN & POCKET

Books for Collectors and Dealers

Cleaning, Repairing and Caring for Books
Robert L Shep

This revised edition has been brought up to date. A practical manual describing in simple and straightforward language how to repair, clean and restore books. Liberally illustrated, the manual has been written with both American and British book bibliophiles in mind. Sources of supplies are listed.

Size: 140 x 210 mm (portrait) 148 pages
ISBN 1 872699 02 2   £10.95

Bookworms – The Insect Pest of Books
Norman Hickin

Revised and updated, this book is for all who have the responsibility for caring for books, whether in an amateur or professional capacity. More especially it concerns the conservation of antiquarian books, collection of books in warm and subtropical climates and where recent storage conditions have been less than ideal. The text includes a detailed study of insect pests, with methods of prevention and treatment.

Size 140 x 210 mm (portrait) 184 pages
ISBN 1 872699 12 X   £24.00

Miniature Books
Louis W. Bondy

Miniature books - that is books not more than 76 mm (3 inches in height) - have always fascinated booklovers. A number of manuscript volumes still exist and the history of miniature books begins with the advent of printing. The author traces their story, from the *Officium Beatae Virginis Mariae* printed by Mathias Moravius in Naples in A.D. 1486 to the present time when new printing methods, and perhaps a growing belief that small is beautiful, have greatly increased the number of enthusiastic collectors.

Size: 140 x 210 mm (portrait) 221 pages
ISBN 1 872699 16 2   £24.00

All titles are available from: Richard Joseph Publishers Ltd.,
Unit 2, Monks Walk, Farnham, Surrey GU9 8HT. Fax: (01252) 734307

SHEPPARD'S
INTERNATIONAL SUBJECT GUIDES

VOLUME I – ART
Applied Art, Art, Art history,
Art Reference, Artists, The Arts

VOLUME II – HISTORY
Egyptology, General History, Local History,
National History, History of Civilisation

VOLUME III – SCIENCE
Anthropology, Archaeology, Astrology, Astronomy
Biology, Botany, Chemistry, Cosmology, Economics,
Geography, Geology, Natural Sciences, Science

VOLUME IV – LITERATURE
Classical Studies, Literary Criticism, Literature,
Literature in Translation

VOLUME V – SPECIAL EDITIONS
First Editions, Limited Editions, Signed Editions,
Fine & Rare Books

VOLUME VI – TOPOGRAPHY & GEOGRAPHY
Atlases/Cartography, Canals & Waterways, Geography,
Hydrography, Topography – Local & General

VOLUME VII – TRANSPORT
Aviation, Maritime & Nautical, Motorbikes, Motoring, Railways,
Steam Engines, Traction Engines, Transport, Vintage Cars

VOLUME VIII – MILITARY
Arms & Armour, Espionage, Firearms,
Military, War, Wargames

DISPLAYED ADVERTISEMENTS
INDEX OF ADVERTISERS

DIRECTORY OF DEALERS IN COLLECTABLES

FREE DEALER ENTRY FORM

Office use only

Trading Name of Business: _____

Address _____

_____

_____

Name(s) of Proprietor(s)_____

Tel:_____ Fax: _____ Established: _____

Type of premises: SHOP ___ MARKET STAND ___ STOREROOM ___ PRIVATE ___

Stock may be viewed: In business hours without appointment __ , by appointment only __ ,
        not at all (postal business only) __ .

Days & Hours of business:_____

STOCK - the Speciality Index is split into two sections - please ensure this is completed

NEW & REPRODUCTION No. items held: VERY SMALL (< 500) __ SMALL (500–1,000) __

  MEDIUM (1–5,000) __ LARGE (5-10,000) __ VERY LARGE (> 10,000) __

GENERAL STOCK with no specialities ___or STOCK with MAJOR SPECIALITIES ___

(List specialities) _____

_____

OLD & ANTIQUE No. items held: VERY SMALL (< 500) __ SMALL (500–1,000) __

  MEDIUM (1–5,000) __ LARGE (5-10,000) __ VERY LARGE (> 10,000) __

GENERAL STOCK with no specialities ___or STOCK with MAJOR SPECIALITIES ___

(List specialities) _____

_____

If possible, please assess the general price-range of your stock (e.g. 50p–£100) _____

Also, do you deal in any of the following:

 Ephemera ___ Prints & Maps ___ Antiquarian & Secondhand Books ___ Postcards ___

Richard Joseph Publishers Ltd, Unit 2, Monks Walk, Farnham, Surrey GU9 8HT.
Tel: (01252) 734347 Fax: (01252) 734307